Dealing with religious difference in kindergarten

Religious Diversity and Education in Europe

edited by

Cok Bakker, Jenny Berglund, Gerdien Bertram-Troost,
Hans-Günter Heimbrock, Julia Ipgrave,
Robert Jackson, Geir Skeie, Wolfram Weisse

Volume 38

Globalisation and plurality are influencing all areas of education, including religious education. The inter-cultural and multi-religious situation in Europe demands a re-evaluation of the existing educational systems in particular countries as well as new thinking at the broader European level. This well-established peer reviewed book series is committed to the investigation and reflection on the changing role of religion and education in Europe, including the interface between European research, policy and practice and that of countries or regions outside Europe. Contributions will evaluate the situation, reflect on fundamental issues and develop perspectives for better policy making and pedagogy, especially in relation to practice in the classroom.

The publishing policy of the series is to focus on strengthening literacy in the broad field of religions and related world views, while recognising the importance of strengthening pluralist democracies through stimulating the development of active citizenship and fostering greater mutual understanding through intercultural education. It pays special attention to the educational challenges of religious diversity and conflicting value systems in schools and in society in general.

Religious Diversity and Education in Europe was originally produced by two European research groups:

ENRECA: The European Network for Religious Education in Europe through Contextual Approaches

REDCo: Religion in Education. A contribution to Dialogue or a factor of Conflict in transforming societies of European Countries

Although books will continue to be published by these two research groups, manuscripts can be submitted by scholars engaged in empirical and theoretical research on aspects of religion, and related world views, and education, especially in relation to intercultural issues. Book proposals relating to research on individual European countries or on wider European themes or European research projects are welcome. Books dealing with the interface of research, especially related to policy and practice, in European countries and contexts beyond Europe are also welcome for consideration. All manuscripts submitted are peer reviewed by two specialist reviewers.

The series is aimed at teachers, teacher educators, researchers and policy makers. The series is committed to involving practitioners in the research process and includes books by teachers and teacher educators who are engaged in research as well as academics from various relevant fields, professional researchers and PhD students (the series includes several ground-breaking PhD dissertations). It is open to authors committed to these issues, and it includes English and German speaking monographs as well as edited collections of papers.

Outline book proposals should be directed to one of the editors or to the publisher.

Helena Stockinger

Dealing with religious difference in kindergarten

An ethnographic study in religiously affiliated institutions

Waxmann 2018
Münster • New York

Der Wissenschaftsfonds.

Publication with the support of the
Austrian Science Fund (FWF): PUB 416-G24

Bibliographic Information of the German National Library
The German National Library lists this publication in the German National Bibliography;
detailed bibliographical data is available on the Internet at http://dnb.dnb.de.

Religious Diversity and Education in Europe, volume 38

ISSN 1862-9547
Print-ISBN 978-3-8309-3983-2
E-Book-ISBN 978-3-8309-8983-7

© Waxmann Verlag GmbH, Münster 2018
Steinfurter Straße 555, 48159 Münster

www.waxmann.com
info@waxmann.com

Cover design: Plessmann Design, Ascheberg
Typesetting: Sven Solterbeck, Münster

Printed on non-ageing paper,
acid-free according to ISO 9706

Printed in Germany

All rights reserved. Reprinting, even in extracts, is prohibited.
No part of this work may be reproduced in any form
or processed, copied or distributed using electronic
systems without the written permission of the publisher.

Preface

I would like to begin by thanking the people who were involved in the development of this study.

Many thanks to the children, the teachers and the directors for their openness in letting me experience one year in the kindergarten as a researcher and for sharing their knowledge with me. Without this cooperation, the present work would not exist in this form.

This publication is the revised version of my dissertation, which was adopted at the University of Vienna in July 2015 and defended in December 2015. For the recognition of my scientific work, the appreciative and motivating support and the valuable insights, I would like to thank my supervisor of the dissertation, Univ.-Prof. i. R. Dr. Martin Jäggle. I would like to thank Univ.-Prof. Dr. Dr. h.c. Norbert Mette and Prof. Dr. Reinhold Boschki for their positive reviews of the dissertation. I thank Univ-Prof. i. R. Dr. Martin Jäggle and Univ.-Prof.[in] Dr.[in] Andrea Lehner-Hartmann for the experiences and activities that were made possible for me during my work as a university assistant at the Institute for Practical Theology, Department of Religious Education and Catechetics, at the University of Vienna in addition to writing my dissertation. At the Institute for Catechetics, Religious Education and Pedagogy at the Catholic Private University Linz, I was able to complete my work, for which I would like to thank Prof.[in] Dr.[in] Ilse Kögler, whose cordiality and interest in my research project created ideal working conditions. I would like to thank my colleagues at the Institute for Practical Theology at the University of Vienna and my colleagues at the Institute for Catechetics, Religious Education and Pedagogy at the Catholic Private University Linz for many conversations I had with them.

I would like to thank the participants of various congresses, conferences and seminars, including the Childhood Conference in Oxford, the Religionspädagogische Sozietät der Evangelisch-Theologischen Fakultät of the University of Vienna, the Empirikertagung in Nuremberg and the ET-Juniortagung in Innsbruck for their support and interest in my research. Through the many conversations with people from different countries, with different nationalities, religions, cultures and from various disciplines, I got to know different perspectives and was thus able to sharpen the profile of my research project. The support of a congress participation abroad and the short-term scientific scholarship of the University of Vienna, as well as the support of a stay abroad by the Bischöflicher Fonds zur Förderung der Katholischen Privat-Universität Linz, made these experiences possible for me. I would also like to thank the staff of the "Warwick Religious Education Unit" at the University of Warwick, in particular Prof. Robert (Bob) Jackson, PhD, DLitt and the staff of the "School of Sociology, Social Work and Social Policy" at Queen's University Belfast, in particular Dr. Dirk Schubotz, who made the respective research stay and subsequent scientific exchange and diverse experience, possible for me. This was feasible because of the employees and Heinz Ivkovits, then director of the Institute for Teacher Education in Religion at the KHP Wien/Krems, and former director Maria Habersack of BAKIP Kenyongasse and the students, who allowed me this flexibility. Thank you.

I would like to thank my friends, especially Andrea Riedl and Sandra Trimmel and my sister Elisa Stockinger, for the many conversations, mutually enjoyed activities and happy get-togethers. In this phase of the dissertation I would like to thank Hubert Mitterhofer in particular for his emotional support.

Many thanks to my parents Elisabeth and Helmut Stockinger. Their belief in my abilities and their unconditional support of my previous life's path has laid the foundation for my personal and professional development. Thank you very much!

Finally, I would like to thank the editors of the "Religious Diversity and Education" series for the inclusion of this publication. I thank Beate Plugge from Waxmann Verlag for her competent work on the publication.

The costs of the publication are borne entirely by the Austrian Science Fund FWF. The book available here in English was originally written in German and subsequently translated. German original quotations, which are not available in English, have accordingly also been translated into English. The German reference in the footnotes indicates that these are translations of the original quotations. For the original German quotations please refer to the book: Stockinger, Helena (2017): Umgang mit religiöser Differenz im Kindergarten. Eine ethnographische Studie an Kindergärten in katholischer und islamischer Trägerschaft in Wien. Münster-New York: Waxmann.

München, December 2016
Helena Stockinger

Content

Preface 5

Introduction 11

Part I: Theoretical Basics and Terminology 12
1. Practical-theological approach 12
2. Starting position of research 13
3. Children's right to difference 15
4. Opportunities and challenges of religious education 16
5. Religious difference in early childhood institutions 18
6. Terminological clarifications 19
6.1 General explanation of terms 20
6.3 Culture 22
6.4 Relationship between culture and religion 23
6.5 Religion and Religiousness 24
6.6 Perception and forms of expression 27
6.7 Religious Education 29
6.8 Plurality – Difference 32
6.9 Religious Difference 36

Part II: State of research 37
1. Research results on dealing with religious difference 37
1.1 Selected studies with children of primary school age 38
1.2 Empirical studies with children in early childhood education ... 42
1.2.1 Eva Hoffmann: Interreligious Learning in Kindergarten? 42
1.2.2 Friedrich Schweitzer, Albert Biesinger, Anke Edelbrock: Tübingen projects 43
1.2.3 David Elkind: Research on the Development of Faith 47
1.2.4 Ina ter Avest: Experiences in dealing with others 48
1.2.5 Daniel Bar-Tal: Concept of an "Arab" in Israel 49
1.2.6 Paul Connolly et al.: Attitude towards groups in Northern Ireland 50
1.3 Summary of research results 53
2. Research question 54
3. Concern of the study 55
4. Developmental psychological findings 56
4.1 Cognitive development of pre-school children 57
4.2 Social and emotional development of pre-school children .. 59
4.3 Importance of developmental psychological findings for the study 60

5.	Possibilities and limits of childhood research	60
5.1	Three levels of recognition processes	64
5.2	Methodological approaches in childhood research	68

Part III: Methodological approaches of the study ... 73
1.	Qualitative-empirical Research	73
1.1	Principles of qualitative empirical research	73
1.2	Data gathering	77
1.3	Triangulation within qualitative research	78
2.	Ethnographic access	80
3.	Grounded Theory	81
3.1	Basic assumptions of the Grounded Theory according to Corbin and Strauss	81
3.2	Data Analysis using Grounded Theory	82
4.	Thematic coding according to Uwe Flick	85
5.	Reasons for access to research	86
6.	Overview of the methods used	89
6.1	Participant observation	90
6.2	Group discussion	91
6.3	Group discussion procedures in childhood research	93
6.4	Interview with experts	94

Part IV: Study Design and Conduct ... 97
1.	Methods used in the investigation	97
1.1	Expert interview with the management of the two kindergartens	97
1.2	Participant observation	98
1.3	Group discussions with the children	99
1.3.1	Group discussions initiated by the children	99
1.3.2	Group discussions initiated by the researcher	100
1.4	Group discussions with the teachers	101
2.	Selection of kindergartens	102
3.	Examination procedure	105
3.1	Field access	105
3.2	Declaration of Consent	106
3.3	Data gathering	107
3.4	Documentation of Data	107
3.5	Transcription of the collected data	107
4.	Reflection on the examination procedure	108
4.1	Reflection on the researcher's understanding of her role	108
4.2	Influencing the context by going into the field	109
4.3	Unintended expert role of the researcher	110
4.4	Availability of time, space and personnel resources	110

Part V: Evaluation		112
1.	Notes on evaluation in this study	112
2.	Presentation of the kindergartens	113
2.1	Catholic Kindergarten	113
2.1.1	Field access	113
2.1.2	Sponsorship	114
2.1.3	Framework conditions	114
2.1.4	Personnel staffing	114
2.1.5	Kindergarten room	115
2.1.6	Socio-demographic data of children	115
2.1.7	Routine	116
2.2	Islamic Kindergarten	117
2.2.1	Field access	117
2.2.2	Sponsorship	117
2.2.3	Framework conditions	118
2.2.4	Personnel staffing	118
2.2.5	Kindergarten room	118
2.2.6	Socio-demographic data of children	118
2.2.7	Routine	120
3.	Short case descriptions	121
3.1	Interview with experts	121
3.1.1	Catholic Kindergarten	121
3.1.2	Islamic Kindergarten	122
3.2	Participant observation (with focus on religious difference)	123
3.2.1	Catholic Kindergarten	123
3.2.2	Islamic Kindergarten	124
3.3	Group discussions with the children	125
3.3.1	Catholic Kindergarten	125
3.3.2	Islamic Kindergarten	128
3.4	Group discussions with the teachers	130
3.4.1	Catholic Kindergarten	131
3.4.2	Islamic Kindergarten	133
4.	Data Analysis	135
4.1	Dealing with religious difference in kindergarten	137
4.1.1	Conceptual reflections on religion and religious difference	138
4.1.2	Recognisable elements of religious difference	141
4.1.3	Verbal communication about religious difference	147
4.1.4	Dominance of a religion	151
4.2	Dealing with and Thematising Religious Difference by Children	152
4.2.1	Interest in religious difference	152
4.2.2	Question of affiliation	157

4.2.3	Dealing with disagreements in discussions	161
4.2.4	Children's aspirations of belonging	163
4.3	Overview of the two core categories	164

Part VI: Discussion 166
1.	The kindergarten as an organisation	166
1.1	Organisation and environment	167
1.2	Kindergarten as a social space	168
1.3	Family and family environment	169
1.4	The kindergarten as a learning organisation	171
1.5	Organisational culture – Kindergarten culture	173
2.	Plea: Development of a culture of recognition of religious difference	176
2.1	Organisational development	178
2.1.1	Developing the kindergarten as a *safe space*	178
2.1.2	Support the development of the respective organisation	193
2.1.3	Offer self-evaluation of the respective kindergarten	196
2.2	Development of teaching	198
2.2.1	Recognising situations in everyday kindergarten life as a learning opportunity	198
2.2.2	Offering factually correct explanations of religious difference	201
2.2.3	Guiding initiatives to promote the handling of difference	203
2.3	Human resources development	205
2.3.1	Recognise the importance and tasks of those working in the kindergarten	206
2.3.2	Take causes of low thematisation of religious difference seriously	210
2.3.3	Promote interreligious aspects of education and training	215
3.	Review – Outlook	221
3.1	View of children	221
3.2	View of the organisation	222
3.3	Research desiderata	223

References 224

List of tables and figures 253

Appendix 254

Abstract 256

Introduction

As an early childhood educational institution, the kindergarten has the task of helping children in their development and contributing to their education. Kindergartens are often the first institutions in which children are confronted with different religions and religious attitudes than those experienced in their family environment, and it is very important that they learn to treat each other with respect and to be sensitive to differences. Taking children's opinions and interests into account and exploring how early childhood educational institutions deal with religious differences contributes to both childhood research and raising awareness of aspects of dealing with religious differences in educational institutions, given the low number of research projects to date. The scientific discipline of religious education, which is primarily focused on[1] people and their respective world, has to focus more on younger children in addition to the focus on young people and take their world and perspectives into account. This study contributes to this. Starting from the findings in the research process and the results on the double-perspective research question of how kindergartens deal with religious difference and how children address religious difference, it brings the perspective of the organisation to the fore, which will have to be taken into account in any case in future work on religious education that deals with people in organisations.

The state of research (Part II) in the field of early childhood education , which is supplemented by selected work from the primary school sector, follows on the basis of basic principles and definitions (Part I), insofar as these are necessary for the understanding of this study. The subsequent methodological approaches and the theoretical overview of the methods used in the study (Part III) form the basis for the study design and implementation (Part IV). The evaluation (Part V) starts with a presentation of the kindergartens, describes short case studies and analyses the data using the fundamentals of grounded theory. The most important results will be discussed in the final discussion (Part VI) in the horizon of the specialist discourse in order to formulate a plea.[2]

---

1 An insight into the first results of the research with an exclusive look at the expert interviews with the directors has already been published: Stockinger, Helena (2014): Religiöse Differenz in elementarpädagogischen Einrichtungen. Was der Religionspädagogik zu denken geben kann. *ÖRF 22*, 85–91.

2 Square brackets in quotations refer to the author's additions, three dots within a square bracket indicate that words were omitted by the author within the quotation. Quotations longer than three lines are indented in the text.

Part I: Theoretical Basics and Terminology

1. Practical-theological approach

Norbert Mette names three main tasks of Practical Theology: an exploration of the 'signs of time', their interpretation in the light of the Gospel and a conceptual design of the resulting priorities for action.[3] In the methodical cyclical four-step[4], an appropriate consideration of the signs of the times[5] includes "orientation" and "seeing", which precede "judgement" and "action". This "orientation" and "seeing" requires a perception of what concerns people today, an attention to contextual and biographical conditions of people and an analysis and reflection of the conditions "under which the truth of faith can become reality in everyday life practice in order to initiate and accompany qualified learning processes of faith on the basis of such insights",[6] which is a particular task for the practical-theological subjects. Any preoccupation with issues that concern men and women in their basic constitution has theological significance.[7] The so-called "anthropological turning point" in theology has brought an intensified recollection of the biblical insight that faith is not primarily about abstract truths, but about people in their concrete existence.[8] Practice is a constitutive dimension of theological practice itself[9] and not the application of a theory.

"Seeing" is preceded by "orientation", in which the initial conditions and the perspective of the researching person are revealed, which is a basic principle for a research process in which researchers are present as subjects.[10] The theological dimension of

---

3   Cf. Mette, Norbert (2005): Einführung in die katholische Praktische Theologie. Darmstadt: Wissenschaftliche Buchgesellschaft, 41.
4   This is based on the three-step seeing, judging and acting developed by J. Cardijn and confirmed by John XXIII in the encyclical "Mater et magistra" (1961, 236). Cf. Boschki, Reinhold (2007): Der phänomenologische Blick: „Vierschritt" statt „Dreischritt" in der Religionspädagogik. In: Boschki, Reinhold/Gronover, Matthias: Junge Wissenschaftstheorie der Religionspädagogik. Berlin: LIT 2007, 25–47.
5   "To carry out such a task, the Church has always had he duty of scrutinizing the signs of the times and of interpreting them in the light of the Gospel." (Gaudium et Spes, Pastoral Constitution on the church in the modern world Gaudium et Spes, promulgated by Pope Paul VI, 7th December 1965. Über die Kirche in der Welt von heute, article 4.
6   Mette, Norbert (2006): Religionspädagogik. Düsseldorf: Patmos, 269.
7   Cf. Boschki, Reinhold (2007): Der phänomenologische Blick. In: Boschki, Reinhold/Gronover, Matthias: Junge Wissenschaftstheorie der Religionspädagogik, 25–47, 32.
8   Cf. Mette, Norbert (2005): Einführung in die katholische Praktische Theologie, 63.
9   Cf. Mette, Norbert (2006): Religionspädagogik, 269.
10 Cf. Boschki, Reinhold (2007): Der phänomenologische Blick. In: Boschki, Reinhold/Gronover, Matthias: Junge Wissenschaftstheorie der Religionspädagogik, 25–47, 39.

research is closely linked to the researching subject.[11] Thus, the research process must never be viewed in isolation from the researchers, as their location flows into the research process. Through the step "Orientation", "the ideology-critical insight into the connection between knowledge and interest is obtained (Jürgen Habermas), as well as the *position determination* demanded by Johann Baptist Metz for each theological activity".[12] Johann Baptist Metz poses the question of where, with whom and for whom theology is practised.[13] "Who drifts where – so: with whom? and in whose interest – for whom? theology?"[14] The situational contextuality in which each researcher is involved and the intended research objectives must be disclosed for the research project.[15] "This implies the contextual, i.e. also the ecclesial, social, economic and political conditions of theological and empirical thinking and research."[16]

Therefore, the understanding of the terms used in the work is disclosed in a separate section.[17] In the decision for qualitative-empirical research, the ethnographic approach combined with grounded theory and thematic coding is chosen, since the research field and the persons acting in it are openly encountered and the subjectivity of the researching person, the intuitions and the behaviour are regarded as fruitful for the gain of knowledge. The chapter "Reflection of the investigation", in which the research process is described from different perspectives, is written in ego form in order to make the subjectivity of the researcher recognisable.[18]

2. Starting position of research

The presence of different religions has become a matter of course in today's society. Dealing with people from foreign countries and cultures in a society, whether they have been recruited as workers, whether they have left their homeland because of (civil) war, persecution, torture, economic hardship or similar, and are dependent on receiving asylum elsewhere or at least temporary refuge, represents a particularly urgent, but also controversial field of probation for partnership behaviour. [19]

---

11 Cf. Klein, Stephanie (2005): Erkenntnis und Methode in der Praktischen Theologie. Stuttgart: Kohlhammer, 115.
12 Boschki, Reinhold (2007): Der phänomenologische Blick. In: Boschki, Reinhold/ Gronover, Matthias: Junge Wissenschaftstheorie der Religionspädagogik, 25–47, 39.
13 Cf. Metz, Johann Baptist (⁵1992): Glaube in Geschichte und Gesellschaft. Studien zu einer praktischen Fundamentaltheologie. Mainz: Matthias-Grünewald-Verlag: Mainz [1977], 71.
14 Metz, Johann Baptist (1992): Glaube in Geschichte und Gesellschaft, 71.
15 Cf. Boschki, Reinhold (2007): Der phänomenologische Blick. In: Boschki, Reinhold/ Gronover, Matthias: Junge Wissenschaftstheorie der Religionspädagogik, 25–47, 41.
16 Ibid., 39.
17 See chapter "Plurality and difference" (Part I, 6).
18 See chapter "Reflection on the conduct of the investigation" (Part IV, 4).
19 Cf. Mette, Norbert (2005): Einführung in die katholische Praktische Theologie, 177.

Religion is currently present in public debates and its influence on the actions and thoughts of individuals is emphasised. It has returned to the forefront of public debate in European societies. It must be taken seriously as a powerful influence on the actions and thoughts of individuals.

> "Religion is thus of great social and political significance, both in ethnic or national conflicts and extremist movements, but also in individual and communal quests for meaning and orientation. As a result, today's young people are most likely to encounter religion in one form or another."[20]

Especially the increasing religious diversity is one of the most important changes of the 21st century.[21]

> "Religious diversity is probably one of the most important changes affecting our lives in the twenty-first century. Yes, those changes began earlier, but the twenty-first century is going to be about the management of religious diversity, doing it well, or getting it terribly wrong. Religious diversity has increased and become a part of daily life, in a way that it probably never was before, or if it was, it was much more isolated than it is now. It has become the new normal in the lives of most people."[22]

With the situation of increased religious diversity often goes

> "a huge potential for conflict that has its roots in diffuse fears of the foreign and is not only used by politically extreme groups to assert their own interests. To counteract this and promote a prosperous coexistence is therefore a central concern that is intensively pursued, especially by the ranks of religions. This begins with the desire to get to know each other better and extends to the point where this is possible and necessary (for example on the occasion of criminal events with religious implications), common religious practice (especially in the form of common prayers). Indeed, religions can make a significant contribution and have helped to promote and strengthen the social climate as a whole, both locally and globally, through peaceful coexistence at the religious level. This requires above all meetings and dialogues between or among members of different religions (both bilaterally and multilaterally), in which the participants learn

---

20 Bertram-Troost, Gerdien/Ipgrave, Julia/Josza, Dan-Paul/Knauth, Thorsten (2008): Encountering religious pluralism in school and society. A Qualitative Study of Teenage Perspectives in Europe. Background and Contextualisation. In: Knauth, Thorsten/Josza, Dan-Paul/Bertram-Troost, Gerdien/Ipgrave, Julia (Ed.): Encountering religious pluralism in school and society. A Qualitative Study of Teenage Perspectives in Europe. Münster et al.: Waxmann, 11–19, 11.
21 For a breakdown of the frequencies of the respective religious affiliations see chapter "Selection of kindergartens" (part V, 6).
22 Bouma, Gary D. (2011): Being Faithful in Diversity. Religions and Social Policy in Multifaith Societies. The Lloyd Geering Lectures 2010. Hindmarsh: ATF, xiii.

from each other in a very concrete way and are thus better able to respect the otherness of others, but can also experience an enrichment for their own religiosity."[23]

Religious learning in modernity is based on the plurality of religious traditions (ad extra and ad intra) and on the plurality of subjective religion.[24] Modernity necessarily pluralises,[25] it means that closed communities become fragile precisely because the others are always there.[26] The plurality of religious positions offers an opportunity to perceive others as people in their otherness.[27] Designs such as those by:

> "Martin Buber and Emmanuel Lévinas from the field of Jewish philosophy, Hans-Jochen Margull from ecumenical Christian theology, Abdoldjavad Falaturi or Abdulkader Tayob from the Islamic field, Paul Ricoeur from a Protestant philosophy or Helmut Peukert from the overlapping field of theology and educational science [...] are aiming for an approach to religion that seeks not its 'own' in conclusion, in deposition or even in enmity to others, but in relation to them."[28]

3. Children's right to difference

The UN Convention on the Rights of the Child[29] enumerates the rights of every child. The second article of the UN Convention on the Rights of the Child addresses the existing difference and makes it clear that this must not be a reason for discrimination. The rights belong to every child,

---

23 Mette, Norbert (2005): Einführung in die katholische Praktische Theologie, 196.
24 Cf. Ziebertz, Hans-Georg (2002): Grenzen des Säkularisierungstheorems. In: Schweitzer, Friedrich/Englert, Rudolf/Schwab, Ulrich/Ziebertz, Hans-Georg: Entwurf einer pluralitätsfähigen Religionspädagogik. Gütersloh/Freiburg i. Br.: Gütersloher Verlagshaus/Herder, 51–85, 53.
25 Cf. Berger, Peter L./Weiße, Wolfram (2010): Im Gespräch: Religiöse Pluralität und gesellschaftlicher Zusammenhalt. In: Weiße, Wolfram/Gutmann, Hans-Martin (Ed.): Religiöse Differenz als Chance? Positionen, Kontroversen, Perspektiven. Münster et al.: Waxmann, 17-26, 19. In this article, Peter L. Berger answers questions by Wolfram Weiße.
26 Cf. ibid.
27 Cf. Gutmann, Hans-Martin/Weiße, Wolfram (2010): Einleitung. In: Weiße, Wolfram/Gutmann, Hans-Martin (Ed.): Religiöse Differenz als Chance? Positionen, Kontroversen, Perspektiven. Münster et al.: Waxmann, 7-14, 9.
28 Gutmann, Hans-Martin/Weiße, Wolfram (2010): Einleitung. In: Weiße, Wolfram/Gutmann, Hans-Martin (Ed.): Religiöse Differenz als Chance?, 7–14, 8.
29 Convention on the Rights of the Child. Adopted and opened for signature, ratification and accession by General Assembly resolution 44/25 of 20 November 1989, entry into force 2 September 1990, http://www.ohchr.org/en/professionalinterest/pages/crc.aspx [22.07.2015].

"without discrimination of any kind, irrespective of the child's or his or her parent's or legal guardian's race, colour, sex, language, religion, political or other opinion, national, ethnic or social origin, property, disability, birth or other status."[30]

Article 14 establishes the right of the child to freedom of thought, conscience and religion and the rights and obligations of parents or guardians "to provide direction to the child in the exercise of his or her right in a manner consistent with the evolving capacities of the child"[31]. Freedom to manifest one's religion or beliefs must be given and "may be subject only to such limitations as are prescribed by law and are necessary to protect public safety, order, health or morals, or the fundamental rights and freedoms of others".[32] Article 29 of the UN Convention on the Rights of the Child emphasises that the child's education shall be directed to:

> "c) The development of respect for the child's parents, his or her own cultural identity, language and values, for the national values of the country in which the child is living, the country from which he or she may originate, and for civilisations different from his or her own; d) The preparation of the child for responsible life in a free society, in the spirit of understanding, peace, tolerance, equality of sexes, and friendship among all peoples, ethnic, national and religious groups and persons of indigenous origin; [...]."[33]

These legal rights point out the rights of children to learn about other cultures, other nations, other religions and differences in society and emphasize the right of children to be prepared for a responsible life in a free society.[34]

4. Opportunities and challenges of religious education

"Since its foundation [...], religious education has stood for the conviction that religion is dependent on education and that the relationship between religion and education can be shaped in such a way that it also meets pedagogical demands".[35] To analyse individual and collective conditions of religious education and training is a basic condition for this. A central concern of the practical theological approaches is "to be as close as possible to what concerns and moves people, especially where questions of the unconditional and the unavailable arise in their lives".[36] Norbert Mette emphasises that religious education has primarily taken on the task of promoting peaceful coexistence

---

30 Convention on the Rights of the Child, article 2.
31 Ibid., article 14.
32 Ibid.
33 Convention on the Rights of the Child. article 29.
34 Cf. ibid.
35 Schweitzer, Friedrich (2006): Religionspädagogik. Gütersloh: Gütersloher Verlagshaus, 64.
36 Mette, Norbert (2005): Einführung in die katholische Praktische Theologie, 26.

and that other practical-theological disciplines still have some catching up to do.[37] Religious education, which is already in its basic form, a bridge discipline between theology and pedagogy, plays an essential role in the canon of theology in communicating the relevance of theology and religious education also for other disciplines. "In reference to the public, religious education stands under the claim to achieve processes of understanding".[38] On the one hand, understanding refers to the different scientific disciplines, on the other hand, understanding between people, between different views, between different religions is a core topic of religious education, which gains special relevance under increased plurality. Migration and individual self-design dynamist plurality insofar as other possible aspects of difference arise, which need to be dealt with. In view of the religious and social situation of plurality, it is the task of religious education[39] to take on new responsibility and shape itself.[40] In addition to the goals of education in faith and ethical education, the third overarching goal in the Christian tradition of education is the capacity for plurality and understanding.[41] "The double orientation towards commonality and difference corresponds to the educational goal of a capacity for plurality, which presupposes distinguished religious education."[42] The difference that arises due to the fact of a capacity for plurality, which offers opportunities and challenges that need to be increasingly addressed with heightened focus in pedagogy and religious education. A basic condition for a pluralistic religious education is the ability to comprehend operations by means of which children, young people and adults construct their faith today.[43] Awareness of difference in religious education is a prerequisite for educational work that promotes the sensitivity and ability of children, young people and adults to learn about differences. Karl Ernst Nipkow mentions two challenges for religious education in modern times,

> "on the one hand, the independence of individuals and thus the *increase of inter-individual difference, i.e. diversity* (maturity, self-determination/autonomy, religious

---

37　Cf. ibid., 196.
38　Ziebertz, Hans-Georg (2002): Gesellschaft und Öffentlichkeit. In: Schweitzer, Friedrich et al.: Entwurf einer pluralitätsfähigen Religionspädagogik, 204–226, 208.
39　The topic of plurality connects the religious education of different countries. Schweitzer, Friedrich (2002): Ausblick: Internationale Perspektiven. In: Schweitzer, Friedrich et al.: Entwurf einer pluralitätsfähigen Religionspädagogik, 229–237, 234.
40　Cf. ibid., 229.
41　Schweitzer, Friedrich (2006): Religionspädagogik. Gütersloh: Gütersloher Verlagshaus, 124.
42　Council of the Evangelical Church in Germany (Ed.) (2014): Religiöse Orientierung gewinnen. Evangelischer Religionsunterricht als Beitrag zu einer pluralitätsfähigen Schule. Eine Denkschrift des Rates der Evangelischen Kirche in Deutschland. Gütersloh: Gütersloher Verlagshaus, 12.
43　Cf. Englert, Rudolf (2002): Dimensionen religiöser Pluralität. In: Schweitzer, Friedrich et al.: Entwurf einer pluralitätsfähigen Religionspädagogik, 17–50, 41.

individualisation) and on the other hand the *increase of social difference* (functionally-differentiated society, ideological-religious pluralism)".[44]

5. Religious difference in early childhood institutions

It has become widely recognised in the meantime that living together in peace in the face of social plurality can only be possible if children are prepared for it through an education for the capacity for plurality.[45] If theology is taken seriously as an existential biography, the phase of childhood must not be ignored.[46] Early childhood institutions are a reflection of society,[47] and as such reflect the diversity of religious communities in the respective country.[48] They are often the first organisations that children visit regularly and in which they meet people who are not from the family environment[49] and where they are confronted with the plurality of religions, world views and values.[50] In kindergarten, religion is not taught as a subject, but can be explored and integrated in significant situations of everyday life,[51] which is why, unlike in school, there is no division into denominational and religious affiliation. The educational mandate of early childhood institutions must be taken seriously and early childhood research must be integrated into the centre of religious education discourses. In order to contribute to the goal of the ability of plurality and understanding, this ability should be promoted in young children. In view of the multi-religious situation already in kindergarten, religious education based on plurality should under no circumstances be waited until

---

44 Nipkow, Karl Ernst (²2009): Pädagogische Grundbegriffe – religionspädagogische Grundmuster. In: Bitter, Gottfried/Englert, Rudolf/Miller, Gabriele/Nipkow, Karl Ernst (Ed.): Neues Handbuch religionspädagogischer Grundbegriffe. Munich: Kösel [2002], 25–30, 27.
45 Cf. Schweitzer, Friedrich (2008): Den Anfang schon verpasst? Religiöse Bildung in der Kindheit. In: Bertelsmann Stiftung (Ed.): Religion und Bildung. Orte, Medien und Experten religiöser Bildung. Gütersloh: Bertelsmann Stiftung, 23–34, 25.
46 Metz, Johann Baptist (1976): Theologie als Biographie. *Concilium 12*, 311–315.
47 Cf. School as a reflection of society.
48 Cf. Hess-Maier, Dorothee (2011): Mein Gott – Dein Gott, kein Gott? Religion in Kita und Elternhaus. In: Biesinger, Albert/Edelbrock, Anke/Schweitzer, Friedrich (Ed.): Auf die Eltern kommt es an! Interreligiöse und interkulturelle Bildung in der Kita, vol. 2. Münster et al.: Waxmann, 13-14, 14.
49 Cf. Woodhead, Martin (2008): Identity at birth – and identity in development. In: Brooker, Liz/Woodhead, Martin (Ed.): Developing Positive Identities. Diversity and Young Children. Early Childhood in Focus (3). Milton Keynes: The Open University, 4.
50 Cf. ibid.
51 Cf. Dommel, Christa (2008): Religion und religiöse Unterschiede als „Weltwissen" im Kindergarten. In: Klöcker, Michael/Tworuschka, Udo (Ed.): Handbuch der Religionen. Kirchen und andere Glaubensgemeinschaften in Deutschland/im deutschsprachigen Raum. Landsberg: Olzog, 1–14, 5.

adolescence.[52] It is clear that "all around the world today, societies are changing ever more rapidly and becoming increasingly diversified. [...] there is growing evidence that the values of social inclusion and respect for diversity are more applicable to young children than has previously been appreciated."[53] This can lead to opportunities for successful cooperation and interaction, but also to misunderstandings and prejudices.[54] Since children's world of experience is marked by plurality, it is important to support children in not feeling threatened by plurality, but in dealing with it productively.[55] The task of religious education is to contribute to the coexistence of children, which is supported by respect and recognition for others. This concern of religious education supports the *development* and *learning* of children and opens further development and learning opportunities.[56]

In order to promote the development and learning of children in a child-friendly manner and to open up development, education and learning opportunities in a world characterised by plurality, empirical basic research is necessary in religious education, which focuses on the world in which children live and how they relate to it and thematise it. This study is based on this ambition.

6. Terminological clarifications

The terms education, the relationship between culture and religion, the terms religion and religiosity, perception and forms of expression, religious education, plurality, difference and religious difference, which are of central importance in this study, are defined differently. The underlying understanding of the terms here are outlined without wishing to present the ambiguity of the terms. With some terms, the researcher's

---

52 Cf. Schweitzer, Friedrich (2008): Den Anfang schon verpasst? In: Bertelsmann Stiftung (Ed.): Religion und Bildung, 23–34, 25.
53 Promoting social inclusion and respect for diversity in young children's environments (2007). *Early Childhood Matters 108*, 5–6, 5. (Authors were not mentioned for this article.)
54 Cf. Schweitzer, Friedrich/Biesinger, Albert/Blaicher, Hans-Peter/Edelbrock, Anke/Haußmann, Annette/Ilg Wolfgang/Kaplan, Murat/Wissner, Golde (2011): Interreligiöse und interkulturelle Bildung in Kindertagesstätten – Befunde aus der Erzieherinnenbefragung. In: Schweitzer, Friedrich/Edelbrock, Anke/Biesinger, Albert (Ed.): Interreligiöse und interkulturelle Bildung in der Kita. Eine Repräsentativbefragung von Erzieherinnen in Deutschland – interdisziplinäre, interreligiöse und internationale Perspektiven. Interreligiöse und Interkulturelle Bildung im Kindesalter, vol. 3. Münster et al.: Waxmann, 29-54, 30.
55 Cf. Gierden-Jülich, Marion (2008): "Von Kindesbeinen an: Von der Notwendigkeit, den Umgang mit Pluralität zu erlernen". In: Schweitzer, Friedrich/Biesinger, Albert/Edelbrock, Anke (Ed.): Interkulturelle und interreligiöse Bildung in Kindertagesstätten. Weinheim/Basel: Beltz, 142–145, 145.
56 Cf. Schweitzer, Friedrich (2006): Religionspädagogik, 14.

understanding changed during the research process. The description of the terms corresponds to the researcher's understanding after the empirical research.

Language forms reality, therefore this publication, which deals with the difference, tries to clearly explicate the difference in language, which is why both the female and the male form are used. Despite this gender-specific mode of expression, difference in some terms is expressed too little, since linguistic naming always brings with it a reduction. "Over-expressions such as children, toddlers, pre-school children or kindergarten children lead to summary treatment and obscure the view of the differences between the girls and boys, of the diversity of the small personalities that educators deal with.[57] According to Hartmut Griese, in an immigration society such as Germany[58] and Austria, it is forbidden to speak pedagogically of "children and young people with a migration background", since the other is to be encountered in its generality and uniqueness and this should be respected and recognised.[59]

The recognition of the uniqueness and diversity of people is the starting point of this research work.

> "On the one hand, it is forbidden to speak undifferentiated of 'the' person, 'the' subject, 'the' identity, because that does not exist in reality; there are people only in the plural and in diversity. On the other hand, the concrete socio-structural conditions must be taken into account, which have a considerable influence on the possibility for people to develop their subject status."[60]

6.1 General explanation of terms

Since the present study was conducted in Austria, the term kindergarten, which is customary in Austria, is used when referring to the specific kindergartens[61] in which the qualitative empirical study was conducted. The kindergarten in Austria is usually an institution for girls and boys from the age of three, in two federal states from two and a half years up to the age of six. In the presentation of other research projects, the term kindergarten or day care centre is used depending on how they are named by the

---

57 Habringer-Hagleitner, Silvia (2009): Geschlechtergerechte Religionspädagogik im Kindergarten. Berlin: LIT. In: Pithan, Annebelle/Arzt, Silvia/Jakobs, Monika/Knauth, Thorsten (Ed.): Gender – Religion – Bildung. Beiträge zu einer Religionspädagogik der Vielfalt. Eine Veröffentlichung des Comenius Instituts. Gütersloh: Gütersloher Verlagshaus/Herder, 306-316, 307.
58 This is documented in the German Immigration Act.
59 Cf. Griese, Hartmut M. (⁴2013): Kinder und Jugendliche mit Migrationshintergrund. In: Deinet, Ulrich/Sturzenhecker, Benedikt (Ed.): Handbuch Offene Kinder- und Jugendarbeit. Wiesbaden: Springer VS Verlag für Sozialwissenschaften [1998], 143–148, 147.
60 Mette, Norbert (2005): Einführung in die katholische Praktische Theologie, 75.
61 The term kindergarten was introduced in 1840 by Friedrich Fröbel and is derived from the understanding that children must be cared for like plants.

respective authors.[62] Otherwise, institutions dedicated to the education and development of children up to the age of six are called early childhood institutions.

6.2 Education

Education is understood as "the mental self-activity through which the subject enters into a relationship to the world of things and persons and to an inner representation of the world and its relationship to the world".[63] The term education focuses on the activity of the child, who promotes his or her own educational processes and acquires more differentiated concepts about himself and herself and the environment. This definition is supplemented by the elementary sense of education formulated by Helmut Peukert, which consists in "gaining identity and the ability to act in a historical-concrete situation in the face of the challenges of the future"[64] and by Peukert's description of education as the will "to enable each other to live in a shared, finite world".[65] Education is seen as the mental self-activity of the respective person, through which the person places himself in a relationship with himself and the world, with the aim of developing the ability to act and identity in the face of the challenges of the future[66] and enabling each other to live in the world. According to Peukert, educational processes prove to be processes of freedom, since in educational processes it is a matter of "transcending oneself into the unknown".[67]

---

62 How these are used in the various studies depends on the context of the country in which the study was conducted.
63 Liegle, Ludwig (2006): Bildung und Erziehung in früher Kindheit. Stuttgart: Kohlhammer, 94.
64 Biehl, Peter (²2005): Die Gottebenbildlichkeit des Menschen und das Problem der Bildung. In: Biehl, Peter/Nipkow, Karl Ernst: Bildung und Bildungspolitik in theologischer Perspektive. Münster: LIT, 9–102, 21.
65 Peukert, Helmut (1987): Die Frage nach der Allgemeinbildung als Frage nach dem Verhältnis von Bildung und Vernunft. In: Pleines, Jürgen-Eckardt (Ed.): Das Problem des Allgemeinen in der Bildungstheorie. Würzburg: Königshausen & Neumann, 69–88, 69f.
66 Peter Biehl writes in his reception of Helmut Peukert: "If education is to rise to the challenge of the future, then it is knowledge of facts and insight into functional contexts, but at the same time resistance to reducing life to them. Education is not only dependent on knowledge and ability, but also on a *renewal of imagination*, as made possible by aesthetic and religious experience; for intersubjective creativity does not arise from appeals directed at the will, but owes above all to the *transformational power of poetic speech*." (Biehl, Peter (2005): Die Gottebenbildlichkeit des Menschen. In: Biehl, Peter/Nipkow, Karl Ernst: Bildung und Bildungspolitik in theologischer Perspektive, 9–102, 25).
67 Cf. Peukert, Helmut (2004): Bildung und Religion. Reflexionen zu einem bildungstheoretischen Religionsbegriff. In: Dethloff, Klaus/Langthaler, Rudolf/Nagl-Docekal, Herta/Wolfram, Friedrich: Orte der Religion im philosophischen Diskurs der Gegenwart. Berlin: Parerga, 363–386, 382.

6.3 Culture[68]

Already in Gaudium et Spes 53, a comprehensive, differentiated definition of culture is presented. "The word 'culture' in its general sense indicates everything whereby man develops and perfects his many bodily and spiritual qualities."[69]

Human culture has a "historical and a social aspect" and often assumes "a sociological and ethnological sense". It is spoken of as a plurality of cultures since.

> "Different styles of life and multiple scales of values arise from the diverse manner of using things, of laboring, of expressing oneself, of practicing religion, of forming customs, of establishing laws and juridic institutions, of cultivating the sciences, the arts and beauty. Thus the customs handed down to it form the patrimony proper to each human community. It is also in this way that there is formed the definite, historical milieu which enfolds the man of every nation and age and from which he draws the values which permit him to promote civilization."[70]

The study focuses on "cultures in the plural" in the use of the term culture, since differences between and within cultures are addressed. Georg Auernheimer[71], an important representative of intercultural pedagogy, describes the culture of a society or social group as its repertoire of means of communication and representation.[72] Culture has both an orientation function and an identity function; "within a culture, differences – and thus identities – are always negotiated discursively."[73] Annedore Prengel summarises in "agreement with other scientists (e.g. Gramsci, Haug, Metscher, Bourdieu, Clarke, Willis, Claessens, Greverus)"[74] which dimensions this cultural understanding implies:

> "Culture is limited to symbolic meanings, but the symbol systems of the material life process, of everyday life, are part of culture. Culture is thus closely related to production methods and class positions. It enables understanding, action orientation and self-assurance. Cultures are constantly changing, even cultures that at first glance seem to be unchanged for a long time."[75]

---

68 In the following, a working definition of culture is assumed without sufficient precision and detail in terms of cultural science.
69 GS, article 53.
70 Ibid.
71 The discourse around the "cultural turn" is not received in this context.
72 Cf. Auernheimer, Georg (1989): Kulturelle Identität – ein gegenaufklärerischer Mythos?. *Das Argument 31*(3), 381–394, 386.
73 Auernheimer, Georg (⁷2012): Einführung in die Interkulturelle Pädagogik. Darmstadt: Wissenschaftliche Buchgesellschaft [1990: Einführung in die Interkulturelle Erziehung], 78.
74 Prengel, Annedore (2006): Pädagogik der Vielfalt, 84.
75 Ibid.

Clifford Geertz emphasises that a person can confront other people and things only on the basis of his own understanding of interpretation and understand them exclusively in his own interpretation system. This framework of interpretation is determined by culture, which is the horizon of human thought and action, and cultural habits have developed into behaviour patterns no longer consciously registered by humans.

> "Becoming human is becoming individual, and we become individual under the guidance of cultural patterns, historically created systems of meaning in terms of which we give form, order, point, and direction to our lives. [...] Man is to be defined neither by his innate capacities alone, as much of contemporary social science seeks to do, but rather by the link between them, by the way in which the first is transformed into the second, his generic potentialities focused into his specific performances."[76]

"To be human here is thus not to be Everyman; it is to be a particular kind of man, and of course men differ."[77] The culture conveyed to man through sign systems first defines the norms and values with which man initially perceives other cultures. The culture is influenced and individually interpreted by one's own experiences and the specific context of the members. Cultural meanings can be chosen according to the situation. This creates subgroups within a culture, which can lead to greater differences between the subgroups of a culture than between the individual cultures themselves.

> "We must, in short, descend into detail, past the misleading tags, past the metaphysical types, past the empty similarities to grasp firmly the essential character of not only the various cultures but the various sorts of individuals within each culture, if we wish to encounter humanity face to face."[78]

6.4   Relationship between culture and religion

Paul Tillich, who decisively influenced the anthropological turn of religious education, describes culture as a form of expression of religion and religion as the content of culture,[79] thus revealing the close connection. Witte determines the interrelationship between religion and culture, characterised by participation and distance. Religion

> "is, on the one hand, less than culture, since it comprises only a part of the human way of life. On the other hand, religion is more than culture, since its counterpart, God, does

---

76   Geertz, Clifford (1973): The interpretation of cultures. Selected essays. New York: Basic Books, 52.
77   Ibid., 53.
78   Ibid.
79   Cf. Tillich, Paul (1962): Religionsphilosophie. Stuttgart: Kohlhammer [first published in: Dessoir Max (Ed.): Lehrbuch der Philosophie, vol. 2. Berlin: Verlag Ullstein 1925].

not merge into the respective world. Religion is part and parcel of the culture in which it is lived. Participation and distance shape the mutual interrelationship."[80]

Culture and religion cannot be explored independently, as they are interrelated. Religion, which is linked to ethical and moral values, has a culturally shaping function. Religion can be seen as part of culture.[81]

6.5 Religion and Religiousness

In view of the multitude of attempts at definition[82] that have already been made, the term religion seems elusive and evades a final definition. It would also be questionable if religious education were to commit itself to a clear concept of religion, since it is the task of religious education to maintain the question of what is considered religion and what recognition it deserves in church, society and among individuals.[83]

Tillich describes religion in a broader sense as life in the dimension of depth, as being touched by something that absolutely concerns us[84] and stresses that man is directly aware of something unconditional.[85] In the narrower sense, Tillich describes religion as a certain expression of what absolutely concerns us that happens in all forms of human culture.[86] The two dimensions that Tillich ascribes to the term religion are divided into two terms in this study. Religiousness here means the depth dimension of human; the term religion refers to Tillich's narrower meaning.

---

80 Witte, Markus (2001): Zu diesem Buch. In: Witte, Markus (Ed.): Religionskultur – zur Beziehung von Religion und Kultur in der Gesellschaft. Beiträge des Fachbereichs Evangelische Theologie an der Universität Frankfurt am Main. Würzburg: Religion und Kultur, 11–17, 11.

81 Zirker, Hans (2001): Religion, Religionskritik. In: Mette, Norbert/Rickens, Folkert (Ed.): Lexikon der Religionspädagogik, vol. 2. Neukirchen-Vluyn: Neukirchener, 1672–1677, 1677.

82 Cf., for example, the different perspectives from which the concept of religion is illuminated: Matthes, Joachim (2005): Das Eigene und das Fremde. Gesammelte Aufsätze zu Gesellschaft, Kultur und Religion. Published by Rüdiger Schloz. Würzburg: Ergon; Schieder, Rolf (2001): Wieviel Religion verträgt Deutschland?. Frankfurt am Main: Suhrkamp; Schreiner, Peter (2012): Religion im Kontext einer Europäisierung von Bildung. Eine Rekonstruktion europäischer Diskurse und Entwicklungen aus protestantischer Perspektive. Münster et al.: Waxmann, 47. The author's briefly presented understanding of the concept of religion is intended to clarify the use of the term in this study.

83 Zirker, Hans (2001): Religion, Religionskritik. In: Mette, Norbert/Rickens, Folkert (Ed.): Lexikon der Religionspädagogik, 1677.

84 Cf. Tillich, Paul (1967): Die religiöse Substanz der Kultur. Schriften zur Theologie der Kultur. Gesammelte Werke, vol. IX. Stuttgart: Evangelisches Verlagswerk, 94.

85 Cf. Tillich, Paul (1964): Die Frage nach dem Unbedingten. Schriften zur Religionsphilosophie. Gesammelte Werke, vol. V. Stuttgart: Evangelisches Verlagswerk, 131.

86 Cf. Tillich, Paul (1967): Die religiöse Substanz der Kultur, 94f.

Religion is a social phenomenon from the ground up.[87] Religion – as Hans Zirker emphasises – can never be that of an individual person, but is a social phenomenon, since personal concern and convictions are also embedded in the social environment. Religion depends on stable communicative forms and forms of action, it expresses its identity in binding terms, for example in holy scriptures, authoritative bodies or prescribed rites and is handed down in interpersonal relationships. Under conditions of common understanding, experiences are gained which are communicated, rejected, or approved.[88]

In contrast to the concept of religion, the concept of religiosity has received less attention in scientific debate.[89] Ulrich Hemel notices the lack of scientific reflection on the phenomenon of religiosity while at the same time taking the use of the term in everyday life for granted.[90] In most attempts at definition, religiosity[91] includes

> "a constitutive subjective element of 'faith', 'religious experience' or 'authenticity', which, in the case of explicit religiosity, is hardly accessible at all only via the subject's self-description (which cannot easily be equated with 'reality'), in the case of implicit religiosity."[92]

Ulrich Hemel[93] distinguishes five dimensions of religiosity.[94] With the dimension of religious sensitivity, he describes the "openness, responsiveness and perceptibility of religious phenomena." The dimension of religious expression "reflects the development of competence to act in the religious sphere, including the ability and willingness to assume religious roles." The dimension of religious content describes the "differentiation of the cognitive sphere" and does not have to be accompanied by a high degree of linguistic and dialogue ability, which describes the dimension of religious communication. The fifth dimension of religiously motivated living describes "the

---

87   Cf. Zirker, Hans (2001): Religion, Religionskritik. In: Mette, Norbert/Rickens, Folkert (Ed.): Lexikon der Religionspädagogik, 1672–1677, 1677.
88   Cf. ibid.
89   Cf. Angel, Hans-Ferdinand (2006): Religiosität – Die Neuentdeckung eines Forschungsgegenstands. In: Angel, Hans-Ferdinand/Bröking-Bortfeldt, Martin/Hemel, Ulrich/Jakobs, Monika/Kunstmann, Joachim/Pirner, Manfred L./Rothgangel, Martin: Religiosität. Anthropologische, theologische und sozialwissenschaftliche Klärungen. Stuttgart: Kohlhammer, 7–15; Rothgangel, Martin (2006): Religiosität als menschliches Gesicht der Offenbarung Gottes. In: Angel, Hans-Ferdinand et al.: Religiosität, 175–198.
90   Cf. Hemel, Ulrich (2001): Religiosität. In: Mette, Norbert/Rickers, Folkert (Ed.): Lexikon der Religionspädagogik, 1839–1844, 1840.
91   Der Begriff Religiosität ist ein diskursiver Begriff, der keinen Tatbestand bezeichnet.
92   Pirner, Manfred L. (2006): Religiosität als Gegenstand empirischer Forschung. In: Angel, Hans-Ferdinand et al.: Religiosität, 30–52, 44.
93   Following Glock, Ulrich Hemel distinguishes five dimensions of religiosity.
94   Manfred L. Pirner, too, considers Hemel's model as suitable for empirical research. Cf. Pirner, Manfred L. (2006): Religiosität als Gegenstand empirischer Forschung. In: Angel, Hans-Ferdinand et al.: Religiosität, 30–52, 47.

subjective relevance of religious orientations for a personality". The latter dimension expresses "the subjective internal relevance of religious reality and the subjective intensity of religious references to life".[95] Ulrich Hemel describes the unfolding religiosity through the competence:

> "to view oneself and the world in the light of religious patterns of interpretation and to recognise these patterns of interpretation as true, valid and guiding for one's own person. Religious competence is, from this point of view, a special form of judgement and action competence in view of one's own life. It has a holistic claim, as it refers to the orientation and meaning of one's own life in its wholeness, from birth to death, from youth to old age."[96]

The description of religious competence, which includes one's own life "from youth to old age"[97], is extended in this study to include childhood, since life in its entirety must not exclude childhood and this religious competence also belongs to children. Children's engagement with the dimensions of religiousness, religious sensitivity, religious expressions, religious content, religious communication and religiously motivated lifestyle and the related questions is also evident in children's theology and philosophy.[98]

In the definition of religion, the social-scientific dimension and in the definition of religiosity, the anthropological dimension should be in the foreground, whereby it is not possible to isolate the two terms from one another.[99] The orientation towards the phenomenon of religiosity increasingly expresses the focus on the subject.[100] With

---

95 Hemel, Ulrich (2006): Religionsphilosophie und Philosophie der Religiosität. In: Angel, Hans-Ferdinand et al.: Religiosität, 92–115, 102.
96 Ibid., 101.
97 Ibid.
98 Cf. Bucher, Anton A./Büttner, Gerhard/Freudenberger-Lötz, Petra/Schreiner, Martin (Ed.) (since 2002): Jahrbuch für Kindertheologie. Stuttgart: Calwer; Blasberg-Kuhnke, Martina (2007): Kindertheologie – Zur pastoralen Bedeutung eines religionspädagogischen Programms. *Diakonia 38*, 305–308, 308; Schluß, Henning (2005): Ein Vorschlag. Gegenstand und Grenze der Kindertheologie anhand eines systematischen Leitgedankens zu entwickeln. *Zeitschrift für Pädagogik und Theologie 37*, 23–35; Kalloch, Christina (2009): Kindertheologie als religionsdidaktisches Prinzip. In: Kalloch, Christina/Leimgruber, Stephan/Schwab, Ulrich (Ed.): Lehrbuch der Religionsdidaktik. Für Studium und Praxis in ökumenischer Perspektive. Freiburg: Herder, 314–327.
99 Cf. Rothgangel, Martin (2006): Religiosität als menschliches Gesicht der Offenbarung Gottes. In: Angel, Hans-Ferdinand et al.: Religiosität, 175–198. These working terms were also used by Martin Rothgangel in his discussions with Friedrich Schleiermacher, Karl Barth, Paul Tillich and Wolfhart Pannenberg and proved themselves as heuristic instruments.
100 Cf. Rothgangel, Martin/Angel, Hans-Ferdinand/Hemel, Ulrich (2006): Die Bedeutung von Religiosität im Horizont religionspädagogischer Theorie und Praxis. In: Angel, Hans-Ferdinand et al.: Religiosität, 199–212, 204.

regard to the dimensions of religiosity, the focus of this study is on children's religious sensitivity to religious difference. This can concern forms of expression, content, communication and lifestyle. The use of the term "religious" refers to both the religion and the religiosity of the children,[101] since these are interrelated.

> "For epistemological reasons, talking about 'identifying' religion or religiosity is problematic and should be avoided. The question whether something is 'really' religion or religiosity suggests an objectifiability of reality that we do not have at our disposal, and misjudges the constructive character of the two terms."[102]

6.6   Perception and forms of expression

Aesthetic[103], phenomenological and action-theoretical concepts[104] guide the concepts of perception and forms of expression in practical theology and religious education. The concepts of perception put a special emphasis on the subjects of perception and the "individual conditions and modes of understanding in the act of perception" are

---

101 In this context, Rudolf Englert's question, based on Feifel, remains critical: "At the moment when certain experiences can no longer be identified as *religious* experiences simply because they are interpreted in a specifically religious language game, the question of the very essence of religion and religiosity arises: what is religion, as it were, in disregard of the concrete manifestations of positive religions (cf. Angel 1999)? Is it possible to arrive at a concept of religion that is still rich in content and practicable in this way? And: Is it permissible to refer the concept of religion or religiosity also to groups of persons in whose own self-interpretation these terms do not occur at all or perhaps even have an extremely negative connotation? Finally: To what extent is this new demarcation of the area of religious education not determined by the 'subliminal apologetic attempt to make religious education and even more religious education unassailable by a very broad, ontologically secured concept of religion' (Feifel 1973, 44)?" This question is also relevant for children of kindergarten age, for whom the concept of religion is often an abstract word. Even if children do not call religious experiences that, they can still have experienced them.

102 Pirner, Manfred L. (2006): Religiosität als Gegenstand empirischer Forschung. In: Angel, Hans-Ferdinand et al.: Religiosität, 30–52, 43.

103 Cf. Kunstmann, Joachim (2002): Religion und Bildung. Zur ästhetischen Signatur religiöser Bildungsprozesse. Gütersloher Verlagshaus.

104 The juxtaposition of an aesthetic and an action-theoretical approach remains inadequate; rather, "the inclusion of the aesthetic dimension leads to a practical-theological theory of action from possible constrictions" and contributes "to grasp their specific concept of action more precisely and to outline the resulting practical tasks more clearly." (Mette, Norbert (2000): Praktische Theologie – Ästhetische Theorie oder Handlungstheorie? In: Abeldt, Sönke/Bauer, Walter/Heinrichs, Gesa/Knauth, Thorsten/Koch, Martina/Tiedemann, Holger/Weiße, Wolfram (Ed.): "… was es bedeutet, verletzbarer Mensch zu sein". Erziehungswissenschaft im Gespräch mit Theologie, Philosophie und Gesellschaftstheorie. Helmut Peukert zum 65. Geburtstag. Mainz: Matthias-Grünewald-Verlag, 37–46, 45).

in the foreground.[105] In the sense of the action scientific approach, action is "open to perception, because it can be understood as an expression of experiences with perceptions, which achieves (again perceptible) effect".[106] "Perception manifests itself through the act of expression, which in turn can become the object of renewed perception."[107] The aesthetic dimension carries believing "action as preserving action [....] in itself, for it is a manifestation of God's practice in human action."[108]

> "In the aesthetic dimension of religious learning processes, an interplay between the acts and forms of expression of learners and forms of expression of tradition is of central importance. Cross-fertilisation can occur when the effect of traditional forms of expression can be activated in the learner's perception. There are two ways to do this: On the one hand, the learners can unconsciously anticipate in their own acts of expression the space of experience and question, from which the forms of expression of faith arose and which has contributed to a multifaceted process of perception and expression at all times. On the other hand, the effect of forms of expression of faith can be activated by a suitable dramaturgy of the teaching/learning processes in such a way that learners can independently associate their own worlds of experience and process them in their own forms of expression."[109]

In the phenomenological approach, in which the perception of reality is seen as being ahead of action,[110] perception is "related to forms of expression and changes into action where the effect of what is perceived begins to manifest itself".[111] Mediating between acting and perceiving faith is "the form of expression of faith: acting faith forms of expression and perceiving faith refers to forms of expression."[112]

In order to "think perception not exclusively from the learning subject, but to get the specific perceptual character of the objects into view",[113] Stefan Altmeyer proposes three steps that complement the perception dimension,

> "that unite in an elemental movement. These are (1) perceptions, (2) experiences with perceptions, (3) effects and (4) expression. This movement from perception to

---

105 Altmeyer, Stefan (2007): Welche Wahrnehmung? Kontexte und Konturen eines praktisch-theologischen Grundbegriffs. In: Boschki, Reinhold/Gronover, Matthias: Junge Wissenschaftstheorie der Religionspädagogik, 214–237, 223.
106 Altmeyer, Stefan (2006): Von der Wahrnehmung zum Ausdruck. Zur ästhetischen Dimension von Glauben und Lernen. Stuttgart: Kohlhammer, 373.
107 Ibid.
108 Ibid.
109 Ibid., 377. This section is italicised in the original.
110 Biehl, Peter (1998): Der phänomenologische Ansatz in der deutschen Religionspädagogik. In: Heimbrock, Hans-Günter (Ed.): Religionspädagogik und Phänomenologie. Weinheim: Deutscher Studien Verlag, 15–46, 15.
111 Altmeyer, Stefan (2006): Von der Wahrnehmung zum Ausdruck, 373.
112 Ibid.
113 Altmeyer, Stefan (2007): Welche Wahrnehmung? In: Boschki, Reinhold/Gronover, Matthias: Junge Wissenschaftstheorie der Religionspädagogik, 214–237, 232.

expression (and back) is as much an elementary component of human self- and world knowledge and thus also a central element of educational processes as it is fundamental for the appropriation, transmission and practice of (Christian) faith."[114]

It is based on sensual perception. To perceive religious forms is considered to be the first step to open up religious reality. The sensations triggered by perception can be thematised and processed into experiences that can be both cognitively and pragmatically linked to other areas of experience.[115] The experiences depend on the subject and the object. The importance of the subject, the object and the community and their interaction are emphasised in this view of perception. It is emphasised that religious education is not limited to perception, but is supplemented by expression, which in turn can be perceived. Perception and the expression of what is perceived are therefore indispensable for religious education.[116]

The close connection between perception and forms of expression in the phenomenological, aesthetic and action-theoretical approach to the concepts makes it clear that the present study can be assigned to the three approaches mentioned. If these views are considered in isolation, they do not do justice to the interrelationship between subjective, objective and community aspects.[117]

6.7 Religious Education

In this publication, religious education is seen as a human right, as enshrined in the Universal Declaration of Human Rights, Article 26:

> "Education shall be directed to the full development of the human personality and to the strengthening of respect for human rights and fundamental freedoms. It shall promote understanding, tolerance and friendship among all nations, racial or religious groups, and shall further the activities of the United Nations for the maintenance of peace."[118]

This right is also formulated in the Charter of Fundamental Rights, Article 10:

> "Everyone has the right to freedom of thought, conscience and religion. This right includes freedom to change religion or belief and freedom, either alone or in community with others, and in public or in private, to manifest religion or belief, in worship, teaching, practice and observance."[119]

---

114 Ibid., 232f.
115 Ibid., 233.
116 Ibid., 234.
117 Ibid., 231.
118 United Nations General Assembly: Universal Declaration of Human Rights 1948 www.un.org/en/universal-declaration-human-rights/ [22.07.2015].
119 Charter of Fundamental Rights of the European Union (2010/364/01). Official Journal of the European Communities, article 10, http://www.europarl.europa.eu/charter/pdf/

The first international document on the rights of the child, the Geneva Declaration of the Rights of the Child, already states that men and women of all nations declare it as their duty and accept to grant the child five rights, irrespective of race, nationality and faith. One of these rights emphasises that the child must maintain the conditions for normal development, both materially and spiritually.[120] "(1) The child must be given the means requisite for its normal development, both materially and spiritually."[121]

In addition to the legal rights, Schweitzer refers to "the importance of religion for a comprehensively understood welfare of the child [...]. Children need religion, especially for their self-development and for the formation of values [...]."[122] From a Christian point of view, he sees this "right of the child"[123] confirmed in Jesus' turn towards the child, which also makes God's relationship to the children recognisable.[124]

---

text_en.pdf. [22.07.2015].

120 "By the present Declaration of the Rights of the Child, commonly known as 'Declaration of Geneva', men and women of all nations, recognising that mankind owes to the Child the best that it has to give, declare and accept it as their duty that, beyond and above all considerations of race, nationality or creed: (1) The child must be given the means requisite for its normal development, both materially and spiritually; (2) The child that is hungry must be fed; the child that is sick must be nursed; the child that is backward must be helped; the delinquent child must be reclaimed; and the orphan and the waif must be sheltered and succored; (3) The child must be the first to receive relief in times of distress; (4) The child must be put in a position to earn a livelihood, and must be protected against every form of exploitation; (5) The child must be brought up in the consciousness that its talents must be devoted to the service of fellow men." Geneva Declaration of the Rights of the Child of 1924, *adopted* Sept. 26, 1924, League of Nations O.J. Spec. Supp. 21, at 43 (1924), http://www.kinderrechte.gv.at/wp-content/uploads/2013/01/genfer_erk-laerung_1924_englisch1.pdf [22.07.2015].

121 Geneva Declaration of the Rights of the Child of 1924, Supp. 21, at 43.

122 Schweitzer, Friedrich (2008): Den Anfang schon verpasst? In: Bertelsmann Stiftung (Ed.): Religion und Bildung, 23–28, 24.

123 Schweitzer, Friedrich (2013): Das Recht des Kindes auf Religion. Gütersloh: Gütersloher Verlagshaus. [This edition is the amended reprint of the book: Schweitzer, Friedrich (2000): Das Recht des Kindes auf Religion. Ermutigungen für Eltern und Erzieher. Gütersloh: Gütersloher Verlagshaus. Second print: 2005]. Cf. also Schweitzer, Friedrich (2010): Children's Right to Religion and Religious Education. In: Engebretson, Kath/de Souza, Marian/Durka, Gloria/Gearon, Liam: International Handbook of Inter-religious Education. Part Two. Dordrecht/Heidelberg/London/New York: Springer, 1071–1086.

124 "*In summary,* it should be noted that the right of the child to religion can be expressly confirmed from a Christian perspective. In Christian-theological interpretation it arises from Jesus' turning towards the child, and this turning towards Jesus shows God's relationship to the children. This can also be expressed in such a way that the very reference to a 'right of the child' can aptly express the closeness between God and child that is characteristic of the Christian faith." (Schweitzer, Friedrich (2013): Das Recht des Kindes auf Religion, 96f.).

To support the child in elementary questions of life,[125] to meet the child's questions openly and to initiate the search process together with the child, which can also be initiated by questions of the adult whose answers are not known in advance, are characteristics of religious education. There are many studies on religious education and education of children.[126]

> "Taking into account the religious dimension of education means […] in the first place, a changed overall attitude towards the child – an attitude that is able to recognise in the child a counterpart who has religious questions, who not only lives in the world of the sensually tangible and palpable, but who also wants to move in a much more far-reaching orientation space of sense concepts and sense experiences."[127]

---

125 Friedrich Schweitzer mentions five major questions in the growing up of the children: "It is particularly about the question of death and dying, the question of one's own identity and its recognition, the question of the reason for moral action, the question of God as well as the question of the religion of others." (Schweitzer, Friedrich (2006): Religionspädagogik, 201). The importance of children's questions is emphasised in several articles and books, cf. for example Oelkers, Jürgen (1994): Die Frage nach Gott. Über die natürliche Religion von Kindern. In: Merz, Vreni (Ed.): Alter Gott für neue Kinder? Das traditionelle Gottesbild und die nachwachsende Generation. Fribourg, Switzerland: Paulusverlag, 13–22; Zimmermann, Mirjam (Ed.) (2013): Fragen im Religionsunterricht. Unterrichtsideen zu einer schülerorientierten Didaktik. Göttingen: Vandenhoeck & Ruprecht; Beer, Peter (2003): Kinderfragen als Wegmarken religiöser Erziehung. Ein Entwurf für religionspädagogisches Arbeiten im Elementarbereich. Munich: Don Bosco.

126 A draft of a paradigm of religious education theory formation and a discussion of questions of religious education is presented by Norbert Mette in his habilitation thesis, cf. Mette, Norbert (1983): Voraussetzungen christlicher Elementarerziehung. Vorbereitende Studien zu einer Religionspädagogik des Kleinkindalters. Düsseldorf: Patmos. Silvia Habringer-Hagleitner presents various models of religious learning and asks about the importance of religion, especially Christianity and places for religious education in the face of a plural society, cf. Habringer-Hagleitner, Silvia (2006): Zusammenleben im Kindergarten. Modelle religionspädagogischer Praxis. Stuttgart: Kohlhammer. Carola Fleck gives an overview of existing curricula in Germany, cf. Fleck, Carola (2011): Religiöse Bildung in der Frühpädagogik. Berlin: LIT. In his work, Johann Hofmeier tries to give an overview of the historical, social and anthropological conditions of religious education, cf. Hofmeier, Johann (1987): Religiöse Erziehung im Elementarbereich. Munich: Kösel, 9. Adolf Exeler already points to forms of religious education, cf. Exeler, Adolf (^{2}1977): Fehlformen religiöser Erziehung. In: Feifel, Erich/Leuenberger, Robert/Stachel, Günter/Wegenast, Klaus (Ed.): Handbuch Religionspädagogik. Vol. 1 (Religiöse Bildung und Erziehung: Theorie und Faktoren). Zurich/Einsiedeln/Cologne, 135–144. Bernhard Grom describes the aims of religious education. His search for meaning comes to the fore, cf. Grom, Bernhard (^{5}2000): Religionspädagogische Psychologie des Kleinkind-, Schul- und Jugendalters. Düsseldorf: Patmos [1981].

127 Schweitzer, Friedrich (2013): Das Recht des Kindes auf Religion, 129.

It is based on an elementary religious learning ability and openness, the basis "for rel[igious] learning, for the development of r[eligious] consciousness a[nd] indirectly for the development of various forms of personal r[eligiosity] a[nd] spirituality."[128] Children are seen as actors in their development who are capable of thinking about questions of life, as is made clear in the approach of theologising and philosophising with children. Theology with children means "to encourage and affirm, to allow them to express their experiences and questions, their faith and doubts, speaking and thinking for themselves."[129] Religious education is seen in today's religious pedagogy in the confrontation with other religions,[130] even if the handling of these varies in the respective concepts of religious education.[131]

6.8 Plurality – Difference

The examination of plurality and difference clarifies in which frame of reference the concept of difference used by the author is to be located and why the concept of difference is used and does not claim to reflect the complex debate on difference, diversity, etc.

Plurality[132] refers to a situation of social, cultural, religious, ideological, etc. diversity in its mere fact[133]. Plurality is a fact that occurs when people meet. When plurality questions the self-evident, new demands for unity and commitment usually prove unsuccessful. Plurality forces us to deal and engage with it, to work on it and to reach agreements through it without which life (together) cannot function.[134]

---

128 Hemel, Ulrich (2001): Religiosität. In: Mette, Norbert/Rickens, Folkert (Ed.): Lexikon der Religionspädagogik, 1839–1844, 1842.
129 Schweitzer, Friedrich (2013): Das Recht des Kindes auf Religion, 145.
130 In earlier religious education works other religions in connection with religious education are mentioned less frequently. Thus, for example, Adolf Exeler emphasises three findings in his description of the situation of religious education in secularised society, whereby other religions are not mentioned (cf. Exeler, Adolf (1983): Religiöse Erziehung als Hilfe zur Menschwerdung. Munich: Kösel 1983, 76–83). Religious education for him means "to provide children with appropriate positive experiences" (Exeler, Adolf (1983): Religiöse Erziehung als Hilfe zur Menschwerdung, 27).
131 Cf. chapter "Development of concepts for dealing with religious difference" (Part V, 2.1.2.3).
132 The fact that plurality is a topic whose importance science has recognised becomes apparent in the constantly growing literature on this topic, which is why these short explanations serve to outline the underlying understanding of the study.
133 Cf. Schweitzer, Friedrich et al. (2002): Entwurf einer pluralitätsfähigen Religionspädagogik, 11.
134 Cf. Ziebertz, Hans-Georg (2002): Grenzen des Säkularisierungstheorems. In: Schweitzer, Friedrich/Englert, Rudolf/Schwab, Ulrich/Ziebertz, Hans-Georg: Entwurf einer pluralitätsfähigen Religionspädagogik, 51–85, 53.

In a situation of plurality, difference occurs. Difference precedes every relationship and only through the otherness of the other is relationship made possible.[135]

> "To enter into a conversation means to bring in one's unique, individual history and unmistakable identity, arising from experiences and decisions, at the same time perceiving and acknowledging the uniqueness of the other and in this situation finding a common understanding both about experiences to be distinguished and about perspectives of possible common action. Education as the ability to come to oneself at a certain level and to reach a consensus with others is only possible as consciousness and concession of difference. Education *is* the consciousness of difference."[136]

That plurality is to be regarded as given finds its expression in difference, "plurality is *difference* at its core".[137] Plurality and difference are interdependent and interrelated. Only those who perceive difference respect plurality [...].[138]

Paul Mecheril and Melanie Plößer describe the "question of the social handling of difference and identity" as one of the "most important topics of political debate and social theoretical reflection of the present".[139]

> "The discovery of difference is a topos that is relevant in pedagogy in many ways. Especially under conditions of the accelerated disintegration of the validity of knowledge in the knowledge society and a pluralisation of life situations and life models, educational action has to do in many ways with the topos of difference and thus with topics such as insecurity, ambiguity, ambivalence, uncertainty and not least with uncertainty and ignorance."[140]

At the latest with the work of Annedore Prengel's „Pädagogik der Vielfalt", the question of difference, diversity and how to deal with it has been placed in the German-language pedagogical discourse.[141]

---

135 An example of this is the close relationship between a parent and a small child, despite their difference. Prengel, Annedore (2006): Pädagogik der Vielfalt, 57.
136 Peukert, Helmut (1984): Über die Zukunft der Bildung. In: Dirks, Walter/Kogon, Eugen (Ed.): Nach 1984: Die Krise der Zivilisation und unserer Zukunft. *Frankfurter Hefte extra* 6, 129–137, 134.
137 Nipkow, Karl Ernst (1998): Bildung in einer pluralen Welt, vol. 1. Moralpädagogik im Pluralismus. Gütersloh: Chr. Kaiser/Gütersloher Verlagshaus, 176.
138 Cf. Nipkow, Karl Ernst (1998): Bildung in einer pluralen Welt, vol. 2. Religionspädagogik im Pluralismus. Gütersloh: Chr. Kaiser/Gütersloher Verlagshaus, 106.
139 Mecheril, Paul/Plößer, Melanie (2009): Differenz. In: Andresen, Sabine/Casale, Rita/Gabriel, Thomas/Horlacher, Rebekka/Larcher Klee, Sabina/Oelkers, Jürgen (Ed.): Handwörterbuch Erziehungswissenschaft. Weinheim/Basel: Beltz, 194-208, 194.
140 Ibid., 194f.
141 Cf. Pohlkamp, Ines (2012): Differenzsensible/intersektionale Bildung – Ein Theorie-Praxis Dilemma? Vortrag im Rahmen der Ringvorlesung „Behinderung ohne Behinderte?! Perspektiven der Disability Studies", University Hamburg, 29.10.2012, 3. http://www.zedis-ev-hochschule-hh.de/files/pohlkamp_29102012.pdf [29.06.2015].

> "The pedagogy of diversity is based on the 'indeterminability of human beings', so it cannot diagnose 'what someone is' nor 'what should become of him or her'. She opposes all objectifications in the form of definitions of what a girl, a boy, a behavioural disorder, a Turkishwoman is. If people are to be characterised, it is in their development dynamics and their environmental context. Only in their processuality and environmental interdependence can people be adequately described."[142]

Following the presentation of the pedagogical movements of intercultural pedagogy, feminist pedagogy and integration pedagogy, Annedore Prengel formulates twelve theses, the facets of the idea of difference, that are valid for the three pedagogical movements:[143] (1) The concept of difference is directed against hierarchies; it is about the development of egalitarian difference. (2) Difference implies "openness to the unpredictable and incommensurable"; it "wants to describe manifold, 'other' independently of the 'one', i.e. both as heterogeneous". (3) Several levels of human heterogeneity are affected, both differences between different groups, as well as subgroups within the groups, between individuals, between intrapsychic and intrasomatic heterogeneity of different personality components. (4) Socialisation and construction theory, non-essentialist concepts, form the basis for the idea of difference. "Individual and collective differences between people are socio-cultural differences, difference refers to social differences, i.e. different ways of living and different ways of processing life experiences." (5) Difference refers to dynamic processes, since ways of life and symbol structures of cultures [and religions] change. (6) Difference has become historical. Knowing our history better means getting to know ourselves better, because we are what we have become. (7) "Difference is not simply there, but the forms of life that do not belong to the dominant culture are silenced, repressed, marginalised, devalued, exploited. Therefore, different ways of life must always be rediscovered, brought to their own language and acknowledged in their value". (8) The right to equality and the right to difference belongs to the "inferior" persons and groups, without them having to be morally better or particularly valuable. (9) "The perception of different experiences thus always remains fragmentary, incomplete and limited and cannot reach the goal of an authenticity conceived as the final truth, precisely because cultural currents and the life stories embedded in them are constantly changing". Man remains indeterminable. Since definitions "do not do justice to the diversity and processual of human reality", the description of the phenomenon of difference also remains imperfect, but "revealing hypotheses can be obtained with regard to the main stream of patterns of interpretation and behaviour in a collective in a broad or narrowly defined social situation". (10) Different cultural lifestyles mutually influence each other. (11) Different forms of life have the same right to exist, to be socially visible, recognised and effective. "The postulate of equality is redeemed in a new radical way by granting equal

---

142 Prengel, Annedore (^{3}2006): Pädagogik der Vielfalt. Verschiedenheit und Gleichberechtigung in Interkultureller, Feministischer und Integrativer Pädagogik. Wiesbaden: VS Verlag für Sozialwissenschaften [1993], 191.
143 Ibid., 181–184.

rights to heterogeneous lifestyles. Equality is therefore a condition of the possibility of difference." (12) "Difference without equality means social hierarchy, cultural devaluation, economic exploitation. Equality without difference means assimilation, adaptation, synchronisation, exclusion of 'others'. From the democratic difference point of view, based on equal rights, everything is not acceptable, everything is arbitrary or indifferent. Rather, a democratic concept of difference provides clear criteria for forming judgements: All those tendencies which are monistic, totalitarian, hegemonic, exploitative and discriminatory in order to destroy the equality of the difference can only be fought from this point of view. Diversity is only realised in a clear statement against ruling assaults. It is committed to the vision of justice."[144]

In summary, the pedagogy tries to "avoid disregard in education" and "promote personal educational processes, as well as qualification and socialisation processes" and "sees itself as pedagogy of intersubjective recognition between equal differences".[145]

The concept of "egalitarian difference"[146] was first adopted by Annedore Prengel[147] in the educational discourse.

> "'Egalitarian Difference' recognises difference without defining the individuals using differences or even classifying them in a hierarchy. It is about the recognition of equality and difference, which cannot be separated. The sole view of equality hides the specific needs of individuals, the sole view of difference hides the fundamental equality as well as the power relationships and powerlessness in relationships."[148]

The emphasis on recognising the difference must not lead to categorising people and the difference between those categories being recognised.[149]

Mecheril and Plößer draw attention to dilemmas that a pedagogy related to plurality and difference has to deal with. On the one hand, inequalities are (re)produced when difference is not recognised; on the other hand, the recognition of difference reproduces power and inequalities.[150] These dilemmas cannot be overcome in the pedagogical handling of difference, which is why a "critical-reflective thematisation

---

144 Ibid.
145 Ibid., 62.
146 Cf. Honneth, Axel (⁶2010): Kampf um Anerkennung. Zur moralischen Grammatik sozialer Konflikte. Frankfurt am Main: Suhrkamp [1992].
147 Prengel, Annedore (1993): Pädagogik der Vielfalt.
148 Jäggle, Martin (2015): Religionsbedingte Heterogenität als Thema der Forschung in der LehrerInnenbildung. In: Lindner, Doris/Krobath, Thomas (Ed.): Vielfalt(en) erforschen. Tag der Forschung 2014. Series: Schriften der Kirchlichen Pädagogischen Hochschule Wien/Krems, vol. 10. Vienna/Berlin: LIT, 28–37, 29f.
149 Cf. Dahlberg, Gunilla/Moss, Peter (2005): Ethics and Politics in Early Childhood Education. London/New York: RoutledgeFalmer, 86.
150 Mecheril, Paul/Plößer, Melanie (2009): Differenz. In: Andresen, Sabine et al. (Ed.): Handwörterbuch Erziehungswissenschaft, 194–208, 206.

of difference is preferred [...]."[151] The relationship between difference and pedagogy is "about an experiential reflection on how difference is pedagogically thematised in such a way that as a consequence of this thematisation less power over others is required."[152] In science, various models have been developed that focus on power and power relations, such as intersectional[153] and difference-sensitive approaches.[154]

Knowing these dilemmas, which are fundamental to the concept of difference and cannot be constantly explicated in the work, but which resonate in any speech about difference, the concept of difference, which is the core of plurality,[155] is chosen for this study.

6.9 Religious Difference

By religious[156] difference – referring to the distinction between religiosity and religion – both the anthropological dimension and the sociological dimension are understood, since these are inseparably connected. This implies that both religion and religiosity are meant in the use of the term "religious".[157] Religious difference is seen as a dimension of difference that is closely interwoven with other dimensions such as cultural and linguistic difference.[158]

---

151 Ibid., 196.
152 Ibid.
153 Cf., for example, Portal Intersektionalität, http://portal-intersektionalitaet.de/startseite/ [22.07.2015].
154 Cf. Pohlkamp, Ines (2012): Differenzsensible/intersektionale Bildung. Lecture, 29.10.2012, http://www.zedis-ev-hochschule-hh.de/files/pohlkamp_29102012.pdf [29.06.2015].
155 Cf. Nipkow, Karl Ernst (1998): Bildung in einer pluralen Welt, vol. 1. Moralpädagogik im Pluralismus, 176.
156 The term "religious" makes it possible to speak of the religiosity of man without establishing a connection to a concrete religion by its very name. Cf. Hemel, Ulrich (2006): Religionsphilosophie und Philosophie der Religiosität. In: Angel, Hans- Ferdinand et al.: Religiosität, 92–115, 94.
157 Cf. chapter "Religion and Religiousness" (Part I, 6.5).
158 Cf. chapter "Plurality and Difference" (Part I, 6.8).

Part II: State of research

1. Research results on dealing with religious difference

Studies on religious difference are few compared to studies on other forms of difference, such as ethnic difference,[159] cultural difference or differences of race,[160] gender difference[161] and linguistic difference. Religious difference is interwoven with other forms of difference,[162] but the focus of this study is on religious difference. Therefore,

---

159 Some of the names are used differently. Often the term ethnic difference already refers to cultural, religious and linguistic difference.
160 For studies on the topic of "race" see, for example Aboud, Frances E. (1988): Children and Prejudice. Oxford: Basil Blackwell; Aboud, Frances E./Doyle, Anna Beth (1996): 'Does Talk of Race Foster Prejudice or Tolerance in Children?'. *Canadian Journal of Behavioural Science 28*(3), 161–170; Aukrust, Vibeke Grøver/Rydland, Veslemøy (2009): 'Does it matter?' Talking about ethnic diversity in preschool and first grade classrooms. *Journal of Pragmatics 41*(8), 1538–1556; García Coll, Cynthia/Lamberty, Gontran/Jenkins, Renee/McAdoo, Harriet Pipes/Crnic, Keith/Wasik, Barbara Hanna/Vázquez García, Heidie (1996): An Integrative Model for the Study of Developmental Competencies in Minority Children. *Child Development 67*(5), 1891–1914; Hirschfeld, Lawrence (1993): The child's representation of human groups. In: Medin, Douglas L. (Ed.): The psychology of learning and motivation Vol. 31. San Diego: Academic Press, 133–183; Kowalski, Kurt (1998): The Impact of Vicarious Exposure to Diversity on Preschoolers' Emerging Ethnic/Racial Attitudes. *Early Child Development and Care 146*(1), 41–51; Ramsey, Patricia (1991): The Salience of Race in Young Children Growing Up in All-White Community. *Journal of Educational Psychology 83*(1), 28–34; MacNaughton, Glenda/Davis, Karina (Ed.) (2009): "Race" and Early Childhood Education. An International Approach to Identity, Politics, and Pedagogy. New York: Palgrave Macmillan; van Ausdale, Debra/Feagin, Joe R. (2001): The First R: How Children Learn Race and Racism. Maryland: Rowman and Littlefield; Van Ausdale, Debra/Feagin, Joe R. (1996): Using Racial and Ethnic Concepts: The Critical Case of Very Young Children. *American Sociological Review 61*(5), 779–793.
161 Braunschweiger Zentrum für Gender Studies/Institut für Pädagogische Psychologie der Technischen Universität Braunschweig (Ed.) (2005): Geschlechtertrennung in der Kindheit: Empirische Forschung und pädagogische Praxis im Dialog. Final report of the project "Identity and gender in childhood", Braunschweig; Pithan, Annebelle (2007): Kinder als Jungen und Mädchen. In: Spenn, Matthias/Beneke, Doris/Harz, Frieder/Schweitzer, Friedrich (Ed.): Handbuch Arbeit mit Kindern – Evangelische Perspektiven. Gütersloh: Gütersloher Verlagshaus, 63–70; Pithan, Annebelle et al. (Ed.) (2009): Gender – Religion – Bildung.
162 For example, the two main results of Alice Pyke's dissertation show that the nationality of pupils and the type of school can influence attitudes towards religious diversity. Cf. Pyke, Alice (2013): Assessing and understanding young people's attitudes toward religious diversity in the United Kingdom. PhD thesis, University of Warwick, 139f.

in the following, research results are listed[163] that implicitly or explicitly address religious difference and are relevant for this study, while retaining the terminology used by the authors of the respective research work. If the research design for this publication is of interest, this will also be described. Since few studies have been carried out in the field of early childhood education, selected research results from the primary school sector, which are of interest for early childhood research are initially discussed.

1.1 Selected studies with children of primary school age

Compared to the field of early childhood education, there is a larger number of studies on children of primary school age in which religious difference plays a role – even if this is not explicitly addressed in the research question. The most important results from five research projects are briefly outlined below.

Gottfried Orth's research interest was that on the one hand, what children think theologically about God and religion, and on the other hand how children deal with the differences that arise among them. In the first meeting the children painted what they understood by "religion", in the second meeting what they understood by "God". Afterwards, in each of the meetings, they presented their picture to the other group members, whereby the pictures acted as a stimulus in bringing the children into conversation with each other. The conversations and the pictures of the students of the fourth grade were evaluated. Looking back on the conversations with four primary school children about the pictures they painted about religion and God, Gottfried Orth notes that non-discriminatory experiences of difference are a matter of course for children.[164] The children perceive the differences between the views, want to get into conversation about them and try to discover commonalities. Gottfried Orth emphasises the importance of religious difference and how to deal with it. "Difference and dealing with difference seem to me to be the central keywords for research and teaching in religious education in the coming years."[165]

A similar research design was used by Heinz Streib, who was concerned with the question of how children process elements in their constructions that they have known from tradition or their surroundings.[166] In a study by Bielefeld University, two children of different religions were interviewed in a primary school. During the interview

---

163 These refer to the publications available at the beginning of the research process.
164 Cf. Orth, Gottfried (2000): Umgang mit religiöser Differenz in Gesprächen über Bilder von Gott. In: Fischer, Dietlind/Schöll, Albrecht (Ed.): Religiöse Vorstellungen bilden. Erkundungen zur Religion von Kindern über Bilder. Münster: Comenius-Institut, 173–186, 182.
165 Ibid., 185.
166 Streib, Heinz (2000): Gottesbilder fallen nicht vom Himmel. Kindliche Malprozesse als Gestaltung von Religion. In: Fischer, Dietlind/Schöll, Albrecht (Ed.): Religiöse Vorstellungen bilden. Erkundungen zur Religion von Kindern über Bilder. Münster: Comenius-Institut, 129–141.

they were asked, without talking to each other, to paint a picture with symbols and pictures that they consider important for their own religion. Afterwards they were to exchange the pictures, explain them and ask questions about them. The session ended with a semi-structured interview asking questions about the differences and similarities between the two religions.[167] A more detailed description of one of the interviews made it clear that the two girls involved (whose parents were rooted in a traditional religion and who identified with its strict religious traditions), entered into a playful interreligious exchange of ideas and images, found similarities and agreements, became aware of the differences, but did not emphasize the differences and failed to argue for the superiority of a religion.[168] The curiosity shown by the girls is an important prerequisite according to Streib for the beginning of an interreligious encounter.[169]

Julia Ipgrave dedicated her study to the cross-religious encounter and religious understanding of children. Her previously unpublished dissertation "Inter faith encounter and religious understanding"[170] includes a research project in England with eight to eleven-year-old children who belonged to the non-Muslim minority at a school. The study was concerned with the religious understanding of the children who met at school and in the discussion groups. "The 'religious understanding' of the thesis title is both the content in terms of what the children understand about religion and about God, and the process by which they come to their understanding within the context of encounter."[171] The children were given playing cards with terms which they were to discover in turn and exchange afterwards. Also, a group was asked to develop questions for further group discussions, which were also discussed afterwards. The results of the study suggest that religious plurality is a matter of course for the children. Differences were identified by the children, but these were not always viewed positively, which Julia Ipgrave attributes to the minority status of the surveyed group within their peers, as responsible for this outcome. The children felt a certain pride in

---

167 Streib, Heinz (2001): Inter-Religious Negotiations: Case Studies on Students' Perception of and Dealing with Religious Diversity. In: Heimbrock, Hans-Guenter/Scheilke, Christoph/Schreiner, Peter (Ed.): Towards Religious Competence. Diversity as a Challenge for Education in Europe. Münster: LIT, 129-149, 134.
168 Ibid., 138.
169 Ibid., 140.
170 Ipgrave, Julia (2012): Inter faith encounter and religious understanding in an inner city primary school. PhD thesis, University of Warwick. The dissertation was not published, however, articles have been published on the dissertation, cf. Ipgrave, Julia (2013): The Language of Interfaith Encounter Among Inner City Primary School Children. *Religion & Education 40*(1), 35–49. Further studies followed this project, which resulted in several publications such as McKenna, Ursula/Ipgrave, Julia/Jackson, Robert (2008): Inter Faith Dialogue by Email in Primary Schools. An Evaluation of the Building E-Bridges Project. Religious diversity and education in Europe, vol. 6. Münster et al.: Waxmann.
171 Ipgrave, Julia (2002): Inter faith encounter and religious understanding in an inner city primary school. PhD thesis, University of Warwick 2002, 8.

their own religion. The children showed creative theological thinking and developed new theologies on how the god of a plural world could be understood.[172] Children's religious thinking seemed to be both flexible and at times inconsistent.[173]

In the project of Friedrich Schweitzer and Albert Biesinger "Strengthen commonalities – do justice to differences", group interviews were conducted with children of primary school age on denominational cooperation at school.[174] In the conversations with the children few prejudices against the other religion were visible. A division into a self-group and a foreign group demonstrated that the understanding of the different groups could result in challenges, because oppositions were often divided along national lines, Muslims and Germans. Religious differences were expressed as national differences, in that Muslims were described as "Turks" facing the "Germans". This could lead to prejudices down the road, if the classifications also correspond to the orientation needs of the children.[175] The children were particularly interested in the sensually perceptible differences between Protestant and Catholic.[176] Even if the children did not know which denomination they belonged to and what the terms Catholic or Protestant meant, they had some experiences that arose from a denominational or ecclesial context.[177] In the study, the children spoke only about the differences between the Christian denominations,which were explicitly asked, but not about the

---

172 Cf. Ipgrave, Julia (2013): The Language of Interfaith Encounter. *Religion & Education* 40(1), 35–49, 43.

173 Ibid., 37.

174 The results of the study are available in two volumes. Schweitzer, Friedrich/Biesinger, Albert (with Boschki, Reinhold/Schlenker, Claudia/Edelbrock, Anke/Kliss, Oliver/Scheidler, Monika) (2002): Gemeinsamkeiten stärken – Unterschieden gerecht werden. Erfahrungen und Perspektiven zum konfessionell-kooperativen Religionsunterricht. Freiburg i. Br./Basel/Vienna: Herder/Gütersloh: Gütersloher Verlagshaus; Schweitzer, Friedrich/Biesinger, Albert/Conrad, Jörg/Gronover, Matthias (2006): Dialogischer Religionsunterricht. Analyse und Praxis konfessionell-kooperativen Religionsunterricht im Jugendalter. Freiburg i. Br.: Herder. For a summary of the results, see Conrad, Jörg (2009): "As a Protestant, you somehow think a little less, somehow. Or "more or less the same" – how children perceive, understand and deal with denominational difference. In: Bucher, Anton A./Büttner, Gerhard/Freudenberger-Lötz, Petra/Schreiner, Martin. (Ed.): Jahrbuch der Kindertheologie: "In den Himmel kommen nur, die sich auch verstehen". Wie Kinder über religiöse Differenz denken und sprechen, vol. 8. Stuttgart: Calwer, 60–70, 68.

175 Schweitzer, Friedrich (2013): Religiöse Bildung als Integrationsfaktor? Aufgaben und Möglichkeiten Interreligiösen Lernens im Kindes- und Jugendalter. In: Rothgangel, Martin/Aslan, Ednan/Jäggle, Martin (Ed.): Religion und Gemeinschaft. Die Frage der Integration aus christlicher und muslimischer Perspektive (RaT-Reihe vol. 3). Göttingen: Vienna University Press by V&R unipress, 149–165, 156.

176 Schweitzer, Friedrich/Biesinger, Albert (with Boschki, Reinhold et al.) (2002): Gemeinsamkeiten stärken – Unterschieden gerecht werden, 25–29.

177 Cf. ibid., 73–75.

differences between different religions.[178] "In this respect, their religious orientation space proved to be clearly limited [...]. In any case, it would be inaccurate to assume that religious affiliations in childhood are not, in principle, and cannot become an object of children's reflection."[179]

In 2006 and 2007, a project was carried out at the Catholic University Kempen in Flanders in cooperation with the Katholieke Universiteit Leuven, in which 10- to 14-year-old children were asked about religion, religious education, ethnocentrism and values using questionnaires.[180] Among other things, the data led to the conclusion that children generally have a positive attitude towards multicultural society. "If they tend to think in black and white terms and are more negative towards religion, then they usually also distribute many points in the category ethnocentrism, or in other words, they are generally more negative towards people who are different."[181]

All these studies encouraged children to deal with religious similarities and differences through stimulus or through the compilation of group discussions and specific questions. The studies point out that children perceive religious differences, address them and enter into an exchange about similarities and differences. How these differences are interpreted differs in the individual studies, as Orth and Streib's research work shows that similarities are sought and that the differences are not particularly highlighted. In Ipgrave's study the children are partly proud of their religion and they are not exclusively positive about the differences mentioned. The work of Schweitzer and Biesinger indicates that few prejudices against the other religion become visible, but a frequent subdivision into a self-group and a foreign group takes place. The project in Flanders emphasises the fundamental positive attitude of the children towards the multicultural society.

---

178 Schweitzer, Friedrich (2009): Wie Kinder und Jugendliche religiöse Differenz wahrnehmen – Möglichkeiten und Grenzen der Orientierung in der religiösen Pluralität. In: Bucher, Anton A. et al. (Ed.): Jahrbuch der Kindertheologie: "In den Himmel kommen nur, die sich auch verstehen", 39–49, 45.

179 Ibid.

180 Dillen, Annemie (2009): Glaubensvorstellungen von Kindern und ihre Wahrnehmung von Multikulturalität. In: Bucher, Anton A. et al. (Ed.): Jahrbuch der Kindertheologie: "In den Himmel kommen nur, die sich auch verstehen", 50–59. Cf. also Henckens, Reinhilde/ Pollefeyt, Didier/Hutsebaut, Dirk/Dillen, Annemie/Maex, Joke/De Boeck, Ellen (2011): Geloof in kinderen? Levensbeschouwelijke perspectieven van kinderen in kaart gebracht. Opzet, methode en resultaten van empirisch onderzoek bij leerkrachten rooms-katholieke godsdienst en hun leerlingen in de derde graad lager onderwijs en de eerste graad secundair onderwijs. Instrumenta Theologica 33. Leuven: Uitgeverij Peeters.

181 Dillen, Annemie (2009): Glaubensvorstellungen von Kindern. In: Bucher, Anton A. et al. (Ed.): Jahrbuch der Kindertheologie: "In den Himmel kommen nur, die sich auch verstehen", 50–59, 57.

1.2 Empirical studies with children in early childhood education

In addition to research results in the primary school sector, results of research with children in the field of early childhood education are of particular relevance. Following her study on interreligious and intercultural learning at primary schools, Erna Zonne emphasises that field research would be interesting to conduct on four- to five-year-old children, particularly because of the great openness of children at this age. In addition, the first encounter with other religions often takes place at this age and the teacher plays an important role. However, researchers consider the teaching of these children to be more challenging at this age, due to the teaching being less structured.[182] Eva Hoffmann, Friedrich Schweitzer, Albert Biesinger and Anke Edelbrock, who have already conducted studies on religious differences in day care centres, emphasize the lack of research on this topic. These studies and others that address religious difference, taking into account the perspective of the children, are presented below.

1.2.1 Eva Hoffmann: Interreligious Learning in Kindergarten?

In 2009, Eva Hofmann published a pilot study on interreligious differences in her work „Interreligiöses Lernen im Kindergarten. Eine empirische Studie zum Umgang mit religiöser Vielfalt in Diskussionen mit Kindern zum Thema Tod" (Interreligious Learning in Kindergarten? An empirical study on dealing with religious diversity in discussions with children on the topic of death), in which she asked children about their ideas about death and life after death in group discussions. The study investigated the following research question: "What do kindergarten children of different religions say in group discussions with regard to the question of what might come after death?".[183] The focus was on what answers children of different religions find in a common conversation and how children deal with any differences that may arise among them.[184] The existence of different religions was not explicitly addressed by the researcher, but religious plurality was implicitly addressed by children of different religions having group discussions with each other, which were initiated by the researcher through an impulse.

Eva Hoffmann came to the conclusion that children encounter the diversity of individual ideas with composure. "Differences are perceived, endured, but not highlighted."[185] The children were prepared "to engage with the foreign, to deal with it, to think about their own ideas and, if necessary, to partially withdraw them in the

---

182 Zonne, Erna (2006): Interreligiöses und interkulturelles Lernen an Grundschulen in Rotterdam-Rijnmond. Münster et al.: Waxmann, 352–354.
183 Hoffmann, Eva (2009): Interreligiöses Lernen im Kindergarten? Eine empirische Studie zum Umgang mit religiöser Vielfalt in Diskussionen mit Kindern zum Thema Tod. Berlin: LIT, 105.
184 Cf. Ibid.
185 Ibid., 91; 221.

face of other considerations or to support them with arguments.[186] The children made no explicit references to religious traditions, and some of the religious references made did not refer to beliefs of their own religious community.[187] Rather, difference was related to individual ideas of the children and not to their religious affiliations and associated conventions, which are marked by little reference to tradition.[188] The individual ideas were very important for some children and they did not give them up easily.[189] Some children showed a certain pride in individually formulated ideas, but not in their religious affiliation.[190] Different religious ideas were thematised[191] and there were no scenes of xenophobic fear or anxiety in Eva Hoffmann's investigation.[192]

1.2.2 Friedrich Schweitzer, Albert Biesinger, Anke Edelbrock: Tübingen projects

The studies by Friedrich Schweitzer, Albert Biesinger and Anke Edelbrock consist of a pilot project and five subsequent subprojects, each published in a book. The pilot project „Mein Gott – Dein Gott" (My God – Your God)[193] by Friedrich Schweitzer, Albert Biesinger and Anke Edelbrock, conducted in 2006 and 2007, integrates a qualitative and a quantitative component and is dedicated to the question of how intercultural and interreligious education takes place in day care centres. In the qualitative part, 37 interviews were conducted and evaluated. Experts, managers in day-care centres in districts with a high proportion of immigrant population, seven Muslim teachers and one Muslim mother were interviewed. The questionnaire was designed on the basis of the results of the interviews. The questionnaires were sent to 940 municipal and 758 denominational institutions, 364 questionnaires were returned, which corresponds to a response rate of 21 percent. Confessional kindergartens offer Christian and religious education, and address to a lesser extent other religions. In non-denominational day care centres, religion is less common and children remain without concrete religious instruction.

---

186 Ibid., 91.
187 Cf. ibid., 213-221.
188 Cf. ibid., 213.
189 Cf. ibid., 215.
190 Cf. ibid., 213.
191 Cf. ibid., 212.
192 Cf. ibid., 217.
193 Schweitzer, Friedrich/Biesinger, Albert/Edelbrock, Anke (2008): Mein Gott – Dein Gott.

The subprojects are divided into a study on the perception of differences in childhood,[194] a parent survey,[195] a representative survey of teachers,[196] a description of best practice models,[197] a description of competences[198] and the discussion of basic and advanced training for the early childhood sector .[199] In the qualitative empirical study „Wie viele Götter sind im Himmel? Religiöse Differenzwahrnehmung im Kindesalter" (How many gods are in heaven? Perception of religious difference in childhood),[200] the children were given the opportunity to speak, whereby the subjective view of the children and their constructions of religious difference became clear. There were 140 children, 71 girls and 69 boys with the average age of four years and nine months, interviewed. 65 Christian children, 49 Muslim children and 20 children without religion participated in the study. The three survey dates were based on different focal points, whereby four aspects of interreligious education were to be examined: Knowledge, experiences, attitudes and language skills. In order to collect these aspects, group interviews were conducted, which were introduced by stimulus such as showing Christian or Islamic symbols as well as pictures or a narrative, like the circumstances surrounding different eating habits. The study focused on Christianity and Islam by showing only religious symbols from these two religions.

In order to determine the children's knowledge and attitudes, discussions were held with a maximum of three children, between ten and twenty minutes. For the category of knowledge, children were asked questions based on photos or pictures, what they could see, whether they had seen something similar before, experienced it themselves

---

194 Edelbrock, Anke/Schweitzer, Friedrich/Biesinger, Albert (Ed.) (2010): Wie viele Götter sind im Himmel? Religiöse Differenzwahrnehmung im Kindesalter. Interreligiöse und interkulturelle Bildung im Kindesalter, vol. 1. Münster et al.: Waxmann.
195 Biesinger, Albert/Edelbrock, Anke/Schweitzer, Friedrich (Ed.) (2011): Auf die Eltern kommt es an! Interreligiöse und interkulturelle Bildung in der Kita. Interreligiöse und Interkulturelle Bildung im Kindesalter, vol. 2. Münster et al.: Waxmann.
196 Schweitzer, Friedrich/Edelbrock, Anke/Biesinger, Albert (Ed.) (2011): Interreligiöse und interkulturelle Bildung in der Kita. Eine Repräsentativbefragung von Erzieherinnen in Deutschland – interdisziplinäre, interreligiöse und internationale Perspektiven. Interreligiöse und interkulturelle Bildung im Kindesalter. Vol. 3. Münster et al.: Waxmann.
197 Edelbrock, Anke/Biesinger, Albert/Schweitzer, Friedrich (Ed.) (2012): Religiöse Vielfalt in der Kita. So gelingt interreligiöse und interkulturelle Bildung in der Praxis. Berlin: Cornelsen Verlag Scriptor.
198 Biesinger, Albert/Schweitzer, Friedrich (2013): Religionspädagogische Kompetenzen. Zehn Zugänge für pädagogische Fachkräfte in Kitas. Freiburg/Basel/Vienna: Herder.
199 Schweitzer, Friedrich/Biesinger, Albert (Ed.) (2015): Kulturell und religiös sensibel? Interreligiöse und Interkulturelle Kompetenz in der Ausbildung für den Elementarbereich. Interreligiöse und interkulturelle Bildung im Kindesalter, vol. 5. Münster/New York: Waxmann.
200 Edelbrock, Anke/Schweitzer, Friedrich/Biesinger, Albert (Ed.) (2010): Wie viele Götter sind im Himmel?.

or practised it.[201] Children were shown cards with drawings of various foods and asked which three they would like to eat and which they would not like to eat. The renunciation of pork was explicitly mentioned in the form of a report from another kindergarten, in which the children were symbolically represented in the context of a role play using simple play figures. In the third part of the interview, the children were asked about their desired seat neighbour and their behaviour in conflict situations. The main questions were: What are you doing? How are the other kids?[202] In order to learn something about the children's experiences, ten to twenty-minute conversations were held with two children or individual conversations were held. Discussions began with a question about Easter. An attempt was made to open up the interreligious dimension by telling the children of other children who spoke of Allah or God. The evaluation of the transcripts followed a content-analytical procedure.

The study made it clear that children think independently about interreligious questions and contexts. Many of the 140 children had little religious knowledge, but five-year-olds already perceived the religious plurality of society and were interested in it, as demonstrated by individual parts of the conversation. Some of the children knew about the existence of religious differences, whereby the sometimes-limited knowledge was combined with questions of orientation.[203] "Again and again it becomes clear that the children independently work on and try to answer such orientation questions, but that the results sometimes remain confusing or unsatisfactory if one considers them from a religious education point of view."[204] Children spontaneously made group assignments and social categorisations, mixing religion and nationality. "Religious differences are most rarely described as religious. What is more typical are confrontations – oppositions between "we" and "they", which follow religious ideas without the correlations appearing to be really clear to the children".[205] One way of establishing links between knowledge and attitudes was through role-playing, which enabled children to put themselves in the situation.[206] The children showed "openness and interest in the other as well as restraint, defence and distancing. Expressions of incomprehension or rejection were more common among children who were unable

---

201 Cf. Dubiski, Katja/Essich, Ibtissame/Schweitzer, Friedrich/Edelbrock, Anke/Biesinger, Albert (2010): Religiöse Differenzwahrnehmung im Kindesalter. Befunde aus der empirischen Untersuchung im Überblick. In: Edelbrock, Anke/Schweitzer, Friedrich/Biesinger, Albert (Ed.): Wie viele Götter sind im Himmel?, 23–38, 26.
202 Ibid., 27.
203 Dubiski, Katja et al. (2010): Religiöse Differenzwahrnehmung im Kindesalter. Eine qualitativ-empirische Untersuchung mit Kindern im Alter zwischen 4 und 6 Jahren. In: Edelbrock, Anke/Schweitzer, Friedrich/Biesinger, Albert (Ed.): Wie viele Götter sind im Himmel?, 122–194, 187.
204 Ibid. What remains open is what unsatisfactory results in religious education mean.
205 Ibid., 189.
206 Dubiski, Katja et al. (2010): Religiöse Differenzwahrnehmung im Kindesalter. Befunde. In: Edelbrock, Anke/Schweitzer, Friedrich/Biesinger, Albert (Ed.): Wie viele Götter sind im Himmel?, 23–38, 31.

to connect with the other group of people they knew"[207] Dubiski, Essich, Schweitzer, Edelbrock and Biesinger summarize at the end of the work "Wie viele Götter sind im Himmel" that "the findings on the question of a religious perception of difference in childhood already raise numerous educational or religious pedagogical challenges in the field of early childhood education"[208] and there is no discernible reason for an exclusion of this aspect. If the differences are addressed, the children's questions are taken seriously and an answer is given, or a common search process initiated by the question,and there are opportunities for successful togetherness and learning from one another, whereas misunderstandings and prejudices can arise if the children's questions are ignored.[209]

In the study „Auf die Eltern kommt es an" (It depends on the parents),[210] discussions with 44 parents were conducted in the qualitative part and 581 questionnaires were completed in the quantitative part. Religion is seldom addressed in parent-teacher discussions, from which it can be concluded that parents pay little attention to religious education in the day-care centre. One third of the respondents agreed that religious education should take place in the day care centre, and one third of the respondents were against it. The importance of communication in relation to questions of religious education between educators and parents becomes clear.

The study „Interreligiöse und Interkulturelle Bildung in der Kita" (Interreligious and Intercultural Education at the Kita)[211] was conducted as a quantitative questionnaire study. 2,838 questionnaires were completed and returned, representing a 28 percent response rate. The survey provided a representative picture of the territory of the Federal Republic of Germany and provided insight into the composition of the children's groups in religious terms, general support for religious education, Christian, Islamic and Jewish, interreligious and intercultural education, the perception of parents, role of the sponsor and the evaluation of education and further training. Children of different religions, the majority of whom are Christian, Muslim or non-denominational, attend both denominational and non-denominational institutions. The importance of intercultural education is rated higher than interreligious education, which is not sufficiently perceived in most institutions. Little importance is attached to Islamic themes and the religious accompaniment of Jewish children is hardly taken into account. In non-denominational institutions, the likelihood of children receiving

---

207 Ibid., 33.
208 Dubiski, Katja et al. (2010): Religiöse Differenzwahrnehmung im Kindesalter. Eine qualitativ-empirische Untersuchung. In: Edelbrock, Anke/Schweitzer, Friedrich/Biesinger, Albert (Ed.): Wie viele Götter sind im Himmel?, 122–194, 194.
209 Cf. Dubiski, Katja et al. (2010): Religiöse Differenzwahrnehmung im Kindesalter. Befunde. In: Edelbrock, Anke/Schweitzer, Friedrich/Biesinger, Albert (Ed.): Wie viele Götter sind im Himmel?, 23–38, 30.
210 Biesinger, Albert/Edelbrock, Anke/Schweitzer, Friedrich (Ed.) (2011): Auf die Eltern kommt es an!
211 Schweitzer, Friedrich/Edelbrock, Anke/Biesinger, Albert (Ed.) (2011): Interreligiöse und Interkulturelle Bildung in der Kita.

religious accompaniment is low, even for Christian children. Regardless of the sponsorship, the teachers are open to religious topics, but this does not have any practical consequences. Due to lack of training and further education, the educators feel insufficiently prepared for interreligious education. Nor do they receive any support from the institution in relation to religious education topics.

> "Overall, the results of the study show that there is a clear backlog demand in the early childhood sector. In future, the task of religious accompaniment for children of different backgrounds and interreligious education must be taken much more seriously than it has been the case up to now. The fact that the early childhood sector is increasingly lagging behind (primary) school is a deficient state of affairs that could by no means be justified by the children's developmental and orientational needs or possibilities."[212]

In the work "Religiöse Vielfalt in der Kita! – Best-Practice-Beispiele" (Religious Diversity in Daycare! Best Practice Examples)[213], the interreligious practice of 17 institutions was presented, where a range of different model profiles was be made visible.

1.2.3 David Elkind: Research on the Development of Faith

In a study with 790 children, David Elkind was interested in the importance of religious identity for children of different ages. He asked the Protestant, Catholic and Jewish children questions like "Are you a... "Is your family ...", "Are all boys and girls in the world...", "Can a dog or cat be a...". How can you tell a person that they are a...? "What is a...?", "How do you become a..." "Can you be an American and a..." at the same time?".[214] At the age of five to seven, children had a global, undifferentiated impression of their religious community, which resembled a family name. When asked what this meant, it became clear that they had only a vague, unclear idea of the faith community.[215]

David Elkind asked the children suggestive questions, which they answered with Yes or No, and only when further questions were asked, some of the questions were open. In the answers to these questions, the mixture of religious, national and racial differences became clear. Moreover, the children exclusively thought that being American prevented one from being Protestants, Catholics or Jews. Elkind explained that the child knew that he or she only had one family name and therefore could not have

---

212 Schweitzer, Friedrich et al. (2011): Interreligiöse und interkulturelle Bildung in Kindertagesstätten. In: Schweitzer, Friedrich/Edelbrock, Anke/Biesinger, Albert (Ed.): Interreligiöse und interkulturelle Bildung in der Kita, 29–54, 54.
213 Edelbrock, Anke/Biesinger, Albert/Schweitzer, Friedrich (Ed.) (2012): Religiöse Vielfalt in der Kita.
214 Cf. Elkind, David (1964): Age changes in the meaning of religious identity. *Review of Religious Research* 6(1), 36–40, 37.
215 Ibid.

two general affiliations at the same time. He spoke of a "nominal conception", thus of belonging to a religious group by name. The children heard terms, but could not associate them with certain characteristics. Primary school children between the ages of seven and nine could clearly distinguish between religious and non-religious affiliations, but the distinctions were based on descriptions of personal observations, the visible differences were thus in the foreground and there were no abstract or rational formulations.[216] Elkind concluded that children from the age of five or six and often earlier are aware of their religious identity,[217] but comprehend it more when they reach adolescence.[218]

1.2.4 Ina ter Avest: Experiences in dealing with others

In this study conducted by Ina ter Avest together with five Bachelor students, children from a kindergarten (four to five years) and a primary school in the Dutch metropolitan area (six to twelve years) were asked questions about their experiences with the other. A four-year-old boy of Turkish descent, a five-year-old girl of Surinamese descent and a five-year-old girl and a five-year-old boy of Dutch descent were interviewed. It was assumed that children had developed their own Theory of Mind based on their experiences. Ina ter Avest chose a very open approach to the conversation, which refers to the day on which the conversation took place. The child was shown a box of dolls and asked who they had already seen that day. The child was asked about two or three familiar people, significant others, and was told it should choose a doll and dress it like these other people. Afterwards, the child chose a doll that represents itself and dressed the doll as the child dresses itself. The child was then asked whether it had met a person it did not know that day or on another day. The child also chose a doll for this person. The conversation continued with the doll that embodied the unknown person and the doll that represented the child itself. Questions were asked, such as "When was the encounter? How did it go? How did the child experience the encounter?".[219] The child was encouraged to repeat the encounter with the dolls, whereupon the child told what the doll felt and thought in this situation, whereby the encounter with the other was reconstructed. Ina ter Avest notes in her pilot study, which addresses whom children perceive as different, that religion

> "is either so 'normal' that they don't say they're not interested in religion yet, or they don't have words yet. They focus on other aspects, such as whether someone is 'nice'. This means that they look at similarities and not so much at differences (yet). Neither

---

216 Ibid., 38.
217 Ibid., 36.
218 Ibid., 40.
219 ter Avest, Ina (2010): Der Andere – fast so wie ich? Der Unterschied zwischen dem Ich und dem Anderen aus der Sicht von Kindergartenkindern. In: Edelbrock, Anke/Schweitzer, Friedrich/Biesinger, Albert (Ed.): Wie viele Götter sind im Himmel?, 89–103, 99.

the attention of the youngest children nor their religious education seems sufficiently developed to explore and discuss this aspect further with adults."[220]

1.2.5 Daniel Bar-Tal: Concept of an "Arab" in Israel

Daniel Bar-Tal[221] explored in studies done in Israel how Israeli children understand the concept of an "Arab", on what basis children form such a concept,[222] what evaluation children make and what the visual prototype of an "Arab" is in the mind of the child. Many of the two and a half to three-year-old children in the study of Bar-Tal had already developed a concept of an "Arab". At this age children internalize the categorical and symbolic principles of language and can learn context-independent words.[223] Children at this age begin to understand that the "Arabs" are a group that can be distinguished from the group of "Jews".[224] They are able to characterise them linguistically with different characteristics and to draw them concretely. Five- to six-year-old children were better able to recognise an "Arab" in a picture than three- to four-year-olds. Not all children between the ages of three and six had knowledge of Arabs, but some of those who could say something about them described them negatively. Due to negative information from parents and other sources about "Arabs", the negative evaluations of the children were not surprising. It became clear that even very young children express negative evaluations which increased starting at the age of six or seven years. In children aged three to six there was a positive correlation between negative attributes and refusal of social contact. Israeli children at the age of four associated something negative with the term "Arab", although the majority of the children could not identify an "Arab" when presenting various photos. The results from the study demonstrate that children learn – especially with very negative intergroup relationships – to establish associations between group names and negative evaluations at the linguistic level alone.

---

220 Ibid., 101.
221 Bar-Tal, Daniel (1996): Development of social categories and stereotypes in early childhood: The case of "the Arab" concept formation, stereotype and attitudes by Jewish children in Israel. *International Journal of Intercultural Relations 20*(314), 341–370.
222 By concepts, the study means mental representations of classes or beings. Cf. Bar-Tal, Daniel (1996): Development of social categories. *International Journal of Intercultural Relations 20*(314), 341–370, 343.
223 Bar-Tal, Daniel (1996): Development of social categories. *International Journal of Intercultural Relations 20*(314), 341–370, 360.
224 Ibid., 361.

1.2.6 Paul Connolly et al.: Attitude towards groups in Northern Ireland

The studies by Paul Connolly[225] et al. in Northern Ireland clearly show the importance of addressing the differences in kindergarten. The research was conducted in parts of Northern Ireland where religious separation and partial violence between Catholic and Protestant believers prevailed.[226] The research results are partly representative for all children in Northern Ireland.

The results of Connolly's "Developing programmes to promote ethnic diversity in early childhood" show significant differences in attitudes between three-year-olds and certain groups. Three-year-old Protestant and Catholic children have already adopted the cultural habits and preferences of their community, even if they first had to learn what they meant and they are mostly unaware of their affiliation to a specific community.[227] "Given that children in Northern Ireland are growing up in a highly divided and segregated society, it is not surprising to find that they are likely to be internalizing the dispositions and cultural habits of their own communities."[228] In "Too Young to Notice",[229] Connolly, Smith and Kelly interviewed 352 children between the ages of three and six in Northern Ireland, using images, photographs and symbols related to the local cultural divide. The children were asked about each item what they knew about it and about some of the items they liked best or if they liked them. Children's awareness of differences was much stronger in terms of symbols or events than in terms of terms such as "Catholic", "Protestant" or certain colours.[230] At the age of six, 34 percent of the children surveyed identified themselves with a community and 15 percent made confessional remarks about the "other side".[231]

In the "Children and the conflict in Northern Ireland" research project, Connolly and Healy used ethnographic methods to better understand the perspective of children

---

225 An overview of the studies of Paul Connolly, who in many of his studies deals with different dimensions of difference, can be found on his homepage. (Paul Connolly, http://www.paulconnolly.net/publications/ [21.07.2015]).
226 In the separation between the two ethnic groups of Northern Ireland, religion became a sign of diversity and a form of distinction between the two traditions. Northern Ireland is an example of a context of fear, mistrust, religious tension and occasional violence.
227 Connolly, Paul/Healy, July (2004): Children and the conflict in Northern Ireland: The Experiences and Perspectives of 3–11 Year Olds. Belfast: Office of the First Minister and Deputy First Minister, 34.
228 Connolly, Paul (2009): Developing programmes to promote ethnic diversity in early childhood: Lessons from Northern Ireland. Working Paper No. 52. The Hague, The Netherlands: Bernard van Leer Foundation, 13.
229 Connolly, Paul/Smith, Alan/Kelly, Berny (2002): Too Young to Notice. The cultural and political awareness of 3–6 year olds in Northern Ireland. A report commissioned by the Northern Ireland Community Relations Council in Partnership with Channel 4. Belfast: Community Relations Council.
230 Ibid., 50.
231 Connolly, Paul (2009): Developing programmes, 14.

and examine the relationship of the social contexts, and they focused on three age groups: Three- to four-, seven- to eight- and ten- to eleven-year-olds.[232] They examined Protestant and Catholic children from two neighbouring regions who had social and economic deprivation and a high level of denominational tension and sporadic violence. Three- to four year-old children developed an awareness of different people and their roles as well as of certain events, objects and symbols they saw. At this age, children's consciousness seemed to be related to immediate experiences that they sought to understand through close observation, role-playing and hearing.[233] Some of the children's role-plays addressed the tension between the two areas, but they were isolated events. The conflict and the separations associated with it did not significantly determine the daily play of the children.[234] "Overall, however, these tended to be relatively isolated incidents. Observing the children over an extended period of time made it clear that the conflict and the divisions associated with it did not tend to figure prominently in their day-to-day play."[235] To understand whether children are unaware of the events and symbols or whether they do not consider them important, each child was interviewed towards the end of the field study by showing items and asking them about them. These interviews confirmed the thesis that children had experiences with and were familiar with the individual items, some had strong opinions on them, but that these did not play an important role in their current lives. The attitudes and preferences of children aged three to four were more clearly defined and communicated among children aged seven and eight, and there was an awareness of the cultural and political importance of football teams, for example. The preference for certain events and symbols associated with their own community forms the basis on which some children develop negative attitudes and prejudices about the other community.[236] "The general preferences they have already internalised towards particular cultural events and symbols now provide the lens through which they come to identify, make sense of and organise a wide range of new experiences."[237] Even if they only understand individual terms and symbols partially, this does not protect many children from perceiving the other community as negative and prejudiced.[238]

Further studies by Connolly with five- to six-year-old children in a primary school in England have shown that girls with light skin tones have a feeling for femininity and attractiveness through negative and stereotypical comparisons with South Asian girls. Similarly, Afro-Caribbean and light-coloured boys tended to emphasise their own masculinity in comparison with South African boys, who they considered weak and

---

232 Connolly, Paul/Healy, July (2004): Children and the conflict in Northern Ireland.
233 Connolly, Paul (2009): Developing programmes, 15.
234 Cf. ibid., 16.
235 Ibid.
236 Connolly, Paul/Healy, July (2004): Children and the conflict in Northern Ireland, 104f.
237 Ibid., 48.
238 Cf. ibid., 48f.

feminine.[239] In the researches, different motivations were determined of why children exclude others. This is not always due to negative prejudices towards others, but can also mean a strong preference of one's own group. This is evident in young Protestant and Catholic children in Northern Ireland who have a clear preference for the culture and tradition of their reference group without negative attitudes towards others.[240]

In summary, Connolly's study results suggest that not addressing the differences of another group can also mean that these differences are currently not important to the children, although they are aware of them. Children are able to distinguish groups from each other and to form concepts and apply them to certain groups of people if opinions about them prevail in their environment. Children often show a strong preference of their own group, as shown by the young Protestant and Catholic children in the study done in Northern Ireland, but this does not have to be accompanied by negative attitudes towards others. The results of the study argue in favour of not using terms in research design that characterise religions, but to use religious celebrations, experiences or symbols as a starting point for conversations.

Due to the importance of the context, the results are not directly transferable to other contexts, which is why studies are necessary in different social and societal contexts. The importance of context for understanding children's attitudes and behaviour is emphasised: "The nature and forms taken by racism and ethnic divisions vary enormously from one context to the next and also at any specific time within a particular context [...]."[241] In addition, Paul Connolly emphasises the influence of the type of research design and research execution on the results. A child-friendly research design, which is not determined by concepts or the experiences of adults, is a prerequisite for being able to perceive and appreciate children's attitudes and experiences accordingly, to which the results of childhood research make an important contribution. Paul Connolly points out that earlier studies to investigate whether existing separations affect young children underestimated the extent to which the children were affected. This can be explained by the fact that adults tried to transfer their way of thinking to children:

> "It is shown that much of the earlier research tended to underestimate the extent to which existing divisions affect young children. This can be explained largely by the fact that researchers have tended to apply adult ways of thinking about the conflict to young children and assessing their attitudes and levels of awareness on that basis."[242]

The importance of listening to young children and understanding their experiences against the background of the social environment around them is perhaps the crux of the research. "Perhaps the key point is the importance of listening to young children

---

239 Cf. Connolly, Paul (2008): Positive identities may lead to negative beliefs. In: Brooker, Liz/Woodhead, Martin (Ed.): Developing Positive Identities, 42.
240 Ibid.
241 Connolly, Paul (2009): Developing programmes, 5.
242 Ibid.

and understanding their experiences and perspectives against wider social environments within which they live."[243]

The early childhood sector can have a significant impact on the lives of young children and it is possible to have positive and demonstrable effects on the characteristics of children and their levels of consciousness.[244] The studies prove "the important role of research in informing our understanding of the impact of ethnic divisions on young children."[245]

1.3 Summary of research results

The above-mentioned research, which took place in different contexts, agrees that children perceive difference and address the difference that occurs, but vary in how children judge this difference. The studies of Bar-Tal in Israel and the studies of Connolly in Northern Ireland have each taken place in a context of enmity towards another group. This rejection by society of a clearly defined group has an effect on children's statements and assessments of this other group. Children are able to adopt and integrate these attributes. They understand that there is another group to which they themselves do not belong, so they are able to form and evaluate concepts about another group. Remaining in one's own group can also be related to a strong preference for these contexts without devaluing the other group. Connolly's results pay special attention to child-friendly examination design, through which it can be ascertained what actually occupies the children. According to the research results of Connolly and Bar-Tal, it remains open how children perceive religious difference in another context. Is religious difference an issue for children when there are no open conflicts?

In Ipgrave's study, some children show pride in their religious affiliation, which can also be connected with the religious minority status of the children surveyed at school, whereas in Hoffmann's survey the children are sometimes proud of their individual ideas, but not of their religious affiliation. In Ina ter Avest's research project, the children do not mention religion and religious difference in their role-plays about others. The question that follows from these research results is that of the context, the effect of the context and the influence of the methodology on children and on their perception and thematisation of religious difference.

The German-language surveys deal with the question of how children react to a certain input in a group with children of different religious affiliations. Due to this stimuli, all studies in German-speaking countries refer to a relatively short duration of field research. The research designs of the presented research work on children of primary school age as well as the studies by Hoffmann, Schweitzer, Biesinger and Edelbrock and Bar-Tal confronted the children with a problem situation, with pictures

---

243 Ibid., 25.
244 Cf. ibid., 27.
245 Ibid., 25.

of people or objects of different religions. Based on these stimuli, they spoke either in group discussions or in individual interviews with the children. Only Connolly's work is devoted to the question of how children address the divisions occurring in the country in their play on the basis of an ethnographic approach and concludes that these are rarely the subject of children's play. In some analyses – such as Connolly and Bar-Tal – the context of the country is addressed, Hoffmann and Ipgrave thematise the environment of kindergartens and schools. None of the investigations takes a closer look at what is happening in the respective institutions. The mentioned meaning of the context refers to the social context, the possible meaning of the organisation is not examined in detail. The focus of the work is exclusively on one group of people, which means that relationships between those acting in the field and the importance of the entire organisation are not taken into account.

The question remains open of how children address religious difference if no direct impulse from the researchers instructs the children to talk about it and how children address religious difference in the context of the respective kindergarten. The present study is based on a look at the organisation of the kindergarten with the question of to what extent it deals with religious difference and how children address this religious difference. This requires a research method that is not limited to stimulus given by researchers, which is carried out over a longer period of time and supplements the view of the children from the perspective of the organisation.[246]

2. Research question

This study takes up the above question by focusing on what is happening in two kindergartens and exploring, on the basis of an ethnographic approach, the thematisation of religious difference by children – without specific research-led impulses. Thus, the practice of kindergarten and the children's perspective on religious difference are investigated in this project, which is why the work is based on a double perspective question:

How are Catholic kindergartens and Islamic kindergartens in Vienna dealing with religious differences and how do children address them?

As is usual in grounded theory studies, this research question crystallised during the course of the research process. The approach to the field was based on a question focused on children, how these religious differences are addressed. Due to the participant observation and the first group discussions with the children, differences in the thematisation of religious differences became apparent, depending on the kindergarten in which the research was carried out. The initial focus on children was extended to the context of the kindergarten, as the entire setting of the kindergarten had to be taken into account in order to better understand the thematisation or non-thematisation of religious difference by the children. The focus on one group in kindergartens

---

246 Cf. part IV "Study design and conduct".

would ignore the diverse relationships in kindergarten and the different influences in kindergarten and thus the view of the selected group of children would be too limited to gain an understanding for them. For this reason, the research question focused on children was extended to include the question of dealing with religious difference in kindergarten.

3. Concern of the study

The aim of this study, on the basis of a Catholic kindergarten and an Islamic kindergarten,[247] is to show tendencies with regard to the dual-perspective question of how kindergartens deal with religious differences and how these are thematised by the children or how they relate to them. Due to the importance of the context, a final theoretical development is not carried out.

> "However, it is important not to develop universal theories on how race and ethnicity affect young children's lives. The nature and forms taken by racism and ethnic divisions vary enormously from one context to the next and also at any specific time within a particular context […]."[248]

If it is known how children address religious difference and how religious difference is dealt with in organisations, empirically founded concepts for interreligious education can be formulated and pedagogical and religious educational implications can be named. The lack of empirical research on which interreligious concepts are based has been noted by several authors.

> "In German-speaking countries there has been a lack of systematic and wide-ranging research into when and how young children begin to refer to differences in people and what implications these differences have for their identity constructions."[249]

Albert Biesinger, Friedrich Schweitzer, Anke Edelbrock and Eva Hoffmann emphasize the importance of research on how children deal with religious difference and the lack of empirical analyses.

> "Empirically, very little is known about how children deal with religious differences, especially with regard to pre-school children. For interreligious education in kindergarten it is therefore crucial to get to know children's perceptions, views and attitudes

---

247 Cf. chapter "Selection of kindergartens" (part IV, 2).
248 Connolly, Paul (2009): Developing programmes, 5.
249 Wagner, Petra (²2010): Vielfalt und Diskriminierung im Erleben von Kindern. In: Wagner, Petra (Ed.): Handbuch Kinderwelten. Vielfalt als Chance – Grundlagen einer vorurteilsbewussten Bildung und Erziehung. Freiburg/Basel/Vienna: Herder [2008], 56–71, 58.

first and foremost, so that a realistic and at the same time child-oriented formulation of educational tasks becomes possible."[250]

Furthermore, according to Eva Hoffmann, there is an urgent need for research into the other priorities of interreligious learning.[251] Thanks to the research projects of Biesinger, Schweitzer, Edelbrock and the study of Hoffmann, results on the handling of religious difference in the German-speaking area are available and given the small number of studies, the shortcomings they have identified can still be ascertained [252].

In order to investigate the research question with the help of a research design that is suitable for children, some developmental psychological findings and relevant insights from childhood research are discussed in Sections 4 and 5.

4. Developmental psychological findings

Developmental psychology tries to present the normal course of development on the basis of research results. The findings "challenge religious education to engage in the experiences, ideas and world approaches of children and young people. They serve the cause of being appropriate for children."[253] However, "developmental psychological possibilities and conditions of intercultural education and training" have been minimally researched.[254] This also applies to interreligious education and training. In the following, only those developmental psychological findings are mentioned that are relevant to the content of the present research work. The examination of these is of particular importance for the conceptual design of the study. During data collection and evaluation, developmental psychological findings were largely ignored in order to respect the individuality of the child and to allow for difference.

For the design of the study, the cognitive development of the child and the various thinking and categorisation achievements associated with it as well as the social and emotional competence of the child are particularly relevant, since these can influence the perception, the communication and the behaviour of the children. These areas are briefly outlined.[255]

---

250 Biesinger, Albert/Schweitzer, Friedrich/Edelbrock, Anke (2010): Religiöse Differenzwahrnehmung im Kindesalter. Befunde aus der der empirischen Untersuchung im Überblick. In: Edelbrock, Anke/Schweitzer, Friedrich/Biesinger, Albert (Ed.): Wie viele Götter sind im Himmel?, 23–38, 24.
251 Cf. Hoffmann, Eva (2009): Interreligiöses Lernen im Kindergarten?, 236.
252 Cf. chapter "Empirical studies with children in early childhood education" (part II, 1.2).
253 Schweitzer, Friedrich (2006): Religionspädagogik, 112.
254 Auernheimer, Georg (2012): Einführung in die Interkulturelle Pädagogik, 126.
255 The developmental psychological findings are presented with a view to the areas of interest for this research without any claim to a complete presentation of the children's development.

4.1 Cognitive development of pre-school children

Piaget's model has had a lasting influence on research in developmental psychology, even though some points of his theses have been criticised and refuted. Piaget adopts a preoperational approach for children aged two to six. In this phase, children are able to "imagine an event or an action in their minds".[256] The child can use symbols and interact competently with the environment.[257]

> "This symbolic function then brings great flexibility into the field of intelligence. Intelligence up to this point refers to the immediate space which surrounds the child and to the present perceptual situation; thanks to language, and to the symbolic functions, it becomes possible to invoke objects which are not present perceptually, to reconstruct the past, or to make projects, plans for the future, to think of projects not present but very distant in space – in short, to span spatio-temporal distances much greater than before."[258]

However, a child in the preoperational thinking phase "has a number of stage-typical limitations in the mobility of thinking and cannot follow the rules of adult logic."[259] According to Piaget's descriptions, the child's thinking in this phase is characterised by centrism and egocentrism. By centrism he means the concentration of the child on one aspect of the situation while neglecting other important characteristics. By egocentrism he means "the inability of children to distinguish other people's views or perspectives from their own".[260] "The actions are centred on the body. I used to call this egocentrism; but it is better thought of as lack of reversibility of action."[261] At this stage of thinking, the child is still incapable of accepting other perspectives than its own, in regards to both spatial perception[262] and communication in the social context. The characterisation of this phase by deficits and less by resources of the child can be

---

256 Schneider, Wolfgang/Lindenberger, Ulman (⁷2012): Entwicklungspsychologie, 190 (formerly Oerter, Rolf/Montada, Leo (Ed.): Entwicklungspsychologie, Weinheim: Beltz ⁶2008 [1983]).
257 Piaget, Jean (1999): The stages of the intellectual development of the child. In: Slater, Alan/Muir, Darwin (Ed.): The Blackwell Reader in Developmental Psychology. Malden-Oxford: Blackwell Publishing, 35–42, 38–40. (From *Bulletin of the Menninger Clinic 26* (1962), 120–128).
258 Ibid., 38.
259 Schneider, Wolfgang/Lindenberger, Ulman (2012): Entwicklungspsychologie, 190.
260 Ibid., 191.
261 Piaget, Jean (1962): The stages of the intellectual development of the child. In: Slater, Alan/Muir, Darwin (Ed.): The Blackwell Reader in Developmental Psychology, 35–42, 39.
262 The three-mountain experiment is being received in this respect. On a table a model is prepared of three adjacent mountains of different shape and height. The child is asked what the doll sitting on the opposite side of the table sees, and it seems clear to the child that the doll sees exactly what the child sees.

criticised. A large number of studies confirm the assumption that Piaget has clearly underestimated the knowledge and skills of preschool children.[263] It was found that young children were capable of taking perspectives if the material was familiar and the instructions were easy to understand.[264] In the classification of objects, children certainly show abstract achievements and can draw correct conclusions about invisible characteristics of objects.[265] Even if the category system of young children is not yet particularly complex, they can classify hierarchically early on and think logically.[266] Thus, children can assign themselves to the parent of the same sex and evaluate the activities according to those of the partner in the same category.

From the age of three there is evidence that preschool children can make thought itself the subject of their thinking.[267] 'Theory of Mind' refers to concepts of everyday psychology that allow children to attribute to themselves and other mental states (knowledge, faith, thinking, feeling). The children realize that other people do not have to have the same worldview and act on the basis of information that does not correspond to their own level of knowledge.[268]

The Maxi story[269] shows a developmental progress in the age range between three and five years. Four- to five-year-old children know that a certain conviction is wrong and that the story figure can still have it.[270] At the age between three and four years the differentiation between appearance and reality and the epistemic adoption of perspectives takes place, which includes the understanding that an object can look different from different perspectives.[271] From the age of about five, children can speak coherently. "Children between 3 and 5 years of age understand better and better how to convey their own intentions to adults, how to adapt their speech to the listener, and how to comply with the rules of communication and, if necessary, adapt to communicative failures."[272] The children's vocabulary is also constantly being expanded. With the

---

263 Schneider, Wolfgang/Lindenberger, Ulman (2012): Entwicklungspsychologie, 191.
264 Cf. Ibid.
265 Cf. Ibid., 192.
266 Cf. Ibid.
267 Cf. Ibid., 197
268 Cf. Ibid.
269 The doll Maxi comes back with his mother and puts the chocolate in the green cupboard. While Maxi leaves the scene, the mother puts the chocolate in the blue cupboard. The children are asked where Maxi is looking for the chocolate when he returns. Almost all three-year-olds say that he will look in the blue cupboard, while the four- to five-year-olds say that he will look for the chocolate in the green cupboard.
270 Ibid., 197.
271 Flavell, John H./Everett, Barbara A./Croft, Karen/Flavell, Eleanor R. (1981): Young children's knowledge about visual perception: further evidence for the level 1–level 2 distinction. *Developmental Psychology 17*(1), 99–103.
272 Schneider, Wolfgang/Lindenberger, Ulman (2012): Entwicklungspsychologie, 196.

start of school, children already have an active vocabulary of 2000 to 3000 words and a receptive vocabulary that is about ten times the active vocabulary.[273]

4.2 Social and emotional development of pre-school children

In the third year of life a development becomes clear in the children's stories about others and their questions about feelings, perceptions and their sensitivities increase.[274] Children of pre-school and early primary school age look for similarities with others and are happy about similarities. The social comparison serves in development on the one hand to determine how one should behave and on the other hand to determine how good one is in a certain task class. "As early as age 4 or 5, children are beginning to recognise differences among themselves and their classmates as they use social comparison information to tell them whether they perform better or worse in various domains than their peers [...]."[275] Pre-school children relate cognitive activity to concrete contents and experiences. Children are able to abstract and classify, differences and similarities can be recognised by the children. Children of early primary school age are beginning to attribute persistent psychological traits to people and no longer interpret their actions only against the background of current desires, intentions and information.[276] Children between the ages of three and four seem to learn the concept of conviction.[277] The point of view of others begins to become self-guidingly effective as early as the age of three, and from the age of four the understanding of other beliefs, which differ from one's own, is further expanded. At the age of five, children develop an understanding of certain emotions such as surprise and joy.[278] At the age of four or five, children can correctly conclude from body movements whether a person is happy, angry or sad.[279] People who are similar to each other tend to see positive things in their counterparts, whereas people who are strangers to each other tend to perceive negative things.[280] At pre-school age, children are able to respond to the wishes of others and are often willing to share the toys with others, although there are considerable individual differences.[281] Several studies have shown that "conflicts between friends are solved

---

273 Cf. Ibid.
274 Dunn, Judy (1988): The Beginnings of Social Understanding. Oxford: Basil Blackwell, 136–147.
275 Shaffer, David R./Kipp, Katherine (⁹2014): Developmental Psychology. Childhood and Adolescence. International Edition. Belmont: Wadsworth, 425.
276 Cf. ibid., 445.
277 Oerter, Rolf/Montada, Leo (Ed.) (2008): Entwicklungspsychologie, 461.
278 Hadwin, Julie/Perner, Josef (1991): Pleased and surprised: Children's cognitive theory of emotion. In: *British Journal of Developmental Psychology 9*(2), 215–234.
279 Shaffer, David R./Kipp, Katherine (⁹2014): Developmental Psychology, 379.
280 Cf. Forgas, Joseph P. (1995): Mood and judgement: The affect infusion model (AIM). *Psychological Bulletin 117*(1), 39–66.
281 Cf. Schneider, Wolfgang/Lindenberger, Ulman (2012): Entwicklungspsychologie, 207.

more often in the service of relationships than between 'non-friends'.[282] Children who manage to adapt to a group are popular.[283]

4.3 Importance of developmental psychological findings for the study

Developmental psychological research illustrates the developmental steps in childhood that take place between the ages of three and six. Pre-school children relate cognitive activities to concrete contents and experiences. This is important for the creation of the research design, which is why the group discussions, some of which were initiated by the researcher, are created immediately after a concrete experience. Due to the vocabulary and language skills of five-year-old children, a linguistic survey is already possible. Nevertheless, non-verbal forms of communication are taken into account in the study; in younger children, data collection should be even more focused on non-verbal data collection. The effect that children tend to perceive negative things when people are strangers, and positive things when people are known, is minimised by group discussions taking place in groups of aquaintances, i.e. only people in groups who also act together in everyday life. Children from the age of four are capable of taking on new perspectives, which is indicated by the results of the Theory of Mind.[284] Children are able to abstract and classify,[285] differences and similarities can be recognised by the children. Children of early primary school age are beginning to attribute persistent psychological traits to people and no longer interpret their actions only against the background of current desires, intentions and information. If there is a difference in the environment, children perceive this from a developmental psychological perspective.

5. Possibilities and limits of childhood research[286]

As long as children were perceived as future adults and research turned exclusively to them as self-developing, the adult phase stood above childhood and society understood itself as an exclusive adult society, whereas childhood was considered a defi-

---

282 Ibid., 208.
283 Puttalaz, Martha/Gottman, John M. (1981): An interactional model of children's entry into peergroups. *Child development 52*, 986–994.
284 Cf. Doherty, Martin (2009): Theory of Mind. How Children Understand Others' Thoughts and Feelings. East Sussex-New York: Psychology Press.
285 Cf. Schneider, Wolfgang/Lindenberger, Ulman (2012): Entwicklungspsychologie, 192.
286 This section is based on the article written by the author: Stockinger, Helena (2013): Die wechselseitige Verwiesenheit einer Kultur der Anerkennung und einer Kindheitsforschung. In: Jäggle, Martin/Krobath, Thomas/Stockinger, Helena/Schelander, Robert: Kultur der Anerkennung. Würde – Gerechtigkeit – Partizipation für Schulkultur, Schulentwicklung und Religion. Baltmannsweiler: Schneider Hohengehren, 191–201.

cient state. The task of childhood research in view of this image of the child was to investigate which conditions and circumstances best contributed to "turning this unfinished work into something finished".[287] The focus was therefore not on the child in its childhood phase, but on the child's future as an adult. "While the plea for the child's own world at the turn of the century – in the tradition of Rousseau – demanded the recognition of its peculiarity as a 'man in development', today the concept of development is rejected as a metaphor of paternalism."[288] In the new paradigm of childhood research, the status of the child as an object is replaced by the status of the child as a subject and childhood "primarily understood as a socially created and certain social category".[289] This conviction, which emerged towards the end of the 20th century to perceive children as subjects and to give childhood its own important status in society characterises childhood research.[290] In contrast to earlier approaches, it tries to explore

---

287 Wilk, Liselotte/Wintersberger, Helmut (1996): Paradigmenwechsel in Kindheitsforschung und -politik. Das Beispiel Österreich. In: Zeiher, Helga/Büchner, Peter/Zinnecker, Jürgen (Ed.): Kinder als Außenseiter? Umbrüche in der gesellschaftlichen Wahrnehmung von Kindern und Kindheit. Weinheim/Munich: Juventa, 29–55, 30.

288 Honig, Michael-Sebastian/Leu, Hans Rudolf/Nissen, Ursula (1999): Kindheit als Sozialisationsphase und als kulturelles Muster. Zur Strukturierung eines Forschungsfeldes. In: Honig, Michael-Sebastian/Leu, Hans Rudolf/Nissen, Ursula (Ed.): Kinder und Kindheit. Soziokulturelle Muster – sozialisationstheoretische Perspektiven. Weinheim/Munich: Juventa, 9–29, 11.

289 Wilk, Liselotte/Wintersberger, Helmut (1996): Paradigmenwechsel in Kindheitsforschung und -politik. In: Zeiher, Helga/Büchner, Peter/Zinnecker, Jürgen (Ed.): Kinder als Außenseiter?, 29–55, 31.

290 In this context, the discourses in the individual disciplines on childhood research cannot be dealt with in detail. For a closer examination of childhood research, see the works and handbooks published on childhood research, which examine the research from the perspectives of sociology, psychology and educational science. Cf. Behnken, Imbke/Zinnecker, Jürgen (2001): Kinder. Kindheit. Lebensgeschichte. Seelze-Velber: Kallmeyersche Verlagsbuchhandlung; Friebertshäuser, Barbara/Langer, Antje/Prengel, Annedore (Ed.) (^{4}2013): Handbuch. Qualitative Forschungsmethoden in der Erziehungswissenschaft. Weinheim/Basel: Beltz Juventa [1997]; Hurrelmann, Klaus/Bründel, Heidrun (^{2}2003): Einführung in die Kindheitsforschung. Weinheim/Basel/Berlin: Beltz [1996]; Keller, Heidi (Ed.) (^{4}2011): Handbuch der Kleinkindforschung. Bern: Huber; Krüger, Heinz-Hermann/Grunert, Cathleen (Ed.) (2002): Handbuch Kindheits- und Jugendforschung. Opladen: Leske + Budrich; Markefka, Manfred/Nauck, Bernhard (1993): Handbuch der Kindheitsforschung. Neuwied/Kriftel/Berlin: Luchterhand; Qvortrup, Jens/Corsaro, William A./Honig, Michael-Sebastian (Ed.) (2011): The Palgrave Handbook of Childhood Studies. Basingstoke/New York: Palgrave Macmillan; Ossowski, Ekkehard/Rösler, Winfried (2002): Kindheit. Interdisziplinäre Perspektiven zu einem Forschungsgegenstand. Baltmannsweiler: Schneider Hohengehren; Wustmann, Cornelia/Bamler, Vera (2010): Lehrbuch Kindheitsforschung. Weinheim/Munich: Juventa.

how children open up[291] to the world and gain orientation. Childhood is thus seen as a form of life whose reality appears historically different and which is shaped and constituted to varying degrees by the children themselves.[292] The term childhood is understood as a social construction[293] that is determined by society. Janusz Korczak, a pioneer in the discussion on children's rights, stresses that children know more about themselves. "We [adults] are much more experienced than children, we know a lot that children do not know, but what children think and feel, they know better than we do."[294] He calls for the lives of adults and children to be equal. "Either the lives of adults – on the verge of children's lives. Or the life of children – on the verge of adult life. When will that moment of openness occur, when the lives of adults and children are on an equal footing."[295]

With regard to childhood research, children must have the right to participate in research, which is also enumerated in the UN Convention on the Rights of the Child.

---

291 The picture of children described is also a prerequisite for children's theology, cf. Bucher, Anton A./Büttner, Gerhard/Freudenberger-Lötz, Petra/Schreiner, Martin (Ed.): Jahrbuch für Kindertheologie. Stuttgart: Calwer, since 2002. In general, the principles of childhood research on which this study is based have many similarities with the principles of children's theology. "The great success of children's theology also fits in with the change in religious education from witnessing to observing. Because the child theologian can limit himself first of all to encouraging children to articulate a problem or an 'answer' of his own, to raise attitudes, to moderate conversations. Like the empiricist, he turns to the religious ideas of *others*. He can largely disregard his own ideas and attitudes. If he 'participates', then according to age and with respect to the developmental psychological prerequisites of the students; his own view, his own 'confessio', can withdraw. He observes and supports the children's mental productions; the plausibility of *his* ideas is (usually) not directly in question." (Englert, Rudolf: Religion gibt zu denken. Eine Religionsdidaktik in 19 Lehrstücken. Munich: Kösel 2012, 40f.).
292 Cf. Hülst, Dirk (²2012): Das wissenschaftliche Verstehen von Kindern. In: Heinzel, Friederike (Ed.): Methoden der Kindheitsforschung. Ein Überblick über Forschungszugänge zur kindlichen Perspektive. Weinheim-Basel: Beltz Juventa, 52–77, 52f.
293 Cf. Qvortrup, Jens (Ed.) (1993): Childhood as a social phenomenon: lessons from an international project: international conference Billund, Denmark, 24–16 September 1992. Vienna: European Centre of Social Welfare Policy and Research.
294 Korczak, Janusz (1999): Sämtliche Werke, vol. 4. Gütersloh: Gütersloher Verlagshaus, 238.
295 Korczak, Janusz (1999): Sämtliche Werke, vol. 4, 459.

Articles 12[296] to 17[297], for example, enshrine the right of children to participate.[298] With the decision of the Federal Constitutional Act on the Rights of Children 2011,[299] the Austrian State is obliged to take into account the opinions of the child in all matters concerning it,[300] which is expressed in Article 4 of the Federal Constitutional Act. "Each child has the right to adequate involvement and consideration of his/her opinion regarding all matters affecting the child in a manner that is commensurate with his/her age and development".[301] Children are able to form opinions on topics, which has been proven in several studies.[302] Children can give information about their childhood, whereby childhood must always be thought of in a social context. Thomas Nigel gives three reasons why it is important to listen to children: Children have a right to be heard, it is good for the children and it leads to better decisions.[303] As article 31 states: "State Parties shall respect and promote the right of the child to fully participate in cultural and artistic life and shall encourage the provisions of appropriate and equal opportunities for cultural, artistic, recreational and leisure activity"[304]

---

296 "1. States Parties shall assure to the child who is capable of forming his or her own views the right to express those views freely in all matters affecting the child, the views of the child being given due weight in accordance with the age and maturity of the child. 2. For this purpose, the child shall in particular be provided the opportunity to be heard in any judicial and administrative proceedings affecting the child, either directly, or through a representative or an appropriate body, in a manner consistent with the procedural rules of national law." (Convention on the Rights of the Child, article 12).

297 "States Parties recognize the important function performed by the mass media and shall ensure that the child has access to information and material from a diversity of national and international sources, especially those aimed at the promotion of his or her social, spiritual and moral well-being and physical and mental health. [...]" (Convention on the Rights of the Child, article 17).

298 Convention on the Rights of the Child, 1989.

299 Federal Constitutional Act on the Rights of Children. In: Federal Law Gazette I, No. 4/2011.

300 For an overview regarding the ratification, acceptance(A), accession(a), succession(d) of the UN Convention on the Rights of the Child see the following website: United Nations. Treaty Collection, http://treaties.un.org/Pages/ViewDetails.aspx?src=TREATY&mtdsg_no=IV-11&chapter=4&lang=en [21.07.2015].

301 Federal Constitutional Act on the Rights of Children, article 4.

302 This can be seen, for example, in the following studies: World Vision Kinderstudie http://www.worldvision-institut.de/kinderstudien-kinderstudie-2013.php [16.07.2015]; Haug, Lena (2011): Junge StaatsbürgerInnen. Politik in Zukunftsvorstellungen von Kindern. Wiesbaden: VS Verlag für Sozialwissenschaften.

303 Nigel, Thomas (2001): Listening to Children. In: Foley, Pam/Roche, Jeremy/Tucker, Stanley (Ed.): Children in Society. Contemporary Theory, Policy and Practice. The Open University, 104–111, 104.

304 Convention on the Rights of the Child, including reservations and declarations. In: Federal Law Gazette No. 7/1993.

The importance of the children's perspective and the childhood[305] phase of life has consequences for the research process. According to Fuhs, "the exploration of children's view of their own world and the world of adults has become a research-theoretical necessity, since it has turned out that children often have different ways of thinking and experiencing, different interests and a different taste than adults."[306] At the same time, it is "an expression of a changed social and political understanding of childhood, which ‚not only since the UN Convention on the Rights of the Child, has provided children with the opportunity to participate in all socially relevant areas at their own level".[307] It is not enough to define children's needs from the adult's point of view; instead, children are to be regarded as people with their own rights in the research process.

5.1 Three levels of recognition processes

The recognition processes is comprised of three levels. With egalitarian recognition, each child is recognised as a subject, as an independent person, and has the same fundamental right to be heard in the research process.

> "When the adults let the children do it and when they take a look themselves, members of both generations, but also members of the same generation can see each other. They mutually recognise each other as viewers. In this perspective, children and adults become visible in a 'symmetrically' named relationship of egalitarian recognition based on elementary equality: Both are people who meet in eye contact from equal to equal, both are vulnerable beings, both need food and other people, both were born, both will die."[308]

Both the researcher and the child have the same dignity and the same rights associated with it. This can be expressed in the research process in appreciation of the person, their statements, their needs, wishes, fears, etc. The persons participating in the research process are at the same level, at the level of the dignity of each person, regardless of performance, age, status, etc. "The idea of recognition in democratic,

---

305 The predominant image of children in a society is also reflected in the images of children in art (cf. Deckert-Peaceman, Heike/Dietrich, Cornelia/Stenger, Ursula (2010): Einführung in die Kindheitsforschung. Darmstadt: Wissenschaftliche Buchgesellschaft).
306 Fuhs, Burkhard (2012): Kinder im qualitativen Interview – Zur Erforschung subjektiver kindlicher Lebenswelten. In: Heinzel, Friederike (Ed.): Methoden der Kindheitsforschung, 80–103, 82.
307 Ibid.
308 Prengel, Annedore (2005): Anerkennung von Anfang an – Egalität, Heterogenität und Hierarchie im Anfangsunterricht und darüber hinaus. In: Geiling, Ute/Hinz, Andreas: Integrationspädagogik im Diskurs. Auf dem Weg zu einer inklusiven Pädagogik. Bad Heilbrunn: Julius Klinkhardt, 15–34, 19.

egalitarian relationships is characterised by a balance of mutual recognition based on the fact that both 'x' and 'y' recognise themselves and the other person."[309]

The differentiating recognition can be seen as follows: If we get to know each other, those involved in the interaction will never get to know each other completely, as the other will always remain indeterminate and unknown. If the researcher is actually involved in childhood research, both the process of research and the result of the research process cannot be predicted. As pedagogical action often has different effects than expected, the process of research can also bring different situations and results if the person conducting the research is open to them and enters the research process unbiased as possible and is aware of the preconceptions . If the diversity of each child is taken seriously, it is not possible to fall back on certainties, every research process means a risk. "Uncertainty is part of the structure of recognition."[310] The assumption that diversity is normal[311] is also a prerequisite in childhood research. In the research process, an encounter with the other person and his or her otherness takes place. Recognition is "related to heterogeneous, i.e. to different, variable, unknown and unpredictable".[312]

In addition to the diversity of children, which makes every research process an open venture, the difference between adults and children in the research process must not be levelled.

> "If it is true that children are different, dealing with children means dealing with otherness. Otherness can be fascinating and experienced as enrichment, it can be alienating and experienced as a threat, it can be annoying or relieve the burden of one's own existence."[313]

As a basic assumption, this difference shapes the theoretical and methodological design of childhood research. If children are defined in a differentiating comparison

---

309 Prengel, Annedore (2007): „Ohne Angst verschieden sein?" – Mehrperspektivische Anerkennung von Schulleistungen in einer Pädagogik der Vielfalt. In: Hafeneger, Benno/Henkenborg, Peter/Scherr, Albert (Ed.): Pädagogik der Anerkennung. Grundlagen, Konzepte, Praxisfelder. Schwalbach/Ts.: Wochenschauverlag, 204.
310 Prengel, Annedore (2005): Anerkennung von Anfang an. In: Geiling, Ute/Hinz, Andreas: Integrationspädagogik im Diskurs, 16.
311 The work "Pädagogik der Vielfalt" by Annedore Prengel was published in 1993, the third edition in 2006. The 4th Würzburg Symposium in 1994 was entitled "Normal ist, verschieden zu sein" and the documentation volume was published in the same year. The expression comes from what was then called curative and special education. "It is normal to be different" was the title of the address given by the then German President Richard von Weizsäcker at the opening event of the conference of the Federal Association for Assistance for the Disabled, 1 July 1993, Gustav-Heinemann-Haus in Bonn.
312 Prengel, Annedore (2005): Anerkennung von Anfang an. In: Geiling, Ute/Hinz, Andreas (Ed.): Integrationspädagogik im Diskurs, 20.
313 Liegle, Ludwig (2006): Bildung und Erziehung in früher Kindheit, 11.

to adults,[314] they are regarded as unfinished adults and not as independent subjects in their own phase of life. The difference that exists between adults and children must be acknowledged without the children being fixed in the childhood that the adults themselves have experienced or have adjusted to meet their idea. Recognition of the difference that exists through intergenerational relations involves recognition of the child in the respective childhood and requires openness and impartiality in order to know the viewpoint of the other person. If the researcher enters the research process with assumptions about being a child or the outcome of the research, this can distort the child's response behaviour in the direction of complacency . The different roles of children and adults must be reflected upon. Adults are far more autonomous and children are more dependent in conducting conversations. Children can be shy towards foreign interviewers. Children are not necessarily able to classify the special structure of the interview situation.

The differentiating recognition between adults and children leads to recognition of the dependency and hierarchical relationship that resonates in relationships between children and adults.

> "If the relationship is to become possible, the older generation must acknowledge that the child is largely dependent on it, that it has very far-reaching power over the child and that it must take responsibility for much of its life. The child must accept nourishment and all other necessities, must in some unconscious way acknowledge the adults as determining power and as givers in order to be able to continue to exist and grow up at all."[315]

Just as there are interdependencies in pedagogical processes, those involved in the research process are also interdependent. Particularly in the research process with children, awareness of existing hierarchies and dependencies is of great relevance, since children often experience adults in an educational framework that is characterised by hierarchies[316] and children depend on "protection, care and support"[317] from adults and are thus dependent on them. All research processes in which interactions with children take place are interrelationships that

> "as social relationships always also contain shares of power and impact of interference on what is to be traded or communicated. Depending on the understanding, trust and interpretation the addressed subjects have towards the person and the interviewer's

---

314 Cf. Fuhs, Burkhard (2012): Kinder im qualitativen Interview. In: Heinzel, Friederike (Ed.): Methoden der Kindheitsforschung, 80–103, 84.
315 Prengel, Annedore (2005): Anerkennung von Anfang an. In: Geiling, Ute/Hinz, Andreas (Ed.): Integrationspädagogik im Diskurs, 20.
316 Cf. Fuhs, Burkhard (2012): Kinder im qualitativen Interview. In: Heinzel, Friederike (Ed.): Methoden der Kindheitsforschung, 80–103, 91.
317 Zeiher, Helga (1996): Von Natur aus Außenseiter oder gesellschaftlich marginalisiert? Zur Einführung. In: Zeiher, Helga/Büchner, Peter/Zinnecker, Jürgen (Ed.): Kinder als Außenseiter?, 7–27, 8.

intentions (contextualisation, interpretation of the situation), their willingness to address the issue and their answers will vary in greater or lesser nuances."[318]

The transparency and recognition of the existing hierarchy can contribute to an honest research process. Annedore Prengel asks "for a way of recognising hierarchical superiority and inferiority in the context of equality and heterogeneity as compatible with democracy."[319] Even if qualitative-empirical studies take place in a spirit of partnership in an appreciative atmosphere, there remains a hierarchy that influences the course of the conversation and the roles of the discussion partners.[320] This influence is to be considered as a possible factor for the behaviour during the entire research and evaluation process. A research situation will always remain asymmetric, as people with different goals and different prior knowledge interact. The researchers usually determine the setting of the research situation, which can affect the balance of power between the persons involved. In the relationship of recognition, power can never be completely avoided, because even if an investigating person recognises another person as someone, for example as a child, he/she grants oneself the power to recognise this, i.e. to recognise the child as a child, and in this execution places oneself above the child. With regard to the power dimension of recognition,[321] it is important to become aware of this subliminal power relationship and to address it. Even if the hierarchy, which is not balanced by the relationship between generations and the different degrees of knowledge about the research process, the openness to present one's own positions and to stand by them can make mutual recognition in diversity possible.

> "It is not possible to speak of the playback of a 'child's perspective' just because the researchers themselves have their say. It must always be taken into account that adult researchers and researched children meet and jointly establish a generational order that must be made the starting point of childhood and the description of children."[322]

Since it is not enough to let children have their say, and the contextual and personal factors of the child and the researcher play an essential role, it is important to consider how childhood research can be best designed so that children can express their opinions, wishes and interests and be heard in their childhood.

---

318 Hülst, Dirk (2012): Das wissenschaftliche Verstehen von Kindern. In: Heinzel, Friederike (Ed.): Methoden der Kindheitsforschung, 52–77, 67.
319 Prengel, Annedore (2005): Anerkennung von Anfang an. In: Geiling, Ute/Hinz, Andreas (Ed.): Integrationspädagogik im Diskurs, 22.
320 Cf. Heinzel, Friederike (2012): Qualitative Methoden der Kindheitsforschung. Ein Überblick. In: Heinzel, Friederike (Ed.): Methoden der Kindheitsforschung, 22–35, 29.
321 Cf. Balzer, Nicole/Ricken, Norbert (2010): Anerkennung als pädagogisches Problem. Markierungen im erziehungswissenschaftlichen Diskurs. In: Schäfer, Alfred/Thompson, Christiane (Ed.): Anerkennung. Paderborn/Munich/Vienna/Zurich: Ferdinand Schöningh, 35–87, 63–72.
322 Heinzel, Friederike (2012): Qualitative Methoden der Kindheitsforschung. In: Heinzel, Friederike (Ed.): Methoden der Kindheitsforschung, 22–35, 24.

"The success of childhood research in the described sense depends therefore in particular on (adult) researchers "understanding" the (manifest) statements of children and interpreting the (often latent) aspects of their background in an appropriate interpretation according to the research question."[323]

5.2 Methodological approaches in childhood research

In qualitative empirical studies of childhood research, various methods are used,[324] although the discussion of methods in childhood research is not complete.[325]

A tolerant, sanction-free atmosphere and an appreciative interaction are important for research with children. "A certain atmosphere comes from the fact that all parties involved take a common attitude towards what they do. In the term 'attitude' are both physical moments and moments of interpretation of the situation."[326] It is advantageous to conduct research in places and with researchers known to the children.

> "The atmosphere and thus the situation is determined by posture, facial expressions and gestures, voice pitch, pitch, speed of speech, etc. But also through expectations, which in turn are generated by a cultural learning process that is linked to certain situations. – Situations are based on a culture of dealing with things and people."[327]

Conditions of the external setting that can influence the children's behaviour during the survey are physical characteristics of the environment such as building, furnishings, light, the design of the external examination situation such as distraction by toys, social characteristics of the environment such as familiarity with the research person, presence of other persons, and the subjective impression of representing and being observed as the centre of attention.[328]

---

323 Hülst, Dirk (2012): Das wissenschaftliche Verstehen von Kindern. In: Heinzel, Friederike (Ed.): Methoden der Kindheitsforschung, 52–77, 54.
324 For an overview of the question of methods in childhood research, see, for example: Heinzel, Friederike (Ed.) (2012): Methoden der Kindheitsforschung.
325 Research with children is also always methodological research, "which – against the background of the changing culture of children and adults – develops, evaluates and critically discusses methodological requirements and procedures" (Fuhs, Burkhard (2012): Kinder im qualitativen Interview. In: Heinzel, Friederike (Ed.): Methoden der Kindheitsforschung, 80–103, 93). There are many methodological considerations, whereby current childhood research also includes research on suitable methods.
326 Scholz, Gerold (2012): Teilnehmende Beobachtung. In: Heinzel, Friederike (Ed.): Methoden der Kindheitsforschung, 116–134, 132.
327 Ibid.
328 Cf. Heinzel, Friederike (1997): Qualitative Interviews mit Kindern. In: Friebertshäuser, Barbara/Prengel, Annedore (Ed.): Handbuch Qualitative Forschungsmethoden in der Erziehungswissenschaft. Weinheim/Munich: Juventa, 396–413.

The possibility of empathy can enable researchers to put themselves in a child's perspective even before research begins, although this can never be done completely because of their own life history and the child's otherness. It would also be helpful if we knew how children interpret researchers and the research process. Children must not be pressured, frightened or forced to respond. Childhood research can fall back on various research results, for example Kelsey Moore, Victoria Talwar and Sandra Bosacki, following their study "Canadian children's perceptions of spirituality: diverse voices", identified limitations of the research design and made suggestions for future research projects.

> "Although the interviews were designed to flow like a natural conversation and the researcher engaged with children candidly and warmly, children may have the need to please the researcher by answering questions in a prescribed manner or sensed a power differential between themselves and the researcher."[329]

When designing the study, the question of complacency must be taken into account and the extent to which children want to please the person conducting the research with their answers must be minimised. The way in which children are asked questions is important; suggestive questions must be avoided because of the great influence of the answers, which is confirmed by the testimonies of the children in court, where it is said "that even three- to five-year-old children can be reliable witnesses in court, provided they are protected from suggestive questions. They often forget details of events, but what they say is usually correct [...]."[330] The younger the children are, the more susceptible they are to suggestive questions, especially when they are asked again and again, and the more distorted their memory becomes toward the direction of questioning.[331] "It is our task as researchers, from both practical and ethical considerations, to ensure that we ask the right questions in our studies, those which are important, and that we conduct our research in a manner that optimises the opportunity for children's perspectives to be listened to – and heard."[332] In order for children to actually participate in research, a research design must be chosen that can express what actually concerns children and minimises the influence of the person conducting the research, even if this can rarely be completely prevented due to the existing hierarchy. "The question of whether we understand children is how the collected 'data' is given

---

329 Moore, Kelsey/Talwar, Victoria/Bosacki, Sandra (2012): Canadian children's perceptions of spirituality: diverse voices. *International Journal of Children's Spirituality 17*(3), 217–234, 231.
330 Siegler, Robert/DeLoache, Judy/Eisenberg, Nancy (^{3}2011): Entwicklungspsychologie im Kindes- und Jugendalter. German edition published by Sabina Pauen. Heidelberg: Spektrum Akademischer Verlag [2005], 5.
331 Cf. ibid.
332 Lewis, Ann/Lindsay, Geoff (2000): Emerging Issues. In: Lewis, Ann/Lindsay, Geoff (Ed.): Researching children's perspectives. Buckingham/Philadelphia: Open University, 189–197, 192.

meaning and how meaning is reconstructed. Children also act as members of society by interpreting social situations."[333] Possible unconscious ideas of the researcher about the child or the research process can influence the response behaviour in the sense of transmission and countertransference of the person interviewed.[334] In order to be aware of this situation and possible influences on the research results, reflexive elements are required throughout the research process, which relate both to the situation and to the relationship of the persons involved in the research process. Since one person can arouse prejudices in the researcher, the reflection of one's own ideas and feelings is an essential component in order to be open to an encounter with the other person and to achieve results that are as reliable and valid as possible. "Adults need to rethink their categories of children when undertaking research as well as when planning and implementing interventions."[335]

It would be an illusion to believe that one can completely distance oneself from any preconceptions, but it requires the consciousness to be subject to them and to take this into consideration in the research process. It is important "to be productive in dealing with the fact that every researcher brings prior knowledge, preconceptions and prejudices into his or her research. The point is not to deny this process, but to control it methodically."[336]

Methodically, the existing hierarchy between adult and child can be weakened by group discussions in which children outnumber numerically, but the children influence each other in their answers, which is why collective and subjunctive experiences and orientations are expressed. Ethnographic field research tries to connect the children themselves with their own world. Methods such as participant observation, document analysis and questioning in the everyday environment are used to "grasp children's everyday cultural practices and decipher the subjective meanings of children's living worlds."[337] In participant observation, the researchers are involved in the process and participate in shaping it. They also influence the actions of the children and select the situations observed, which is why a situation cannot be described neutrally. Children have a right to know what the observers are planning and who they are. Ethnographic descriptions are often made possible by video recordings. On the basis of video observations, the performance of children's actions such as physicality or theatricality

---

333 Heinzel, Friederike (2012): Qualitative Methoden der Kindheitsforschung. In: Heinzel, Friederike (Ed.): Methoden der Kindheitsforschung, 22–35, 31.

334 Cf. Hülst, Dirk (2012): Das wissenschaftliche Verstehen von Kindern. In: Heinzel, Friederike (Ed.): Methoden der Kindheitsforschung, 52–77, 68.

335 West, Andy/O'Kaine Claire/Hyder, Tina (2008): Diverse childhoods: Implications for childcare, protection, participation and research practice. In: Leira, Arnlaug/Saraceno, Chiara (Ed.): Childhood: Changing Contexts. Bingley: Emerald Group Publishing Limited, 268–292, 288.

336 Scholz, Gerold (2012): Teilnehmende Beobachtung. In: Heinzel, Friederike (Ed.): Methoden der Kindheitsforschung, 116–134, 123.

337 Fuhs, Burkhard (2012): Kinder im qualitativen Interview. In: Heinzel, Friederike (Ed.): Methoden der Kindheitsforschung, 80–103, 82.

can be taken into account.[338] Movie recording depends on the selected perspective. In participant observation, the diversity of roles is recognised by those involved in the interaction.

> "Participation in participant observation thus means becoming part of the culture. Nevertheless, the researcher remains a different person than the others, an accepted observer. He participates in the negotiation of meanings. From this point of view, the researcher does not have to be able to act like a local."[339]

Also, child-specific forms of communication such as drawings, role plays, dream journeys, conversations with a hand puppet,[340] games and statements in spontaneous conversation situations[341] are an expression of the children, which can give an insight into the perspective of the children. Focus groups are a popular method of research with children, but it is not popular with all children, so it may make sense to think about the children who participate in the research and make decisions about the form of communication with regard to the children. "You may find it more useful to think about the particular children you are engaging with – the communication forms they like to use, the contexts in which they are, their own characteristics."[342]

The questions that concern adults may not be children's questions, but children's questions are equally important. "It is all too easy for adults to concentrate on getting the answers to the questions that concern them without considering that a child may have other issues to discuss that may be equally, if not more important."[343] Robert Coles describes a conversation with Anna Freud, which well describes the challenges and opportunities of childhood research:

> "She knew how daunting it can be to sit, with a particular line of questioning in mind, in a room before a child, only to find an utter lack of interest on the part of the boy or girl, whose politeness or charm conceals detachment from adults trying to press matters too urgently. She also knew that other children can be rather too obliging and forthcoming – ready in an instant, it seems, to grab at whatever direction is offered by

---

338 Cf. Heinzel, Friederike (2012): Qualitative Methoden der Kindheitsforschung. In: Heinzel, Friederike (Ed.): Methoden der Kindheitsforschung, 22–35, 29.
339 Scholz, Gerold (2012): Teilnehmende Beobachtung. In: Heinzel, Friederike (Ed.): Methoden der Kindheitsforschung, 116–134, 130.
340 Eva Hoffmann presented an empirical-qualitative study on dealing with religious diversity with children on the subject of death, in which the children get into conversation with a hand puppet, cf. Hoffmann, Eva (2009): Interreligiöses Lernen im Kindergarten?.
341 Cf. Liegle, Ludwig (2006): Bildung und Erziehung in früher Kindheit, 25.
342 Tisdall, E. Kay M./Davis, John/Gallagher, Michael (2009): Introduction. In: Tisdall, E. Kay M./Davis, John/Gallagher, Michael: Researching with Children and Young People. Research Design, Methods and Analysis. Los Angeles/London/New Delhi/Singapore/Washington DC: SAGE, 1–10, 7.
343 Nigel, Thomas (2001): Listening to Children. In: Foley, Pam/Roche, Jeremy/Tucker, Stanley (Ed.): Children in Society, 104–111, 109.

a teacher, a doctor, someone who comes armed with questions, paper, pencils, crayons. She reminded me at great length that day, drawing confessionally on her failures as well as her successes, how important it would be, in a study of young spirituality, to set aside my preconceptions and let the children 'do with the opportunity what they will.' – share what sense (if any) they make out of life. 'I often think,' Miss Freud went on, 'that we must work harder conceptually with our research data when we are at our desks writing than we do when we are sitting with the children and asking our questions of them.' She paused and then added a delightful explanation: 'Perhaps it is because then [when we are writing up our work] they are not there to help us!'"[344]

---

[344] Coles, Robert (1990): The Spiritual Life of Children, Boston: Houghton Mifflin Company, 99f.

Part III: Methodological approaches of the study

1. Qualitative-empirical Research

The interest of religious education is to deal with the various questions of the respective contexts and biographies of people in both a hermeneutic and empirical way.[345]

> "The subject area of Practical Theology is 'religious practice' and in order to understand and explain this subject, empirical methodology is appropriate. Behind this is the idea that religious practice is also like a text that must be decoded with the help of appropriate methods."[346]

This study takes a closer look at the world of kindergarten by means of the qualitative-empirical approach,[347] whereby the children and the kindergarten organisation are of interest. "The religious-educational interest in contemporary experiences converges with the objective of qualitative empirical research to comprehend subjectively experienced and interpreted reality."[348]

1.1 Principles of qualitative empirical research

> "Rapid social change and the resulting diversification of life worlds are increasingly confronting social researchers with new social contexts and perspectives. These are so new to them that their traditional deductive methodologies – deriving research questions and hypotheses from theoretical models and testing them against empirical evidence – are failing due to differentiation of the objects. Thus, research is increasingly forced to make use of inductive strategies: Instead of starting from theories and testing them, **"sensitizing concepts"** are required for approaching the social context to be studied. However, contrary to widespread misunderstanding, these concepts are themselves influenced by previous theoretical knowledge."[349]

---

345 Cf. Mette, Norbert (2006): Religionspädagogik, 159f.
346 Ziebertz, Hans-Georg (2011): Vorwort. In: Ziebertz, Hans-Georg (Ed.): Praktische Theologie – empirisch. Methoden, Ergebnisse und Nutzen. Berlin: LIT, 3-4, 3.
347 Research results and conceptual considerations on qualitative research can be found in the Zeitschrift für Qualitative Forschung. The ZQF (formerly ZBBS, Zeitschrift für Qualitative Bildungs-, Beratungs- und Sozialforschung) is published by the Centre for Qualitative Education, Counselling and Social Research and brings together conceptual approaches and results of qualitative research (Zeitschrift für qualitative Forschung, http://www.budrich-journals.de/index.php/zqf [21.07.2015]).
348 Porzelt, Burkard (2000): Qualitativ-empirische Methoden in der Religionspädagogik. In: Porzelt, Burkard/Güth, Ralph (Ed.): Empirische Religionspädagogik. Grundlagen – Zugänge – Aktuelle Projekte. Münster: LIT, 63-81, 78.
349 Flick, Uwe (⁴2009): An Introduction to Qualitative Research. London u.a.: Sage.

"Qualitative research is a field of inquiry in its own right."[350] Central principles of qualitative social research are "openness", "research as communication", the "process character of research and object", the "reflectivity of object and analysis", "explication" and "flexibility".[351] The basic attitude of openness includes being open-minded towards the investigators, the examination situation and the methods to be applied. Qualitative social research often has an explorative function and hypotheses are not formed before the investigation.[352] "In contrast to the quantitative approach, qualitative social research is not a method that tests hypotheses, but generates hypotheses".[353] When research is seen as communication, social phenomena are processual.[354] This process affects both the research act and the research object. Qualitative social research is primarily interested in "patterns of interpretation and action" that "possess a certain collective binding character".[355]

> "Patterns of acting and interpreting [...] are constituted by the social actors, just as they create social reality with the help of patterns of interpretation and action. To document this constitutional process of reality, to reconstruct it analytically and finally to explain it through understanding comprehension is *the* central concern of qualitative social research and its founding interpretative sociology."[356]

Every meaning reflexively refers to the whole and "understanding individual acts" presupposes "understanding the context", which means that "*constitution* and *understanding of meaning*" are circular.[357] Explication is the expectation of social researchers to "disclose as far as possible the individual steps of the research process".[358] Qualitative research is characterised by a flexible approach, which makes it possible "to adapt to the particular characteristics of the subject matter".[359] Qualitative social research is characterised by "particularly great flexibility".[360]

---

350 Denzin, Norman K./Lincoln, Yvonna S. (^{4}2011): Introduction. Disciplining the Practice of Qualitative Research. In: Denzin, Norman K./Lincoln, Yvonna S. (Ed.): The SAGE Handbook of Qualitative Research. Thousand Oaks/London/New Delhi/Singapore: SAGE, 1–19, 3 [Denzin, Norman K./Lincoln, Yvonna S. (1994): Handbook of Qualitative Research. Thousand Oaks/London/New Delhi: SAGE].
351 Lamnek, Siegfried (^{5}2010): Qualitative Sozialforschung. Weinheim/Basel: Beltz [1988], 19–25. Since in some areas Lamnek's book published in 1995 is more detailed, it is also partly quoted from it, see Lamnek, Siegfried(^{3}1995): Qualitative Sozialforschung, vol. 1. Methodologie. Weinheim: Beltz [1988].
352 Lamnek, Siegfried (^{5}2010): Qualitative Sozialforschung, 20.
353 Ibid.
354 Cf. ibid., 21.
355 Ibid.
356 Lamnek, Siegfried (1995): Qualitative Sozialforschung, vol. 1, 24f.
357 Ibid., 25.
358 Lamnek, Siegfried (2010): Qualitative Sozialforschung 23.
359 Ibid., 24.
360 Lamnek, Siegfried (1995): Qualitative Sozialforschung, vol. 1, 27.

> "Qualitative inquiry seeks to discover and to describe in narrative reporting what particular people do in their everyday lives and what their actions mean to them. It identifies meaning-relevant *kinds* of things in the world – kinds of people, kinds of actions, kinds of beliefs and interests – focusing on differences in forms of things that make a difference for meaning."[361]

A challenge of qualitative methodology lies in agreement on common standards.[362] Qualitative and quantitative research differ in their empirical approaches to experience data.[363] Communication is standardised for quantitative methods and the experience and observation categories are clearly defined. In qualitative procedures, it is crucial "that the different relevance systems of researchers and those being investigated are taken into account systematically and in a controlled manner".[364] In order to contribute to an understanding between quantitative and qualitative methodology, Przyborski and Wohlrab-Sahr apply the "classical" quality criteria of quantitative research in modified form to qualitative research.[365] Qualitative methods are valid insofar as they are based on the common sense constructions of the investigated persons and on the everyday structures and standards of understanding.[366] Reliability is ensured in qualitative methods "by proving the law of reproduction of the elaborated structures and by systematically incorporating and explicating everyday standards of communication".[367] By formalising and standardising the steps of survey and evaluation, the intersubjective verifiability and thus the objectivity of empirical methods is increased.[368] Qualitative research can be understood as "subjective without giving up objectivity".[369] Objectivity arises "in the qualitative paradigm, not by ignoring subjectivity, but by taking it into account".[370] The people who take part in the investigation must "have their say".[371]

It is important to reflect on the researcher's previous understanding: Particular attention must be paid to the language, as the language of the person examined may differ from the language of the person conducting the research.[372] Language and action

---

361 Erickson, Frederick (⁴2011): A history of qualitative inquiry in social and educational research. In: Denzin, Norman K./Lincoln, Yvonna S. (Ed.): The SAGE Handbook of Qualitative Research, 43–59, 43.
362 Cf. Przyborski, Aglaja/Wohlrab-Sahr, Monika (2014): Qualitative Sozialforschung. Ein Arbeitsbuch. Munich: Oldenbourg Verlag, 21.
363 Cf. ibid.
364 Ibid., 22.
365 Cf. ibid., 21-28.
366 Ibid., 24.
367 Cf. ibid., 26.
368 Cf. ibid., 28.
369 Porzelt, Burkard (2000): Qualitativ-empirische Methoden. In: Porzelt, Burkard/Güth, Ralph (Ed.): Empirische Religionspädagogik, 63–81, 78.
370 Lamnek, Siegfried (1995): Qualitative Sozialforschung, vol. 1, 229.
371 Ibid., 240.
372 Girtler, Roland (³1992): Methoden der qualitativen Sozialforschung. Vienna/Cologne/Weimar: Böhlau [1984], 34.

are directly related. Only by knowing the specific linguistic symbols that are important for the group can access be found to their thinking or culture.[373] Qualitative research is an intersubjective process in which the researcher and the person participating in the research produce socially constructed truths.[374] It takes interpretation to understand the statements of people, "the world interpreted by man can only be 'understood' by those who interpret it in the same way".[375] Qualitative research "focuses on fathoming the individual complexity of *a few individual cases in as differentiated and detailed a manner as possible.*"[376]

> "The individual cases examined are as such individual and situational. However, their fluoroscopy is not an end in itself. Qualitative research ultimately also aims at cross-case structural statements on the experience, interpretation and action of certain groups of people and subcultures. Out of a few individual cases ever examined and compared with each other, such structural statements cannot be proven to be generally valid. However, as long as they are proven and considered with methodical care and coherence of content, they can represent object-related starting points for a (more) general theory, despite all their precariousness and limitations. Before such a theory can be considered proven, it must be corrected, modified and completed by further empirical findings."[377]

Qualitative research is looking for rules that underlie social action. "The goal of a 'qualitative' sociology or ethnology [...] is not to classify human action under any laws, but to seek those rules that determine social action."[378] This coincides with the aim of qualitative research oriented towards religious education. This research

> "wants to get very close to the subjects, the children, young people, women and men, to let them have their say, not to impose categories on them from outside, but to listen to their stories, reports of experience, perceptions, interpretations, images etc., in order to understand their subjective approaches to reality and rehabilitation region".[379]

---

373 Cf. ibid.
374 Cf. King, Katherine/Hemming, Peter J. (2012): Exploring Multiple Religious Identities through Mixed Qualitative Methods. *Fieldwork in Religion* 7(1), 29–47, 30.
375 Girtler, Roland (1992): Methoden der qualitativen Sozialforschung, 20.
376 Porzelt, Burkard (2000): Qualitativ-empirische Methoden. In: Porzelt, Burkard/Güth, Ralph (Ed.): Empirische Religionspädagogik, 63–81, 65.
377 Ibid.
378 Girtler, Roland (1992): Methoden der qualitativen Sozialforschung, 35.
379 Boschki, Reinhold (2007): Der phänomenologische Blick. In: Boschki, Reinhold/ Gronover, Matthias (Ed.): Junge Wissenschaftstheorie der Religionspädagogik, 25–47, 42.

1.2 Data gathering

In field research, it is necessary to familiarize oneself with the conditions of the research field before entering the field, as well as to deal with one's own role as a researcher in this research field. The reflection on the conditions of the research field can possibly accompany the entire research process.[380]

It is often not possible to clarify who belongs to the field before research begins, which is why the research field is partly expanded and redefined in the course of research.[381] In the role of the researcher, the researcher must strike an appropriate balance between distance and involvement in the respective field of research.

> "Just as in the beginning it is about overcoming distance and building trust, in the process and end of research it is perhaps much more about creating distance and reducing involvement. One will undoubtedly have to find one's own way between observing distance and empathic closeness in any kind of research."[382]

Throughout the entire process, the researcher assumes the social role of the researcher "who leaves the field at some point and carries out new research in other places".[383] The aim is to clarify with all persons associated with the research field their willingness to cooperate and to inform them about the role of the researcher and his research intention.[384] If contact with the interviewees cannot be established by the researchers themselves, the assurance of anonymity is particularly important.[385] Field research requires a communicative attitude and openness as well as an attitude of authenticity and interest[386] towards the persons participating in the study. Through direct contact with the subjects of the investigation, one's own communicative attitude can be made clear, which is reflected in openness towards the investigators. This begins with the flexibility of the appointment agreement and can "under certain circumstances go as far as taking up proposals in connection with the survey situation or with regard to the design of the investigation. But above all, it goes hand in hand with an effort to understand."[387] It is important "to listen carefully to the respondent and to support the flow of speech in his or her personal way by 'mhm', nodding, laughing, eye contact

---

380 Cf. Przyborski, Aglaja/Wohlrab-Sahr, Monika (2014): Qualitative Sozialforschung, 40.
381 Cf. ibid., 42.
382 Cf. ibid., 45.
383 Cf. ibid.
384 Cf. ibid., 55.
385 Cf. ibid., 56.
386 Cf. ibid., 57f.
387 Cf. ibid., 57.

and the like".[388] The professional role of researchers is reflected in the "maintenance of the tension between researching distance and empathic participation."[389]

What influences the perception of the researcher and how is relevant in a phenomenological study. One's own perspective plays an essential role.[390] Significant,

> "to observe not only others but also oneself during research, and not only the behaviour of others, but also the change of one's own position. For the research process, this means systematically breaking away from the role of the participant and becoming an observer. This can be integrated into the research work at the conceptual level by, for example, alternating phases of intensive field research with phases of distanced analytical work."[391]

The circularity of the qualitative research process forces a permanent reflection of the entire research process and its partial steps in the light of the other steps.[392] It is important to consider what kind of data material is generated by a certain method, with which method the data material is evaluated and how the use of a certain evaluation method influences the type of results.[393]

1.3 Triangulation within qualitative research

In triangulation, different perspectives are adopted in an effort to answer the research question, whereby these should be "treated and applied on an equal footing and in an equally consequent way".[394] Triangulation allows an increase in knowledge, so that, for example, triangulation "should produce knowledge on different levels, which means they go beyond the knowledge made possible by one approach and thus contribute to promoting quality in research."[395] Norman Denzin, who presented a systematic conceptualisation of triangulation, mentions four basic types of triangulation, the data triangulation, the investigator-triangulation, theory-triangulation and methodological triangulation[396] and considers them as a strategy of validation, which he changes due to expressed criticism of this understanding and sees triangulation[397] as a strategy on

---

388 Cf. ibid., 69.
389 Ibid., 48.
390 Zonne, Erna (2006): Interreligiöses und interkulturelles Lernen an Grundschulen, 164.
391 Cf. Przyborski, Aglaja/Wohlrab-Sahr, Monika (2014): Qualitative Sozialforschung, 47.
392 Cf. Flick, Uwe (2012): Qualitative Sozialforschung. Eine Einführung, 126.
393 Cf. Bock, Karin (2010): Kinderalltag – Kinderwelten. Rekonstruktive Analysen von Gruppendiskussionen mit Kindern. Opladen/Farmington Hills: Barbara Budrich, 115.
394 Flick, Uwe (⁴2009): An Introduction to Qualitative Research, 445.
395 Ibid, 445.
396 Cf. Denzin, Norman K. (1989): The research act. A Theoretical Introduction to Sociological Methods. New Jersey: Prentice Hall 1989, 236–241.
397 Ibid., 235.

the way to a deeper understanding of the investigated object and thus as a step on the way to more knowledge.[398]

> "The goal of multiple triangulation is a fully grounded interpretive research approach. Objective reality will never be captured. In-depth understanding, not validity, is sought in any interpretive study. Multiple triangulation should never be eclectic. It cannot, however, be meaningfully compared to correlation analysis in statistical studies."[399]

The use of triangulation extends and deepens the interpretative basis of every study: "However, its use, when coupled with sophisticated rigor, will broaden, thicken, and deepen the interpretive base of any study."[400] The limitations resulting from the use of a method or the performance of an examination by a researcher can be partially overcome by triangulation. "By combining methods and investigators in the same study, observers can partially overcome the deficiencies that flow from one investigator or one method."[401]

In data triangulation,[402] researchers directly search for different sources for obtaining relevant data. The data obtained comes from different places, from different times or from different people.[403] Investigator triangulation[404] means that proposals and interpretations are made in groups to broaden, correct or verify the subjective view of the interpreter.[405] "Investigator triangulation simply means that multiple, as opposed to single, observers are employed."[406] In theory triangulation,[407] it must be considered that different methods are based on different basic theoretical assumptions, which must be taken into account, which is why Denzin suggests that data should be viewed from different theoretical perspectives.[408] Methodological triangulation[409] distinguishes between the "within-method" and the "between-method". While the within-method

---

398 Cf. Flick, Uwe (⁹2012): Triangulation in der qualitativen Forschung. In: Flick, Uwe/von Kardorff, Ernst/Steinke, Ines: Qualitative Forschung. Ein Handbuch. Reinbek bei Hamburg: Rowohlt Taschenbuch [2000], 309–318, 311; Denzin, Norman K.: The research act. A Theoretical Introduction to Sociological Methods. New Jersey: Prentice Hall 1989, 246f.
399 Denzin, Norman K. (1989): The research act, 246.
400 Ibid., 247.
401 Ibid., 235.
402 Cf. ibid., 237-239.
403 Ibid., 237.
404 Ibid., 239.
405 Cf. Flick, Uwe (2012): Triangulation in der qualitativen Forschung. In: Flick, Uwe/von Kardorff, Ernst/Steinke, Ines: Qualitative Forschung. Ein Handbuch, 309–318, 312.
406 Denzin, Norman K. (1989): The research act, 239.
407 Cf. ibid., 239-243.
408 Cf. Flick, Uwe (2012): Triangulation in der qualitativen Forschung. In: Flick, Uwe/von Kardorff, Ernst/Steinke, Ines: Qualitative Forschung. Ein Handbuch, 309–318, 315.
409 Denzin, Norman K. (1989): The research act, 243f.

uses different subscales within a questionnaire,[410] for example, the between-method combines several methods.[411] The reason for the combination of different methods is that the weaknesses of one method are often the strengths of another method and through the combination the advantages of the respective method can be utilized[412] and the disadvantages of the respective method can be overcome. An implicit triangulation in ethnographic studies can be spoken of when different methods are combined within the framework of a longer participation in a research field. Explicit triangulation takes place when ethnographic methods of longer participation and observation in a field explicitly involve the use of, for example, interviews with individual actors on separately agreed upon dates.[413]

If the concept of triangulation is taken seriously, the combined methods are understood to be equivalent and "one method is not regarded in advance as the central and the other as a preliminary stage or illustration [...]."[414]

2. Ethnographic access

"An ethnographically motivated childhood research is about describing and learning to understand children's cultural orders."[415] Christian Lüders attempts to describe three essential characteristics of ethnographic research: Longer participation, flexible research strategy and ethnographic writing and recording.[416] Ethnographers are convinced that situational practice and local knowledge can be made available for analysis through long-term participation. "It is precisely the interest in the insider perspective that forces the ethnographer to expose himself to, adapt to, and in a certain sense subjugate to the respective situational orders and practices."[417]

Because of this long-term participation, it is not possible to exclusively assume the "role of the distanced, seemingly neutral observer", but productive ethnographies "are based on developed, trusting relationships and lived participation", which requires

---

410 Ibid., 243.
411 Cf. Flick, Uwe (2012): Triangulation in der qualitativen Forschung. In: Flick, Uwe/von Kardorff, Ernst/Steinke, Ines: Qualitative Forschung. Ein Handbuch, 309–318, 309.
412 Cf. Denzin, Norman K. (1989): The research act, 244.
413 Cf. Flick, Uwe (2012): Triangulation in der qualitativen Forschung. In: Flick, Uwe/von Kardorff, Ernst/Steinke, Ines: Qualitative Forschung. Ein Handbuch, 309–318, 314.
414 Cf. ibid.
415 Lange, Jochen/Wiesemann, Jutta (2012): Ethnografie. In: Heinzel, Friederike (Ed.): Methoden der Kindheitsforschung, 262–277, 264.
416 Lüders, Christian (2012): Beobachten im Feld und Ethnographie. In: Flick, Uwe/von Kardorff, Ernst/Steinke, Ines: Qualitative Forschung. Ein Handbuch, 384–401, 391–399.
417 Ibid., 391.

a balance between closeness and distance.[418] This implies the necessity to adapt to the situational conditions and to maintain a "balance between cognitive interests and situational requirements", since a too "rigid adherence to methodical principles of behaviour [...] could block access to important information."[419]

> "In terms of data collection, ethnography usually involves the researcher participating, overtly or covertly, in people's daily lives for an extended period of time, watching what happens, listening to what is said, and/or asking questions through informal and formal interviews, collecting documents and artefacts – in fact gathering whatever data are available to throw light on the issues that are the emerging focus of inquiry."[420]

The analysis of the collected data is not a clear stage of research, but runs through the entire research process.

> "This iterative process is central to the 'grounded theorising' promoted by Glaser and Strauss, in which theory is developed out of data analysis, and subsequent data collection is guided strategically by emergent theory. [...] it is important to recognise that there is no formula or recipe for the analysis of ethnographic data. [...] Data are materials to think with."[421]

3. Grounded Theory

3.1 Basic assumptions of the Grounded Theory according to Corbin and Strauss

Barney Glaser and Anselm Strauss developed the grounded theory in the 1960s and repeatedly pointed out that they consider this theory and its steps to be flexible.

> "Our principal aim is to stimulate other theorists to codify and publish their *own* methods for generating theory. We trust that they will join us in telling those who have not yet attempted to generate theory that it is not a residual chore in this age of verification. Though difficult, it is an exciting adventure. In our own attempt to discuss methods and processes for discovering grounded theory, we shall, or the most part, keep the discussion open-minded, to stimulate rather than freeze thinking about the topic."[422]

Thus, the procedures of grounded theory are not unchanging rules, but guidelines that can provide orientation, which is why numerous different uses of grounded theory

---

418 Cf. ibid., 392f.
419 Ibid., 393; Flick, Uwe (2011): Triangulation. Eine Einführung, 12.
420 Hammersley, Martyn/Atkinson, Paul (³2007): Ethnography. Principles in practice. London/New York: Routledge [1983], 3.
421 Ibid., 159.
422 Glaser, Barney G./Strauss, Anselm (1967): The Discovery of Grounded Theory. Strategies for Qualitative Research. New York: Aldine Publishing, 8f.

have emerged in recent decades.[423] Glaser and Strauss also diverged in the use and perspectives of grounded theory, so that we can speak of two variants of the procedure, the variant of Glaser and that of Strauss, or of Strauss and Corbin or Corbin and Strauss.[424] With the "communicative abilities, the researcher becomes the central 'instrument' of inquiry and knowledge".[425] He or she takes on certain roles in the field, whereby the information to which the researcher has access depends on the role taken.[426]

The grounded theory is designed "to make new discoveries in the social world and also to theoretically grasp and name social phenomena that have not yet been described, or for which there are no scientific concepts and theories.[427] The research process is characterised by openness, which is why theories, hypotheses and methods arise in the research process. The method of grounded theory is based on an open question that is broad and unspecific, which is intended to change and accentuate the question in the research process. This also means that the methods are selected during the research process.[428] The data collection and evaluation is circular. The findings of grounded theory should be comprehensible. Science and practice are combined in the process of grounded theory. For example, "medium-range theories relating to the subject and field are aimed at, the aim being which is more to the benefit of a particular field of practice than to a high general validity".[429] The subjectivity of the person conducting the research is regarded as a source of theoretical knowledge. The "subjectivity and liveliness of people in the field of investigation"[430] is also acknowledged. "The theory, which is formulated in abstract terms, is combined in grounded theory with descriptions of the life and self-declarations of the subjects, which thus become exemplarily visible in their uniqueness and liveliness."[431]

3.2 Data Analysis using Grounded Theory

> "I realize there is no one 'reality' out there waiting to be discovered [...]. However, it is not the event itself that is the issue in our studies, because each person experiences

---

423 Mey, Günter/Mruck, Katja (²2011): Grounded Theory Methodology: Entwicklung, Stand, Perspektiven. In: Mey, Günter/Mruck, Katja (Ed.): Grounded Theory Reader. Wiesbaden: VS Verlag für Sozialwissenschaften [2007], 11–48, 13–22.

424 For the methodological and methodical differences between Barney Glaser and Anselm Strauss, see Strübing, Jörg (²2011): Zwei Varianten von Grounded Theory? Zu den methodologischen und methodischen Differenzen zwischen Barney Glaser und Anselm Strauss. In: Mey, Günter/Mruck, Katja (Ed.): Grounded Theory Reader, 262–277.

425 Flick, Uwe (2012): Qualitative Sozialforschung. Eine Einführung, 143.

426 Ibid.

427 Cf. Klein, Stephanie (2005): Erkenntnis und Methode in der Praktischen Theologie, 261.

428 Cf. ibid., 245.

429 Ibid., 261f.

430 Ibid., 262.

431 Ibid.

and gives meaning to events in light of his or her own biography or experiences, according to gender, time and place, cultural, political, religious, and professional backgrounds."[432]

In this quotation from Corbin and Strauss it becomes clear that it is always a reality interpreted by people that can be discovered. It is not the event itself that is the subject of the study, but the meanings that the respective persons attach to it, based on their biographies and experiences. "In developing a grounded theory, we are trying to capture as much of the complexity and movement in the real world as possible, while knowing we are never able to grasp all of it."[433] The "conceptualisation of data" is fundamental to grounded theory.[434]

> "Categories emerge during the process of conceptualising analysis of the data. They are defined less in terms of fixed at any point in data analysis, but develop through the conceptualisation and coding of the data, through the ordering of the codes and the increasing clarification of their relationships to each other."[435]

Categories can group together a variety of codes, allowing them to integrate even contradictory hypotheses and variants, thereby trying to do justice to the complexity of social reality.[436] Category formation is rooted in the data from the beginning of open coding to the description of the core category, which makes different readings possible. "Diversity is not a lack, a sign of blurriness or arbitrariness, but a sign of *critical, process-oriented thinking* that gains *a certain temporary stability only through categories*."[437] Three steps can be identified in grounded theory: open coding, selective coding and axial coding. With open coding, the individual words or sequences are coded, with axial coding, categories are developed that include as many codes as possible and with selective coding, the core category is identified.

> "Often researchers have difficulties in summarising the central statements of the study in view of 'all the important details'. Here one should ask, which 'history' is contained in the data. In a few sentences, the researcher summarises the results of the study for an interested reader. The main questions for these minutes are: What is this about? What did I learn from the examination? What is the focus of attention? What are the connections? The central story revolves around the category, develops it succinctly

---

432 Corbin, Juliet/Strauss, Anselm (³2008): Basics of Qualitative Research. Los Angeles/London/New Delhi/Singapore: Sage Publications, 10.
433 Strauss, Anselm/Corbin, Juliet (1990): Basis of Qualitative Research. Grounded Theory Procedures and Techniques. London u.a.: Sage, 111.
434 Muckel, Petra (²2011): Die Entwicklung von Kategorien mit der Methode der Grounded Theory. In: Mey, Günter/Mruck, Katja (Ed.): Grounded Theory Reader [2007], 333–352, 338.
435 Ibid., 338f.
436 Cf. ibid., 350.
437 Ibid., 349.

and shows the connections to other important categories. After defining the core category, its properties and dimensions, other relevant categories are systematically and schematically related to the core category (e.g. in the sense of the coding paradigm). Once the relations of the central categories have been formulated, their respective characteristics and dimensions can be compared in terms of regularity and pattern."[438]

Corbin and Strauss define the analysis as a process of generating, developing and confirming concepts, with the process progressing over time and with the acquisition of data. "Analysis is a process of generating, developing, and verifying concepts – a process that builds over time and with the acquisition of data."[439] The first analysis of grounded theory should ideally take place after the first data collection, which enables the researcher to identify relevant concepts and to hear and observe them with more sensitivity. The decision as to which data will be collected next is based on the data already available.

> "Theoretical sampling is the process of data collection for generating theory whereby the analyst jointly collects, codes, and analyses his data and decides what data to collect next and where to find them, in order to develop his theory as it emerges. This process of data collection is *controlled* by the emerging theory, whether substantive or formal. The initial decisions for theoretical collection of data are based only on a general sociological perspective and on a general subject or problem area […]."[440]

The grounded theory is collected from the data and illustrated with characteristic examples from the data.[441]

> "Generating a theory from data means that most hypotheses and concepts not only come from the data, but are systematically worked out in relation to the data during the course of the research. Generating a theory involves a process of research. By contrast, the *source* of certain ideas, or even 'models,' can come from sources other than the data. […] But the generation of theory from such insights must then be brought into relation to the data, or there is great danger that theory and empirical world will mismatch."[442]

Systematic use of comparative analysis enables a rich, integrated and dense grounded theory, in which the development of the theory is not completed too quickly.[443] The theory is developed from the data, without this being based on a certain theoretical approach.

---

438 Böhm, Andreas (⁹2012): Theoretisches Codieren: Textanalyse in der Grounded Theory. In: Flick, Uwe/von Kardorff, Ernst/Steinke, Ines: Qualitative Forschung. Ein Handbuch, 475–485, 482f.
439 Corbin, Juliet/Strauss, Anselm (³2008): Basics of Qualitative Research, 57.
440 Glaser, Barney G./Strauss, Anselm (1967): The Discovery of Grounded Theory, 45.
441 Cf. ibid., 5.
442 Ibid., 6.
443 Cf. ibid., 256.

"In short, our focus on the emergence of categories solves the problems of fit, relevance, forcing, and richness. An effective strategy is, at first, literally to ignore the literature of theory and fact on the area under study, in order to assure that the emergence of categories will not be contaminated by concepts more suited to different areas. Similarities and convergences with the literature can be established after the analytic core of categories has emerged. While the verification of theory aims at establishing a relatively few major uniformities and variations on the same conceptual level, we believe that the generation of theory should aim at achieving much *diversity* in emergent categories, synthesised at as *many levels* of conceptual and hypothetical generalisation as possible. The synthesis provides readily apparent connections between data and lower and higher level conceptual abstractions of categories and properties."[444]

The grounded theory was adapted accordingly in the course of time. Thus "Charmaz (1990) [...] detailed ('dense') case studies as a starting point for the development of theory"[445] and Flick (1996) selects groups in advance, which are examined because he assumes that different views on a certain topic can be found in different groups.[446]

4. Thematic coding according to Uwe Flick

The method of thematic coding was developed by Uwe Flick based on Strauss (1991) and works with pre-defined groups derived from the question.[447] "The research issue is the social distribution of perspectives on a phenomenon or a process. The underlying assumption is that in different social worlds or groups, differing views can be found."[448] In order to asses this assumption and to develop a theory on group-specific views and experiences, Strauss' approach must be modified in such a way that the comparability of the empirical material is increased.[449]

> "Sampling is oriented to the groups whose perspectives on the issue seem to be most instructive for analysis, and which therefore are defined in advance [...] and not derived from the state of interpretation as Strauss's procedure. Theoretical sampling is applied in each group in order to select the concrete cases to be studied."[450]

The thematic coding is used as a multi-level procedure for the interpretation of the material. In the first step, the cases are interpreted in a series of individual case analyses. Short descriptions of the respective case, which specify the motto of the case, a

---

444 Ibid., 37.
445 Böhm, Andreas (2012): Theoretisches Codieren. In: Flick, Uwe/von Kardorff, Ernst/Steinke, Ines: Qualitative Forschung. Ein Handbuch, 475–485, 485.
446 Cf. ibid., 484f.
447 Cf. Flick, Uwe (2012): Qualitative Sozialforschung. Eine Einführung, 402.
448 Flick, Uwe (2009): An Introduction to Qualitative Research, 318.
449 Ibid.
450 Ibid.

presentation of the persons with regard to the question and the central topics, provide an initial orientation and have heuristic value for the subsequent analyses.[451] The procedure is based on an in-depth analysis of the individual case. In this way, the relations that the respective person deals with the topic of the study[452] is preserved. For each case, a category system is developed and further elaborated by openly and then selectively coding according to Strauss.

> "Here, selective coding aims less at developing of a grounded core category across all cases than at generating thematic domains and categories for the single case first. After the first case analyses, you will cross-check the developed categories and thematic domains linked to the single cases. A thematic structure results from this cross-check, which underlies the analysis of further cases in order to increase their comparability."[453]

Similar codes are grouped into individual groups and specific topics are identified for each group. The constant comparison of the cases on the basis of the structure developed makes it possible to sketch the spectrum of content in which the interviewees deal with the respective topics. The procedure of thematic coding

> "specifies Strauss's (1987) approach to studies, which aims at developing a theory starting from the distribution of perspectives on a certain theme, issue, or process. Group-specific correspondences and differences are identified and analyzed. In contrast to Strauss's procedure, however, the first step consists of a single case analysis: only in the second step will you undertake group comparisons beyond the single case (e.g., an interview). By developing a thematic structure, which is grounded in the empirical material for the analysis and comparison of cases, you will increase the comparability of interpretations. At the same time, the procedure remains sensitive and open to the specific contents of each individual case and the social group with regard to the issue under study."[454]

5. Reasons for access to research

The research project described here is based on an ethnographic approach to the research field of kindergarten, combined with the basics of the data collection and evaluation method of grounded theory[455] and thematic coding. The common denominator in this is that research is understood as an open process in which data collection and evaluation are interlinked and the principle of triangulation is pursued.

---

451 Cf. ibid., 319.
452 Cf. ibid., 319.
453 Ibid., 319.
454 Ibid., 322f.
455 Corbin, Juliet/Strauss, Anselm (³2008): Basics of Qualitative Research.

In data collection and evaluation, the basics of thematic coding and grounded theory[456] are linked together. The procedure of thematic coding brings a structuring and an overview into the wealth of data and enables a better traceability of the individual methods of data collection than would be possible with exclusive access to the data material via grounded theory. Following the thematic coding approach, two kindergartens were selected, on the basis of which different ways of dealing with religious differences were to be expected. "Sampling is oriented to the groups whose perspectives on the issue seem to be most instructive for analysis, and which therefore are defined in advance".[457] In order to ensure comparability, the research fields are characterised not only by differences but also by a number of common features,[458] and topics are defined while at the same time being open to the respective, related points of view.[459] Theoretical sampling "is applied in each group in order to select the concrete cases to be studied."[460] The first step of thematic coding focuses on the cases included, which are interpreted in a series of individual case analyses,[461] whereby brief case descriptions of the respective case are prepared for initial orientation. In this study, these case descriptions are prepared for the methods carried out with different people, such as group discussions with children and teachers, the expert interview and the participant observation of the two kindergartens. In these case representations, a short description of the participating persons and, if relevant, the respective situation and the central topics that are addressed is made.[462] In addition to the case descriptions, all the data collected and transcribed are openly coded in the sense of grounded theory. Both the case descriptions and the coding and categorisation of the data are carried out in close proximity to field research in order to enable theoretical sampling within the two kindergartens, in which the findings determine the further course of data collection and the methodological procedure. The case descriptions and open coding are extended by axial coding, which takes place in constant comparison of case descriptions and codes from open coding and finally leads to the elaboration of a core category in selective coding. The creation of codes and the categorisation are accompanied by ongoing memos. Since the research question on which the study is based is a double perspective, it became apparent in the process of axial coding that these two parts of the research question must first be answered separately in the analysis before they can be linked together and interrelationships can be recognised. All these described steps are not to be understood as linear and clearly distinguishable from each other, but are

---

456 Cf. Glaser, Barney G./Strauss, Anselm (1967): The Discovery of Grounded Theory; Strauss, Anselm/Corbin, Juliet: Grounded Theory. Grundlagen Qualitativer Sozialforschung. Weinheim: Psychologie Verlags Union 1996.
457 Flick, Uwe (2009): An Introduction to Qualitative Resarch, 318.
458 Cf. chapter "Selection of kindergartens" (part IV, 2).
459 Flick, Uwe (2012): Qualitative Sozialforschung. Eine Einführung, 402.
460 Flick, Uwe (2009): An Introduction to Qualitative Research, 318f..
461 Flick, Uwe (2012): Qualitative Sozialforschung. Eine Einführung, 403.
462 Cf. ibid.

interlinked in a circular procedure throughout the entire study: Figure 1 tries to outline this procedure.

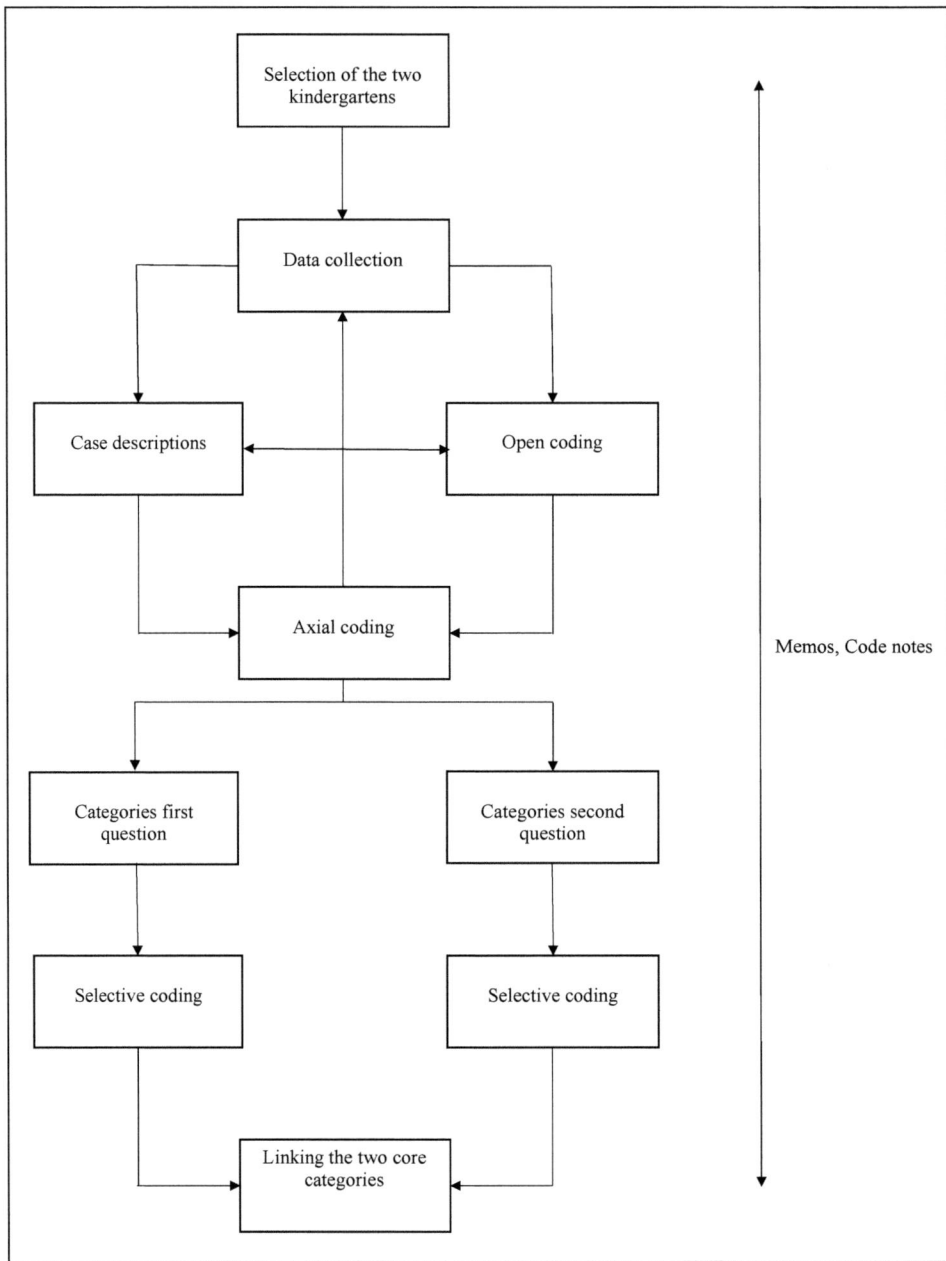

Fig. 1: Presentation of the procedure by linking the research approaches of grounded theory and thematic coding

6. Overview of the methods used

Triangulation plays an indispensable role in grounded theory, thematic coding and the ethnographic approach.[463] The grounded theory, for example, considers that "theory generated from diverse slices of data never fits or works as well, as theory generated from diverse slices of data (...)"[464] According to grounded theory, theoretical saturation is reached when the inclusion of further data and methods no longer brings new findings, thus triangulation also reaches the limit of theoretical saturation.[465] An essential characteristic of the ethnographic approach is the flexible research strategy that also characterises grounded theory.[466]

The study is also based[467] on the insight that triangulation leads to a deeper understanding of what has been investigated and should justify and increase knowledge through further findings. Therefore, data triangulation, investigator-triangulation, theoretical triangulation as well as methodological triangulation in the sense of between-method triangulation are applied.[468] Data triangulation is carried out by collecting the data from the study from various sources. Discussions and interviews with different actors take place at different times of the year in the field of the two kindergartens. The data obtained are put up for discussion by various interpretation groups and, in discussions with people from different professional, religious and national backgrounds, the best possible interpretation of the data is sought in order to come close to the concerns of the investigator triangulation.[469] Methodological triangulation is applied in the sense of between-method triangulation. The use of various methods, participant observation, expert interviews and group discussions allows a broad view of the research field. By dealing with each method used, the theoretical basis of the individual methods is taken into consideration and thus the theoretical triangulation is carried out.[470]

Both explicit and implicit triangulation are used in the study. Thus, separate appointments are arranged with the kindergarten teachers for the group discussion or

---

463 Both triangulation and ethnographic research have long attracted attention in the discussion of methods, see Flick, Uwe (2011): Triangulation. Eine Einführung, 51.
464 Glaser, Barney G./Strauss, Anselm (1967): The Discovery of Grounded Theory, 68.
465 Cf. Flick, Uwe (2012): Triangulation in der qualitativen Forschung. In: Flick, Uwe/von Kardorff, Ernst/Steinke, Ines: Qualitative Forschung. Ein Handbuch, 309–318, 318.
466 Lüders, Christian (2012): Beobachten im Feld und Ethnographie. In: Flick, Uwe/von Kardorff, Ernst/Steinke, Ines: Qualitative Forschung. Ein Handbuch, 384–401, 391–399.
467 Cf. Flick, Uwe (2012): Triangulation in der qualitativen Forschung. In: Flick, Uwe/von Kardorff, Ernst/Steinke, Ines: Qualitative Forschung. Ein Handbuch, 309–318, 311; 318.
468 Cf. chapter "Triangulation within Qualitative Research" (part III, 1.3).
469 The triangulation of investigators in its full form, in which various researchers also go into the field and apply methods, could not be carried out due to the creation of this study as a dissertation, which is carried out by one person.
470 The theoretical implications of the methods used are explained in more detail in the following chapter.

with the heads of the kindergartens for the expert interviews, while the group discussions with the children result in the sense of implicit triangulation.

In order to do justice to the theoretical triangulation, an overview of the basics, the areas of application and the theoretical implications of the methods[471] used is given before the selection of the methods[472] is explained in the following chapter. Before conducting the study, the researcher dealt with the various methods used in qualitative empirical research in order to select the appropriate methods in the course of the research which seem sensible with regard to the course of research to date. After completion of the field research, it is known which methods are used, which is why only the methods actually used, the participant observation, the group discussion and the expert interview are outlined below.

6.1   Participant observation

Qualitative research requires the ability to observe.[473]

> "This observation can – depending on the question and procedure – play a more or less important role as a separate form of survey and complement other types of survey – be it interviews or group discussions. In order to make this possible, it is important to formalise the process of observation as far as possible and thus make it intersubjectively comprehensible."[474]

In participant observation,[475] the person conducting the research enters into a communication process that is determined by what he or she brings with him or her as a person.[476]

---

471 For detailed methodological discussions see Tashakkori, Abbas/Teddlie, Charles (Ed.) (²2010): SAGE Handbook of Mixed Methods in Social & Behavioral Research Overview of contemporary issues in mixed methods research. Thousand Oaks/London/New Delhi/Singapore: SAGE Publications [2003]; Johnson, R. Burke/Onwuegbuzie, Anthony J. (2004): Mixed Methods Research: A Research Paradigm Whose Time Has Come. *Educational Researcher 33*(7), 14–26; Flick, Uwe/von Kardorff, Ernst/Steinke, Ines (Ed.) (2012): Qualitative Sozialforschung. Ein Handbuch; Flick, Uwe (2012): Qualitative Sozialforschung. Eine Einführung.
472 Cf. part IV "Study design and conduct".
473 Cf. Przyborski, Aglaja/Wohlrab-Sahr, Monika (2014): Qualitative Sozialforschung, 49.
474 Ibid.
475 For a more intensive study of the participant observation, see, for example, Bachmann, Götz: Teilnehmende Beobachtung. In: Kühl, Stefan/Strodtholz, Petra/Taffertshofer, Andreas (2009): Handbuch Methoden der Organisationsforschung. Quantitative und Qualitative Methoden. Wiesbaden: VS Verlag für Sozialwissenschaften, 248–271.
476 Cf. Przyborski, Aglaja/Wohlrab-Sahr, Monika (2014): Qualitative Sozialforschung, 44.

> "Participating observers move into a field to seek answers to research questions they have designed in advance. These research questions usually have the character of problem questions, so they are open and not closed."[477]

In the course of the participant observation the research questions can be specified.[478]

> "Observation means purposeful, attentive and systematic perception. The sensations that affect the observer are given a shape. Although these may first develop intuitively during the participating observation, the core of the participating observation consists of the systematic search for sensations in which previously discovered configurations can be rediscovered. Participant observation thus changes from rather passive perception to active search."[479]

The observation protocols are texts by researchers "who, with the linguistic means at their disposal, subsequently condense their 'observations' and memories, classify them into contexts and pour them into comprehensible protocols in text form".[480] Whether structured observation sheets make sense depends largely on the question and phase in the research process. "The more differentiated an observation sheet is, the more comprehensive is not only what it takes into account, but also greater is the danger that something unforeseen is neither perceived nor noted in it."[481] In order not to limit the sensitivity for new things too much, descriptive observation rather dispenses with structured arcs, whereas with selective observation, completely relevant aspects that were worked out in advance are captured.[482]

6.2 Group discussion

In the Anglo-American world, the method of group discussion[483] can be traced back to the 1930s. The studies carried out by social psychologist Kurt Lewin and his stu-

---

477 Merkens, Hans (1992): Teilnehmende Beobachtung: Analyse von Protokollen teilnehmender Beobachter. In: Hoffmeyer-Zlotnik, Jürgen H.P. (Ed.): Analyse verbaler Daten. Über den Umgang mit qualitativen Daten. Opladen: Westdeutscher Verlag, 216–247, 218.
478 Merkens, Hans (1992): Teilnehmende Beobachtung. In: Hoffmeyer-Zlotnik, Jürgen H.P. (Ed.): Analyse verbaler Daten, 216–247, 218.
479 Ibid.
480 Lüders, Christian (2012): Beobachten im Feld und Ethnographie. In: Flick, Uwe/von Kardorff, Ernst/Steinke, Ines: Qualitative Forschung. Ein Handbuch, 384–401, 396.
481 Flick, Uwe (2012): Qualitative Sozialforschung. Eine Einführung, 288f.
482 Cf. ibid., 289.
483 For a more detailed description of the group discussion see, for example, Przyborski, Aglaja/Wohlrab-Sahr, Monika (2014): Qualitative Sozialforschung, 88–102; Bock, Karin (2010): Kinderalltag – Kinderwelten, 102–122; Liebig, Brigitte/Nentwig-Gesemann, Iris: Gruppendiskussion. In: Kühl, Stefan/Strodtholz, Petra/Taffertshofer, Andreas (2009): Handbuch Methoden der Organisationsforschung, 102–123; Lamnek, Siegfried (²2005): Gruppendiskussion. Theorie und Praxis. Weinheim: Beltz; Loos, Peter/Schäffer,

dents are considered to be the oldest form of qualitative organisational analysis in history. At the beginning of the 1950s, the group discussion procedure was used as a survey method for the first time in German-speaking countries.[484] With Werner Mangold's[485] new conception of the group discussion procedure, the research of collectively anchored orientations in contrast to individual opinions of individuals came to the fore. Ralf Bohnsack put the group discussion procedure on a theoretical-methodological basis.[486]

Group discussion procedures are characterised by an interweaving of two discourses, firstly the discourse of the researchers with the investigated and secondly the discourse of the investigated, the group discussion participants among themselves.[487] In groups of aquaintances, their members also find themselves outside the research situation in social contexts and interact with one another, which is why they share a concrete, collectively shared basis of experience to which questions can be directly connected.[488] Through group discussion procedures, an attempt is made to reconstruct cultural collective action practice in the groups of aquaintances in order to capture reflexive and action-guiding knowledge.[489] "The group discussion procedure is therefore intended to reconstruct collective orientations in certain groups, since these can be seen as the cultural practice of several actors and can be brought into a context."[490]

Burkhard (2001): Das Gruppendiskussionsverfahren. Theoretische Grundlagen und empirische Anwendung. Opladen: Leske + Budrich; Bohnsack, Ralf/Przyborski, Aglaja/Schäffer, Burkhard (^{2}2010): Das Gruppendiskussionsverfahren in der Forschungspraxis. Opladen/Farmington Hills: Barbara Budrich [2006]; Dreher, Michael/Dreher, Eva (2013): Gruppendiskussionsverfahren. In: Flick, Uwe/von Kardorff, Ernst/Keupp, Heiner/von Rosenstiel, Lutz/Wolff, Stephan (Ed.): Handbuch qualitative Sozialforschung: Grundlagen, Konzepte, Methoden und Anwendungen. Munich: Psychologie Verlags Union, 186–188.

484 Cf. Pollock, Friedrich (Ed.) (1995): Gruppenexperiment: Ein Studienbericht. Bearbeitet von Friedrich Pollock. Mit einem Geleitwort von Franz Böhm. Frankfurter Beiträge zur Soziologie, on behalf of the Institut für Sozialforschung published by Theodor W. Adorno and Walter Dirks, vol. 2. Frankfurt am Main: Europäische Verlagsanstalt.

485 Cf. Mangold, Werner (1960): Gegenstand und Methode des Gruppendiskussionsverfahrens: aus der Arbeit des Instituts für Sozialforschung, vol. 9 Frankfurt am Main: Europäische Verlagsanstalt.

486 Cf. Bohnsack, Ralf/Nentwig-Gesemann, Iris/Nohl, Arnd-Michael (Ed.) (^{3}2013): Die dokumentarische Methode und ihre Untersuchungspraxis. Grundlagen qualitativer Sozialforschung. Wiesbaden: VS Verlag für Sozialwissenschaften; Bohnsack, Ralf/Przyborski, Aglaja/Schäffer, Burkhard (^{2}2010): Das Gruppendiskussionsverfahren in der Forschungspraxis.

487 Cf. Przyborski, Aglaja/Wohlrab-Sahr, Monika (2014): Qualitative Sozialforschung, 105f.

488 Cf. Liebig, Brigitte/Nentwig-Gesemann, Iris (2009): Gruppendiskussion. In: Kühl, Stefan/Strodtholz, Petra/Taffertshofer, Andreas: Handbuch Methoden der Organisationsforschung, 102–123, 105.

489 Cf. Bock, Karin (2010): Kinderalltag – Kinderwelten, 105.

490 Bock, Karin (2010): Kinderalltag – Kinderwelten, 112.

The introduction of the group discussion procedure is based on four hypotheses, which are: opinions always arise as an interaction between the individual and society. It is only through the confrontation with the other that attitudes become conscious. By creating situations that are linked to the reality in which the settings are exchanged and activated, these settings can be determined.[491] Opinions and attitudes are subject to the fluctuations of emotional life, which is why many of the opinions and attitudes not expressed can be traced back to psychological barriers and rationalisations.

The principles of group discussion chairmanship formulated by Bohnsack support the conduct of group discussions according to a basic methodological principle. The questions asked in group discussions are to be addressed to the entire group, exclusive topics and no propositions are to be given and no intervention is to be made in the speeches. Questions must be kept vague and asked in such a way that detailed representations are generated. The immanent demand, which refers to already given topics, is followed by the phase of exmanent demand, in which questions relevant to research are introduced after the climax of the discussion, and the directive phase, in which contradictory or prominent passages can be connected with.[492] There are different forms of chairmanship, formal chairmanship, thematic control and control of dynamics.[493] The formal chairmanship keeps a list of speakers and determines the beginning, the course and the end of the discussion. If new questions are also introduced and the discussion is steered, this is a matter of thematic control. In controlling the dynamics, the interaction also extends to stimulating the conversation by asking stimulating questions, polarising them and specifically addressing cautious participants in the discussion.[494]

6.3 Group discussion procedures in childhood research

Group discussion procedures are regarded as suitable procedures for getting to know "children in their everyday cultural practices".[495] They make it possible to explore how the "production process of social reality is made up by children and which deeper conditions of being or contexts of experience lead to the development of specific action-guiding structures".[496] Nentwig-Gesemann was able to point out

---

491 Cf. Bock, Karin (2010): Kinderalltag – Kinderwelten, 103.
492 Cf. Bohnsack, Ralf (2012): Gruppendiskussionen. In: Flick, Uwe/von Kardorff, Ernst/Steinke, Ines: Qualitative Forschung. Ein Handbuch, 369–384, 380–382.
493 Described amongst others in Flick, Uwe (2011): Qualitative Sozialforschung, 254.
494 Cf. Flick, Uwe (2011): Qualitative Sozialforschung, 254.
495 Nentwig-Gesemann, Iris (2002): Gruppendiskussionen mit Kindern. Die dokumentarische Interpretation von Spielpraxis und Diskursorganisation. *Zeitschrift für qualitative Bildungs-, Beratungs- und Sozialforschung 3*(1), 41–63, 41.
496 Nentwig-Gesemann (2007): Sprach- und Körperdiskurse von Kindern – Verstehen und Verständigung zwischen Textförmigkeit und Ikonizität. In: Friebertshäuser, Barbara/von Felden, Heide/Schäffer, Burkhard (Ed.): Bild und Text. Methoden und Methodologien

"that this is a new quality of data material in which the so-called 'act of focusing' gains particular importance. The first conclusion to be drawn from this is that children probably use a discourse practice that is somehow different and not easily comparable to that of young people and/or adults – either because it appears 'covert' or because children may even somehow follow their own (language and order) logic in the production of communication in group discussions."[497]

In the main part of the group discussion, the interviewees play the role of attentive listening persons who intervene with neither thematic nor with evaluative interventions in the course of the discourse, so that the children can find the topics important to them and work on them in their everyday language in the familiar form of the discourse.[498]

"Their role arises from the focus on *generating self-sufficiency* in relation to verbal interaction, the discourse of children. The children's group should be able to adjust to their common experience contexts, to their central experience centres and relevance systems, which are of central importance for the collective orientation framework and its reconstruction."[499]

There are few methodological reflections on the application and evaluation of group discussions, which is considered a central theoretical deficiency and a practical research problem.[500] In recent years, some research has been carried out with children using the group discussion method. Experience with groups of children has shown that it is often easier to enter into forms of practice with children in which, for example, they re-enact what happens with puppets and only then move on to reconstructive forms of discourse.[501] One method that has proven to be helpful in lowering the hierarchy in conversation is the personal doll training method.[502]

6.4   Interview with experts

The question of who is considered an expert is answered in connection with the respective field of action and taking into account the research spectrum of the empirical survey.[503] The term expert can be defined approximately as follows:

---

visueller Sozialforschung in der Erziehungswissenschaft. Opladen/Farmington Hills: Barbara Budrich, 105–120, 118.
497 Bock, Karin (2010): Kinderalltag – Kinderwelten, 118.
498 Cf. Nentwig-Gesemann, Iris (2002): Gruppendiskussionen mit Kindern. *Zeitschrift für qualitative Bildungs-, Beratungs- und Sozialforschung* 3(1), 41–63, 46.
499 Ibid.
500 Ibid., 45f.
501 Cf. Przyborski, Aglaja/Wohlrab-Sahr, Monika (2014): Qualitative Sozialforschung, 106.
502 Ibid. Persona-Doll-Training, http://www.persona-doll-training.org/ [21.07.2015].
503 Cf. Bogner, Alexander/Menz, Wolfgang (^{2}2005): Das theoriegenerierende Experteninterview. Erkenntnisinteresse, Wissensform, Interview. In: Bogner, Alexander/Littig,

"The expert has technical, process and interpretative knowledge relating to his specific professional field of action. In this respect, expert knowledge does not consist solely of systematic, reflexively accessible specialist knowledge, but to a large extent shows the character of practical or action knowledge, into which various and quite disparate maxims of action and individual decision rules, collective orientations and social patterns of interpretation flow. The knowledge of the expert, his orientations for action, relevance, etc. also show – and this is decisive – the chance to become hegemonic in practice in a certain organisational functional context, i.e., the expert has the possibility to (at least partially) enforce his orientations. By making the knowledge of the expert practical, it structures the conditions for action of other actors in its field of action in a relevant way."[504]

Bogner and Menz distinguish three different typologies of the expert interview, the "explorative",[505] the "systematising" and the "theory-generating" expert interview.[506] Explorative interviews with experts can provide an initial orientation in a field, raise the researcher's awareness of the problem or provide information for the preparation of a guideline.[507] "In this sense, explorative interviews help to structure the research area thematically and to generate hypotheses."[508] Explorative interviews should be conducted as openly as possible, "but for reasons of demonstrative competence alone, it is advisable to structure at least central dimensions of the course of the interview in advance in a guideline."[509] The systematic interview with experts aims at "systematic and complete information gathering".[510] In contrast to the explorative expert interview, the focus here is on the thematic comparability of the data. In the context of multi-methodological approaches, this form of expert interviews has become a central survey instrument. The theory-generating interview aims "at the communicative exploration and analytical reconstruction of the 'subjective dimension' of expert knowledge."[511] In this survey, the experts are asked because their knowledge has the power to be effective in that "their action orientations, their knowledge and their assessments (co-)structure the conditions for action of other actors in a decisive way and thus expert knowledge has the dimension of social relevance."[512]

Beate/Menz, Wolfgang (Ed.): Das Experteninterview. Theorie, Methode, Anwendung. Wiesbaden: VS Verlag für Sozialwissenschaften [2002], 33–70, 46.
504 Ibid. This section is italicised in the original.
505 Cf. ibid., 37.
506 Cf. ibid., 36-39.
507 Ibid., 37.
508 Ibid.
509 Ibid.
510 Ibid.
511 Ibid., 38.
512 Ibid., 45.

A guideline can "guarantee the openness of the course of the interview", if this "is not handled as a compelling process model of the discourse".[513]

> "Guideline-oriented discussion guidance does justice to both the researcher's thematically limited interest in the expert as well as the expert status of the other person. The work involved in developing a guideline rules out the possibility of the researcher presenting himself as an incompetent interlocutor. [...] The orientation on a guideline also rules out the possibility that the conversation gets lost in topics that do nothing to the point and at the same time allows the expert to extemporize his cause and view of things."[514]

A permanent mediation between the course of the interview and the guideline is necessary.[515]

> "In principle, the consequence and attempted solution of the tension between structuring needs on the one hand and the interest in as much 'openness' and 'spontaneity' as possible on the other can be seen in guidelines. Whether and how guidelines are used must and can therefore actually only result from the research interest and the orientation of an interview method."[516]

It is possible to formulate "general rules for the construction of guidelines that offer at least a rough quality standard",[517] even if not this, but rather "successful use determines the quality of a guideline".[518] For the questions asked, the theoretical relevance, the content dimension, the appropriate type of stimulus and question, the adequate wording, the structure of the guideline, the question types and the relationship between the questions need to be clarified.[519]

---

513 Meuser, Michael/Nagel, Ulrike (2005): ExpertInneninterviews – vielfach erprobt, wenig bedacht. Ein Beitrag zur qualitativen Methodendiskussion. In: Bogner, Alexander/Littig, Beate/Menz, Wolfgang (Ed.): Das Experteninterview [2002], 71–93, 78.
514 Meuser, Michael/Nagel, Ulrike (2005): ExpertInneninterviews – vielfach erprobt, wenig bedacht. Ein Beitrag zur qualitativen Methodendiskussion. In: Bogner, Alexander/Littig, Beate/Menz, Wolfgang (Ed.): Das Experteninterview, 71–93, 77.
515 Cf. Flick, Uwe (2012): Qualitative Sozialforschung. Eine Einführung, 223.
516 Ullrich, Carsten, G. (2009): Deutungsmusteranalyse und diskursives Interview. *Zeitschrift für Soziologie 28*(6), 429–447, 436.
517 Ibid.
518 Ibid.
519 Ibid., 436f.

Part IV: Study Design and Conduct

Empirical research has an explorative function in this study. It serves the perception and sensitisation for fundamental questions to religious difference in early childhood education as well as the pointing out of tendencies, how children thematise religious difference. In the following, the research design and the research process are outlined, in which data collection, data evaluation and the adaptation of the research situation are mutually dependent.

1. Methods used in the investigation

In field research, neither the course of the research nor the end of the research is known at the beginning of the research process. The willingness and the desire are given to realize triangulation in the four basic types[520] described. Decisions about sampling and the applied methods are made in the sense of grounded theory, thematic coding and ethnographic research in the course of the research. Thus, the methods used and the respective preparations for the application of the methods can only be described in retrospect after the field research has been completed. At the beginning, discussions were held with the director of the respective house, during which appointments for the expert interview were fixed. After these interviews, the phase of observation followed, during which both the group discussions initiated by the children and the researcher took place. Afterwards, the group discussions were held with the teachers.

1.1 Expert interview with the management of the two kindergartens

After distinguishing between Bogner and Menz, the expert interview is an explorative interview. It helps to structure the research area thematically and to generate initial hypotheses.[521]

In the first week of field research in kindergarten, the researcher conducted an expert interview with the head of the Catholic kindergarten and the head of the Islamic kindergarten, which was based on the following guideline:
- What religious affiliations do the children have in the kindergarten?
- What is the place of religion in kindergarten groups?
- How is religion expressed in kindergarten?
- How are different religions thematised?
- In which situations do children address religion of their own accord?

---
520 Cf. Denzin, Norman K. (1989): The research act, 236–241.
521 Cf. Bogner, Alexander/Menz, Wolfgang (2005): Das theoriegenerierende Experteninterview. In: Bogner, Alexander/Littig, Beate/Menz, Wolfgang (Ed.): Das Experteninterview, 33–70, 37.

- Would you please tell me about a situation in which the different religions became a challenge?
- Would you please tell me about a situation in which the different religions were an opportunity?
- Which festivals are celebrated in the kindergarten?
- How are celebrations celebrated in kindergarten? Who celebrates? Who does not celebrate? What opportunities do children who do not celebrate have?
- What space do forms of expression of religions have in everyday kindergarten life (e.g. prayers, songs, etc.)?
- When are prayers said?
- What prayers are said?
- How do you deal with different religious eating habits in kindergarten?

1.2 Participant observation

As is usual in ethnographic work,[522] the observations are recorded in field notes and a regular research diary is kept. Interaction sequences are recorded literally. For the observation protocol, the scheme of Przyborski and Wohlrab-Sahr[523] is modified. The following columns are available in the observation log: Place, time, observations, context information, own perception/reflexion and if necessary theoretical reflection. The observations are noted directly in the field; if possible, the other information is also added, otherwise it is added as soon as possible. After the day at the kindergarten, the observation protocol is supplemented with missing information and the recordings are digitised.

In order not to restrict the participant observation in advance, but to make it as open as possible in the sense of an explorative study, the two-part research question without formulating exact criteria serves as a basis for the participant observation.[524] Based on previous literature research and her own experiences in kindergarten, the researcher has certain expectations as to where and how religious difference can be expressed. Since the observation behaviour may therefore also be influenced, the areas are disclosed in which the researcher considers the recognisability of religious difference to be probable: Language, pictures, interior design, conversations of the teachers, topics in the morning circle, selection of the celebrations, ways of celebrating and conversations with parents.

---

522 Przyborski, Aglaja/Wohlrab-Sahr, Monika (2014): Qualitative Sozialforschung, 49.
523 Cf. ibid., 50.
524 Cf. Flick, Uwe (2012): Qualitative Sozialforschung. Eine Einführung, 289.

1.3 Group discussions with the children

Group discussions with children are of particular interest, as the collective action orientation can be well expressed in them.[525] The decision for group discussions is made because they try to minimise the hierarchical gap between the researcher and the children,[526] because attitudes of persons are determined both individually and collectively and because this collectivity is given clear weight in group discussions. Since attitudes develop by interaction with others, group discussion are considered an adequate method to engage in conversation with children about religious difference. In addition to the children's statements, the group dynamics can thus also be subjected to an analysis in conversation.

Since group discussions initiated by the researcher have the disadvantage because of the hierarchy between the researcher and the children and the form and content of the impulse influence the further course of the group discussion, the study refrains, as far as possible, from group discussions initiated by the researcher and pays particular attention to discussions that children conduct among themselves with the teacher or researcher. If, after the group discussion initiated by the children, information is still missing which is determined by continuous transcription and coding, the researcher initiates group discussions. The stimulus given by the researcher is kept as low as possible by drawing on an experience shared by the children in the group from everyday kindergarten life and asking the children to tell about it. Open questions are particularly important in group discussions with children.[527]

1.3.1 Group discussions initiated by the children

The advantage of the group discussions, which are started by the children, is that the children's contributions are not influenced by questions or stimulus from the researchers. Since the questions and the way the researcher asks questions influence the children's answers, the children's influence is reduced in group discussions in which the researcher is exclusively observing. Possible unconscious intentions and requests for answers by the researcher, to which the children may attempt to respond in group discussions, play no role in group discussions initiated by the children.[528] Since the

---

525 Cf. Liebig, Brigitte/Nentwig-Gesemann, Iris (2009): Gruppendiskussion. In: Kühl, Stefan/Strodtholz, Petra/Taffertshofer, Andreas: Handbuch Methoden der Organisationsforschung, 102–123, 105.

526 Cf. chapter "childhood research" (part II, 5) where the hierarchical gap is outlined.

527 Cf. Houskamp, Fisher, Stuber (2004): Spirituality in children and adolescents: research findings and implications for clinicians and researches. *Child & Adolescent Psychiatric Clinics of North America*13(1), 221–230, 223. Questions concerning the children's perspective on spiritual experiences make even more sense than clinical interviews.

528 Since the researcher is present at the children's conversation, it cannot be assumed that the children are completely uninfluenced.

researcher is not active in these group discussions, but has an exclusively observational role, he or she documents the discussions taking place and supplements the framework conditions immediately after the end of the discussion.

1.3.2 Group discussions initiated by the researcher

If no theoretical saturation is achieved on the basis of the information from the expert interviews, the participants' observation and the group discussions initiated by the children themselves, which is determined by continuous transcription and coding, situations are identified with the help of the participant observation in which religious difference could become recognisable for children in the respective kindergarten and these are selected as discussion causes for the group discussions with the children.

In group discussions initiated by the researcher, the children are asked whether they would like to participate, and a discussion is only conducted with them if there is an explicit affirmative answer. The discussions take place in familiar rooms in the kindergarten and in groups of aquaintances with two to four children each,[529] whereby the composition of the group is agreed to in advance with the kindergarten teacher. The number of conversations depends on the time and space available in everyday kindergarten life, as the researcher tries not to disrupt the daily routine in the kindergarten.

Before the group discussions begin, the children are shown the audio device and told: "The device records what you say so that I can remember it later." They are asked if it is okay if the device is switched on and what has been said is recorded. If children do not know what an audio device is and want to know more about the device, they can say or sing something at the beginning and listen to what they have recorded before the group discussion with the actual topic is opened.

Children are influenced by their experiences and refer to sensually perceptible differences,[530] which is why conversation is timed to directly follow an experience of the children, so that a common experience forms the starting point for the conversations with the children. This common starting point is the forms of expression and life of religion, which lie in the world of experience of the children and which they experience.[531] The group discussions initiated by the researcher are formally conducted so that the children have the opportunity to talk to each other. The children are asked to tell about the situation they have experienced. This free narrative of the children, which is not influenced by objects brought along or a consciously set stimulus, shows what children find relevant to tell. If the conversation goes in a direction that deviates greatly from the research question, the course of the conversation stalls or religious difference is not addressed by the children, a thematic control takes place by the

---

529 Cf. chapter "Group discussion" (part III, 6.2).
530 Cf. McKenna, Ursula/Ipgrave, Julia/Jackson, Robert (2008): Inter Faith Dialogue by Email in Primary Schools; Elkind, David (1964): Age changes in the meaning of religious identity. *Review of Religious Research* 6(1), 36–40.
531 Religion cannot be limited to these, but this approach is chosen to talk to children.

researcher asking open questions.[532] If questions are asked, this is done by means of a guideline[533] that is flexibly adapted to the respective situation and not rigidly followed, and which only addresses those questions that are not answered in advance by the children. If children ask questions during the discussion, special attention will be paid to them. In order not to limit the discussion to the cognitive level, various methods are used that are appropriate to the situation. In some group discussions, for example, a hand puppet is used to reduce the hierarchy between the teacher and the children by acting as an intermediary.[534] In the course of the group discussion, drawings are also made, songs sung or things illustrated with a small doll, provided that the children want to do so and accept the methodical offer, which is left to them. The questions and the methods are adapted to the situation and the children participating in the discussion. The methodical implementation of the group discussions as well as the situations according to which group discussions are conducted are not fixed in advance, but result in the course of the research process.

1.4 Group discussions with the teachers

Group discussions are held with the teachers working together in a kindergarten, whereby the composition of the discussion groups corresponds to groups of aquaintances. Due to the authority given between the director and the teachers, the group discussion with the teachers is conducted without the director. During the discussion, the teachers are asked questions similar to those asked to the director in an expert interview, albeit more closely aligned with everyday kindergarten life. The guidelines for the Catholic kindergartens and for the Islamic kindergartens vary. These marginal differences are marked with a slash.

Introduction: Since you know the children and the kindergarten life much better than I do, I ask you to share your experiences, views and impressions on some questions:
- Children are different. How can this be seen in kindergarten?

---

532 Cf. chapter "Group discussion" (part III, 6.2).
533 Questions that appear in the guide and are adapted to the situation: Which festival was celebrated?, What was celebrated at the festival?, How did you celebrate the festival?, Who participated in the festival?, Who did not participate in the festival?, Why did you not celebrate the festival?, Why did some people not participate?, What did you like about the festival?, What did you not like?, What is particularly important at the festival?, What do you do in the Koran lesson?, Who goes to the Koran lesson?, Who does not go to the Koran lesson? Why do you go to the Koran lesson?, Why do you not go to the Koran lesson?, Why do not all go to the Koran lesson?
534 After a festival, the researcher thematises that a friend of hers is present today who is interested in the festival and asks whether the children would like to tell the friend something about the festival. The hand puppet is introduced and the children are welcomed by it. At the end of the discussion the doll says thanks and goodbye.

- Children recognise differences. In your opinion, which ones are recognisable to them?
- What differences do children talk about?
- What differences do you address in everyday kindergarten life?
- In your opinion, which differences should be discernible in kindergarten and which not?
- How do you thematise religious differences? (What makes it difficult to address religious differences?)
- How can religious differences become apparent to children?
- What is the place of religion in your kindergarten groups?
- There are children who are not Catholic/Muslim. What place do their religions and worldviews have in your kindergarten groups?
- In which situations do children address religion of their own accord?
- How are different religions thematised in kindergarten?
- When do children address different religions?
- Please tell me about a situation in which different religions have become an issue.
- Please tell me of a situation in which challenges or conflicts arose due to the different religions.
- Please tell me of a situation in which opportunities arose due to the different religions.
- Which children do not take part in the celebration of Christian festivals/the teaching of the Koran? Why don't they participate?
- How do children who do not take part in celebrations/who do not take part in Koran lessons mention their absence?
- How do the children attending the festival/the Koran lesson mention the absence of some children?
- How do you think other religions should be considered in kindergarten in the future?
- What do you think should happen to festivals of other religions in kindergarten?
- What support do you wish to be able to implement this (training, concepts)?

2. Selection of kindergartens

Kindergartens in Vienna,[535] the capital of Austria, are selected. Compared to the other federal states of Austria, the city of Vienna is characterised by a high degree of religious plurality. The last census, in which the data on religious affiliation in Austria and

---

535 According to Statistics Austria data, 8,445 institutional childcare facilities (excluding seasonal day care centres) existed in the 2013/14 school year, of which 4,692 were kindergartens, 1,450 nursery schools, 1,167 day care centres and 1,136 mixed-age childcare facilities. As of 15 October 2013, 333,326 children were enrolled in day-care centres throughout Germany, 211,141 of whom attended kindergarten groups (http://www.

the federal states were collected, was carried out in 2001;[536] more recent figures are available on the basis of censuses or estimates. The following table lists the population of Austria and the population of Vienna according to the religious creed of 2001. The percentages calculated from the figures listed at Statistics Austria are rounded to one decimal place.[537]

Table 1: Population of Austria and population of Vienna by religious affiliation by the last conventional census 2001[538]

Religious affiliation	Austria		Vienna	
	Persons	Percentage	Persons	Percentage
Roman Catholic	5,915,421	73.6	762,089	49.2
Protestant	376,150	4.7	72,492	4.7
Old Catholic	14,621	0.2	7,134	0.5
Jewish	8,140	0.1	6,988	0.5
Islamic	338,988	4.2	121,149	7.8
Other	255,681	3.2	116,970	7.5
Without religious confession	963,263	12.0	397,596	25.7
Not specified	160,662	2.0	65,705	4.2
Total population	8,032,926	100.0	1,550,123	100.0

Recent counts or extrapolations of the respective religious communities of the number of Catholic, Protestant and Muslim religions as well as the data from Statistics Austria for the entire population show the following picture.[539]

---

statistik.at/web_de/statistiken/bildung_und_kultur/formales_bildungswesen/kindertagesheime_kinderbetreuung/index.html [01.06.2015]).

536 The 2001 census was the last conventional census in Austria to be conducted via questionnaires and has been replaced by register censuses. (cf. http://www.statistik.at/web_de/frageboegen/registerzaehlung/weitere_informationen/faq/index.html [30.04.2015]). In the following register counts the information about religious affiliation is missing. "Religious affiliation: could not be collected on the basis of an ordinance of the responsible Federal Minister pursuant to §1 Paragraph 3 RZG". The "competent BM may order a complete survey of the colloquial language in a person-related form and a complete survey of the religious confession in a non-personal form by order, if this is absolutely necessary for the fulfilment of federal tasks". (Statistics Austria, http://www.statistik.at/web_de/frageboegen/registerzaehlung/weitere_informationen/faq/index.html#index7 [30.04.2015]).

537 This results in a slight blurring of the percentage values.

538 Source: Statistics Austria, http://www.statistik.at/web_de/statistiken/bevoelkerung/volkszaehlungen_registerzaehlungen_abgestimmte_erwerbsstatistik/bevoelkerung_nach_demographischen_merkmalen/022885.html [19.11.2014].

539 Since the figures indicate the number of religious affiliations in different years, the percentages are not shown in the table.

Table 2: Population of Austria and population of Vienna by religious affiliation by own census or projection[540]

Religious affiliation	Austria	Vienna
Catholic[551]	5,308,515	1,246,608
Protestant[552]	309,137	53,375
Muslim[553]	573,876	216,345
Total population[554]	8,401,940	1,714,227

Vienna offers a variety of childcare options. Parents can choose between private childcare[545] and municipal kindergartens[546]. For this research work, two private kindergartens were chosen, whose sponsorships are religiously declared.

One of the selected kindergartens is run by a Catholic association, and one kindergarten is run by an Islamic institution.[547] In the sense of thematic coding, two kindergartens are selected in which different perspectives are expected in relation to the research question, which seem particularly informative for the analysis.[548] In the Catholic kindergarten, the majority of children are Catholic, with the minority of children in the kindergarten belonging to various religions. The majority of the children in the Islamic kindergarten are Muslim, the minority of other children are Christian.[549]

In order to ensure comparability, the two kindergartens should have some similarities, hence the kindergartens have a similar catchment area and are located in the same district of Vienna, which suggests a similar socio-economic status of the

---

540 The year of the respective estimate or count is indicated by the respective religion.
541 Announcement of the statistical data for 2013 by the Austrian Bishops' Conference (Catholic Church Austria, http://www.katholisch.at/site/kirche/article/102078.html[21.07.2015]).
542 According to the census of the Protestant Church in Austria 2014 (Protestant Church in Austria, http://www.evang.at/kirche/zahlen-fakten [21.07.2015]).
543 Extrapolation for the year 2012. Cf. Kolb, Jonas/Mattausch-Yıldız, Birgit: Muslimische Alltagspraxis in Österreich. Ein Kompass zu religiöser Diversität. Zwischenbericht für das Projektjahr 2013. University of Vienna. Department for Islamic-Theological Studies, https://iis.univie.ac.at/fileadmin/user_upload/p_iis/muslimische_alltagspraxis_in_oesterreich.projektbericht.pdf [21.08.2015].
544 Data of the register-related survey 201 by Statistics Austria, http://www.statistik.at/web_de/statistiken/bevoelkerung/volkszaehlungen_registerzaehlungen_abgestimmte_erwerbsstatistik/bevoelkerungsstand/index.html [30.04.2015].
545 City Administration of Vienna, http://www.wien.gv.at/bildung/kindergarten/private-angebote/index.html [21.07.2015].
546 City Administration of Vienna, http://www.wien.gv.at/bildung/kindergarten/staedtisches-angebot/index.html [21.07.2015].
547 In the following these are referred to as the Catholic and the Islamic kindergarten.
548 Cf. Flick, Uwe (2012): Qualitative Sozialforschung. Eine Einführung, 402.
549 For the exact number of children belonging to which religion, see chapter "Socio-demographic data of children" (part V, 2.1.4 and 2.2.4).

families. The kindergartens have a policy to accept children regardless of their religious affiliation, the directors of the kindergartens express religious difference positively, and respect for all children explicitly appears in both concepts. In addition to the emphasis on the uniqueness and dignity of each child, the mission statement of the Catholic kindergarten[550] explicitly mentions respectful treatment of different worldviews and cultures, openness for new things, and welcome of children belonging to other religious communities. It is also anchored in the mission statement that religious beliefs are expressed in the concrete form of everyday life and that different lifestyles stimulate mutual interest, mutual approach, and help to better understand each other. In the mission statement of the Islamic kindergarten the ethical and moral education is emphasised. It is emphasised that children and their religion are accepted and supported without prejudice by allowing them to learn their religion playfully and to freely develop their religious identity. Particular emphasis is placed on social skills such as tolerance, respect for people and compassion.[551]

3. Examination procedure

Since the researcher, her approach and her impressions have a significant influence on the way of conducting the examination, this and the following chapter are written in the first-person form in order to express the subjectivity in these two chapters in particular.

3.1 Field access

The path into the field is "to be understood (and designed) as a never-ending task that must be carried out in cooperation, i.e. together with the supposed objects of research".[552] It is advisable "to insist not only on the field, but also on one's own naivety in order to be able to use one's – actual or supposed – ignorance methodically for as long as possible".[553] The aim of the access work, is on the one hand to eliminate the distance between the researcher and the field, and on the other hand to maintain and use the difference as a resource for gaining knowledge. The social location of the researcher is often characterised by two steps: First, the general connectivity is checked. "The question is whether the recognisable characteristics of the person

---

550 The „Religionspädagogische BildungsRahmenPlan" is used as a reference for the mission statement, see St. Nikolaus Kindertagesheimstiftung, Wien/Caritas für Kinder und Jugendliche, Linz: Religionspädagogischer BildungsRahmenPlan für elementare Bildungseinrichtungen in Österreich. Linz: Unsere Kinder 2010.
551 Due to anonymity, the source of the indirect quotations is not cited.
552 Wolff, Stephan (2012): Wege ins Feld und ihre Varianten. In: Flick, Uwe/von Kardorff, Ernst/Steinke, Ines: Qualitative Forschung. Ein Handbuch, 334–349, 336.
553 Ibid., 349.

(gender, age, ethnicity) and their concerns, as well as aspects of the organisational environment from which the researcher comes, are compatible with local views of the world, interests and processes."[554] In the second step, an agreement is reached on certain roles for participants. Agreements on an accepted observer role can be helpful, which offers the possibility of withdrawing from the field and asking questions that seem obvious.[555]

Due to my training as a kindergarten teacher my social positioning was easily possible for those working in the field, which is why I had to pay particular attention to maintaining the distance between myself and the actors in the field. Since interns are often involved in the field of kindergarten and mostly observe them, and also carry out their own activities, I could be perceived as an intern by outsiders and by teachers, although they knew about my role in the research process. This helped me to preserve "naivety" and to ask questions.[556]

3.2   Declaration of Consent

The teachers of the kindergartens were asked to sign declarations of consent that the data collected may be used for research and teaching activities.[557] I sent letters to the parents asking for their consent for the research project and assuring them that the data collected will be used anonymously. The teachers agreed to hand these letters over to the parents and ask them to sign the consent forms.[558]

> "I agree to my child taking part in a study on "Living together" at the University of Vienna. In the course of this research project, individual conversations and group conversations are conducted with children and drawings are made, whereby the activities are recorded by means of audio and video recordings. With my signature I agree that the data collected may be used for research and teaching purposes."[559]

The parents and the teachers gave their consent for the research project and the use of the collected data.

On my first day, I told the children why I was in kindergarten. I told them that I was interested in what they thought and asked them if it was all right with them for me to write down some of the things they say and do. When I initiated group discussions with children, I asked the children again if they would like to participate in a conversation, and if it would be all right with them if I recorded it.

---

554 Ibid., 340.
555 Cf. ibid., 346f.
556 Cf. ibid., 349.
557 Cf. chapter "Appendix".
558 For the exact wording of the declarations of consent, see the "Appendix" section.
559 Cf. chapter "Appendix".

3.3 Data gathering

Phases of intensive field research alternated with phases of distanced analytical work[560] in order to maintain the necessary distance while being involved in the field. After a few weeks of field research, I did not go to kindergarten for some time in order to transcribe the data collected and to study related literature.

In both kindergartens, an expert interview was conducted at the beginning, participants were observed in both kindergartens throughout a kindergarten year and group discussions were held with children, which on the one hand were initiated by the children, on the other hand if additional information with regard to the research questions seemed useful, by me. The fieldwork was concluded by a group discussion with the teachers of the respective kindergarten. The methods chosen, the time of the survey and the selection of the group were based according to grounded theory on the data already collected and coded. All those involved in kindergarten activities were able to communicate well in German.

3.4 Documentation of Data

"The use of recording devices makes the fixing of data independent of the researcher's point of view as well as that of the subjects studied."[561] The group discussions I initiated with the children, the expert interview and the group discussions with the teachers were recorded using an audio device. Since children were interested in what was recorded, time had to be planned in which this could be listened to in excerpts. During spontaneous group discussions, in which I played an observing role, I documented directly and supplemented the framework conditions immediately after the end of the discussion.

During the participant observation, field notes[562] were made and a research diary was kept, which was supplemented and expanded at the end of each day in the kindergarten.

3.5 Transcription of the collected data

The data collected is transcribed using the TiQ "Talk in Qualitative Social Research" transcription method.[563] The punctuation marks indicate the intonation and are not used grammatically. The lines are numbered, which serves to find and quote transcript passages. The first and last names of the children, the teachers, the directors, the locations and other regional information are made anonymous. In the transcript protocol,

---

560 Cf. Przyborski, Aglaja/Wohlrab-Sahr, Monika (2014): Qualitative Sozialforschung, 47.
561 Flick, Uwe (2012): Qualitative Sozialforschung. Eine Einführung, 372.
562 Cf. Flick, Uwe (2012): Qualitative Sozialforschung. Eine Einführung, 374–377.
563 Przyborski, Aglaja/Wohlrab-Sahr, Monika (2014): Qualitative Sozialforschung, 167–170.

the first letter of the name was supplemented with the letters "w" for female and "m" for male (e.g. Anika = Aw). All files were transcribed and encoded. My sounds supporting the course of the conversation were not included in the transcript, as this would make the readability of the transcripts more difficult.

The following characters were used:[564]

L	The beginning of an overlap of speeches is marked.
(.)	Short pause under one second
(3)	Pause duration in seconds in brackets
<u>Yes</u>	Emphasis
Yes	Volume in relation to the usual volume
°Yes°	Quiet in relation to the usual volume
.	Decreasing intonation
?	Question intonation
,	Increasing intonation
Yes:	Elongation of sounds
@(.)@	Brief burst out laughing
@yes@	laughingly speaking
@(3)@	Duration of laughter in seconds in brackets

4. Reflection on the examination procedure

4.1 Reflection on the researcher's understanding of her role

"The describers are involved with their own person in the processes they describe. *The vulnerability of children and young people also makes the adults* who deal with them *particularly vulnerable.*"[565]

As a trained kindergarten teacher, it was a challenge for me at the beginning to not act like a kindergarten teacher but as a researcher. The separation between the requirements that the presence in the kindergarten usually requires and the tasks of the researcher had to be clearly explained to the teachers and repeatedly emphasised, because they were not familiar with the role of a researcher. Sometimes the role as a researcher made me uncomfortable, because I could not meet the expectations of the teachers and the children due to my role as researcher. In order to keep my distance as a researcher, I was not able to integrate myself, into the team as the teachers wanted me to. The kin-

---

564 Only the characters that appear in the transcripts are listed. For the complete list, see ibid. 168f.
565 Bizer, Christoph (1993): Auf dem Weg zu einer praktischen Anthropologie des Kindes und des Jugendlichen. In: Riess, Richard/Fiedler, Kirsten (Ed.): Die verletzlichen Jahre. Handbuch zur Beratung und Seelsorge an Kindern und Jugendlichen. Gütersloh: Gütersloher Verlagshaus/Herder, 743-756, 747.

dergarten teachers and assistants employed in the kindergarten, who knew that I was a researcher in the kindergarten but also knew that I was a trained kindergarten teacher, often requested that I take on tasks in certain situations or help out in another group due to a lack of staff in the facilities. In the sense of the balance between distance of the researcher's role and involvement in everyday life and empathic participation,[566] I took on these tasks, provided they were compatible with my participating role of observation. If I could not comply with the request with reference to my research project, the teachers understood and accepted this. Also, I could not always meet the children's wishes to play with them, in order to draw my attention to the situation that could bring an increase in knowledge with regard to my research question, whereby the children accepted the explanation that I would like to watch at the moment.

In several statements of the kindergarten teachers it became clear that despite the explanation of the project and the request of the research and the distribution of letters with the short description of the project, my role was still questioned by the teachers, and they partly ascribed to me the role of an intern, which was not corrected by me because I could preserve naivety and ask seemingly self-explanatory questions.[567]

4.2   Influencing the context by going into the field

Those involved in kindergarten activities knew that my research deals with religious diversity, since I thought it appropriate in the sense of research ethics to disclose this, but the exact research question was not explained. By going into the field and roughly naming the topic of my research project, without consciously initiating this, I created a discussion with the topic among the acting people in the kindergarten. In a conversation with other directors, the director of the Catholic kindergarten told them about my project, and why she had to take a stand on dealing with religious diversity. The celebration of the Festival of Eid Al-Adha in the Catholic kindergarten was perhaps based on the effort to address religious diversity because of my presence in the kindergarten and to contribute to my research project. The children in the Islamic kindergarten were more interested in my religion and my religious expressions due to my presence at Koran lessons.

> "As long as we deal only theoretically with religious education, we can avoid a difficulty that immediately causes us problems in the concrete educational everyday life. It consists in the fact that understanding a situation and intervening in a situation cannot be separated. In practice, we always have a connection of both: our observation is at the same time an intervention, as educators we understand implicitly or explicitly. We never know whether what we see is an expression of the child or a reaction to an

---

566   Cf. Przyborski, Aglaja/Wohlrab-Sahr, Monika (2014): Qualitative Sozialforschung, 48.
567   Cf. Wolff, Stephan (2012): Wege ins Feld und ihre Varianten. In: Flick, Uwe/von Kardorff, Ernst/Steinke, Ines (Ed.): Qualitative Forschung. Ein Handbuch, 334–349, 349.

intervention on our part. The very fact of our presence is an intervention and provokes a formation of meaning in the child, and vice versa."[568]

This influence can be seen as a strength of ethnographic work. By bringing about changes in one's own presence or a certain behaviour, it is possible to observe how one's own presence affects people in the field, which can provide further information about the research field.

4.3   Unintended expert role of the researcher

Despite several references to my role as a researcher and my task to assess the current state of kindergarten and not to achieve changes or interventions, I was often asked for advice in everyday life as a psychologist, theologian or educator. Both the heads of the kindergartens and the teachers partly perceived me as an authority by asking me questions about the design of the practice or trying to justify their practice. This became clear, for example, when a kindergarten teacher, while writing texts for the children, pointed out her spelling mistakes to me or the kindergarten director apologised after a festival for the way in which it had been celebrated, because in her opinion it had not been successful.

4.4   Availability of time, space and personnel resources

I tried to influence the normal kindergarten life as little as possible through my presence. The group discussions I initiated proved to be a challenge both in terms of time and space. Since the group discussions were to take place in rooms that were familiar to the children and where recording via audio equipment was possible, group discussions were dependent on the availability of these rooms. Since many activities often took place at the same time and the Catholic kindergarten had few rooms, group discussions had to be held in the director's room twice. Despite the assurance that the children were familiar with this room, it was unusual for them to be in this room. It was not my intention to hold discussions in rooms that the children were not familiar with. In the director's room the conversations were interrupted several times because the telephone rang and the kindergarten director came into the room and conducted a telephone conversation. Despite these interruptions and the non-optimal framework conditions, the children were concentrated during the conversation. Apart from the two discussions on Saint Martin's, which took place in this room, all discussions were held in rooms familiar to the children.

---

568 Schori, Kurt (1998): Religiöses Lernen und kindliches Erleben. Eine empirische Untersuchung religiöser Lernprozesse bei Kindern im Alter von vier bis acht Jahren. Stuttgart/Berlin/Cologne: Kohlhammer, 145.

Depending on the presence of the children, two to four children took part in each of the group discussions I initiated. Which children taken part the group discussions was agreed upon in advance with the teachers. Since the daily routine in the kindergarten was often characterised by many activities and the children had to take part in consecutive appointments, I partly refrained from group discussions with the children, since they had to be concentrated long before and needed a different activity or movement.

Unfortunately, a discussion started by the children in the Islamic kindergarten had to be interrupted because the children were asked to tidy up.

Separate appointments were arranged for the group discussions with the teachers and the expert interview, during which the participants had one hour to attend.

Part V: Evaluation

1. Notes on evaluation in this study

The computer program Atlas.ti was used to provide support.[569] This program offers several ways to accomplish tasks that pursue the goal of a systematic approach to unstructured data. Atlas.ti can be used to provide support in maintaining an overview of a large, complex amount of data and to discover the complex phenomena underlying the data.[570] "The main principles of the ATLAS.ti philosophy are best encapsulated by the acronym VISE, which stands for Visualisation, Integration, Serendipity, and Exploration."[571] Due to the wealth of data collected, the Atlas.ti program offers support in saving the individual data sets in an organised way, finding central categories and displaying relationships graphically.

In order to show with the names of the codes from which primary document the data originated, each code was extended by an abbreviation of the respective document.[572] The abbreviations were not included in the categorisation, as the codes were treated equally, regardless of the document from which the codes originated.[573] The abbreviations were only used for clarity and traceability of the codes to the transcribed data. The complete transcripts cannot be published because of the assurance of anonymity.[574] In the chapter "Short case descriptions", the individual methods used are described.[575] In the section "Data evaluation" selected short passages of the transcript are printed to illustrate the statements.[576] In the interest of legibility, the codes of the individual categories are not listed. Since the evaluation is represented by short case descriptions and taking into account the fundamentals of grounded theory, there are some duplications in the presentation.

In order to ensure the most plausible reading of the data, the researcher presented her preliminary results in various interpretation groups. Research work was discussed

---

569 Cf. Friese, Susanne (QUARC Consulting) (2014): Atlas.ti 7. User Guide and Reference. Berlin: ATLAS.ti Scientific Software Development GmbH. For methodological considerations see Friese, Susanne (²2014): Qualitative Data Analysis with Atlas ti. London: Sage Publications Ltd [2012].
570 Cf. Friese, Susanne (QUARC Consulting) (2014): Atlas.ti 7, 9.
571 Ibid., 10.
572 For example, the abbreviation KKL stands for "Catholic Kindergarten Director" (katholischer Kindergarten-Leiter), which describes the expert interview conducted in the Catholic kindergarten with the management.
573 Cf. Flick, Uwe (2012): Triangulation in der qualitativen Forschung. In: Flick, Uwe/von Kardorff, Ernst/Steinke, Ines (Ed.): Qualitative Forschung. Ein Handbuch, 309–318, 314.
574 If you have any questions regarding individual data, please contact the author by e-mail: h.stockinger@ku-linz.at.
575 Cf. chapter "Short case descriptions" (part V, 3).
576 Cf. chapter "Data evaluation" (part V, 4).

with scientists from the disciplines of theology, educational science, Islamic, Catholic and Protestant religious education, sociology and education in both German and English-speaking countries. The research work was also discussed with practising teachers and worked on in various working groups. People of different religions and nationalities participated in the interpretation groups.[577] In order to leave the Austrian context and to get to know perspectives from other countries on the results of the research, the author went on research stays at the University of Warwick in England and at Queen's University Belfast in Northern Ireland, during which regular exchange about the research work took place. This frequent presentation of preliminary interpretations led to a frequent revision of the interpretations and to their extension due to new perspectives. In the struggle for the most plausible interpretation of the data, it became clear that depending on the context in which the work was presented and put up for discussion, different results of the work were of interest and different focalisations were made. That is why the individual steps are documented in the evaluation in order to do justice to the complexity of the collected data in the best possible way and not by exclusively presenting the core category of the context, possibly interesting results for other contexts are not mentioned in the work.

2. Presentation of the kindergartens

In the presentation of the selected kindergartens, some information is dispensed due to reasons of anonymity.

2.1 Catholic Kindergarten

2.1.1 Field access

The pedagogical director of a Catholic foundation, who has an overview of the kindergartens in Vienna, was asked whether it would be possible to carry out the research project in one of the foundation's kindergartens and asked to name a kindergarten that meets the above criteria.[578] Permission was given to carry out the research, a kindergarten and the contact address of the head of the selected kindergarten were named. The researcher contacted the head of the kindergarten by telephone and she agreed to the research project in the kindergarten. In September 2013, the researcher visited the kindergarten for the first time and held a discussion with the two kindergarten teachers

---

577 The results were discussed at the following conferences and discussion rounds: Seminar of the University of Warwick, Interdisciplinary Conference in Oxford, Conference of the AKRK-Sektion Empirische Religionspädagogik in Nuremberg, Religionspädagogische Sozietät in Vienna, Bonner Graduate Class Seminar in Linz, discussions with kindergarten teachers and scientists from various disciplines, etc.
578 Cf. chapter "Selection of kindergartens" (part IV, 2).

and the director in which the researcher outlined the research interest, promised anonymity and asked all participants for their consent. The teachers were asked to inform the author of any observations that might be interesting with regard to the research question, as this would be beneficial for research. A short description of the researcher and a description of the research project were posted on the information board as parent information. The researcher introduced herself personally to the kindergarten assistants, explained the research interest to them and assured them of the anonymity of the collected data. The researcher introduced herself to the children personally as well as in the morning circle and was immediately accepted by them and asked to play with them.

2.1.2 Sponsorship

The kindergarten is assigned to a Catholic foundation whose concept is binding for the respective kindergartens. In addition to the repeated emphasis on the uniqueness of each child, its mission statement explicitly enumerates respectful treatment and openness towards other cultures and religions, and the fact that religious beliefs and difference are part of everyday kindergarten life and differences are not concealed.[579]

2.1.3 Framework conditions

The kindergarten is run in two groups with an open concept during the free play period. This allows the children to choose between the two group rooms, so that all children know each other and all teachers. At the morning circle and at lunch the children are in their home group.

The non-Catholic parents are comfortable in choosing the Catholic kindergarten for their children and are concerned that their child might not be able to attend this kindergarten because of their religious affiliation and are relieved when this is not the case.

2.1.4 Personnel staffing

The kindergarten groups are each assigned a group-leading kindergarten teacher and a kindergarten assistant, who changes groups if necessary. If there is a shortage of staff, the kindergarten director supports the groups. All kindergarten staff are Catholic.

---

[579] A reference to the source is not possible in this case due to the guaranteed anonymity. Cf. ibid.

2.1.5 Kindergarten room

The kindergarten is located on the second floor of a house. The house, in which there are also rooms of the parish for the Boy Scouts, the youth groups and the youth are located, is spatially connected with the church with a direct access.

The kindergarten has two group rooms, which are supplemented by a corridor which is available to the children during the free play time. In a group room, there is a reading corner, a building and construction corner, a small world game and a small space for role-playing games. In the other group room, there is also a building and construction corner and a small room for painting work. In both group rooms, there are four tables where the children can play, paint or work and where the meals are eaten. In the corridor, there is a building and construction corner with larger building blocks and a table.

The group room is often decorated according to the seasons or for the next Christian festival, whereby the children are involved in the design of the room decoration.

2.1.6 Socio-demographic data of children

In the presentation of the sociodemographic data, the difference between the children already becomes clear, even when it is limited to the usual sociodemographic data collected at this point. The stated percentages are rounded to one decimal place.[580]

Table 3 gives an overview of the children's religious affiliation, as communicated to the researcher by the kindergarten's director.

At the beginning of the kindergarten year in September 2013, two children were going to be six years old, eight children five years old, thirteen children four years old and twenty children three years old. There were no children with special needs in the groups.

Table 3: Religious affiliation of children in the Catholic kindergarten

Religious affiliation	Number	Percentage
Roman Catholic	20	44.4
Islamic	8	17.8
Without religious confession	8	17.8
Serbian Orthodox	5	11.1
Romanian Orthodox	1	2.2
Sikhs	1	2.2
Hindoo	1	2.2
Christian special community	1	2.2
Total number	45	100.0

---

580 Due to the rounding, the percentage figures are slightly blurred.

Table 4 lists the origin of the children.

Table 4: Countries of origin of the children in the Catholic kindergarten

Country of origin	Number	Percentage
Poland	11	24.4
Serbia	8	17.8
Turkey	6	13.3
Austria	5	11.1
Croatia	4	8.9
Slovakia	4	8.9
India	1	4.1
Egypt	1	2.2
Kosovo	1	2.2
Romania	1	2.2
Slovenia	1	2.2
Spain	1	2.2
Nepal	1	2.2
Total number	45	100.0

2.1.7 Routine

The kindergarten day starts at seven o'clock when the first set of children are brought by their parents. During the free play time between eight and nine o'clock all the children have the option to eat breakfast, and all are asked if they want to eat something. Both group rooms and the corridor are available to the children during the free play period. Between nine and half past nine o'clock the morning circle begins, which lasts approximately half an hour. The children's attention is focused by singing and story time. If there is a birthday to celebrate, this is done in the morning circle and a cake that was baked by the kindergarten teachers and some of the children is eaten afterward. After the morning circle, depending on the weather conditions, everyone goes into the garden or to a public playground in the vicinity or the free play time is continued. Around noon all the children have lunch together. After lunch, the children are divided into three groups. The children in the first year of kindergarten gather in a group room to sleep, the "middle"[581] children are in the other group room and a story is read to them. They have the option to sleep or to amuse themselves quietly. "School beginners"[582] are read a story in another room or they listen to a radio play, rest on

---

581 Recorded in the research diary, 56. "Middle children" are children in their second kindergarten year.
582 Recorded in the research diary, 57. "School beginners" means children in their final year of kindergarten.

mattresses and then, if they have not fallen asleep, fill out worksheets, draw something or look at books. After this approximately one-hour rest period, the children continue their free time in the group rooms or visit the garden again. In the afternoon, a snack is prepared for the children and they are asked to eat something. The kindergarten is open until 5 pm.

2.2 Islamic Kindergarten

2.2.1 Field access

Access to the Islamic kindergarten[583] was provided by the professor of Islamic religious education at the University of Vienna, who referred the researcher to a kindergarten that met the criteria. The author contacted the director of the kindergarten by telephone and was invited by him to have at first, a clarifying discussion in which the research interest of the project was briefly described and general conditions were clarified. After this brief conversation with the director, the kindergarten researcher was introduced to the individual kindergarten teachers, with the director mentioning that the researcher was from the university and was carrying out a kindergarten project. In the respective group, the researcher introduced herself to the kindergarten teacher and the assistant in more detail, outlined her research interests and asked the kindergarten teacher some questions about religious celebrations and the children's religious affiliation in the kindergarten. Afterwards, the researcher introduced herself during the morning circle to the children personally, asked the children their names and was immediately accepted by the children.

2.2.2 Sponsorship

The Islamic kindergarten which is still in development, belongs to a foundation that runs the association that finances the kindergarten. This was founded by the pedagogical director himself. This gives the director the opportunity to design and develop a concept in consultation with the association.[584]

The mission statement enumerates "ethical and moral education on a religious basis" as an important aspect of the concept of kindergarten; children should "get to know religion through play and be accepted and supported".[585]

---

[583] The list of kindergartens and day care centres of the Islamic Faith Community in Austria (IGGiÖ) can be found on their homepage. (Islamic community in Austria, http://www.derislam.at/?c=content&cssid=Kinderg%E4rten/Hort%20&na vid=460&par=40 [09.07.2013]).

[584] A more detailed description of the foundation is waived due to the assurance of anonymity.

[585] The source information is not disclosed due to the guaranteed anonymity. Cf. chapter "Selection of kindergartens" (part IV, 2).

2.2.3 Framework conditions

The kindergarten is divided into seven groups, whereby the children are exclusively in their own group room during the free play time. For example, social contacts within the kindergarten are limited to people in the same group of the kindergarten; however, some children know each other due to family relationships or activities outside the kindergarten.

In the Islamic kindergarten, requests from non-Muslim parents as to whether their child can attend the kindergarten are exceptional cases, although attendance of non-Muslim children in Islamic kindergarten is desired, since the kindergarten wants to be "open to all"[586].

2.2.4 Personnel staffing

Two adults with pedagogical training are assigned to each kindergarten group. In the group on which the research is mainly focused, a kindergarten teacher has a Catholic religious affiliation and the kindergarten assistant has an Islamic religious affiliation. The kindergarten assistant wears a headscarf, while the kindergarten teacher wear make-up, has a tattoo and often wears tank tops. The two responsible persons are all in the kindergarten room, get along very well and share the work. Since both adults working in the group have completed pedagogical training and there is no difference in the distribution of tasks between the kindergarten teacher and the assistant, we will refer to both of them as teachers in the following.

2.2.5 Kindergarten room

The kindergarten room is decorated according to the seasons, for example in spring cardboard flowers can be seen in the entire kindergarten room, in winter the room is decorated with cotton wool snowflakes. The teachers are responsible for the design of the kindergarten room, the children are not involved.

The room is divided into several areas, the largest area is occupied by the set-up tables, which are used for various games during the free play time and for eating during meals. A table is declared as a painting table by placing a base on it, other tables can also be used for painting. The room also has a reading area, a role-playing area, a small world game area and a building and construction area.

2.2.6 Socio-demographic data of children

A total of 136 children attend kindergarten. Table 5 lists the religious affiliation of the children in the entire kindergarten as well as in the kindergarten group selected

---
586 Expert interview with the head of the Islamic kindergarten, 34.

for the study, in which the majority of the study took place, both in figures and as a percentage.[587]

Table 5: Religious affiliation of children in the Islamic kindergarten

Religious affiliation	Kindergarten total		Kindergarten group	
	Number	Percentage	Number	Percentage
Islam	124	91.2	22	91.7
Christianity	12	8.8	2	8.3
Total number	136	100.0	24	100.0

The following table shows the origin of the children, as communicated to the researcher.

Table 6: Countries of origin of the children in the Islamic kindergarten[588]

Country of origin	Kindergarten total		Kindergarten group	
	Number	Percentage	Number	Percentage
Turkey	95	69.9	17	70.8
Egypt	14	10.3	2	8.3
Libya	6	4.4		
Poland	4	2.9	1	4.2
Chechnya	3	2.2		
Albania	2	1.5		
Austria	2	1.5		
Romania	2	1.5	1	4.2
Serbia	2	1.5		
Ghana	1	0.7		
Jordan	1	0.7	1	4.2
Pakistan	1	0.7		
Russia	1	0.7		
Syria	1	0.7	1	4.2
Tunisia	1	0.7	1	4.2
Total number	136	100.0	24	100.0

At the beginning of the kindergarten year, three children were six years old, seventeen children five years old and four children four years old. There were no children with special needs in the groups.

---

587 The percentages are rounded to one place for clarity, resulting in slight blurring.
588 The countries of origin are sorted by frequency, with the same frequency the ranking is done alphabetically.

2.2.7 Routine

The kindergarten opens at seven o'clock. By nine o'clock at the latest, all children should have been brought to kindergarten; if children are repeatedly late, the teacher speaks to the parents. At approximately nine o'clock a common snack for all children takes place. Each child has its own place marked with a name sticker, where it sits at each meal. The ingredients for the meal are taken from the kitchen by a teacher and consist of halal[589] food and tea. The teacher calls the children one by one to wash their hands and sit in their place. Meanwhile, the teachers prepare the bread for the children or cut the fruit, depending on what food is provided for the day. After all the children have washed their hands, the teacher names the children who can get the food and tea. After the grace, the children eat, with little to no talking. The children who have finished eating wash their hands again and can choose games in the kindergarten room. Two children help the teacher wipe the tables after the meal, and a child accompanies the teacher when she takes the dishes back to the kitchen. The children's free play time is interrupted by a bell ringing and a song sung by the teacher, so that all children gather in the morning circle, in which the children and the teachers sing different songs and play various games. After the morning circle, the free play time is continued, during which the teacher sometimes offers the children a work activity. Around noon the children are asked in turn to wash their hands, while a teacher takes the food prepared in the kindergarten from the kitchen and prepares it on the plates. After grace, the children who want a meal pick it up from the teacher one by one. During the meal, long, intensive conversations are prevented by the teacher, while some comments are fine. After lunch half of the children rest on mattresses, which are distributed in the group room, while the other half are picked up by the Koran teacher. They go to the Koran room from Monday to Thursday and to the mosque on Friday. After approximately half an hour the two groups change. When all the children are back in the group room, another teacher will read stories to some children in a separate room. In the course of the afternoon there is another afternoon meal, with the same schedule as in the morning. Most children are picked up between 3:30 pm and 5:30 pm.

During the free play time, a radio station with music and news is often switched on, but the children do not pay attention to it.

---

589 The Arabic word ḥalāl means "Allowed; permitted, permissible, lawful, legitimate, permitted possession" (Wehr, Hans (⁴1968): Arabisches Wörterbuch für die Schriftsprache der Gegenwart. Wiesbaden: Otto Harrassowitz [1952], 180).

3. Short case descriptions

The key data and the structure of the study design are already explained.[590] In the following, based on the concept of thematic coding,[591] brief case descriptions of the interviews, the group discussions and the participant observation are presented, including the methodological implementation, the methods, the participating persons and the central topics. The case descriptions are kept descriptive, so that insight into the course of the individual methods is granted, since by this the following analysis can be better illustrated and disclosed after the bases of the grounded theory. These descriptions ensure that despite the reduction and abstraction of the data, the survey situations can be identified on the basis of the grounded theory.

3.1 Interview with experts

3.1.1 Catholic Kindergarten

The twenty-five-minute conversation took place on 13th September 2013 from 8:25 a.m. to 8:50 a.m. in the director's room, where it was possible to hold a conversation without interruption. The kindergarten director answered all questions in detail and expressed herself very positively towards me and the project.

The personal attitude, the visions for the future and the reality in the kindergarten are mixed in the interview, in which the dissatisfaction of the kindergarten director with the current situation becomes clear. She would like to bring about changes in kindergarten, which is difficult because of traditional procedures. The daily life in the kindergarten is marked by Catholic rituals and celebrations, Catholic prayers are said before the meal, the celebrations of the Christian year are celebrated and the Catholic church is visited. Prayers of other religions are not spoken, festivals of other religions are not celebrated and the visit to a mosque in the last kindergarten year is emphasised, which indicates a lack of other activities. All children are invited to Christian festivals. If the parents do not want their child to attend, they can pick the child up before the party. The director would like to involve other religions more in the planning and implementation of everyday kindergarten life and is aware of the importance of a careful and respectful approach to knowing elements of another religion. Thus, she would not want to celebrate some festivals in the church because of her consideration of Muslim parents. The religious offer should be suitable for everyone involved in the kindergarten and children should not be forced to participate in something that is different than what they experience in their home. Pork is generally not included in the food offered. If parents indicate that their child needs to eat the vegetarian meal, the presumed religious reason for it is not brought up for discussion.

---

590 Cf. part IV "Study design and conduct".
591 Cf. chapter "Thematic coding" (part III, 4).

3.1.2 Islamic Kindergarten

The twenty-five-minute conversation took place on the 16th December 2013 from 3:05 p.m. to 3:30 p.m. in the room of the director of the kindergarten. The window of the room was tilted, so background noise made transcription difficult, yet still be understood. The conversation was briefly interrupted by a kindergarten teacher coming into the room, but continued after the brief interruption. The director answered all questions in detail and thanked the researcher several times for the questions asked. During the interview, he repeatedly asked the interviewer questions, e.g. whether certain offers in kindergarten corresponded to the interviewer's opinion. These were answered as neutrally as possible or addressed with a further question; in the case of a very direct enquiry, these were answered briefly.

The kindergarten should be open to children of all nations and religions, which is why religion is offered as a voluntary additional benefit in the form of religious education, whereby parents decide whether their child should attend it. Religious education takes place for twenty to thirty minutes in a specially reserved room, a trained teacher teaches the children and the lessons take place at a daily scheduled time. Since only a small religious offer is possible for three- to six-year-old children, the content and method of religious education should be adapted to the age of the children and an appropriate amount of time should be chosen for the religious offering. In class, they learned the commandments and prohibitions of Islam and sung "little verses from the Holy Qur'an", which "slowly connect the children with prayers".[592] There is a clear distinction to the Koranic school, "We do not have Koranic schools",[593] and proselytism should not take place. The aim of the lessons is to prepare children with a "small background"[594] for school. They should learn to interact properly and become "healthy believers,"[595] not "fundamentalists or atheists".[596]

The rest of kindergarten life should be uninfluenced by religion and the religious attitudes of the teachers. Religious festivals are not celebrated in the kindergarten, only stories about the festivals are told and symbolic gifts are presented to the children. The different levels and the wishes of the parents form the starting point for the planned activities, whereby a middle way is chosen between the various requirements of the parents, which is particularly evident in the offer of halal prepared food. All those involved in kindergarten activities should be satisfied with the offers in the kindergarten and the kindergarten should serve as a "bridge"[597] for parents to reduce fear of Austrian society and build trust. Children and parents need time to build this bridge,

---

592 Expert interview with the head of the Islamic kindergarten, 12f.
593 Ibid., 195f.
594 Ibid., 195.
595 Ibid., 178.
596 Ibid., 178f.
597 Ibid., 93f.

as they come from "different social classes"⁵⁹⁸ in their home countries, which is why "Austrian culture to a certain extent, very consciously"⁵⁹⁹ is taught in kindergarten. The kindergarten does not want to proselytize, but the children should learn to deal properly with each other.

3.2 Participant observation (with focus on religious difference)

The participant observation took place continuously in both kindergartens during the kindergarten year 2013/2014. Phases of intensive participant observation alternated with phases of initial evaluations and literature studies to ensure the scientific distance.⁶⁰⁰ The researcher got to know the children and the everyday life of the kindergarten on the basis of the participant observation and was able to weigh the necessity for the use of further methods on the basis of continuous coding and categorisation. The most important observations relating to the research question are now briefly presented.

3.2.1 Catholic Kindergarten

Focus on everyday kindergarten life: Catholic festivals are prepared by the teachers and director and songs and role plays are rehearsed together with the children. Parents are invited to some festivals, who play an exclusively observing role at the festival. During the Festival of Eid Al-Adha, a Muslim woman tells the story of the sacrifice with the help of paper figures and gives the children sweets. The children listen with concentration. A child asks whether this story "really" happened,⁶⁰¹ which the Muslim woman affirms, whereupon some children make astonished sounds.

Conflicts due to religious differences are not discussed together, but ended with reference to the sponsorship of the kindergarten. One mother complains that her child makes a sign of the cross in kindergarten, whereupon the teacher thinks that this is customary in a "Catholic kindergarten"⁶⁰² and there are other kindergartens where this sign is not used. The teachers do not continue to discuss this conflict with each other, nor is it discussed with the children, although some children have observed this conflict.

Focus on children: After the festivities, the children are busy with their games, there are no conversations about the festivities. In Advent, some children play with the Advent path, which is set up in the kindergarten. During the prayer before the meal, all the children fold their hands and say the grace in the Catholic tradition, and all the

---

598 Ibid., 92.
599 Ibid., 90f.
600 Cf. Przyborski, Aglaja/Wohlrab-Sahr, Monika (2014): Qualitative Sozialforschung, 47.
601 Research diary, Catholic kindergarten, 120.
602 Ibid., 86.

children sing along to the songs taken from the Catholic tradition. The children who are not supposed to eat the offered food receive a sandwich for lunch. At Catholic festivals, some children are picked up beforehand, the other children do not mention the absence of the children in everyday kindergarten life, nor do the children picked up mention their absence at certain activities.

3.2.2 Islamic Kindergarten

Focus on everyday kindergarten life: The kindergarten day-to-day life intended by the director, which should be uninfluenced by religion, is not always followed, since a dua[603] is prayed before the meal and children talk about religious education and religious affiliation. At the secular festivals, religious elements are interwoven in the kindergarten, so at the summer festival suras are sung and a workshop deals with the Koran. All other participants in kindergarten life refer to religious education as Koran instruction.[604]

Attending the Koran lessons is partly used as a disciplinary measure, in which only children who are described as "good" are allowed to join the Koran lessons. If during the teaching of the Koran one of the children is perceived as "bad", it is sent back to the group room. The Koran teacher is respected by most children because of her knowledge. The children like to attend the Koran lessons, are attentive during the Koran lessons and follow the teacher's instructions. In the Koran lessons the Arabic characters as well as single Arabic words and sentences are studied, the main focus is on the studying of suras, whereby the teacher recites them and the children repeat them.

Focus on children: The Muslim children in the Islamic kindergarten address their own religious affiliation and ask about the religious affiliation of the teachers and the researcher. Without prior impulse, they tell that Muslims wear a headscarf and non-Muslims do not. Thematised are own celebrations or own religious practices, for example the fasting, which some children would also like to do. They are interested in how festivals of other religions are celebrated, asking the Christian teacher about them and combining Christian festivals with terms of Islamic festivals. They talk about the mosque in the kindergarten and talk about the teaching of the Koran or ask the teacher who is allowed to participate in the teaching of the Koran on the respective day. The nationality and religion of the children are mixed in their conversations. Before visiting the mosque, the children carry out the prayer washes independently, with two children taking leadership over the correct sequence of prayer washes. The

---

603 The Arabic word duʿāʾ means "call; invocation of God; prayer; request, blessing [...]; curse [...]", (Wehr, Hans (1968): Arabisches Wörterbuch, 255).
604 In the following, depending on who made certain statements, the teaching is called Koran or religious education.

two children leading speak to the children in a strict tone and order them to carry out the prayer washes.

The Christian children in the group do not mention celebrations, religious attitudes or practices without prior stimulus .

3.3   Group discussions with the children

In the following, those group discussions are described that resulted from the children's conversations or were initiated by a stimulus or a question from the researcher. As there is no clearly structured daily routine in a kindergarten, unlike in school, the framework conditions for group discussions varied according to day and group. Each group discussion lasted no longer than twenty minutes. The concentration of the children varied according to topic, time and group composition. The children were very interested in what they were saying, which was recorded specially during the first discussions, and the children had the opportunity to study the audio equipment and listen to parts of what they had said. All group discussions took place in a pleasant atmosphere, the children were in a good mood, cheerful and enjoyed the group discussions. This was also shown by telling the rest of the group of the discussions why many children wanted to talk to me. The children enjoyed the group discussions, which is reflected in the following entry in the research diary:

> "The two boys enthusiastically told about the conversation in the group afterwards, which meant that many children wanted to come with me, which, however, was no longer possible due to the upcoming lunch."[605]

The individual group discussions are described in this chapter in an overview, whereby the participants, the framework conditions and – if the discussion is characterised by high interaction – the discourse organisation are mentioned.

3.3.1   Catholic Kindergarten

Longer group discussions took place after St. Martin's day, after Easter, after Eid Al-Adha and during Advent. The children enjoyed extensive conversations about common experiences such as a visit to a farm or a birthday party. Discussions about the religious festivals remained concentrated on the researcher with the exception of individual passages.

Group discussion about St. Martin's with Mw, Sw and Ew: The discussion with Mw, a five-year-old Christian girl, Sw, a five-year-old Muslim girl and Ew, a four-year-old Muslim girl, took place in the director's room the day after St. Martin's. Although the

---

605   Research diary, Catholic kindergarten, entry 17th Oct. 2014.

questions were addressed to everyone, the discussion was dominated by the speeches of Mw.

An important topic of the group discussion is the absence of Sw at St. Martin's, which Mw mentioned at the beginning of the conversation, whereupon Sw emphasised her presence at St. Martin's with a loud voice. Mw tries to clarify the disagreement and asks Sw if she celebrated St. Martin's at home, which she negates. The difference of opinion between the two children persists throughout the conversation and continues to flare up. Sw wants to convince Mw of her presence by telling her about the rehearsal of St. Martin's. Mw underpins her opinion with clues such as the absence of Sw at a dance performed at the festival. As an explanation for the absence of Sw, Mw takes up a conflict talk that took place the day before in the kindergarten corridor, in which the mother of Sw, together with a relative who had acted as interpreter, explained to the kindergarten teachers that Sw should not make a cross in the kindergarten and that the kindergarten teachers should prevent this. Mw doesn't know why Sw shouldn't make a cross, because she didn't hear anything else.

Group discussion about Saint Martin's with Aw, Bw and Rw: In the second group discussion, also on the day after the celebration of St. Martin's, with five-year-old Catholic Aw, the five-year-old Catholic Bw and the five-year-old Muslim Rw. The conversation was conducted in the group room before lunch, while the other children were in the garden. The girls were concentrated during the conversation, which was briefly interrupted once because the plates were brought to the group room for the lunch that followed. The conversation was supported by drawing elements and a small St. Martin doll.

Aw is convinced that Rw was not present at the party and justifies this with Rw's lantern, which is still in kindergarten, while all other lanterns are already at home. Bw does not know an explanation for Rw's absence. Rw does not comment on Bw's reproachful sounding statement and hardly speaks during the group discussion. Rw also does not answer the question asked by Bw to Rw a little later whether she had been present at St. Martin's. Only towards the end of the group discussion did she barely mention her absence at the party with the words "was not".[606] Otherwise, the children talk about the horse ridden by the boy who played Martin and the croissants they had to eat. Bw is pleased to tell that all children have a lantern, but is uncertain about her own statement and asks whether the children at school also have a lantern, whereby she gives herself an affirmative answer.

The *group discussions about Eid Al-Adha* were held on the day on which the feast took place, and a birthday party was also celebrated on the same day. As it was an eventful day for the children, the duration of the group discussions was kept short.

---

606 Group discussion about the Martin's day with Aw, Bw and Rw in the Catholic kindergarten, 114

Group discussion about Eid Al-Adha with Bw and Rw: The conversation with the five-year-old girls, the Catholic Bw and the Muslim Rw, was conducted with the children in a separate room after the celebration. Bw's speeches dominated the discussion, with Rw also repeatedly taking part in the discussion.

Bw immediately states that she only attended the festival for a short time because, while the others were celebrating the festival of Eid Al-Adha, she had designed the pre-school folder with a teacher. Rw, who kept silent about her own absence during the discussion about St. Martin's and only at the end quietly addressed this in two words, says at the beginning of this discussion that she had not been present at this celebration.

Bw mentions chocolate sweets and pictures that they would have received as gifts from a woman who attended kindergarten, and Rw also reports on chocolate.

Group discussion about Eid Al-Adha with Lm, Bm and Sw: The discussion between Lm, a four-year-old Catholic boy, Bm, a five-year-old Muslim boy and Sw, a four-year-old Catholic girl took place in the director's room. The director accompanied the children into the room, who had awakened after the afternoon rest. The framework conditions were not optimal, which is why the researcher kept the conversation short and ended it when she realised that the children were no longer interested in the discussion.

The children talk about sweets they received from a woman who came to kindergarten.

Group discussion about Eid Al-Adha with Km and Om: Km and Om, two Catholic five-year-old boys, took part in the discussion. The discussion was held in a separate room immediately after the festival of Eid Al-Adha. Om dominated the conversation because of his flow of words.

Om reports in detail about the visit on the farm during the last week. He mentions about the festival that a woman told a story and gave chocolate and a picture to everyone. Km also tells about the sweets he received. When asked, Om knows that he does not celebrate the festival of Eid Al-Adha at home, but he does not know the reason for this. He does not know who's celebrating this festival. In the same sentence, he refers to the director, who did not know anything about the festival either, but it was in her calendar.

Group discussion about Eid Al-Adha with Mw and Pw: The discussion with Mw and Pw, two five-year-old Catholic girls, took place, without interruption, in a separate room in the afternoon after the festival of Eid Al-Adha. Both girls participated in the discussion to about the same extent.

The children talk about the birthday party that took place on the same day and then tell about chocolate that they have received from a woman. Both Mw and Pw state that they were not present at the festival of Eid Al-Adha because they created a pre-school folder with another teacher during this time .

Group discussion about Advent wreath with Mw, Lm and Fm: The discussion took place in a separate room familiar to the three children Lm and Fm, two five year old Catholic boys and Mw, a five-year old Catholic girl. The discussion took place before the morning circle with the children.

Lm says that the poor don't have an Advent wreath. Fm takes up this idea and emphasises that the poor and blacks do not have an Advent wreath because they are poor. Lm supplements this statement with the elderly, who also do not have an Advent wreath because they are also poor. That the elderly, the poor and the blacks do not have an Advent wreath is confirmed by the whole group.

Group discussion about Easter with Bw and Mw: Bw and Mw, two Catholic five-year-old girls, took part in the discussion. The discussion was held after Easter and the Easter meal with the children in the garden, whereby the stimulus came from the researcher. Mw asks the researcher why she was not present at Easter. She lists who of the children have not been to Easter, although she does not know the reason for their absence. Bw tells of the songs they have sung during the festival and Mw recalls the chocolate they have received.

Group discussion about the Easter with Km, Lm and Vm: A discussion was held with the children before lunch in the group room. The two Catholic, four-year-old boys Km, Lm and the Catholic, three-year-old boy Vm took part in it.

Km tells of milk and water they have drunk. Lm thinks that Jesus does not celebrate the feast, he does not know the reason for this. Both Km, Lm and Vm are of the opinion to celebrate the festival themselves.

3.3.2 Islamic Kindergarten

In the Islamic kindergarten, group discussions with the children on teaching the Koran[607] and discussions took place the day after the Easter holidays. The children had many discussions among themselves on other topics such as linguistic difference and difference of origin. These discussions were documented in the research diary.[608] The discussions about religious difference in which the researcher was involved and in which the children focused on for a longer period of time are described below.

Group discussion on Koran lessons with Sw and Nw: The discussion took place with the five-year-old Muslim girl Sw and the five-year-old Muslim girl Nw at the drawing table.

---

607 Since the children and the teachers talk about Koran lessons, this name is chosen in the text.
608 The conversations in which children talked to each other about other than religious difference are not explained in this work because of the focus on the research question.

Sw starts on her own to draw several boxes on a piece of paper and to name them after rooms in the kindergarten like doll corner, building corner, toilet and kitchen. She asks the researcher to write the names of the rooms in a box. The researcher asks for more rooms, whereupon the two girls list several rooms. Since the two no longer name any rooms, the researcher asks a question about the Koran Room. Sw knows who goes to the Koran room and lists the three people who do not go to the Koran lesson, stating as an explanation that they are not Muslims.

Group discussion on Koran lessons with Ew, Tw, Lw and Bm: Another discussion was conducted at the drawing table with three five-year-old Muslim girls Ew, Tw and Lw and the five-year-old Muslim boy Bm.

The attention of the children sitting near the researcher is turned to her and they ask the researcher to draw something for them, whereupon the researcher begins to draw some boxes on a piece of paper. When asked by the children about the drawing of the researcher, she explains she is drawing the different rooms of the kindergarten and asks the children what rooms there are in the kindergarten. The children list several rooms such as cloakroom, building corner, kitchen and bedroom. After the children have finished the enumeration of the rooms, the researcher asks if there is a Koran room, which the children affirm and begin to discuss intensively. The children talk about the mosque in the kindergarten and talk about where the mosque is. The girls participating in the discussion agree that Bm is not allowed to go into the Koran room because he is bad and bad children are not allowed to attend Koran lessons and are not allowed to go to the mosque, as this is reserved exclusively for good children. Bm defends himself against this statement and emphasises that he, too, is going to Koran lessons. The children do not agree on the content of the teaching of the Koran. Bm thinks they would read the Koran. Ew contradicts this, because the Koran will not be read, but recited and she will tell the teacher Bm's wrong opinion.

Group discussion on Koran lessons with Im and Dw: The discussion was conducted with the five-year-old Muslim boy Im and the five-year-old Christian girl Dw, who do not attend Koran lessons after lunch. The two of them were in the cosy corner while all the other children were sitting at the table waiting to be picked up for Koran lessons.

Dw states that all children would go to the Koran lessons, which is reinforced by Im. She herself, however, would not attend Koran lessons because she was not a Muslim. Im insists he is a Muslim, but goes to Koran lessons with another group.

Group discussion on Koran lessons with Jw and Pw: The discussion was conducted with Jw, the other five-year-old Christian girl in the group, and Pw, a five-year-old Muslim girl at the drawing table. Both Jw and Pw painted something and the discussion resulted from what they said.

Jw is aware that she and a second girl are not going to Koran lessons and everyone else in the group is attending. She thinks that the others would go to Koran lessons because they are "mosques".⁶⁰⁹ "To be a mosque" means for Jw that all the children who are these must go to the Koran room. When asked who she and the other girl are, the girl answers with her origin or her language.

Group discussion on Koran lessons with Nw and Lw: The discussion took place with Nw and Lw, two five-year-old Muslim girls, at the drawing table, whereby the discussion resulted from what the children said. As a reason why she goes to Koran lessons, Nw states that she is still small and generalises that all small children go to Koran lessons.

Group discussion after Easter with Fw, Rw and Ew: The conversation was started by the children at the drawing table and three five-year-old Muslim girls took part: Fw, Rw and Ew.

The children talk about Easter and mention in this context that they are Muslim. They ask the researcher if and how she celebrated Easter. Since the researcher answered Ew's question as to whether she had celebrated Easter in the affirmative, she was asked whether she is not a Muslim. The children are also interested in why she is not a Muslim and they ask whether her mother is not a Muslim. The children tell the researcher whether their parents are Christians or Muslims, and Fw explains that her father is hodja, asking the other girl what it is called in German, whereupon Rw says that it is also called hodja in German. Fw asks exactly how Easter is celebrated. When the researcher mentions the visit to the church, Fw replies with "Dingdongdingdong"⁶¹⁰ and in response to the story of Easter eggs Fw mentions her cousin, who also has Easter eggs, and continues to ask about chocolate. Ew tells about the chocolate she received and ate. Fw is excited about having eaten chocolate too. Afterwards, she tells that she is a Muslim and her mother wears a headscarf, whereas Christians do not wear headscarves. Ew then asks Fw whether she is a Christian, whereupon Fw replies that she is not a Christian but has watched a Christ film. The children then ask the researcher if she can speak Turkish or Arabic.

3.4   Group discussions with the teachers

The group discussions with the teachers formed the final part of the field research in the kindergarten and took place at the end of the school year 2013/2014: The researcher was already well known to the teachers and a relationship of trust had been established. The teachers in both groups answered the questions asked in detail and came together in a conversation, whereby both discussions lasted 45 minutes each and then had to be ended because the teachers had to return to their responsibilities as teachers. Both group discussions were characterised by a good, open atmosphere in which there was a lot of laughter. The speaking time of all the teachers was balanced.

---

609   Group discussion on Koran lessons with Jw and Pw in the Islamic kindergarten, 6.
610   Group discussion after Easter with Fw, Rw and Ew in the Islamic kindergarten, 18.

During the discussion, there was no intervention in the speaking time or the distribution of the teachers' speeches.[611] In the Catholic kindergarten, the group discussion was held with the two kindergarten teachers leading the group, since they determined the daily routine in the kindergarten, while the assistants had clearly assigned tasks and were not involved in pedagogical decisions. In the Islamic kindergarten, the group discussion was conducted with the kindergarten teacher and the pedagogically trained kindergarten assistant, since no difference could be seen in their pedagogical areas of responsibility.

3.4.1 Catholic Kindergarten

The group discussion with the two teachers in the Catholic kindergarten took place without interruption after the children's meal in the director's room during the rest period. A longer speech block of one teacher followed a longer speech block of another teacher. The following topics were discussed by the teachers:

The individuality of the children is emphasised by addressing the diversity of the children. Every child brings his or her own rituals and habits and knows different family situations. Diversity should therefore be regarded as normal and there should be no fear of it, otherwise the children cannot be given a positive view of diversity. Because of fear and prejudice towards others, there is often no willingness to look beyond one's own prejudices, which can lead to the assumption that others are malicious, which does not reflect reality.

The non-Catholic parents are not bothered by the Catholic sponsorship of the kindergarten, but are rather concerned that their child is not allowed to attend the kindergarten because of his or her denomination or religion and are relieved to learn that this is not the case. A teacher emphasises the importance of describing in detail the possibilities and religious offerings available in the kindergarten, such as the availability of food or visits to churches, so that parents can use this information to decide whether their child should attend the kindergarten. The other teacher considers the problems of this approach, as it could result in exclusively Catholic and Islamic kindergartens.

The challenges associated with religious difference in everyday kindergarten life are described. One mother, for example, has expressed the desire to ban her child from the making sign of the cross, which the teacher in question rejected with reference to the tradition of the "Catholic kindergarten"[612] and made it clear to her that the children attending the kindergarten did not have to make the sign of the cross, but could not be forbidden to do it. The mother's consideration to look for another kindergarten for her child was supported by the teacher by referring the mother to several Islamic kindergartens in the area. The mother finally decided against a change in kindergarten

---

611 Cf. chapter "Group discussion" (part III, 6.2).
612 Interview with the head of the Catholic kindergarten, 70.

and the child stayed in kindergarten. The teachers agree that it must be accepted that children can see the sign of the cross in kindergarten and take part on a voluntary basis. One teacher tried to explain the existence of different prayer attitudes and allowed the children to hold their hands the way they are used to at home. Nevertheless, the children sometimes make a sign of the cross, although they do not do so at home.

The teachers do not know whether the parents and children would approve of the celebration of their religion in kindergarten. They see it as the task of parents to explain the religious expressions of the respective religion to the children and think they themselves possess too little and exclusively superficial knowledge about other religions, which is why they prefer to keep quiet about them instead of telling the children "nonsense".[613] A teacher is in favour of not celebrating all the celebrations in the kindergarten, as there would be too many, but of briefly discussing in the morning circle which celebration is celebrated on the respective day and giving the children who celebrate this celebration the opportunity to tell about it. The other teacher points out that she has already tried to do this, but that the children in the morning circle, when she thematises festivals, tell nothing about them. She suspects that the reason for this is that the children are embarrassed to talk about it because they notice that they are a little different. The teacher also receives no answer from the children to the question of which places of worship the children visit. The children are not really interested in other religions, they listen, but are more interested in other things. This was shown, for example, during a walk past a mosque and the teacher tried to explain something about it to them, but the swan swimming by interested the children more. During a mosque visit last year, the non-Muslim children were first interested in the mosque, but soon joined the Muslim children running around the mosque. The older women, who had allowed the children to run around, told only the teachers about the mosque. After the visit, the teacher had the feeling that she had been in a gym class. The teacher was disconcerted by this situation because she had never been to a mosque before and the behaviour that the children showed in the mosque would not have been allowed in a church, since children behave "normally" in the church.[614] The children sometimes ask why certain children do not eat meat, to which the teacher refers to the prohibition of the mother of the child as a reason. This explanation "works quite well"[615] and in the opinion of the teacher it is the same when children have allergies or diabetes. With the admission of a child into the kindergarten, a suitable meal for this child must be ensured and the child is not to be presented with only a sandwich, which is difficult to implement in a small kindergarten, since many different requirements, in particular internal Islamic requirements, have to be met regarding the food. For the planned Eid Al-Adha it was difficult to find a person who was willing to celebrate it with the children, as some Muslim parents seemed not to know about the festival or to be unable to communicate it linguistically. Almost all parents and children come

---

613 Group discussion with teachers in the Catholic kindergarten, 267.
614 Ibid., 209.
615 Ibid., 63f.

to the Christian festivals in the kindergarten, and the teacher asks herself how far the absence of festivals is motivated by religion or has temporal reasons, whereby she suspects the latter. The teachers are unsure which children were not present at festivals. In their opinion, the explanation why a child could not be present at a party should be given to the child at home. The teachers consider the children too jumpy and excited to notice the absence of some children at a party. If they did notice the absence, they would believe that the absent children were ill or had something else to do. The children may have noticed the three remaining lanterns, but would not register them properly because they were busy with their own lantern. Children would notice more clearly the headscarves of some mothers or the dot on a mother's forehead than the religious difference among children. As an example of situations in which children noticed religious differences in children, the teachers tell of a child who came back from holiday with a bald head and another child who came to kindergarten with henna-painted hands and the children compared this with tattoos that they painted on themselves or that they got from the doctor. Otherwise, children address topics such as the headscarf at home and not in kindergarten. Although scarves lie in the role-playing corner, children do not put them on as headscarves.

The teachers agree that they do not need any support in kindergarten in terms of religious diversity.

3.4.2 Islamic Kindergarten

In the Islamic kindergarten, the group discussion with the two teachers was held during the time when the children were in Koran lessons and was briefly interrupted once by the entry of another teacher. The discussion could be held in the group room because the children who did not take part in the Koran lessons went to another group. The teachers often alternated in their speeches, partly adding words that the other teacher could not think of and referred to what had already been said by reinforcing it, adding examples or a different point of view.

The teachers tell that children talk to each other and to the teachers about religious topics. Thus, even if the teacher is not present, they address what should not be done because it is ḥarām[616]. They ask the teacher why she does not wear a headscarf and why she wears makeup or painted her fingernails because this is not allowed in Islam. When a girl told her that the non-Muslim people would go to hell or the "fire thing"[617], the teacher explained the existence of different religions and pointed out that she herself would also go to heaven, even if she is not a Muslim. The Muslim teacher says that the children give back what they hear from their parents. Normally children in Islam would not fast, but some children would like to fast because they see this in

---

616 The Arabic word ḥarām means "forbidden, illicit; forbidden, sin, inviolable; holy, holy; cursed, cursed" (Wehr, Hans (1968): Arabisches Wörterbuch, 155).
617 Group discussion with teachers in the Islamic kindergarten, 114.

their parents. Many children who want to fast did without breakfast, but eat again at noon. The Muslim teacher believes that children do not have to fast. They can start slowly, but are still too small and it is problematic if they do not drink because it can be very hot in the kindergarten in summer. Muslim parents sometimes bring some cakes to the kindergarten that contain gelatine, which is why the teachers always check the ingredients of the cakes before the meal. According to the statements of the teachers, challenges based on religion only arise with the parents, not with the children. Some parents are very strict with their children for religious reasons, although some rules do not apply to children. For example, a child who wears only thick long clothes in summer and no short-sleeved T-shirts or shorts is mentioned. The teacher spoke to the mother and asked her to put on a thin robe, otherwise it would be too hot for the child in summer. It was important for a Muslim father to be greeted with "Salaam aleikum", which the Christian teacher refused because she was not a Muslim. At the beginning, the teacher greeted the father with "Grüß Gott" [may God bless you], but finally changed to the greeting formula "Good morning".

The children noticed the absence of some children in Koran lessons and asked the reason for this and understood it when the teachers explained it to them several times. The teachers told the children that some children were not Muslim and belonged to a different religion, which is why they did not attend Koran lessons but stayed in the group room. If the children were given sweets in Koran lessons, the Christian children would also be given some so that they would not feel left out. When walking past a church, the teacher explains to the children its importance for Christian people, which can be compared with the importance of the mosque for Muslim people. She herself would go into this building to pray as a Christian. If the kindergarten is closed for a few days over Christmas and Easter, the children ask why. At Easter, they asked the Christian teacher if this was the Austrian Ramadan, after which the teacher tried to explain to them that it was a different festival. They also asked if Santa Claus existed. Some children receive a gift at Christmas or are threatened with none if they misbehaved. The Muslim teacher tells of Muslim parents who tell their children that there is no Santa Claus or Easter bunny in whom the Christian children believe. The Muslim teacher compares this with the belief in the tooth fairy, which may be good for the imagination but does not correspond to the truth. The Christian teacher interjects that there is also no Santa Claus and no Easter bunny, but the Christ Child. In conversation with children, she compares Muhammad in Islam with Jesus in Christianity and cites the birth of Jesus as the reason for celebrating Christmas.

The Eid, Mother's Day, each child's birthday, a summer party, carnival and celebrations after the end of a project are celebrated in the kindergarten year. Father's Day is not celebrated because the teachers do not only want to celebrate with the fathers, but gifts are prepared for both Father's and Mother's Day. Depending on the festival, it is celebrated by the entire kindergarten or in a group. Carnival is not celebrated at the same time and is called costume party because of the parents. Since this festival is great fun for the children, it would be a pity if this festival was not celebrated. At Muslim festivals such as Eid Al-Adha, the Christian children are also given gifts, and at Christmas or Easter, the Muslim children are also given gifts. At Easter, for example, the Christian children receive a chocolate bunny and the Muslim children chocolate because some Muslim parents do not want the children to have a rabbit, because it is not an Islamic festival. Care is taken to discuss the Christian religion with the Christian children and to present them with gifts. The Christian children are accepted by everyone. In kindergarten, all religions are respected and tolerated, which differs from some Islamic kindergartens where children are sometimes not allowed to draw a Christmas tree. Children should be integrated into the country and know, for example, the reason for the Christmas decorations. For Eid Al-Adha, for which the kindergarten is also closed, a gift for the parents is prepared with the children and the parents are invited. Religion means a great deal in kindergarten and occupies a large place.

The teachers agree that they do not need any support in terms of religion and religious diversity, but emphasize the importance of mutual support for the people working in the kindergarten group in everyday kindergarten life.

4. Data Analysis

The categories that emerged from the data are shown below. The collected data are first openly coded, demonstrating the open coding procedure using a short example before presenting the results of axial and selective coding.[618] The data analysis refers exclusively to the qualitative-empirically collected data, all statements are anchored in these and the reality of life of both kindergartens is systematically depicted and tendencies of the kindergartens are described. Additional data collection in the two selected kindergartens would not have led to any further statements with regard to the research question, therefore the categories presented are considered saturated. In other contexts there are probably other differentiations which were not found in the two kindergartens in Austria. The presentation is supplemented by a few short transcript sections.

Data analysis is presented in two parts, according to the underlying double perspective research question. The first part describes "Dealing with religious difference in kindergarten", while the second part focuses on "Dealing with and addressing religious difference by children" and a concluding part looks at and links these two areas together.

All collected data were openly encoded, whereby this was done in units of meaning, which was possible with the help of the computer program Atlas-Ti. Parallel to the coding, code notes explaining the codes or containing further thoughts, as well as memos were made. The memos, most of which also received questions, proved helpful in the categorisation process.

---

618 Due to the assurance of anonymity, the respective transcripts are not published, but only a few short examples, mostly paraphrased, are inserted for illustration.

In the following, a short sequence of a speech[619] from a group discussion with the teachers illustrates the procedure of open coding, how this was carried out on all collected data.[620]

124   ¹Hw: I don't know. Like from her. Is e./²I have the feeling (.) yes. Ahm./³That she really understands that/⁴and
125   that this is well explained to her at home, why./⁵So for her is no problem, (.)/⁶or she does
126   not act up,/⁷when she is picked up/⁸but happily she says by:::e,/⁹I go home
127   now/¹⁰and that is not an issue at all. Yeah, well. (1)/¹¹Because she also notices that we rehearse/¹²and
128   so on, well./¹³And she already knows that a celebration is a party /¹⁴and she also knows in retrospect, well
129   yesterday was a celebration and so./¹⁵But for here it is actually no problem./¹⁶Well, I believe/¹⁷that the parents
130   explain it really well to her at home. (2)/¹⁸Yes. My impression.

1   I don't know. Like from her. Is e.: CODE: KKL_Expression of uncertainty
2   I have the feeling (.) yes. Ahm.: CODE: KKL_Impression of the teacher; code note: expression of own emotion, no secured statement
3   That she really understands that: CODE: KKL_Thematisation of the child's absence; code note: Child understands why he or she does not take part in the festival
4   and that it is well explained to her at home, why: CODE: KKL_Declarations for the child are made at home; code note: own absence is explained at home; memo: Does this imply that this is not explained in kindergarten?
5   So, for her, this is not a problem (.): CODE: KKL_Thematisation of the child's absence; code note: Absence from celebrations is no problem for the child; memo: Does "no problem" mean that it is not problematised by the child?
6   or she does not act up: CODE: KKL_Thematisation of the child's absence; code note: no fuss about absence from celebrations; memo: If child doesn't act up, no one has any "problems" with the child?
7   when she is picked up: CODE: KKL_Pick up the child
8   but happily she says by:::e,: CODE: KKL_Reaction of the child to her own absence; code note: Child says happily goodbye before celebration. Memo: Who does the child say goodbye to?
9   now I go home: CODE: KKL_Reaction of the child to her own absence; code note: Child mentions her intention instead of the festival.

---

619   Interview with the head of the Catholic kindergarten, 124-130.
620   The slashes and the small digits have been inserted exclusively in this example to mark the subdivision of the coded sentence parts.

¹⁰ and that is not an issue at all. Yeah, well: CODE: KKL_Thematisation of the child's absence. Code note: Absence is not an issue; memo: What does it mean that it is not an issue? For the child, for the kindergarten etc.?

¹¹ Because she also notices that we rehearse: CODE: KKL_Children's knowledge about religious offerings; memo: What does "realise" mean? Is the child rehearsing?

¹² and so on, well: CODE: KKL_Children's knowledge about religious offerings; memo: What exactly does the child notice of the rehearsal?

¹³ And she already knows that it is a celebration: CODE: KKL_Children's knowledge about religious offerings; memo: Celebrating the festival is not hidden from the child. What does the child know about the celebration?

¹⁴ And she also knows in retrospect, well, yesterday was a celebration and so: CODE: KKL_Children's knowledge about religious offerings; memo: How does the director know this?

¹⁵ But for her it is actually no problem: CODE: KKL_Thematisation of the child's absence; memo: "actually" as relativisation?

¹⁶ Well, I believe: CODE: KKL_Evaluation by the teacher; memo: Statement not assured, no communication with the parents or the child about it?

¹⁷ that the parents explain it really well to her at home: CODE KKL_Declarations for the child are made at home; code note: Explanations of why children are absent from celebrations.

¹⁸ Yes. My impression: CODE: KKL_Impression of the teacher. Reinforcement that it is an impression; memo: no secured statement, not discussed with parents?

4.1 Dealing with religious difference in kindergarten

In the following sections, those categories are shown which contain many codes and thus appear as those which best match the data after several breaks and new layers of categories, based on axial coding (chapter 4.1.1–4.1.3) and selective coding (chapter 4.1.4). When we speak of major religions or minor religions in the following, this refers to the description of the distribution of religious affiliations in the respective kindergarten. The major religion in the Catholic kindergarten is Christianity, the major religion in the Islamic kindergarten is Islam.[621]

---

621 For these terms a purely descriptive designation was chosen, which refers to the frequency of the occurrence of the respective religion in the respective kindergarten. For reasons of readability, "the greater frequency of religion" and "the lesser frequency of religion" are replaced by the formulations "major religion" and "minor religion".

4.1.1 Conceptual reflections on religion and religious difference

- Reflections on religion in kindergarten
    - Religion of sponsorship as part of everyday life
    - Religion of the sponsorship as a separate, voluntary additional offer
    - No obligation to participate in the offers of the religion of the sponsorship
    - Tentative attempts to include minor religions

- Incompleteness of conceptual considerations
    - Dissatisfaction with current practice
    - Questioning current practice
    - Discrepancy between conceptual considerations and reality
    - A look at challenges

Reflections on religion in kindergarten

The directorsf of the two kindergartens have different considerations how religion is supposed to occur in kindergarten.

Religion of sponsorship as part of everyday life
In the kindergarten, religion is an integral part of the everyday life and is offered in various religious events during the kindergarten life. For example, religion occurs in regular Christian grace prayers, in stories that are told or read aloud, and in songs that are practised and sung with the children. Christian festivities in particular are celebrated intensively, as the children are prepared for them by working and rehearsing songs and poems and celebrate the religious festival together. The group room is decorated according to Christian festivities. During the Advent season, an Advent wreath is placed in a corner of the kindergarten room, as well as a path that Mary and Joseph take, a candle and an Advent calendar. Religion plays an important role in the transmission of values. Religion should permeate kindergarten life. By joining the kindergarten to a parish community, the church can also be used. The relationship with the priest, who sometimes visits the kindergarten, is considered important. The importance of religion in kindergarten is also anchored in the mission statement of the kindergarten association.[622]

Religion of the sponsorship as a separate, voluntary additional offer
In the Islamic kindergarten, religion should occur exclusively as a voluntary additional service in "religious education"[623] and be excluded from the rest of everyday life. Religious education is offered daily, lasts about twenty to thirty minutes, takes place in a room reserved for it, at a fixed time and with a colleague trained for it, who

---

[622] Cf. chapter "Selection of kindergartens" (part IV, 2).
[623] Expert interview with the head of the Catholic kindergarten, 6–8; 41f.

is supported by sporadic conversations with the director. With religion as a voluntary supplementary benefit in kindergarten, parents decide whether their child should participate in religious education. No one is obliged to attend religious education. By locating religion in religious education, religion should be clearly distinguishable from the rest of kindergarten life and play no role in it, which should make the work according to the guidelines of general pedagogy possible. The religious convictions of the teachers should not play a role in their pedagogical work. Religion is also largely avoided as a theme at the festivals: common celebrations are celebrated like a closing party or a festival of lights; before Christmas holidays, for example, a theme related to winter is chosen in order to dispense with religious references. This avoids conflicts with parents about why children have to celebrate a Christian or an Islamic feast. This is important in so far as the satisfaction of all participants in the kindergarten is aimed for.

The kindergarten wants to be open to everyone, and is connected to the hope that more "Austrian children"[624] will attend the kindergarten regardless of their religious background. The mixture of all children should enable a better understanding of the country as well as mutual understanding and the children should learn to deal properly with each other. The kindergarten provides a "bridge to society [....]",[625] which is intended to reduce fear of and build trust in society, which the head of the kindergarten emphasises.

No obligation to participate in the offers of the religion of the sponsorship
The children are not forced to participate in offers of the religion of sponsorship, but they have the opportunity to participate if they want to. In Catholic kindergartens, children of other religions are not required to participate in religious activities, but there are no alternative religious activities for these children. There is no pressure exerted and no one is obliged to say prayers or take part in celebrations. Nevertheless, there is uncertainty as to whether all of the parents are aware of this or whether some feel obliged to let their child participate in these activities, because they are concerned about the negative impact on the child.

In the Islamic kindergarten, no child is obliged to take part in Koran or religious education, but the parents decide on the child's participation.

Tentative attempts to include minor religions
In some cases, there are tentative considerations to include religions that do not correspond to the religion of the institution's sponsors and are less represented in the kindergarten in the everyday life of the kindergarten. Suggestions are made on how this can be achieved, e.g. by saying different prayers, visiting different places of worship and thematising festivals. These proposals are supported by tentative attempts to

---

624 Ibid., 186.
625 Ibid., 93f.

integrate other religions into everyday life, such as a one-time visit by the Catholic kindergarten to a mosque.

Incompleteness of conceptual considerations

The considerations as to how religion and religious difference should occur in kindergarten are not complete and do not form a consistent concept. This is demonstrated by dissatisfaction with current practice, which is being called into question. There is a discrepancy between the conceptual considerations and the practice in kindergarten, and the focus is on the challenges. Only the major religions are emphasised in the considerations, wishes are expressed in part as to how religious difference can become part of a fruitful dialogue.

Dissatisfaction with current practice
The dissatisfaction with current practice and the desire for change illustrate the incompleteness of the conceptual considerations. The director of the Catholic kindergarten is aware of the low level of involvement with other religions in kindergarten. She wants to change this in the future and presents possibilities and ideas that she would like to realize in kindergarten in order to integrate other religions into everyday kindergarten life. The kindergarten director especially criticises the existing practise concerning celebrations and prayers without having been specifically asked for comments, and addresses suggestions for improvement. In her opinion, openness for everyone must go hand in hand with the satisfaction of all those involved in kindergarten activities. For the director, it is questionable whether parents of other religions could be expected to celebrate celebrations in a church with a dominant crucifix on the wall. It is uncomfortable for her to invite Muslim parents to a church with the dominant sign, as they are often reserved and in some cases do not understand everything linguistically and might feel compelled to join in the celebrations. In the future, there should be more emphasis on the way of celebrating other religions' festivals, the involvement and invitation of parents at festivals, the recitation of prayers of other religions and visits to places of worship of other religions. It is conceivable for her to celebrate in a neutral way so that everyone could agree with the way the festival was being celebrated. She could accept parents expressing dissatisfaction with the celebration in the church, since in her opinion celebrations do not always have to be celebrated in the church, but could also take place in the group room.

Questioning current practice
During the interview, the director of the Islamic kindergarten asks the researcher whether the form of religious education offered is suitable for the children and whether it makes sense from her point of view. Together with the Islamic community of faith, he is looking for what children should be taught in kindergartens and what rituals should occur. He points to many open questions in this area that need to be analysed.

In his opinion, the MA 11 and the control authority of the city of Vienna, need to consider how religion should occur in kindergarten, as well as the term "mosque kindergartens". He hopes for a professional proposal, whereby a discussion with Catholic and Protestant kindergartens about their concepts could also be helpful, so that in Islamic kindergartens the extent of religious offerings could be similar to those in these kindergartens. No consideration is given to how different religions could be addressed, since he does not think it makes sense to make offers for children of other religions because of the children's current religious affiliation. Since the kindergarten wants to be a bridge to society, however, Christian festivals are thematised, since the children need to get to know the Austrian customs.

Discrepancy between conceptual considerations and kindergarten practice
Some aspects of the conceptual considerations of the management of the kindergartens are not reflected in everyday kindergarten life and the teachers do not know about them.

Thus, religious education is exclusively described as such by the director of the kindergarten and called Koran lessons by all others in the kindergarten. The concern of the director to keep religion out of everyday life is not strictly followed in the Islamic kindergarten. Thus a dua is spoken before each meal, secular celebrations contain religious elements and religious celebrations are partly celebrated. The teachers address religion in everyday kindergarten life and the children bring religion into everyday life through their questions and comments.

In Catholic kindergartens, where the conceptual considerations envisage religion as an integrated factor of everyday kindergarten life, this shows up relatively little. Thus, table prayers are said, sometimes songs with religious content are sung and the Christian feasts are celebrated, which take place as a repetitive, little –reflected upon ritual.

A look at challenges
A look at the opportunities offered by religious diversity overlooks the challenges posed by religious diversity. Both the directors and the teachers pay particular attention to the resistance and conflict potential of religious diversity. According to those working in the kindergarten, children have no problem with religious difference, which is why the focus is on the desires and needs of parents or on established traditions in dealing with religion. The children's perspective is not taken into account in decisions on how to deal with religious diversity.

4.1.2 Recognisable elements of religious difference

- Festivals
    - General festivals with non-communicated religious elements
    - Religiously declared festivals of the major religion

- Festivals of the minor religions
- Secular festivals instead of religious festivals
- Information about festivals without celebrating them

- Visibility of religion in everyday kindergarten life
    - Religious symbols and pictures in the kindergarten room
    - Clothes and Jewellery
    - Food offer

- Religious offers
    - Religious education/Koran lessons
    - Getting to know places of worship
    - Storytelling

- Prayers
    - Prayers of major religion
    - Unified Prayers
    - Prayers of the minor religions
    - Secular sayings as a substitute for prayers

Festivals

General festivals with non-communicated religious elements
Festivals without a religious background are celebrated, whereby religious elements occur during the course of the celebration, about which no communication is made in advance. Thus, the biggest festival in the Islamic kindergarten year is the "summer party", for which the children and the teacher prepare and rehearse for a long time in order to present a show to the parents. Religion is the theme of this festival, which is celebrated as a closing and summer party, inasmuch as the children sing two suras to their parents during the performance, whereby the non-Muslim children do not sing along with them but remain in the group. During the station operation, which includes several stations with games and music, one station is dedicated to the Koran. In this one the children recite the suras they know. Non-Muslim children do not have to complete this workshop to receive their final gift. Other religions are not discussed at the summer festival.

Religiously declared festivals of the major religion
There are festivals in the kindergarten that are religiously declared and assigned to a certain religious tradition. The Christian festivals of the church year are celebrated in the Catholic kindergarten. These celebrations are celebrated either in the church, in the group room or in another room available in the building. In principle, Christian festivals are celebrated with all children, but no one has to join in and no pressure is to be exerted. If it is known that parents do not want to let their child join the party, they

will be informed so that they do not bring the children to the kindergarten on the day of the celebration, or pick them up before the party; there is no alternative activity for the children. At festivals that take place outside the everyday life of the kindergarten with the parents, such as St. Martin's or St. Nicholas, the parents can decide whether they want to participate in the party with their child. The teachers are exploring ways of dealing with the situation that "still fits the child".[626] The absence of some children at religious festivals and the reasons for the absence are not discussed with their parents, colleagues or children. The reason why parents pick up their children before the festival is thought to be the part the church plays in the celebration. The question is asked whether the celebration should take place in the church or in a neutral place, such as a hall. Despite the director's reservations about celebrating in the church because many Muslim children are in kindergarten, St. Martin's is celebrated with reference to tradition, in the church.

In Islamic kindergartens, religious festivals are not celebrated so that individual children do not feel isolated.

Festivals of the minor religions
The offer of festivals of the minor religions in kindergarten is being considered. The head of the Catholic kindergarten would like to offer festivals of different religions in the kindergarten in the future, whereby no concrete planning for the celebration of festivals of other religions is available. In the course of the year, the director tries to make preparations so that the Eid Al-Adha can be celebrated. It proves difficult to find Muslim parents who will tell the children in kindergarten about the Eid Al-Adha. The teachers attribute this to the fact that the parents themselves either know too little about the festival or do not have the German language skills to tell the children something about it. Therefore, a Muslim friend of the kindergarten director is invited to the kindergarten to celebrate the Eid with the children in the final year of kindergarten. After the festival, the teachers are not sure whether the children have understood the festival, even if the invited woman "has done it nicely".[627] The celebration of the Eid Al-Adha takes place on the same day as the celebration of a birthday party, and some children are unable to participate in the Eid Al-Adha due to an activity occurring at the same time. The festival is therefore of little importance, even if the director is striving to celebrate a festival of a minor religion.

Secular festivals instead of religious festivals
Festivals with an original religious background are changed and reinterpreted in such a way that this background is no longer recognisable. Religious symbols are not used. Festivities are selected that can be celebrated by all children equally. For example, the Islamic kindergarten celebrates a "polar bear festival" instead of Christmas or a "sun, moon and star festival". The reasons given for celebrating a secular festival are that

---

626 Interview with the head of the Catholic kindergarten, 67.
627 Group discussion with teachers in the Catholic kindergarten, 224.

no one should feel excluded, everyone could participate in the festival equally and all children can feel satisfaction and gratitude. Celebrating secular festivals would also prevent parents from complaining about why children have to take part in Christian or Islamic festivals.

Information about festivals without celebrating them
Information about festivals of both the major religion and the minor religions is provided to the children without celebrating the festivals in kindergarten. In the Islamic kindergarten, Christian as well as Islamic festivals are thematised by describing the background of the festivals and giving the children symbolic gifts. Gifts can vary between Christian and Muslim children; for example, at Easter the Christian children receive a chocolate bunny and the Muslim children chocolate. Therefore, there is no criticism from parents as to why festivals are celebrated by different religions.

Visibility of religion in everyday kindergarten life

Religious symbols and pictures in the kindergarten room
Religious symbols and pictures can be visible in the kindergarten room. In the Catholic kindergarten, the group room is decorated and equipped with materials in reference to the next Christian festival. This is expressed by works on the theme, by festive decorations brought along by the kindergarten teacher, such as an Advent wreath, a manger, an arranged path to the manger with Mary and Joseph and an Advent calendar at Advent time, and by books on religious festivals such as Christmas or St. Martin's. Only symbols or festive design of the major religion can be found in the kindergarten. Symbols, pictures or characters of other religions do not appear. The kindergarten building is connected to a Catholic church by a corridor.

In the Islamic kindergarten there are no religious symbols in the group room, neither to Islam nor to other religions. The group room is decorated according to the season. There are no books dealing directly with religion. In the Islamic kindergarten, there is a Koran room, where the religious or Koran lessons for the Muslim children take place, and a mosque, where the children go to Friday prayer. In the Koran Room information about the Prophet Muhammad and Arab suras is on the wall.

Clothing and Jewellery
Religious differences in kindergarten can be seen in the clothes and jewellery of children, teachers or parents. In the Catholic kindergarten, some children wear a necklace with a cross or a bracelet with Catholic motifs. Some parents wear a headscarf or have a bindi on their forehead. Situations arise in which children notice differences, such as a child whose hands were once painted with henna and a girl who has returned from vacation with a bald head due to a religious ritual.

In the Islamic kindergarten, the Muslim teacher wears a headscarf, the Christian teacher often wears short-sleeved T-shirts, is tattooed, sometimes uses nail polish and is often wearing make-up or puts on make-up in front of the children.

Food offered

The children's eating habits differ during meals together, which is taken into account differently in the kindergartens. An attempt is made to reduce the complexity of the different requirements by selecting food that as many children as possible can eat. Pork is generally not offered in the Catholic kindergartens. Children who only eat halal meat receive a sandwich on days when meat is included in the meal, as the size of the kindergarten makes it impossible to provide an alternative, warm meal for them. Food preference of the parents is discussed, i.e vegetarian, during the registration process, and the religious reason is assumed by the kindergarten director and is not asked by her and is not brought up for discussion by the parents. In the Islamic kindergarten, only halal prepared food is offered and all children are served the same food, whereby the teachers take personal preferences of the children into consideration when distributing the food. Due to the internal Islamic diversity, which is expressed in different meal requirements of the parents, the director attempts a middle path in the different requirements in the offer of the halal prepared meal. Teachers in the Islamic kindergarten endeavour to take the religious attitudes of parents seriously and to make them clear in their own behaviour. They check whether the cakes parents bring to the children are halal.

Religious offers

In this context, all activities in which the children get to know their own religion better or learn something about other religions are seen as religious offers. Different religious offers are made, so Koran/religious lessons take place, churches are visited and stories with a religious background are told.

Religious education/Koran lessons

Only Islamic religious education is offered, for which a separate room, an assigned time window on the day and a teacher for Islamic religious education are available. The children learn the Arabic alphabet, simple sentences in Arabic and suras of the Koran. Catholic or Protestant religious education is not offered in the house – on the grounds that almost 95 percent are Turkish-Muslim children – although the director believes that children become "better and healthier"[628] through religion.

Getting to know places of worship

Getting to know about places of worship is another offer in the kindergartens. The church is regularly visited by the Catholic kindergarten, especially during festive sea-

---

628 Expert interview with the head of the Islamic kindergarten, 190f.

sons, as it is spatially connected to the kindergarten building by a corridor. When visiting churches, not every child has to make a sign of the cross with holy water. The one-time visit to a mosque did not meet the teacher's expectations, as the children were allowed to run in the mosque and the visit rather resembled a gym class. The other teacher reports of her experience that children, if they passed a mosque during a trip, were not interested in her explanation about the mosque.

In the Islamic kindergarten, the Muslim children regularly visit the mosque. The teacher thematises churches when they happen to pass by a church during an excursion. She tells the children that because of her religion she goes into this building to pray, which she thinks the children would be interested in. Consciously initiated visits to places of worship other than the mosque are not offered.

Storytelling
Stories with a religious background are told in the Catholic kindergarten at Christian festivals or played with the children as role-plays. Stories of other religions are not discussed in the kindergarten year with the exception of the Eid Al-Adha.

In the Islamic kindergarten, the children are told the background to the Islamic and Christian festivals. In the Koran lessons the children are told about the life of Muhammad.

Prayers

Prayers of major religion
In the Catholic kindergarten, a prayer of thanks is given before each meal, as thanks can be expressed in any religious orientation, but only Christian prayers are said, sung or danced and the prayer is often concluded with a sign of the cross. The prayers before the meal or the snacks are selected from a foundation of Christian prayers. The hand position in prayer in the Catholic kindergarten is the same for all children, as all children fold their hands. Children are not forced to pray along because they are not compelled to participating in something they experience differently at home.

In the Islamic kindergarten, the children pray a dua in Arabic before eating, with the teachers sometimes saying that the non-Muslim children do not have to pray the dua. Nevertheless, most of the time all children adopt an open position of prayer and pray along. The Christian teacher does not pray, for part of the dua she talks to another teacher while the children pray dua, which does not disturb the children.

Unified Prayers
Prayers are generally formulated so that no one will take offence. No child should feel uncomfortable when praying and think that this does not fit.

Prayers of the minor religions
Prayers of the minor religions are formulated exclusively as a possibility for the future. The director of the Catholic kindergarten is aware that no prayers are said of other religions and that no prayers of other religions are heard. She knows that it is up to the people working in the kindergarten to integrate prayers of other religions into the processes and that this is a possibility in the future. To explain why prayers of other religions have not yet been addressed, she cites the lack of knowledge of German and the shyness of children of other religions. In addition, a conscious approach requires detailed preparations, information, the consent of the persons concerned and, if necessary, the invitation of the parents.

Secular saying as a substitute for prayer
Instead of a prayer from a religious tradition, a secular saying is said before the meal, as sometimes happens in the Catholic kindergarten. In the Islamic kindergarten, before each meal, a secular saying is spoken by all the children together with the dua.

4.1.3 Verbal communication about religious difference

- Communication about religious difference in specific situations
- Avoiding communication about religious difference
- Causes for low communication about religious difference

Communication about religious difference in specific situations

In the Islamic kindergarten, the religious habits of Muslim children and parents are discussed. For example, they check whether food brought by the children is halal. Before visiting the mosque, the children are instructed to put on a top with long sleeves. If a child wears a headscarf, it is noticed by the teacher and the child is asked if he or she has grandma's headscarf, because the mother never wears one. The teachers deal with the religious habits of their parents. If they notice negative effects on the child, they might approach the parents with the request to change the behaviour that is having a negative effect on the child. The Christian teacher refuses to use an Arabic greeting, although a father of a child requested the greeting . The greeting "Grüß Gott" [may God bless you], was not accepted by the father which is why she welcomes the father with "Good morning", who accepts this over time.

In the Catholic kindergarten, parents who do not agree to their child's participation in religious festivals are called so that they can pick up their child before the festival or not bring it to the kindergarten on the day in question.

Avoiding communication about religious difference

There is a lack of communication about religious difference and an avoidance of situations that could clarify religious difference .

During the registration interview, the head of the Catholic kindergarten does not ask the parents about the reason for the children's vegetarian diet, although she suspects religious reasons. It would be okay for the director if parents did not want to celebrate festivals in church. However, the parents do not express an opinion and the director does not ask the parents for their opinion. The director does not know what Muslim women think about the celebrations in the church and fears that they wrongly think they have to participate because otherwise this will have negative consequences for the children.

Conflicts that arise, such as the complaint of a mother who does not want her child to make a sign of the cross, are not discussed with the children or with the teachers.

The desire to celebrate festivals other than Christian festivals in the kindergarten originates from the kindergarten director and the celebration of the Eid Al-Adha is initiated by her. The kindergarten teachers do not communicate clearly with each other in advance how, for example, the Eid Al-Adha is to be organised and who is to be present. One week before the planned celebration of the Eid, the kindergarten director and a kindergarten teacher have a short talk in which the kindergarten director discusses the Eid planned for next week, whereupon the kindergarten teacher expresses her incomprehension as to why all children should be involved in it. This objection remains unthematised. Directly before the festival, there is a brief disagreement as to which teachers should attend the festival, as the director wishes all teachers to be present, while one teacher considers it more important to support the assistant in the garden. The teachers do not know whether the parents would like to celebrate the festivals of their religion in kindergarten and do not discuss this with the parents. It is perceived by a teacher that children are embarrassed to talk about their religious expressions because they notice that they are different. This statement is not used as an occasion to work on this with the children. In kindergarten, it is not discussed if children do not take part in festivals because of their religious affiliation, but parents are expected to explain this to the children at home, however, this expectation is not discussed with the parents. The desire not to address religious differences is also evident in the offered food. Thus, in the Catholic kindergarten, generally no pork is offered and in the Islamic kindergarten, one tries to go the middle way in the strictness of the offered halal meal in order not to offend anybody.

Causes for avoiding communication about religious difference

In both kindergartens, the kindergarten director is aware that religious difference exists, but there is a tendency in everyday kindergarten life to avoid situations in which religious difference could be discernible and experienced by the children. The reasons given for low communication about religious difference are not to be understood exclusively and clearly differentiated from one another, but often apply to individual persons for several reasons.

- Equal treatment for all children
- Avoiding challenges and conflicts
- Satisfaction of all involved
- Commitment to tradition
- Reference to sponsorship
- Lack of knowledge
- Religious education as a means of conveying values
- Religion as staging
- Religion as a "matter of privacy"

Equal treatment for all children
To prevent children from experiencing non-affiliation and isolation, religious difference is not discussed and it is attempted to treat all children equally. This is given as a reason for celebrations without a religious background, so that all children can participate equally and feel that they belong. This practice is not intended to exclude children. No child should feel that he or she is not part of the group and that he or she is different.

Avoiding challenges and conflicts
Religious difference is seen from the perspective of being a challenge. Therefore, it is considered an advantage if religious difference is not addressed, as this can provoke conflicts and problems. A conflict between a mother and a teacher about the sign of the cross in kindergarten is neither discussed among kindergarten teachers nor with the children, although some children have heard the conversation. The silence about the conflict was guided by the hope that it would resolve itself.

Satisfaction of all involved
An attempt is made to strike a balance between the different demands of the parents so that everyone involved in kindergarten activities is satisfied. The director of the Islamic kindergarten wishes the satisfaction of all involved in the events of the kindergarten. The choice of halal food is based on an averaged strict interpretation to meet the needs of all parents. Sensitive handling of the internal Islamic diversity and the wishes and religious attitudes of the parents, who are the customers, is necessary, because their satisfaction is decisive for the attendance of the kindergarten.

Commitment to tradition
In the Catholic kindergarten, the celebration of festivals continues in the way it is traditionally done in the kindergarten, with a strong tradition of how and where certain festivals are celebrated. With reference to St. Martin's, the question is asked whether

the celebration should take place in the church or in a neutral place, such as a hall. Despite the director's reservations about celebrating in the church because many Muslim children are in kindergarten, St. Martin's is celebrated in the church, as it has always been A change would cause an uproar, lead to conflict and be a challenge, which is why the director does not encourage it.

Reference to sponsorship
The religious orientation of the kindergarten in a clearly declared religious sponsorship is used as a reason why only the religion of the sponsorship and not religious difference is addressed in the kindergarten.

Lack of knowledge
Another reason for the low thematisation of religious difference is a lack of knowledge about other religions. Since it is impossible to obtain sufficient information about all religions, the different religions are not discussed. The teachers know superficially about some aspects of the religions to which they do not belong, but are too insecure to talk to children or parents about their religion and to discuss religious differences. Fearing to say something wrong, they remain silent about different religions and religious differences. The teachers do not want to tell the children about a religion that they do not practice themselves, because they find it difficult if religious expressions and rituals are explained by a person who is not familiar with them.

Lack of knowledge can lead to irritation and alienation of kindergarten teachers by another religion, for example when visiting a mosque and the children are allowed to run in the mosque. This disconcerting situation and the feeling that the original intention did not lead to success with the children, leads to irritation of the teacher and does not motivate for further attempts to include other religions.

Religious education as a means of conveying values
Religious education is focused on teaching values. The director of the Catholic kindergarten emphasises the importance of communicating values that would affect all children, since all children should learn to thank, all should know that bread should not be thrown away and one should be respectful of nature and the environment. Religious difference is not important in this context, but the common, all that unites is emphasised, the different religions are reduced to mediating values and thus unified, homogenised, as it is expressed in the sentence "Muslims also find sharing good"[629].

Religion as staging
Religious themes are often staged by the children rehearsing role plays or dances in everyday life and presenting them to their parents without being able to give the religious reason for this performance. The focus is on the performance and representation of the kindergarten, not the religious dimension of the festival. Consideration for reli-

---

629 Research diary, Catholic kindergarten, excerpt from conversation with director, 195.

gious difference would change the design of the festival and there would be the danger of not conveying a uniform image of the kindergarten. The children are not involved in the decision on the form of the religious organisation of the celebrations, they are involved exclusively by the rehearsal of the songs or dances given by the teachers and by demonstrating these at the celebration. The festivals planned with the parents are preceded by a long and intensive period of preparation, which ends with a dress rehearsal. At the festival, the children sing to their parents, present a play or dance for them. These celebrations are characterised by performance character, and the parents are proud of the presentation performed by their children. These celebrations, whether religious or secular, are a children's performance for parents. How the children like the festival and whether it is a children's festival remains of secondary importance. This becomes particularly clear during the rehearsals for the performance as well as during the performance, in which children cry and do not want to take part, but still have to do so. Religious difference is a disturbing factor in this access to religion, which is not taken into account.

Religion as a "matter of privacy"
The teachers see it as the task of the parents to educate the children religiously and to provide them with information about their religion, since the kindergarten cannot do this, because the teachers cannot know about all religions. Moreover, too many religious topics and too many religious celebrations would not do justice to the interests of children. Without asking parents and children if they want to celebrate their religion in kindergarten, it is assumed that parents are not interested. The teacher suspects that the parents do not want an unbeliever, as she thinks to be in the eyes of some parents, to educate their children religiously. The responsibility to tell the children about religious expressions of the minor religions in kindergarten lies with the parents. If children are not allowed to participate in certain festivities in the kindergarten or to perform certain gestures, such as the sign of the cross, it is up to the parents to explain the reason for this to the children.

4.1.4 Dominance of a religion

Dominance of the major religion – little recognition of the minor religions

In dealing with religious difference in kindergarten, the dominance of the major religion , which is also the religion of the respective sponsorship, can be established in both kindergartens as a superordinate category. The way in which religion is addressed in kindergarten and how religious differences are dealt with shows a preference for the major religion and little recognition of the minor religions. Even if those working in kindergarten – as shown in the first category, "Conceptual considerations of religion and religious difference"[630] – express themselves positively towards religious differ-

---

630 Cf. category "Conceptual reflections on religion and religious difference" (part V, 4.1.1).

ence, the thematisation of religious difference is largely avoided, except for a few tentative attempts that can be traced back to committed teachers and not to organisational anchoring. Various reasons are cited for this, such as equal treatment of all children, avoidance of challenges and conflicts, shaping religion to the satisfaction of all those involved, traditionality of the shaping of religion, lack of knowledge, religion as a mediation of values, religion as a staging and religion as a "matter of privacy". Everyday kindergarten life is marked by the major religion and the discernability of religious difference is largely avoided in everyday kindergarten life and where religious difference is nevertheless recognisable, an attempt is made to avoid communication about it. This is evident in all dimensions of the categories of "discernible elements of religious difference"[631] and "verbal communication about religious difference"[632]. The selection and organisation of the festivals, the spoken prayers, the visibility of religion in everyday kindergarten life and the religious offerings in kindergarten refer to the major religion, whereas the minor religions are not taken into account. The lack of communication about religious difference is shown by avoiding conversations with other teachers, parents or children about their religion or religious expressions and by not addressing conflicts about religious difference.

4.2 Dealing with and Thematising Religious Difference by Children

In this chapter, all those categories are represented, which treat the handling of the children with and the thematisation of religious difference by them. After axial coding (chapter 4.2.1–4.2.3), the core category (4.2.4) is described. When children of the major and minor religions are spoken of, this refers to the distribution of the children's religious affiliations in the respective kindergarten. The major religion of children in Catholic kindergarten is Christianity, the major religion of children in Islamic kindergarten is Islam.

4.2.1 Interest in religious difference

In the Catholic kindergarten, children tend not to focus on religion and religious difference, while in the Muslim kindergarten children often focus on religion and religious difference and are curious about how other religions are lived. For the children in the Islamic kindergarten, it seems self-evident that there is religious difference, whereas in the Catholic kindergarten, there is no topic that is openly discussed in the kindergarten.

- No discernible interest in religious difference
  - Little thematisation of religious difference without stimulus

---

631 Cf. category "Recognisable elements of religious difference" (part V, 4.1.2).
632 Cf. category "Verbal communication about religious difference" (part V, 4.1.3).

- Initiated and faltering discussions about religious difference
- Little knowledge of religious difference

- A matter of course of and interest in religious difference
  - Self-initiated and self-paced discussions on topics of religious difference
    - Religious affiliation and religious expressions
    - Festivals
    - Absence from Koran lessons
  - Knowledge of religious difference
  - Attempt to understand unknown religious expressions

No discernible interest in religious difference

The children in the Catholic kindergarten do not address religious differences on their own initiative. If the researcher sets stimulus, the conversations remain faltering and concentrated on the researcher and religious difference is not explicitly discussed.

Little thematisation of religious difference without stimulus
Without the impulse of the researcher, their own religious affiliation, religious expressions and religious differences are not discussed by the children in the Catholic kindergarten. Neither before nor after the celebrations take place are these thematised by the children among themselves, the children turn to their games. Only in the pre-Christmas period, while a nativity scene is set up in the kindergarten and a path to the crèche is depicted, the children sometimes sit in front of the crèche and talk about it. A Christian child at home asks why the mother of a child wears a headscarf, in kindergarten the child does not ask this question.

Initiated and faltering conversations about religious difference
If the researcher asks questions during a discussion, the children provide answers to them, the discussions remain sluggish and, with a few exceptions, in which the food or the horse at St. Martins' is the subject of discussion, concentrate on the researcher. In the group discussion about the Eid Al-Adha, for example, the children answer the questions and then change the topic, whereby no sequence in the conversation about the Eid Al-Adha becomes self-evident. The celebration of Eid Al-Adha does not seem to arouse any special interest among the children.

Little knowledge of religious difference
Children in the Catholic kindergarten who notice religious differences, which becomes clear in discussions initiated by the researcher, often have no explanation for them. The children do not know why some children should not make a sign of the cross. They also lack an explanation as to why some children are not present at festivals, although they participated in the rehearsal. The children are not aware that some festivals are not celebrated by everyone. Thus, the Christian children in the Catholic kin-

dergarten know after the celebration of the Eid Al-Adha in the kindergarten that they do not celebrate the festival at home, but they are not aware that some children in the kindergarten celebrate this festival because they are Muslim. Neither the children who did not take part in the religious offers nor the children who noticed the absence of some children mention an explanation for their absence. In a discussion, when asked by the researcher, which people do not have an Advent wreath, the children named the poor, the blacks and the elderly because they are poor. At the Eid Al-Adha, the children in the Catholic kindergarten are not sure why they received chocolate, they think either because of sharing or because they were good. The children do not know that Muslims celebrate this festival which is why the Eid Al-Adha is being celebrated in the Catholic kindergarten.

A matter of course of and interest in religious difference

The Muslim children in the Islamic kindergarten address religious difference as a matter of course and are interested in different forms of religious expression.

Self-paced and self-initiated conversations on topics of religious difference
The Muslim children in the Islamic kindergarten talk about topics of their religion or religious difference without given stimulus in different situations, such as eating, drawing or playing free time, which shows their interest in religious difference and its self-evident thematisation.

Religious affiliation and religious expressions
The Muslim children in the Islamic kindergarten ask about the religious affiliation of other children, the teachers and the researcher. The question of whether the researcher is a Muslim is asked in the Islamic kindergarten in the middle of playing or after visiting the mosque. After visiting the mosque, the children ask the researcher why she goes to Koran lessons, although she is not a Muslim. One child's remark that the researcher is an aunt and not a Muslim answered the question for the children. They make it a subject of their own accord that they are Muslim. For the children, being Muslim means going to Koran lessons and wearing a headscarf for some children. The children mention that certain things like gelatine or alcohol should not be eaten or drunk because they are ḥarām and they ask the Christian teacher if she eats pork. Furthermore, some children say that discos are ḥarām because of the alcohol, or nail polish, make-up or short dresses are ḥarām, they laugh about a picture of a woman wearing a bikini in the newspaper "Heute"[633], since it is ḥarām, and when a girl wears a very short skirt, the children point out to her that she must not dress like that.

Arabic-speaking children are proud to be able to speak Arabic and are admired by the other children in the Islamic kindergarten for their ability.

---

633 Free Viennese newspaper.

Festivals
The Muslim children in the Islamic kindergarten thematise festivals which occur in the Christian yearly circle, they know when a Christian festival has taken place and are curious how the festival has been celebrated. They are interested in the way of celebrating non-Islamic festivals and understand that the festival can be important for people who are not Muslim. This becomes clear, for example, in a situation in which a Muslim girl asks the researcher questions about Easter and then paints a picture with an Easter bunny and gives it to her with the words "I know, you love Easter".[634] The children know that Muslims do not celebrate Easter and ask the researcher if she celebrates Easter. In response to her affirmative answer, they ask if she is not a Muslim.

1 Fw: Did you have Easter yesterday? Yes or no?
2 I: Yes
3 Fw: Aren't you a Muslim?
4 I: No.[635]

The children establish a connection between the celebration of Easter and religious affiliation. They know that they did not celebrate Easter because they are Muslims.

Absence from the Koran lessons
Religious difference becomes particularly recognisable for children in the Islamic kindergarten in the fact that not all children participate in the Koran lessons. Most of the Muslim children explain whether children are Muslim or not by their presence in Koran lessons. Participation in the teaching of the Koran indicates religious affiliation to Islam. The children cite non-affiliation to certain groups as the reason for their absence from Koran lessons.[636]

Knowledge of religious difference
The children in the Islamic kindergarten know about the fact of religious difference. The reference point for declarations on religious expressions among children is Islam. They distinguish whether they are Muslim or not, another religion is not mentioned by the children. The children state that they belong to Islam as a reason whether certain festivals are celebrated, whether a headscarf is worn and whether certain commandments are observed. For many children, the headscarf is a criterion for distinguishing whether women are Muslim or not. A child tells at lunch that his mother can't go swimming.

484   I always go swimming with Dad. Because my mom has a headscarf, she's Muslim. She can't.[637]

---

634 Group discussion after Easter with Fw, Rw and Ew in the Islamic kindergarten, 43.
635 Group discussion after Easter with Fw, Rw and Ew in the Islamic kindergarten, 1-4.
636 Cf. section "Knowledge of religious difference" (part V, 4.2.1).
637 Research diary, Islamic kindergarten, 483.

The Muslim children in the Islamic kindergarten know Christian celebrations, which they do not celebrate. They know about the prayer washes and the mosque and that some commandments are not obeyed by people who are not Muslim. They know the prohibition of certain behaviours in Islam such as wearing short skirts or nail polish, wearing make-up or drinking alcohol. The children correct each other, if a part of a sura is recited wrongly. Before visiting the mosque, they ask each other if they had done the prayer washes correctly. Some girls control the other children during the prayer washes and explain to them in a commanding tone what they should do, whereupon all children obey. In one situation, a Muslim child claims that another child is going to hell because it is not Muslim. The children control each other in religious rituals.

The children identify belonging to a certain group as a reason for attending or not attending Koran lessons and are aware that not all people go to Koran lessons.[638] The Christian children in the group know that they themselves do not go to Koran lessons because they are not Muslims, with one child using the word mosque instead of the word Muslims. The Christian children are also aware that all the other children in the group are going to Koran lessons. For the two Christian girls, being Muslim means going to Koran lessons. The Muslim children who notice the absence of some children have explanations for this in the Islamic kindergarten. The following reasons are given by the Muslim children in the Islamic kindergarten for attending or not attending Koran lessons, with each child stating only one reason:

Being Muslim: Some Muslim children mention that they go to Koran lessons because they are Muslims, whereas some of the group are not Muslims and therefore do not attend Koran lessons. The children know which children of the group do not go to Koran lessons and list their names. A boy does not take part in Koran lessons with the rest of the group because he or she is of a different age and therefore takes part in Koran lessons with another group. He clearly explains that he is a Muslim, he is going to Koran lessons with another group.

Children's behaviour: In a conversation, the distinction between good and bad children is made, whereby only the good children go into the Koran room, but the bad children do not. The children also name the child who, because of its behaviour, is not allowed to attend Koran lessons, which the child concerned is resisting.[639]

38	I:	Who goes to the mosque?
39	Ew:	**Me**, me (points)
40	Bm:	˪Me (points)
41	Tw:	˪**Me**. Me. (points)
42	Ew:	All

---

638 Cf. section "Knowledge of religious difference" (part V, 4.2.1).
639 On the day of the conversation, the Koran teacher and a teacher discuss that all children should have been well in the Koran lesson and that if a child is bad, it will be taken out of the Koran lesson by the teacher. Bm is called by his name and asked to be good. The day before a child was not allowed to go to Koran lessons because of his behaviour.

43 Bm: I'm going too. I'm going too.
44 Ew: Bad child doesn't go, good goes.
45 Tw: Bad child doesn't go, only good. (.) But Bm not. Bm was bad.
46 Bm: Me too.[640]

Height or age: As a reason why she goes to Koran lessons, a girl states that she is still small and generalises that all small children go to Koran lessons.

7 Nw: Koran lessons. yes. (.) Because I'm still small, when someone is small, they go to Koran lesson.[641]

Attempt to understand unknown religious expressions
The children in the Islamic kindergarten show understanding for other religions or religious attitudes. In the conversations, the children look for similarities on the one hand, and on the other they are aware of many differences between the two religions.

Muslim children in the Islamic kindergarten connect their own religion with the Christian religion and seek points of contact from their world of experience. They try to understand Christian festivals by referring to Islamic festivals by combining concepts, so they call the pre-Easter Lent Ramadan and Easter as Easter Bayram. The teacher corrects the girl by telling her that the festival is only called Easter, not Easter bayram, whereupon a boy says Easter holidays.

387 Ew: **Easter** Bayram with Auntie, Easter Bayram
388 T: This is not Bayram, only Easter.
389 Ew: Easter
390 Bm: °Easter holidays°[642]

Without the researcher asking, the children tell her that they are Muslims, but have nevertheless received chocolate and sweets for Easter. The children are interested in the teacher's stories about other churches, they associate the ringing of the bell with the word "church".

In the Catholic kindergarten, children compare a child's henna-painted hands with tattoos given to them by the doctor or with paintings they paint on themselves with felt-tip pens.

4.2.2 Question of affiliation

How children address their own religion and religious expressions differs both between the two kindergartens and between the children of the major and the minor

---

640 Group discussion on the Koran lesson with Ew, Tw, Lw and Bm in the Islamic kindergarten, 38-46.
641 Group discussion on the Koran lesson with Sw and Nw in the Islamic kindergarten, 7.
642 Research diary, Islamic kindergarten, 387–390.

religions. While children of the major religion feel belonging to the religious offers of the respective kindergarten and participate in these, the children of the minor religions are often excluded from these. The desire for belonging becomes apparent in the children of the minor religions by not disclosing difference, remaining silent about their own religion and religious expressions and adapting their behaviour to the behaviour of the children of the major religion , whereas the children of the major religion do not ask themselves the question of belonging. This becomes clear when they reveal religious differences, address their own religion or religious expressions and confront children who are absent at festivals with their absence.

- Desire to belong
  - No disclosure of religious difference
  - Silence about one's own religion or religious expressions
  - Adaptation to the behaviour of the major religion

- Natural affiliation
  - Disclosure of religious differences
  - Thematisation of one's own religion or religious expressions
  - Inquiries to children absent at celebrations

Desire to belong

Children of the minor religion in the Catholic kindergarten do not talk about their own religion or religious expressions. Neither in their behaviour nor in their verbal communication does it become clear that they have a different religious affiliation and that certain Christian expressions do not correspond to those of their religion. The desire of the children of the minor religions to belong to this group can be seen in the lack of thematisation of religious forms of expression in kindergarten, which they experience differently at home, in the non-thematisation of their own absence in religious offerings, in silence about religious forms of expression and in adaptation to the behaviour of the children of the major religion .

No disclosure of religious difference
Children of the minor religions in the Catholic kindergarten neither address issues when they have been absent from festivals, nor do they ask questions in kindergarten that arise because of unknown religious expressions.

For example, children sometimes deny their absence at festivals or only quietly discuss them at the end of the conversation. Instead of addressing the fact that they have not been present at certain festivals, the children keep up the appearance of having been there. The Muslim children who were not present at the Feast of St. Martin's do not want to disclose this afterwards. This is made clear by the fact that they do not comment on their absence or only mention it quietly and cautiously towards the end of the conversation.

Children who are interested in the unfamiliar religious activities in kindergarten do not address this in kindergarten. For example, a Muslim girl in kindergarten does not talk about the sign of the cross, but tells about it at home.

Silence about one's own religion or religious expressions
The children of the minor religion in the Catholic kindergarten do not bring up their religious affiliation on their own in the kindergarten. The Muslim children in Catholic kindergarten do not mention any of the areas thematised by the Muslim children in the Islamic kindergarten. The festivals they celebrate or the practices they participate in at home are not even discussed, even if the teacher asks them to. If they know certain religious expressions based on tradition lived at home, this is not told to the others in the kindergarten. A Muslim girl mentions that she has already heard the story told during the Eid Al-Adha, but does not want to say from where.

The children of the minor religions in the Islamic kindergarten do not thematise their own religious affiliation, there is only a distinction that they are not Muslims or not a mosque and therefore do not participate in Koran instruction. They identify their own affiliation with their origin or language. Other religious expressions are not described by the Christian children in kindergarten.

3	I:	Who goes to Koran lessons?
4	Jw:	All of them, except me and Dw.
5	I:	Why do they all go and you don't?
6	Jw:	Because we're not a mosque. The others are mosques.
7	I:	What are you?
8	Jw:	Romanian and Dw is Polish.
9	I:	What does it mean that all the other children are mosques?
10	Jw:	They have to go **there** (she points in the direction of the Koran room)[643]

Adaptation to the behaviour of the major religion
In the behaviour of the children of the minor religions it is not recognisable that these belong to another religion. They adapt to the rituals lived in the kindergarten of the respective major religion, so that in the Catholic kindergarten, all children say the offered Christian prayers and adopt the same attitude of prayer by folding their hands. All children sing the same songs, design gifts for Christian festivals and are involved in the preparation of festivals for which they are assigned specific roles during dances or role plays. The festivals are celebrated equally by all children, provided that the children are not picked up in advance by their parents.

---

643 Group discussion on the Koran lessons with Jw and Pw in the Islamic kindergarten, 3–10.

Natural affiliation

The children of the major religion naturally take part in the offers prepared in the kindergarten. For the children in the Islamic kindergarten, it goes without saying that the majority of the group is Muslim and goes to Koran lessons. In the Catholic kindergarten, it is normal for all children to participate in the activities offered in the kindergarten; if a child does not participate, it is noticed by the children and the absence of the child is considered strange and the children have no explanation for it. If children of the major religion are prevented from certain offers, they bring this up for discussion, their affiliation does not seem to be called into question.

Disclosure of religious difference
The absence of the children at festivals of the minor religions or other activities is openly discussed. A child who did not mention her absence at St. Martin's for an extensive period of time states not having been present at the Eid Al-Adha because she had created her pre-school folder during this time.

```
61   I:    how did you enjoy the festival?
62   Mw:   no, because we weren't there
63   I:    why weren't you there
64   Mw:   I was at XXX
65   Pw:   I wasn't there either
[…]
68   Mw:   at the XXX too, we're making a pre-school folder[644]
```

The Christian children notice that they only celebrate the Eid Al-Adha in kindergarten and not at home. A child in the Catholic kindergarten notices that the director did not know anything about the festival either, but that it was on her calendar.

Thematisation one's own religion or religious expressions
Children of the major religion address their own religion or their religious expressions, even if this thematisation differs between the children in the Islamic and the Catholic kindergarten. The Muslim children in the Islamic kindergarten report on the teaching of the Koran, the mosque, the festivals they celebrate, as well as religious commandments. The Christian children in the Catholic kindergarten when asked about their religion, address the Christian festivals.

Inquiries to children absent at celebrations
In the Catholic kindergarten, the children of the major religion notice the absence of children at festivals and discuss this absence. For explanations, if they cite any, they suspect that a child is on holiday or sick and therefore cannot take part in the festival,

---

644 Group discussion on the Eid Al-Adha with Mw and Pw in the Catholic kindergarten, 61–65; 68.

once a conflict between a mother and a teacher was assumed as the reason for a child's absence.

37	Mw:	Hm. Her mother and what's her cousin's name said not to make the
38		sign of the cross going in and out because (.) and further I don't know.
39	I:	I: Why do you think she said that?
40	Mw:	I only heard that, I didn't hear anything else[645]

As evidence of the absence of children at festivals, the Christian children cite that the absent children did not stand in their designated place for a dance or that the child's lantern was still in kindergarten and not, as with all other children, already at home. Absent children are accused of not being present at the celebration in group discussions after the celebration. In the Catholic kindergarten, the theme of absence always refers to a single child. Some of the children are listed who generally did not attend kindergarten on that day and therefore did not take part in the celebration. After Easter, the researcher is asked why she was not present at Easter.

Only during a conversation about the Advent wreath do the children generalize and think that the elderly, the black and the poor do not own an Advent wreath because they are poor.

51	I:	Which people have no Advent wreath?
52	Fm:	The poor
53	Lm:	˪ The poor
54	Fm:	The poor and the black
[…]		
57	Fm:	Because they are poor (2)
58	I:	Why are they poor
59	Fm:	Because they have nothing. (2)
60	I:	Who does not yet have an Advent wreath?
61	Lm:	The elderly
62	Fm:	because they are also poor.[646]

4.2.3 Dealing with disagreements in discussions

The children deal differently with differences of opinion that arise in discussions. In some cases, differences of opinion are left uncommented next to each other. Children often try to resolve differences of opinion that arise in discussions, emphasising their own opinions or seeking unanimity. Differences of opinion occur especially when one child makes a statement about another child and that child contradicts it.

---

645 Group discussion on St. Martin's with Mw, Sw and Ew in the Catholic kindergarten, 37–40.
646 Group discussion on Advent wreath with Mw, Lm and Fm in the Catholic kindergarten, 51–54; 57–62.

- Emphasis of one's own opinion
  - Differentiation from what was said before
  - Conviction through argumentation
  - Presenting the teacher's differences of opinion

- Efforts to achieve unanimity
  - Giving in of a child
  - Creative explanation of disagreements
  - Complementing other children's ideas

Emphasis of one's own opinion

During the discussions, situations arise in which children have different opinions, which remain in the further course of the discussion.

Differentiation from what was said before
In some cases, the children set themselves apart from what was said before by emphasising that this does not apply to them. If the child makes a statement about himself or herself, this distinction is not called into question by the other children. Thus, in a conversation about the Advent wreath, a girl clearly distinguishes herself from the statements of the previous speaker, which is not commented on further.

Convincing through arguments
Some children try to support their own opinions with evidence and convince others of the correctness of their statements. Thus, the children justify a child's absence from the celebration by concrete evidence to prove his or her absence. The lantern, which is still in the kindergarten, serves as an indication of the girl's absence from the celebration or is referred to the girl's empty space at the dance of lights.

Presenting the teacher's differences of opinion
Another way of dealing with disagreements is to consult the teacher. In this way, children with different understandings of what is done in the Koran lessons, whether the Koran is read or learned, turn to the teacher, who is to determine the correct opinion.

Efforts to achieve unanimity
In other situations, children try to resolve differences of opinion so that there are no disagreements.

Giving in of a child
Disagreements can be resolved by one child agreeing with another child's opinion. Grammar improvements are taken over by children and sometimes children can be persuaded by their kindergarten mates and change their mind.

Creative explanation of disagreements
In some of the conversations, children try to clarify differences of opinion in a creative way. For example, one girl tries to clarify the difference of opinion about the presence or absence of another child by the fact that this girl, who is convinced of her presence, may have celebrated at home and thus only thinks she was at the kindergarten.

In another disagreement over the location of the celebration of St. Martin's, one girl says that the celebration took place in the garden, whereas another girl claims that the celebration took place in the church and then connects the two opinions in such a way that she believes that the celebration took place first in the church and then in the garden.

Complementing other children's ideas
In some conversations, the children take up ideas of other children and continue them, as for example in the conversation of the children about the Advent wreath.

4.2.4 Children's aspirations of belonging

The aspirations of children of the minor religions to belong – The natural affiliation of children of the major religion

Children notice religious differences due to different religious expressions, and the communication about them differs between children of the major and the minor religions in the respective kindergarten. Children of the major religion, where relevant to them, express themselves about their own religion and religious expressions and show interest in religious difference. Children of the minor religions do not address their own religion and religious expressions, and they tend not to differ in their behaviour from children of the major religion,[647] making their religious difference unrecognisable in kindergarten. The children who show interest in religious difference in the category "Relevance of religious difference"[648] are exclusively children of the major religions, whereby especially the children of the major religion in the Islamic kindergarten naturally address religious difference and are interested in religious difference.

While the children of the major religion together with their religious expressions feel belonging to the kindergarten, children of the minor religions are silent about their religion and their religious expressions and do not stand out in their religious difference. Children of the major religion address their own religion much more frequently than children of the minor religion. Thus, Muslim children in the Islamic kindergarten often express themselves about their religion and their religious expressions and ask questions about other religions, whereas Muslim children in Catholic kindergarten do not mention their own religion or religious expressions and do not ask questions about other religions in kindergarten. Children of the minor religions in Catholic

---
647 Cf. chapter "Question of affiliation" (part V, 4.2.2).
648 Cf. chapter "Relevance of religious difference" (part V, 4.2.1).

kindergarten do not differ in their behaviour from children of the major religion, so the same prayers are said, the same festivals are celebrated and the children's parents take part in the religious offers, unless they decide that they may not participate in certain festivals. The desire for the children of the minor religions to belong can be seen in the fact that this difference is not revealed: they do not thematise the fact that they were not present at festivals and if they are approached by children of the major religion, they deny having been absent.[649] The children of the minor religions do not thematise their own religious affiliation or religious expressions, even if the teacher invites them to.[650] The self-evident affiliation of children of the major religion is demonstrated by revealing[651] behaviours that differ from others and by asking questions to children who have not participated in certain activities and accuse them of having been absent.[652] There are connections between the aspirations of the children of the minor religions or the natural affiliation of the children of the major religion and the communication and behaviour of the children.

4.3 Overview of the two core categories

**Relationship between the dominance of the major religion
and the aspirations of children to belong**

In the last step of the evaluation, parallels between the two core categories "dominance of the major religion – little recognition of the minor religions" and "striving for belonging – self-evident belonging" are presented.

In both kindergartens, children show a different dynamic in the thematisation of religion and religious difference. In the Islamic kindergarten, the children's dynamism in addressing religion and religious difference is not used, whereas in the Catholic kindergarten, the children have no dynamics in addressing religion or religious difference. In both kindergartens there are no structures as to how religious difference is recognisable and how it is thematised, and the directors and teachers of the kindergartens have no concept of how to thematise religious difference in kindergarten.[653] Although the teachers express themselves positively towards religious difference, there is no discussion of the minor religions or religious difference except for a few tentative efforts. The dominance of the major religion in kindergarten is expressed in the fact that everyday kindergarten life is shaped by it, the recognisability of religious difference is minimised and communication about it is largely avoided, which

---

649 Cf. chapter "Question of affiliation" (part V, 4.2.2).
650 Cf. ibid.
651 Cf. section "Disclosure of difference" in chapter "Question of affiliation" (part V, 4.2.2).
652 Cf. section "Inquiries to children absent at celebrations" in chapter "Question of affiliation" (part V, 4.2.2).
653 Cf. chapter "Conceptual reflections on religion and religious difference" (part V, 4.1.1).

becomes clear in the categories "recognisable elements of religious difference"[654] and "communication about religious difference".[655] Despite the dominance of the major religion in kindergartens, there are situations in which children notice religious difference. The children's communication about recognised religious differences differs between the children of the two kindergartens and between the children of the major and the minor religions. Children of the major religion refer to recognisable elements of religious difference in the Islamic kindergarten, mediated in everyday kindergarten life, in the Catholic kindergarten in consciously initiated group discussions or at home. Children of the minor religions do not seem to see kindergarten as the place where religious difference or their own religion can be thematised. The minor religions is only recognisable in the respective kindergarten to the extent that the children concerned are not allowed or do not participate in something. Neither the teachers nor the children discuss their own religious expressions or customs in kindergarten. The children of the minor religions in kindergarten cannot experience their own religion as an enrichment, but exclusively as a deficit. The desire to belong to the respective dominant major religion, as is the case in both kindergartens, is expressed by children of the minor religions not thematising religious difference as well as their own religion or religious expressions and adapting their behaviour to that of children of the major religion.[656] Children take the price of telling untruths for the sake of belonging and not being noticed. Thus, the children of the minor religions do not differ in their behaviour from the children of the major religion. This behaviour is consistent with the structure of the kindergarten, where the major religion dominates and the minor religions are not recognised.

---

654 Cf. chapter "Recognisable elements of religious difference" (part V, 4.1.2).
655 Cf. chapter "Dominance of a religion" (part V, 4.1.4).
656 Cf. chapter "Question of affiliation" (part V, 4.2.2).

Part VI: Discussion

> "The empirical approach is aimed at describing and explaining hermeneutic-communicative practice as it actually proceeds [...]. In this context, however, it is also oriented towards examining and changing this practice by shifting its boundaries towards the [...] normative and eschatological perspective [...]. The empirical results of this research must finally be evaluated in the light of hermeneutic-communicative practice [...]."[657]

In the context of the two core categories possible connections can be seen: The organisation of kindergarten with the respective organisational culture and the children's desire for belonging, which is expressed in dealing with and in the thematisation of religious difference by the children, seem to be connected, which suggests an appropriate meaning of the organisation. "Educational science and sociology as well as educational research in general observe educational processes at different levels: at the macro level of society, at the meso level of organisations, and at the micro level of interactions [...]".[658] But the level of the organisation of the kindergarten and its influence has not been considered in any of the previous studies on religious difference in the field of early childhood education.[659] The studies outlined in the state of research focus on the one hand on the statements of the children or the teachers (micro level) and the wider environment of society (macro level). Therefore, in the following explanations, the organisation (meso level), which alongside the actors in kindergarten and society is an essential factor for dealing with religious difference and which is inseparably interwoven with the micro and macro levels, is examined in more detail on the basis of the research results.

1. The kindergarten as an organisation

The concept of organisation used in the following is based on the institutional concept of organisation, which directs the view of the entire system.

> "The concept of institutional organisation not only reveals the organisational structure, the formal order, but also the whole social structure, the planned order and unplanned

---

657 Ven, Johannes A. van der (²1994): Entwurf einer empirischen Theologie. Kampen: Kok [1990], 89f.
658 Brüsemeister, Thomas (2008): Bildungssoziologie. Einführung in Perspektiven und Probleme. Wiesbaden: VS Verlag für Sozialwissenschaften, 11.
659 Cf. part II "State of research".

processes, the functions but also the dysfunctions of organised work processes, the emergence and change of structures, the goals and their contradictions."[660]

Schreyögg names three central elements of an institutional concept of organisation.[661] Organisations pursue a "specific purpose orientation", which does not need to be identical to the purposes of the organisation members. As a rule, organisations pursue "several, partially contradictory goals".[662] In addition, organisations have a "regulated division of labour" and "consist of several persons (or more precisely: of actions of several persons) whose task activities are shared and coordinated according to a certain pattern [...]".[663] Organisations are structurally organised and have "persistent boundaries" that enable a distinction to be made between the internal and external organisational world. This boundary is deliberately established and shows a certain stability.[664]

The outlined presentation of the institutional concept of organisation makes it clear that early childhood institutions are organisations. In addition to the propagated and necessary view of the child in early childhood institutions, this view of the organisation must be promoted.

1.1 Organisation and environment

"Systems constitute and maintain themselves by creating and maintaining a boundary (a difference) to the environment in the form of generalised expectations of behaviour. Once the system has created the border itself, it can change or remove it at any time, at least in principle. In relation to the organisation, this means that it determines, through its specific differentiation, what the environment is to it, in particular which segments of the environment are more important and which are less, which links between certain parts of the environment are important, etc."[665]

Edgar H. Schein identifies the establishment of boundaries and the identification of relevant environments as one of the greatest difficulties of organisations.[666]

With regard to early childhood institutions, the global environment in particular, and in this case the political-legal environment and the socio-cultural environment,[667] has an influence on the organisation, whereas the organisation can also influence the

---

660 Schreyögg, Georg (^{3}1999): Organisation. Grundlagen moderner Organisationsgestaltung. Mit Fallstudien. Wiesbaden: Gabler [1996], 10.
661 Ibid., 9f.
662 Ibid., 9.
663 Ibid.
664 Ibid., 10.
665 Ibid.
666 Schein, Edgar H. (^{3}1980): Organizational Psychology. Englewood Cliffs/New Jersey: Prentice Hall [1965], 188.
667 The technological, ecological and macroeconomic environment can also have an influence on early childhood institutions , cf. Schreyögg, Georg (1999): Organisation, 312f.

environment. "Constructing early childhood education and care services as democratic and social spaces for autonomy, belonging and connectedness, also means connecting to the local social and cultural context in which the institution is placed."[668]

1.2 Kindergarten as a social space

Organisations can reflect social tendencies. Early childhood institutions are democratic and social spaces interwoven with local social, cultural and religious contexts. For example, society's attitude towards religions or religious differences can influence the organisation of kindergartens. In 2010, a survey was conducted in Germany, the Netherlands, France, Denmark and Portugal to gauge the feeling of the population towards other religions. The question was asked whether there are reservations about the foreign immigration or whether diversity is seen as an opportunity and how high the acceptance of non-Christian communities is. About 1,000 people in each country provided information. In comparison, the "attitude of Germans towards foreign religious communities, especially Islam [...] is much more critical than in all other countries studied".[669] Religious diversity was seen by the majority as the cause of conflicts. "While most Europeans see religious diversity as a cultural enrichment, only just under half of Germans agree."[670] This critical view of religious diversity in society can mean that in kindergartens, which are a reflection of society, religious difference is met with scepticism. A legal equality of different churches and religious societies does not guarantee the same degree of social recognition.[671] The significantly larger number of children of Muslim parents enrolling in a Catholic kindergarten than the number of Christian children enrolling in an Islamic kindergarten could be a reflection on the society's attitude toward Christianity or Islam.[672] The social recognition of the different religions is also reflected in the recognisability of the different religions in public space. In his ethnographic research project on religious diversity in urban space, Martin D. Stringer identifies four themes on the basis of which everyday, uninitiated religious diversity is discussed. These topics relate to clothing, buildings and

---

668 Kjørholt, Anne Trine (2011): Rethinking young children's rights for participation in diverse cultural contexts. In: Kernan, Margaret/Singer, Elly (Ed.): Peer Relationships in Early Childhood Education and Care. London/New York: Routledge, 38–48, 46.
669 Pollack, Detlef/Friedrich, Nils (2013): Religiöse Vielfalt – Bedrohung oder Chance. *Forschung. Spezial Demografie 38*(1), 34–37.
670 Ibid., 36.
671 Cf. Jäggle, Martin (2007): Religiöse Pluralität in Europa – Religionen – Religionslosigkeit. In: Bock, Irmgard/Dichtl, Johanna/Herion, Horst/Prügger, Walter (Ed.): Europa als Projekt. Berlin: LIT, 51-67, 52.
672 Cf. chapter "Framework conditions" (part V, 2.1.3 and 2.2.3). This statement is a conjecture that is not anchored in the data.

the built environment, street festivals and recent media events.[673] In Austria, Christian festivals are present in public space and are announced by decorations, whereas other festivals are not present. This means that the children cannot experience them, unless other children or adults thematise them. In this respect, the recognisability of religions in the public can influence what concerns children and what they thematise. Thus, Christianity is highly perceptible in public space due to various festivals and the church buildings, while other religions, if the gaze is not consciously directed at them, cannot be perceived by the public. Even if the (religiously) plural society is the context of Europe,[674] one's own environment is generally perceived as monoreligious or even monoconfessional, since the other religious communities are ignored.[675]

1.3 Family and family environment

"Children generate the image of the world from the information, images and experiences available to them in their immediate environment."[676] In addition to their recognisability in public spaces, children's attitudes are significantly influenced by influences and caregivers outside kindergarten, such as their parents:[677]

> "In socialisation, the family plays a prominent role. Parents are still the strongest identification partners for the growing child. In their ability to provide a space of affection and solidarity that is constitutive for individual identity building, the family is hardly replaceable."[678]

The importance of parents is also emphasised in the Tübingen study, whose title "Auf die Eltern kommt es an!" (It depends on parents!)[679] already expresses this.

---

673 Cf. Stringer, Martin D. (2013): Discourses on Religious Diversity. Explorations in an Urban Ecology. Farnham: Burlington, 29.
674 Cf. Jäggle, Martin (2007): Religiöse Pluralität in Europa. In: Bock, Irmgard et al. (Ed.): Europa als Projekt, 51–67, 59.
675 Cf. ibid., 58; Jäggle, Martin (2006): Schritte auf dem Weg. In: Bastel, Heribert et al. (Ed.): Das Gemeinsame entdecken – Das Unterscheidende anerkennen, 31–42, 32.
676 Gramelt, Katja (2010): Der Anti-Bias-Ansatz. Zu Konzept und Praxis einer Pädagogik für den Umgang mit (kultureller) Vielfalt. Wiesbaden: VS Verlag für Sozialwissenschaften, 127.
677 Depending on the family situation, different persons can be the close caregivers of the child.
678 Mette, Norbert/Steinkamp, Hermann (1983): Sozialwissenschaften und Praktische Theologie, 60.
679 Biesinger, Albert/Edelbrock, Anke/Schweitzer, Friedrich (Ed.) (2011): Auf die Eltern kommt es an!. In the qualitative part of the study, 44 interviews were conducted with parents of children attending various day care centres (Braun, Anne/Blaicher, Hans-Peter/ Haußmann, Annette/Wissner, Golde/Ilg, Wolfgang/Biesinger, Albert/Edelbrock, Anke/ Kaplan, Murat/Schweitzer, Friedrich/Stehle, Andreas (2011): Was Eltern erwarten und

"All in all, it becomes clear that interreligious education in the day care centre really depends on parents. The work with the children in the facilities can and should be accompanied by a parallel offer for parents. Many educational tasks can only be successfully taken up if the work is directed at children and parents at the same time. And last, but not least: This can also be a decisive enrichment for the entire facility!"[680]

The culture and religion of the respective family influence the children's world. In early childhood institutions, both parents and teachers are responsible actors in a common task,[681] whereby parents can be involved in the pedagogical work of early childhood institutions.[682] The exchange between parents and teachers, as well as an insight into the children's world are prerequisites for pedagogically appropriate action,[683] "[...] practitioners must endeavour to work in partnership with the child's family in an atmosphere of mutual respect [...]".[684] Educational partnership involves working together to ensure the best possible development of the child, which may include the joint search for child-compatible expressions and communication on religious aspects that appear negative for the child's development. However, this educational partnership can prove difficult in religious matters. Lisa Lischke-Eisinger's[685] study shows that the experi-

---

erfahren – Religiöse und interreligiöse Bildung in der Kita aus Elternsicht. In: Biesinger, Albert/Edelbrock, Anke/Schweitzer, Friedrich (Ed.): Auf die Eltern kommt es an!, 43–120, 45). In the quantitative part, 6,000 questionnaires were sent in German and 1,200 in Turkish. 590 parents filled out the questionnaire, which is why it is not possible to speak of representative results. (Braun, Anne et al. (2011): Was Eltern erwarten und erfahren. In: Biesinger, Albert/Edelbrock, Anke/Schweitzer, Friedrich (Ed.): Auf die Eltern kommt es an!, 43–120, 88–90).

680 Biesinger, Albert/Schweitzer, Friedrich (2011): Wer Kinder religiös und interreligiös fördern will, muss ihre Eltern in der Kommunikation mit ihnen unterstützen. In: Biesinger, Albert/Edelbrock, Anke/Schweitzer, Friedrich (Ed.): Auf die Eltern kommt es an!, 203–206, 206.

681 Cf. principles of Reggio pedagogy.

682 Cf. de Graaff, Fuusje/van Keulen, Anke (2008): Making the road as we go. Parents and professionals as partners managing diversity in early childhood education. The Hague: Bernard van Leer Foundation.

683 Cf. Biesinger, Albert/Edelbrock, Anke/Schweitzer, Friedrich (2011): Preface. In: Biesinger, Albert/Edelbrock, Anke/Schweitzer, Friedrich (Ed.): Auf die Eltern kommt es an!, 9–11, 9.

684 Karstadt, Lyn/Medd, Jo (2000): Children in the family and society. In: Drury, Rose/Miller, Linda/Campbell, Robin: Looking at Early Years Education and Care. Professional roles in early childhood. London: David Fulton Publishers, 35–40, 35.

685 Lisa Lischke-Eisinger's work focuses on teachers as professionals in the field of early childhood education . On the basis of interviews with kindergarten teachers, the question "how the requirements and objectives formulated in the education plan are interpreted and experienced in practice and what challenges they pose for the individual educators" is examined. (Lischke, Eisinger, Lisa (2012): Sinn, Werte und Religion in der Elementarpädagogik. Religion, Interreligiosität und Religionsfreiheit im Kontext der Bildungs- und Orientierungspläne. Wiesbaden: Springer VS, 17).

ence of working with parents differs greatly from teacher to teacher.[686] Among some teachers, uncertainties and negative feelings predominate and successful conversations rarely occur. Inhibitions to seeking a conversation with parents about their religious and ideological attitudes become noticeable. The dialogue between kindergartens and homes seems to be difficult for teachers to initiate.[687] When conversations take place, some parents do not readily agree to tell about their own religion. Thus it was also difficult in the Catholic kindergarten to find a person to make the Eid Al-Adha accessible to the children.[688] The Tübingen study also shows that only 22 percent of the parents who completed the questionnaires imagine telling about their religion in the children's group, for 59% this is not at all or not very true.[689] The reason for this may be that many Muslim parents do not feel able to teach their child the Islamic faith, as the research project of Haci-Halil Uslucan shows. Thus in North Rhine-Westphalia, 27.3 percent of the parents questioned thought they could teach their children the Islamic faith themselves, while 70 percent did not believe they were capable of doing so.[690]

1.4 The kindergarten as a learning organisation

Every organisation, including every early childhood institution, is interdependent with the environment.[691] At the same time, each organisation is in itself a learning organisation with a momentum of its own in which developments and changes are possible, provided that the organisation members are open to them. Burkard Sievers emphasises that

> "organisations can ultimately only be successfully changed in the sense of organisational development if the roles of organisational members are also included in such a change. However, since roles – as already mentioned – form the point of intersection or link between personal and social systems, a change of roles can only occur through corresponding simultaneous processes of change or learning of the personal and social systems or persons and organisations involved."[692]

---

686 Cf. Lischke-Eisinger, Lisa (2012): Sinn, Werte und Religion in der Elementarpädagogik, 384.
687 Cf. Ibid.
688 Cf. Group discussion with teachers in the Catholic kindergarten, 230–237.
689 Cf. Braun, Anne et al. (2011): Was Eltern erwarten und erfahren. In: Biesinger, Albert/ Edelbrock, Anke/Schweitzer, Friedrich (Ed.): Auf die Eltern kommt es an!, 43–120, 101.
690 Cf. Uslucan, Haci-Halil (2008): Religiöse Werteerziehung in islamischen Familien. Commissioned by: Federal Ministry for Family Affairs, Senior Citizens, Women and Youth. Berlin, 35.
691 Cf. chapter "Kindergarten as a social space" (part VI, 1.2) and chapter "Family and the family environment" (part VI, 1.3).
692 Sievers, Burkard (2000): Organisationsentwicklung als Lernprozeß personaler und sozialer Systeme – oder: Wie läßt sich OE denken? In: Trebesch, Karsten (Ed.): Organisationsentwicklung. Konzepte, Strategien, Fallstudien. Stuttgart: Klett-Cotta, 33–49, 42.

There is no generally accepted definition of the term organisational development[693].[694] For Edgar Schein, organisational development is above all a philosophy, a perspective and an attitude towards human systems and human problems[695] and at the same time scientific in that the processes are emphasised. Burkard Sievers emphasises the importance of learning of the organisation in organisational development.

> "Organisational development can be understood as a strategy or program for initiating, controlling and guaranteeing complex learning processes of system change and development. [...] Organisational development is a strategy through which the organisation aims to learn through the organisation of learning."[696]

Learning processes can only be achieved if "members as individuals" and "the organisation as a system" are included.[697] Organised learning covers both individual changes in behaviour on the part of members' personal systems and the social system of the organisation.[698] If organised learning processes

> "also refer to the organisation as a social system and its structures, processes and subsystems, i.e. insofar as the process of organised learning is oriented towards the learning of the organisation, such learning can be understood as optimising the potential of organisations to solve problems."[699]

According to Gerhard Fatzer, the most important goal of organisational development is to make organisations capable of learning or to free correspondingly blocked resources.[700] Transformation of the organisation is a main goal of organisational development. Fatzer cites the following basic principles: dual objectives (performance, improvement of the quality of working life), long-term, participatory, process-oriented approach, diagnosis, rolling planning, feedback, conflict management and holistic approach.[701]

---

693 See Cummings, Thomas G. (Ed.) for a discussion of the different perspectives on organisational development (2008): Handbook of Organization Development. Thousand Oaks/London/New Delhi/Singapore: Sage Publications.
694 Trebesch, Karsten (2000): 50 Definitionen der Organisationsentwicklung. In: Trebesch, Karsten (Ed.): Organisationsentwicklung, 50–62, 53.
695 Cf. Schein, Edgar H. (2000): Organisationsentwicklung: Wissenschaft, Technologie oder Philosophie?. In: Trebesch, Karsten (Ed.): Organisationsentwicklung, 19–32, 31.
696 Sievers, Burkard (2000): Organisationsentwicklung. In: Trebesch, Karsten (Ed.): Organisationsentwicklung, 33–49, 48.
697 Cf. ibid., 44.
698 Cf. Ibid., 45.
699 Ibid.
700 Cf. Fatzer, Gerhard (1993): Organisationsentwicklung als Beitrag für die lernfähige Organisation. In: Fatzer, Gerhard (Ed.): Organisationsentwicklung für die Zukunft. Ein Handbuch. Cologne: Edition Humanistische Psychologie, 125–127, 125.
701 Fatzer, Gerhard (1993): Einleitung. Organisationsentwicklung und ihre Herausforderungen. In: Fatzer, Gerhard (Ed.): Organisationsentwicklung für die Zukunft, 13–34, 23.

> "Learning is the detection and correction of error. An error is any mismatch between our attentions and what actually happens. […] Behind this view of learning is a view of human nature and organizations. Human beings design their intentions and their actions. They are designing systems. Organizations design their strategies and they design the implementation of the strategy."[702]

1.5 Organisational culture – Kindergarten culture

Organisational development is oriented towards the idea of learning, innovation, adaptation and change in response to constantly changing technological, social, economic and political conditions. As a stabilising force in human systems, culture is one of the most difficult aspects to achieve. The challenge is to conceptualise a culture in which innovation, learning, adaptation and change are stable elements.[703] Schein defines the culture of a group as shared basic assumptions that the group has learned in solving problems.

> "A pattern of shared basic assumptions that the group learned as it solved its problems of external adaptation and internal integration, that has worked well enough to be considered valid and, therefore, to be taught to new members as the correct way to perceive, think, and feel in relation to those problems."[704]

Edgar Schein distinguishes several levels on which a culture can be analysed: the level of artefacts, the level of values and the level of basic assumptions. The artefacts on the surface include all phenomena that can be seen, heard and felt when encountering a new group with an unknown culture.[705] These artefacts refer to a value or belief that, if shared by the members, can be called a "shared value" or "belief" and suggests underlying basic assumptions.[706] The values of the founder become the basis of the corporate culture, – if the company is successful. To understand a corporate culture, it is therefore best to look at the history and personal values of the company's founder.[707] The basic assumptions are often implicit and, as overarching standards that are not formally passed on, control the behaviour of the organisation members.[708]

---

702 Argyris, Chris (^{2}1999): On Organizational Learning. Malden/Oxford/Carlton: Blackwell Publishing [1992], 165.
703 Cf. Schein, Edgar. H. (^{2}1992): Organizational Culture and Leadership. San Francisco: Jossey-Bass, xiv.
704 Ibid., 12.
705 Ibid., 17.
706 Ibid., 19.
707 Cf. Schein, Edgar H. (2009): Führung und Veränderungsmanagement. Bergisch Gladbach: Andreas Kohlhage, 27.
708 Cf. Kauffeld, Simone/Ebner, Katharina (^{5}2014): Organisationsentwicklung. In: Schuler, Heinz/Moser, Klaus (Ed.): Lehrbuch Organisationspsychologie. Bern: Hans Huber ^{5}2014, 457–507, 465.

> "Basic assumptions, like theories-in-use, tend to be those we neither confront nor debate and hence are extremely difficult to change. To learn something new in this realm requires us to resurrect, reexamine, and possibly change some of the more stable portions of our cognitive structure […]."[709]

Such learning is difficult because re-examining the basic assumptions destabilises the cognitive and interpersonal world and triggers basic fears.[710]

> "The culture of an organisation and its visible and unconscious facets have a great influence on the members of the organisation: they serve as standards of behaviour, provide orientation and ultimately create identity. The culture is lived by members of an organisation – even if they are not aware of all facets […]."[711]

The content of the organisational culture reflects the problems affecting each group, "dealing with its external environment [...] and managing its internal integration [...]".[712]

Taking into account the findings on the organisational culture, it can be assumed that the culture that can be found in the kindergarten influences the behaviour of those involved in the kindergarten. Due to the visible artefacts and the conscious values, it can be concluded that the basic assumptions were not consciously reflected. Thus, in kindergarten, where the children and parents of the minor religions say nothing about their own religion, adapt to the expressions of the larger, dominant religion and try not to attract attention,[713] no culture of recognition of religious difference could be developed. This is expressed in visible artefacts and conscious values of which the unconscious basic assumptions can be concluded. If the topic of religious difference is omitted by teachers in early childhood institutions,[714] this visible artefact can lead to the basic assumption that religious difference is of little importance in kindergarten. For children and parents, the barrier to address religious difference is higher if religious difference does not play a role in the culture of the organisation and is not addressed, if the opportunities of religious difference are not anchored in the artefacts, the values or the unconscious basic assumptions, but is experienced exclusively as a problem. If the culture of the kindergarten excludes the positive view and the dealing with religious difference, it is up to the children to find their way of coping in such a culture. In this study, the children of the minor religions remain silent about their own religion or their

---

709 Schein, Edgar. H. (1992): Organizational Culture and Leadership, 22.
710 Cf. ibid.
711 Kauffeld, Simone/Ebner, Katharina (2014): Organisationsentwicklung. In: Schuler, Heinz/Moser, Klaus (Ed.): Lehrbuch Organisationspsychologie, 457–507, 466.
712 Schein, Edgar. H. (1992): Organizational Culture and Leadership, 49.
713 Cf. chapter "Overview of the two selective codes" (part V, 4.3).
714 Cf. chapter "Dominance of a religion" (part V, 4.1.4).

own religious expressions.⁷¹⁵ A similar trend can be seen in Julia Ipgrave's⁷¹⁶ research project, in which thirteen to seventeen-year-old schoolgirls reacted with silence to the teasing of classmates about their religion or religious habits. The pupils were not excluded from school, but their religion, an important area in their lives, did not occur in everyday school life.⁷¹⁷ Religious children sometimes feel unable to communicate the importance of their faith at school.

> "In one school participating in a recent Warwick project, for example, it was noticed that the evangelical Christian students did not talk about their religion in class. Their teachers observed that 'they generally keep their head down' or 'we try to give them a chance to say their piece in lessons [but] they're usually quiet.'"⁷¹⁸

If an organisation tries to acknowledge religious difference, it may be easier for children and parents to address their own religion and religious expressions if they so wish. The importance of organisational culture becomes clear in a conversation with Hopi children, which was recorded by Robert Coles⁷¹⁹. He had conversations with Hopi children at a school, where the children were not with the heart. He was told by a Hopi mother that his prolonged presence would make the children even less willing to give answers and the children at school won't ever want to talk about "the private events of their lives in this building. They learn how to read and write here; they learn their arithmetic here, but that is that. You are asking them about thoughts they put aside when they enter this building."⁷²⁰ He then visited the children in their home, where after one or two months the children made a different impression, they smiled, started conversations and showed him places that were important to them.⁷²¹

> "Here, for example, is what I eventually heard (in 1975) from a ten-year-old a Hopi girl I'd known for almost two years: 'The sky watches us and listens to us. It talks to us and it hopes we are ready to talk back. The sky is where the God of the Anglos lives, a teacher told us. She asked where our God lives. I said, 'I don't know'. I was telling

---

715 Cf. chapter "Children's aspirations of belonging" (part V, 4.2.4).
716 Cf. Ipgrave, Julia (2014): Relationships between local patterns of religious practice and young people's attitudes to the religiosity of their peers. In: Arweck, Elisabeth/Jackson, Robert: Religion, Education and Society. London/New York: Routledge Taylor & Francis Group, 13–25.
717 Cf. ibid., 18.
718 Ipgrave, Julia (2013): The Language of Interfaith Encounter. *Religion & Education 40*(1), 35–49, 47.
719 Robert Coles had conversations with children from different countries, where the children went at least to primary school, but were not yet in high school. These religious testimonies of mostly eight- to twelve-year-old and some six- or thirteen-year-old children were collected by him over thirty years and described in his work "The Spiritual Life of Children" (cf. Coles, Robert (1990): Boston: Houghton Mifflin Company)
720 Ibid, 24.
721 Cf. ibid., 25.

the truth! Our God is the sky, and lives wherever the sky is. Our God is also the sun and the moon, too and our God is our [the Hopi] people, if we remember to stay here [on the consecrated land]. This is where we're supposed to be, and if we leave, we lose God'. *'Did she also explain the above to the teacher?' 'No.' 'Why?' 'Because – she thinks God is a person. If I'd told her, she'd give us that smile.'* 'What smile?' 'The smile that says to us, 'You kids are cute, but you're dumb; you're different – and you're all wrong![...]'."[722]

In these situations it becomes clear that this Hopi girl excludes from school what she thinks and only at home does she open up with what she is concerned with. The culture of the school, which becomes clear to the child in the artefact of "that smile" and which is based on the value behind it and its basic assumptions ("you kids are cute, but you're dumb", "that you're different and you're all wrong", "they don't listen to hear us"). In an organisation where the child assumes exactly that, it is not surprising if he or she does not communicate about anything that occupies him or her.

This raises the question of which measures can bring about positive changes so that each child feels recognised in his or her own individuality in kindergarten and experiences it as an organisation in which the topics that concern him or her are given a recognised space. Taking into account the importance of organisation and organisational culture, the development of early childhood institutions seems necessary to contribute to an organisation and organisational culture that opens up an area of recognition of religious difference.

2. Plea: Development of a culture of recognition of religious difference

In the kindergartens, due to the dominance of the respective major religion, an organisational disadvantage of the children of the minor religions becomes apparent. This must be counteracted and a space made available to the children in which they can thematise their religion or religious attitudes. The procedure in the kindergartens, in which the respective major religion is preferred, can be seen as discrimination,[723] since children of the major religion are provided with different possibilities of belonging and religious education compared to the children of the minor religions. This is alarm-

---

722 Ibid., 25. Italics by the author.
723 The Vienna Anti-Discrimination Act prohibits direct and indirect discrimination and harassment of natural persons on the grounds of ethnicity, religion, belief, disability, age, sexual orientation, gender identity and gender, in particular also on the grounds of pregnancy and parenthood, as well as the incitement of a person to such discrimination. Cf. Gesetz zur Bekämpfung von Diskriminierung (Wiener Antidiskriminierungsgesetz) (Law to Combat Discrimination, Vienna Anti-Discrimination Act), Paragraph 2, City Administration of Vienna: http://www.wien.gv.at/recht/landesrecht-wien/rechtsvorschriften/html/i5000000.htm [21.07.2015]).

ing because children are entitled to non-discrimination. This is also being followed up in the debate on inclusion.[724]

In view of the results of the present study, considerations are given below as to how the development of a culture of recognition and thus the overall development of early childhood institutions can be promoted so that this can do justice to children and their religious differences in the best way. The culture of the organisation and the thematisation of religious difference by the children seem to be related, which is why the development of a culture of recognition of people with their religious affiliation and their religious difference is the basis for an equal treatment and can form the basis so that children of the minor religions also feel belonging to the kindergarten in their religious difference and they can thematise religious difference, if it concerns them.[725]

In order to realise a culture of recognition in early childhood institutions, it is necessary to develop early childhood institutions that follow school development processes.[726] In the area of school development, a distinction can be made between organisational development, teaching development and personnel development.[727] This division into three parts is transferred to early childhood institutions. The view on the development of organisations, personnel and teaching offers seems to be an important basis for pedagogical and religious pedagogical action in early childhood institutions, which has been given too little consideration in previous work in the field of early childhood institutions.[728]

Based on the empirical findings, these three areas are subdivided to reflect on the process of developing a culture of recognition of people of all religions and religious differences in early childhood institutions.

The development of a culture of recognition can take place in a kindergarten that is regarded as a learning organisation. General patent recipes are not possible, since pedagogical and religious pedagogical action is characterised by acting context-sensitive. "School development" is always a process over a longer period of time. Time and energy are important factors that should be taken into account at the design stage.[729] The three areas of organisational development, personnel development and teaching

---

724 Cf. Prengel, Annedore (2010): Inklusion in der Frühpädagogik. Bildungstheoretische, empirische und pädagogische Grundlagen. Munich: Deutsches Jugendinstitut e. V. (DJI); Pithan, Annebelle/Schweiker, Wolfhard (Ed.) (2011): Evangelische Bildungsverantwortung: Inklusion. Ein Lesebuch. Münster: Comenius-Institut.
725 Cf. chapter "Overview of the two core categories" (part V, 4.3).
726 Cf. Dalin, Per/Rolff, Hans-Günter/Bucher, Herbert (^{4}1998): Institutioneller Schulentwicklungs-Prozeß. Ein Handbuch. Soest: Verlag für Schule und Weiterbildung [1990].
727 Cf. Rolff, Hans-Günter/Buhren, Claus G./Lindau-Bank, Detlev/Müller, Sabine (^{4}2011): Manual Schulentwicklung. Handlungskonzept zur pädagogischen Schulentwicklungsberatung (SchuB). Weinheim/Basel: Beltz [1998], 14.
728 Cf. chapter "Research results on dealing with religious difference" (part II, 1).
729 Schley, Wilfried (1998): Schule als lernende Organisation. In: Altrichter, Herbert/Schley, Wilfried/Schratz, Michael (Ed.): Handbuch zur Schulentwicklung. Innsbruck/Vienna: Studienverlag, 13–53, 27.

development cannot be clearly distinguished from one another; the areas are interdependent and influence one another, so that change at one level can also contribute to change at another level, because these are systemically linked to one another.[730]

2.1 Organisational development

2.1.1 Developing the kindergarten as a *safe space*

> "[Children] will always need safe places for learning. They will always need launching pads from which to follow their curiosity into the larger world. And they will always need places to make the transition from their childhood homes to the larger society of peers and adults."[731]

The concept of *safe space* can be helpful to enable educational institutions to deal constructively with difference. Due to the different understandings, the term safe space, as it is to be understood here, must be clearly distinguished from other uses: It is not based on the understanding of safe spaces, in which spaces are required in which disadvantaged persons are separated from each other and from other persons. This understanding of safe spaces is demanded by different organisations and wants to help people to be among themselves and not to be discriminated against. However, fears and a clear distinction from others often determine behaviour in such areas. Such a separation makes it difficult for educators in educational contexts to respond appropriately and constructively to cases of discrimination and insults.[732]

In contrast to this, the concept of safe spaces, as used here, wants to be a metaphor for spaces in which difference is permitted and in which this openness and appreciation is shown. In order to enable learning with and from each other, spaces are necessary in which difference is permitted, sensitively perceived and thematized.

An early childhood education that is oriented towards the metaphor *safe space* provides an environment in which to express, explore, communicate, tell and hear difference, promote dialogue-oriented ways of learning and can contribute to reconciliation away from hatred and violence.

---

730 Cf. Rolff, Hans-Günter/Buhren, Claus G./Lindau-Bank, Detlev/Müller, Sabine (2011): Manual Schulentwicklung, 15–18.
731 Senge, Peter/Cambron McCabe, Nelda/Lucas, Timothy/Smith, Bryan/Dutton, Janis/Kleiner, Art (2012): Schools that learn. A Fifth Discipline Fieldbook for Educators, Parents, and Everyone who Cares About Education. New York: Crown Business, 4.
732 Stengel, Barbara S.: The Complex case of Fear and Safe Space, in: Studies in Philosophy and Education 29/6 (2010) 523–540, 524–528.

"Organising a 'safe space' can allow a school to:
- provide a secure environment to foster self-expression;
- explore differences outside a context of insecurity, fear and tension;
- share, tell and listen without ready-made statements;
- foster dialogue-oriented ways of learning;
- begin a process of reconciliation free from hatred and violence."[733]

The concept of *safe space* can be a principle for dealing with diversity, including religious difference in early childhood institutions, and can contribute to an atmosphere in which difference is addressed without hurting each other.

"The concept of 'safe space' is a guiding principle for intercultural activities in the classroom. It can create an atmosphere where differences can be expressed without hurting 'the Other'. It means to provide space for equal participation, to foster self-expression, for sharing stories and for mediating conflicts."[734]

Educational institutions can be places, *safe spaces*, in which dealing with religious diversity can be learned and thematised.

"The school is a potentially 'safe place' where respectful and intelligent dialogue about religious and worldview issues can be learned and experienced. […] The whole school culture needs to be modified through the co-operation of staff, pupils, and parents in order to define and justify ideals of mutual understanding and respect and to plan ways of approaching them."[735]

Organisations have a groundbreaking responsibility to work with all stakeholders to show respect for diversity. "The socially valuable good that schools and other educational institutions have to distribute out of their own power and resources is called 'intersubjective recognition' of each individual person in their unique situation in life".[736] In organisations such as schools or early childhood institutions, children can be encouraged to meet, learn from each other and practice solidarity, respect for diversity and democratic skills.

"[The school] may be one of the most important institutions we have to help us build a democratic conversation about the future. A physical, local school where community members are encouraged to encounter each other and learn from each other is one of the last public spaces in which we can begin to build the intergenerational solidarity,

---

733 Schreiner, Peter (2007): A "safe space" to foster self-expression. In: Keast, John (Ed.): Religious diversity and intercultural education: a reference book for schools. Strasbourg: Council of Europe Publishing CDED, 57–66, 58.
734 Ibid.
735 Schihalejev, Olga (2014): Contextuality of young people's attitudes and its implication for research on religion: a response to Julia Ipgrave. In: Arweck, Elisabeth/Jackson, Robert: Religion, Education and Society, 27–30, 29.
736 Prengel, Annedore (2006): Pädagogik der Vielfalt, 61.

respect for diversity and democratic capability needed to ensure fairness in the context of sociotechnical change. Moreover, the public educational institution may be the only resource we have to counter the inequalities and injustice of the informal learning landscape outside school."[737]

The study by Avest and Miedema[738] also points to the importance of a safe learning environment in which children can feel the basic principles of living together. "Remarkable in our empirical data is that both teachers in their subjective educational theories and independent of the denominational religious identity of the school, emphasise the need of a safe learning environment in order to learn to live together in a multi-ethnic and multi-religious society."[739]

2.1.1.1 *Safe space* for addressing religious difference

Communication is a key factor in organisational development[740] and plays a key role in dealing with religious difference.[741]

> "Communication is nothing static, nothing that will ever be ready, no attainable, satisfying final state, no creatable paradise that only needs to be defended and maintained. Communication is always in flux, an open process, permanently endangered in its existence by many turbulences."[742]

Religious difference increases the need for communication about religion and religions.[743] People get to know each other in dialogue. "Otherness is not threatening, but awakens the desire for communication. It is precisely because one or the other is different that we need communication."[744] Kindergarten as a place of communication

---

737 Facer, Keri (2011): Learning Futures. Education, technology and social change. London: Routledge, 28.
738 ter Avest, K.H. Ina/Miedema, Siebren (2010): Learn Young, Learn Fair. Interreligious Encounter and Learning in Dutch Kindergarten. In: Engebretson, Kath/de Souza, Marian/Durka, Gloria/Gearon, Liam (Ed.): International Handbook of Inter-religious Education. Part One. Dordrecht/Heidelberg/London/New York: Springer, 513–527; ter Avest and Miedema give an insight into religious education in an Islamic and a Protestant primary school in the Netherlands, where the children were four and five years old.
739 Ibid., 522.
740 Doppler, Klaus (2000): Kommunikation als Schlüsselfaktor der Organisationsentwicklung. In: Trebesch, Karsten: Organisationsentwicklung, 281–307.
741 Cf. chapter "Verbal communication about religious difference" (part V, 4.1.3).
742 Doppler, Klaus (2000): Kommunikation als Schlüsselfaktor der Organisationsentwicklung. In: Trebesch, Karsten: Organisationsentwicklung, 281–307, 306.
743 Cf. Jäggle, Martin (2007): Religiöse Pluralität in Europa. In: Bock, Irmgard et al. (Ed.): Europa als Projekt, 51–67, 57.
744 Prengel, Annedore (2006): Pädagogik der Vielfalt, 56. Annedore Prengel formulates this in reference to Guzzoni, Ute (1981): Identität oder nicht: zur kritischen Theologie der

implies the possibility for discussions between teachers and children without concrete instructions or intentions.[745] In many situations in kindergarten, communication about religious difference, fears and desires is an opportunity to get to know each other, oneself and the different religions better and to consider design forms in kindergarten together. Discussions between the teachers, with the directors, with the parents and with the children promote an open approach to religious difference. If the people working in the kindergarten have different religious affiliations, communication about their different religious traditions makes sense in the kindergarten.

> "Conflict theories have taught us that there is a need to create a space and atmosphere of safety and security if a constructive dialogue is to take place between those who are different from each other."[746]

The present study refers to the tendency to focus exclusively on the major religion, but not on the minor religions and religious differences.[747] Mecheril and Plößer come to the conclusion, in their analysis of social-constructivist[748] and deconstructive[749]

Ontologie. Freiburg i. Br.: Alber, 343.

745 Singer and de Haan realised in their study that few educators participated in children's conversations during lunchtime or free play time, but mostly talked to a single child by giving instructions or asking the child about food wishes or offering toys. Cf. Singer, Elly/de Haan, Dorian (2011): Fostering a sense of belonging in multicultural childcare settings. In: Kernan, Margaret/Singer, Elly (Ed.): Peer Relationships in Early Childhood Education and Care. London/New York: Routledge, 88-101, 96. In the study, too, the teachers rarely talk to the children without a connection to a specific assignment or offer.

746 Schreiner, Peter (2007): A "safe space" to foster self-expression. In: Keast, John (Ed.): Religious diversity and intercultural education, 57–66, 58.

747 Cf. chapter "Dominance of a religion" (part V, 4.1.4).

748 In the social constructivist view of difference, differences are understood as socially generated. "Social constructivist research is therefore not about the recognition/identification of differences and identities caused by differences, but about the investigation of processes in which social realities are produced by recourse to categories of differences." Educational organisations and pedagogical actors can ask themselves "to what extent they themselves are involved in 'doing difference', what attributions they make, how they make difference and thus inequality in their daily and necessarily recognising work through salutations, assignments, diagnoses, spatial settings, etc. [...] Because 'doing difference' always also means 'doing inequality', it is ultimately necessary to examine which resources are available to the subjects (especially in those identity positions which are not the predominant and not the privileged) for their representational work, or how pedagogy can advocate their accessibility or their valorisation". (Mecheril, Paul/Plößer, Melanie (2009): Differenz. In: Andresen, Sabine et al. (Ed.): Handwörterbuch Erziehungswissenschaft, 194–208, 200–202).

749 The deconstructive view of difference is more interested "in the political effects that an affirming, differences confirming approach brings with it. [...] Deconstructive strategies thus question the symbolic order itself; they aim at the multiplication of identities and the extraction of identity logics from dichotomous and oppositionally structured patterns of

approaches, that the practices of fading out difference criticised in research on differences and in the pedagogies of difference make it clear that the consideration and recognition of difference is necessary.[750]

> "A pedagogy related to difference and diversity has to do with dilemmas. Educational processes (re-)produce inequalities in a context preformed by differences, if these differences are not recognised and acknowledged. On the other hand, the recognition of differences reproduces power relations in two ways: The recognition of others (e.g. the recognition of gay or lesbian lifestyles) acknowledges others that they could only become in a hierarchical order (e.g. heterosexism), whereby paradoxically this hegemonic order is confirmed. Recognition as a practice of identification always goes hand in hand with the problem of definition; it is a medium of self- and external identification inherent in a moment of classifying violence."[751]

This dilemma

> "is constitutive for the connection between difference and pedagogy. In this respect, the relationship between difference and pedagogy is not about the question: 'Difference: yes or no', but an experiential reflection on how differences are thematised pedagogically in such a way that as a consequence of this thematisation less power over others is required."[752]

Against this background and the results of the study, which show that religious difference can be discernible in kindergarten,[753] the question arises as to which thematisation is conducive to recognition of a culture. Only differences that are recognisable in kindergarten or that are thematised can be recognised. Religious difference is often overlooked in organisations, which is strange in view of the openness towards cultural

---

difference. At the same time, they sensitize the reader to the stipulation that accompanies each differentiation and motivate a critical-reflective handling of one's own (pedagogical) actions, norms and rules, insofar as these are always also used to update current orders and produce exclusions [...]". Thus, on the one hand, deconstructive strategies "make it possible to question the binary framework of difference, both by demonstrating its violent character and by giving 'it's right' to the forms of life that are regarded as different, abnormal, indeterminate or unliveable. On the other hand, the demands for reproduction, indeterminacy and liquefaction threaten to negate such everyday worldly self-understandings of individuals who, by asserting their essential identity as 'women', 'gays' or 'Turks', do not conform to the new fluid ideal of identity." (Mecheril, Paul/Plößer, Melanie (2009): Differenz. In: Andresen, Sabine et al. (Ed.): Handwörterbuch Erziehungswissenschaft, 194–208, 202–205).

750 Cf. Mecheril, Paul/Plößer, Melanie (2009): Differenz. In: Andresen, Sabine et al. (Ed.): Handwörterbuch Erziehungswissenschaft, 194–208, 205.
751 Ibid., 206.
752 Ibid.
753 Cf. chapter "Recognisable elements of religious difference" (part V, 4.1.2).

difference, and can have an impact on[754] everyday life in the organisation. As difference is recognised in the organisations, it can gain significance for the child's own contact with difference. Children and adults belonging to a religion are also different in their religiousness, which can be seen in different forms of expression. Children experience difference in their lives and that they do not fit in everywhere. The kindergarten offers the opportunity to make this experience in *safe space* and to work through it with the children. "From a perspective of recognition of difference, it is therefore necessary to stand up for structures in which individuals can live and also change their social subject status."[755] Anchoring the handling of religious difference in the organisation relieves the teachers on whom the responsibility rests as to whether and how religious difference is dealt with in kindergarten and how this is recognisable. Even if perfect justice can never be achieved in kindergarten, it is important to strive for it and to develop a *safe space* in which children are recognised in their individuality and their difference and in which they can address topics that concern them. "While most early childhood settings appear to be calm and friendly places on the surface, there may be a great deal of underlying inequality in practice, as both adults and children inevitably bring with them own perceptions and prejudices to the setting and in their interactions with one other."[756] A culture of recognition "in which the other can remain in its otherness and is not made sublimely uniform to one's own"[757] would be a goal perspective.

> "When the attitude of recognition of the separateness and uniqueness of individuals determines the climate of a study group, community emerges. Intersubjectivity arises from subjectivity. Each person's attention to his or her own specificity awakens the ability to become aware of the specificity of others. Common ground is created by 'processes of transition between the heterogeneous'"[758]

Anchoring forms of dealing with and addressing religious difference in the organisation influences a culture that is characterised by openness and recognition of religious difference. An action is performed in a specific environment within which the situation

---

754 Cf. Jäggle, Martin (2000): Wie nimmt Schule kulturelle und religiöse Differenz wahr? Grundsätzliche Vorbemerkungen und Einblick in ein Forschungsprojekt in Wien. In: Porzelt, Burkard/Güth, Ralph (Ed.): Empirische Religionspädagogik, 119–138, 120.
755 Mecheril, Paul/Plößer, Melanie (2009): Differenz. In: Andresen, Sabine et al. (Ed.): Handwörterbuch Erziehungswissenschaft, 194–208, 198f.
756 Ang, Lynn (2010): Critical perspectives on cultural diversity in early childhood: building an inclusive curriculum and provision. *Early Years: An International Research Journal* *30*(1), 41–52, 48f.
757 Mette, Norbert (2005): Einführung in die katholische Praktische Theologie, 59.
758 Prengel, Annedore (2006): Pädagogik der Vielfalt, 186.

of action is interpreted.[759] The respective context can influence which difference and how children address difference.[760]

> "From a pedagogical perspective, which advocates the recognition of difference and thus of the capacity to act of others, it must be noted that capacity to act depends on social contexts which correspond to the capacity to act of the individual."[761]

An early childhood education oriented on the metaphor of *safe space* can be a place where children are recognised in their uniqueness and difference, including religious difference, and where religious difference can be addressed.

2.1.1.2 *Safe space* for minor religions

The recognition of the cultural and religious background of children is important for the identity development of children, both of the major and minor religions.

> "Two objectives of educational activities in school are to provide support for identity formation and to foster mutual understanding. This necessitates a clear recognition of the cultural and religious background of the pupils and students in school because this is an important part of an identity for both minorities and for the majority in a society."[762]

As the study has shown, unlike children of the major religion, the children of the minor religions do not express themselves about their religion or their religious expressions[763] and their religion is given little attention by the organisation of the kindergarten and in the behaviour of the teachers.[764] This silence of the children of the minor religions about their religion can also be seen in other research projects. "In a classroom where the majority are Christian, there may be the tendency for those of other religions to

---

759 Cf. Collmar, Norbert (2004): Schulpädagogik und Religionspädagogik. Handlungstheoretische Analysen von Schule und Religionsunterricht. Göttingen: Vandenhoeck & Ruprecht, 34.
760 For example, Robert Jackson's study shows the link between attitudes to religious diversity and places of young people in the UK. "Place makes a big difference to young people's attitudes to religious diversity in the UK." Cf. Religion and Society, http://www.religionandsociety.org.uk/uploads/docs/2012_12/1355390760_Jackson_Phase_2_Large_Grant.pdf [07.02.2014].
761 Mecheril, Paul/Plößer, Melanie (2009): Differenz. In: Andresen, Sabine et al. (Ed.): Handwörterbuch Erziehungswissenschaft, 194–208, 198.
762 Schreiner, Peter (2007): A "safe space" to foster self-expression. In: Keast, John (Ed.): Religious diversity and intercultural education, 57–66, 57.
763 Cf. chapter "Question of affiliation" (part V, 4.2.2).
764 Cf. chapter "Dominance of a religion" (part V, 4.1.4).

fall silent, so these students need to be given an equal platform with their peers."[765] In her research project in Estonia, Olga Schihalejev also notes the tendency not to reveal her own religious attitudes but to keep them private.[766] "Religiously affiliated students valued […] preferred mostly to use a code of conduct to keep their religious convictions private."[767] Julia Ipgrave's research project also reveals a strong contrast between contexts in which religious expression behaviour is kept away from interaction and those in which it is valued and allowed to make a contribution to life at school. This has an impact not only on personal well-being, but also on the general well-being of the school communities, which benefit from the full participation of the members.

> "There is a sharp contrast between contexts where religious expression is stigmatised and excluded from teenage interaction and those where it is valued and permitted to contribute to the life of school. The issue is not just the personal well-being of individuals who might be marginalised or discriminated against (although that is of concern), but also the general well-being of school communities that seek to include and benefit from the full participation of all members."[768]

Inclusion and integration, not assimilation are required. Religious students should have the opportunity to address their religious perspective and not hide it.

> "Cohesion and diversity require inclusion and integration, but not assimilation; as different members of society come together, they should retain the distinctions that constitute diversity. These distinctions run deeper that mere identity-signifiers (Sikh, Christian, Muslim), they entail strongly felt reasons and motivations. Therefore, "religious' students should not have to put aside their religious perspectives to engage with their peers and those peers have an obligation (in the interests of inclusion) to be responsive to them and their contributions."[769]

A community can only be diverse if young people with different religious and ideological convictions share their experiences with their colleagues and contribute to public discourse through their religiousness.[770] Barbara Asbrand emphasises the importance of the fact that one's own religion may occur in the organisation. She states that it is of fundamental importance for all children, and in particular for children belonging to the minority, that their experiences from their family context and also their religiousness

---

765 Engebretson, Kath (2009): In your shoes: inter-faith education for Australian religious educators. Ballan: Connor Court Publishing, 166.
766 Cf. Schihalejev, Olga (2010): From Indifference to Dialogue? Estonian Young People, the School and Religious Diversity. Münster et al.: Waxmann.
767 Ibid., 151.
768 Ipgrave, Julia (2014): Relationships between local patterns. In: Arweck, Elisabeth/Jackson, Robert: Religion, Education and Society, 13-25, 23.
769 Ibid.
770 Cf. ibid., 24.

occur in class.[771] Children have similarities in other areas, so they do not have to be on the level of religion. The commonalities of the children are sought on a level other than religion. Similarities can be found in their individual life histories and children's relationships with their environment, while differences are at the level of religions.[772]

The different ways of life have to be discovered in relation to religion, to give them a language and to recognise their value. The realisation that ignoring difference (e.g. in school) leads to the production of inequality and confirms inequalities, promotes the demand for sensitivity to differences and heterogeneity.[773]

In her formulated theses on difference, Annedore Prengel states that difference[774] is not simply there, but that the lifestyles that do not belong to the dominant culture have been silenced, repressed, marginalised, devalued, exploited. Therefore, different ways of life must always be rediscovered, brought to their own language and acknowledged in their value.[775]

Children have the right to address their respective religions and their religious expressions and not to have to assimilate to the habits of the dominant religion in the respective context. Children are confronted with different religious symbols, traditions and forms of action and have a need for appropriate information and participation. When children of different world religions live together in the group, the children have a right to be heard and told about their respective traditions.[776]

This is to be clearly distinguished from forcing children to tell something about their religion or to view them as representatives of the respective religion, who are constantly asked about their own religion.

> "Many children are excited to share their family religious or spiritual practices and traditions, and encouraging them can be easy. Others might not be as comfortable. Many children say they feel burdened or singled out by teachers who ask them many questions about their religion as a means to inform the group. Being from a Muslim

---

771 Cf. Asbrand, Barbara (2008): Zusammen leben und lernen im Religionsunterricht. Eine empirische Studie zur grundschulpädagogischen Konzeption eines interreligiösen Religionsunterrichts in der Grundschule. Frankfurt am Main: Verlag für Interkulturelle Kommunikation, 172.
772 Cf. Ibid., 229.
773 Cf. Mecheril, Paul/Plößer, Melanie (2009): Differenz. In: Andresen, Sabine et al. (Ed.): Handwörterbuch Erziehungswissenschaft, 194–208, 197.
774 Prengel, Annedore (2006): Pädagogik der Vielfalt, 181–184. For a summary, see chapter 1.9. "Plurality – Difference" in the present study.
775 Cf. Prengel, Annedore (2006): Pädagogik der Vielfalt, 183.
776 Cf. Habringer-Hagleitner, Silvia (2006): Zusammenleben im Kindergarten, 337.

family, for example, does not necessarily make the child a representative or spokesperson for the entire religion."[777]

A culture of recognition in kindergarten goes hand in hand with structures in kindergarten within which it is possible to address one's own religion and religious expressions. In dealing with different religions and the openness towards the thematisation of different religions, no group may be ascribed an otherness.

> "Based on theoretically informed reading of our ethnographic data, we suggest that some students and staff members are Otherised in the interreligious encounters in schools. We also argue that the conditions of dialogue are different for those who are constructed as Others. Finally, such Othering that is related to unproblematised notions about religion and dialogue works against the aims of togetherness and mutual learning of interreligious dialogue."[778]

The discussion of religious difference must not lead to a negative attribution of otherness and thus to the establishment of an identity of another person.

> "According to the credo of difference-sensitive approaches, justice does not come about if the multiplicity of life situations, assets, needs and identities are measured by a single yardstick. […] the 'otherness' of minorities, their linguistic and cultural lifestyles, will be judged by the majority as a deficiency."[779]

Difference can be used to devalue or exclude other children, any characteristic of the child can lead to devaluation and exclusion.[780] Possibly, children experience in early childhood institutions,

> "that certain ways of being (symbolised through appearance, clothes, possessions, activities etc.) are favoured over others, that certain language groups are more valued than others, that certain family compositions are more 'normal' than others or that certain expectations of a 'polite attitude' are more appreciated than others."[781]

---

777 Follari, Lissanna (2015): Valuing Diversity in Early Childhood Education. Boston et al.: Pearson Education, 175.
778 Riitaoja, Anna-Leena/Dervin, Fred (2014): Interreligious dialogue in schools: beyond asymmetry and categorisation? *Language and Intercultural Communication 14*(1), 76–90, 77.
779 Mecheril, Paul/Plößer, Melanie (2009): Differenz. In: Andresen, Sabine et al. (Ed.): Handwörterbuch Erziehungswissenschaft, 194–208, 199.
780 Cf. Wagner, Petra (2010): Vielfalt und Diskriminierung im Erleben von Kindern. In: Wagner, Petra (Ed.): Handbuch Kinderwelten, 56–71, 58.
781 Cf. Woodhead, Martin (2008): Identity at birth. In: Brooker, Liz/Woodhead, Martin (Ed.): Developing Positive Identities, 4.

This can become particularly difficult if a group – consciously or unconsciously, openly or hidden – is not accepted. Children of minor religions often tell of negative experiences that they have because of their religious affiliation.[782]

> "While some children are valued and sought after because of the ways their religion is different from the majority of the class, many more children share stories of feeling marginalised and made fun of because of foods, dress, prayers or modesty values which set them apart from other children."[783]

Discrimination against children in certain areas can have a negative impact on the child's development.[784] "Action directed at changing discriminative attitudes and promoting positive self-identity in minorities must be directed at all institutions that make up our society. Child care centres may be especially important as it is during the pre-school years when attitudes towards outgroup members first form."[785] Two fundamental dimensions of social recognition are self-recognition and recognition by others, whereby self-recognition can only develop in structures of recognition by others.[786] The uniqueness of individuals must be recognised.

> "If the recognition of the other is a necessary pole for the subject's self-knowledge and recognition in social life, if the commitment to one's own identity must necessarily run through, 'unconditional solidarity' with the others, then a distinction from others cannot in any way be justified philosophically or theologically. In this case, such a possibly powerful distinction from others is not a model for identification processes. And then the plurality of religious positions provides an opportunity to perceive others as people in their otherness and to embark on a path of mutual recognition."[787]

If the children's religion and the resulting religious difference have no place in the kindergarten – if it is important to them – a part of them has no place.

Characteristics of belonging are produced through the formation of social differences, which is why affiliations must always also be negotiated.[788] In addition to the

---

782 Abo-Zena, Mona M. (2012): Faith from the fringes: Religious minorities in school. *Kappanmagazin 93*(4), 15–19.
783 Follari, Lissanna (2015): Valuing Diversity in Early Childhood Education, 176.
784 Cf. resilience research.
785 Perlman, Michal/Kankesan, Tharsni/Zhang, Jing (2010): Promoting diversity in early child care education. *Early Child Development and Care 180*(6), 753–766.
786 Cf. Mecheril, Paul/Plößer, Melanie (2009): Differenz. In: Andresen, Sabine et al. (Ed.): Handwörterbuch Erziehungswissenschaft, 194–208, 198.
787 Gutmann, Hans-Martin/Weiße, Wolfram (2010): Einleitung. In: Weiße, Wolfram/Gutmann, Hans-Martin (Ed.): Religiöse Differenz als Chance?, 7–14, 9.
788 Cf. Riegel, Christine/Geisen, Thomas (2007): Zugehörigkeit(en) im Kontext von Jugend und Migration – eine Einführung. In: Riegel, Christine/Geisen, Thomas (Ed.): Jugend, Zugehörigkeit und Migration. Subjektpositionierung im Kontext von Jugendkultur,

criteria of belonging, it is also negotiated what consequences it has in each case if someone is regarded as belonging or is excluded as not belonging, which can entail different possibilities for action and perspectives for shaping one's way of life.[789] Which role the question of affiliation plays depends on whether a person experiences himself as belonging or not.

> "Even if the examination of affiliations is relevant for all people, it is always very different – depending on the (affiliation) context and the social and biographical positioning. However, for those whose affiliation is taken for granted, the question of affiliation plays a different role than for those whose affiliation is controversial or even rejected. Thus, the topic becomes relevant above all for those who are categorised as "others" and not recognised as belonging."[790]

Kindergartens can be oriented on the metaphor of *safe spaces* in which children can address what concerns them and are recognised. This includes that one's own religious affiliation is not experienced as a deficiency, in that this is only recognisable in the non-participation in certain offers,[791] but the development of structures in kindergarten, which enable the children to experience their religious affiliation as a resource, which can be thematised in kindergarten and can contribute a part to living together in kindergarten.

2.1.1.3 *Safe space* for participation of children

The study shows a tendency to ignore the perspective of the children in contrast to the challenges that arise in everyday kindergarten life and not to pay attention to the children's perspective in conceptual considerations. Dealing with religious difference in kindergarten is not influenced by what children need in relation to religious difference, but is initially focused on the challenges that may arise due to religious difference and attempts are made to avoid them.[792]

Children comment on topics that concern them, they like to be asked for their opinion and deal with questions that go beyond the immanent, which is illustrated by the results of several studies. Thus Jan W. van Deth, Simone Abendschön, Julia Rathke and Meike Vollmar[793] focus their research on young children and their polit-

---

Ethnizitäts- und Geschlechterkonstruktionen. Wiesbaden: VS Verlag für Sozialwissenschaften, 7–23, 7.
789 Cf. Ibid.
790 Ibid., 8.
791 Cf. chapter "Question of affiliation" (part V, chapter 4.2.2).
792 Cf. chapter "Conceptual reflections on religion and religious difference" (part V, 4.1.1).
793 van Deth, Jan W./Abendschön, Simone/Rathke, Julia/Vollmar, Meike (2007): Kinder und Politik. Politische Einstellungen von jungen Kindern im ersten Grundschuljahr. Wiesbaden: VS Verlag für Sozialwissenschaften.

ical knowledge, abilities and orientations.[794] The interviews[795] showed that young primary school children already have political knowledge, skills and orientations and are enthusiastic when their opinions are of interest.[796] Whether topics are known is hardly influenced by age and gender.[797] Children differ in their assessment of religious forms of expression and action and have different knowledge of them.[798] Lena Haug's study, in which 230 children between the ages of four and ten painted pictures of their future ideas, also shows that children are concerned about political issues.[799] In further studies, in which children were asked about the values of society, children expressed their opinions.[800] With regard to religious difference, children have different religious frameworks of orientation, which is expressed in different knowledge about religion and religious difference.[801] While some children know a lot about their own religion, other children tell nothing about their own religion. In the study „Gemeinsamkeiten stärken – Unterschieden gerecht werden" (Strengthen commonalities – do justice to differences), children answer the questions asked about differences in Christian denomination, but do not talk about differences between religions, from which Schweitzer derives a clearly limited religious orientation framework for children, which does not mean, however, that religious affiliations are or cannot become an object of children's reflection. He states that, under different conditions than in religious education in Baden-Württemberg, difference perception in childhood could

---

794 The close interweaving of religious and political issues plays an important role in religious education.
795 Following expert interviews, in-depth interviews were conducted with 21 six to seven-year-old children who were at the end of the last kindergarten year or at the end of the last school year. Subsequently, a children's questionnaire was developed, which was presented to children in 17 selected primary schools in Mannheim. In September/October 2004, 744 children were interviewed; in June and July, 725 children were interviewed. 634 children completed both questionnaires.
796 Cf. van Deth, Jan W. et al. (2007): Kinder und Politik. Politische Einstellungen von jungen Kindern im ersten Grundschuljahr, 22.
797 Cf. ibid., 210.
798 Ibid., 175. With regard to religious practices such as going to church or going to mosque, children's opinions are ambivalent as to whether this should be rewarded as good citizenship. Political issues and problems, which include issues such as wearing headscarves and migration, are less well known to children of Turkish origin and children from socio-economically weaker backgrounds than to children from other backgrounds.
799 Haug, Lena (2011): Junge StaatsbürgerInnen.
800 Cf. World Vision Kinderstudie 2013, http://www.worldvision-institut.de/kinderstudien-kinderstudie- 2013.php; LBS-Gruppe: LBS-Kinderbarometer Deutschland 2016: So sehen wir das! Stimmungen, Trends und Meinungen von Kindern aus Deutschland; Albert, Mathias/Hurrelmann, Klaus/Quenzel, Gudrun/TNS Infratest Sozialforschung (2010): Jugend 2010–16. Hamburg: Deutsche Shell Holding GmbH.
801 Cf. chapter "Relevance of religious difference" (part V, 4.2.1).

possibly go further,[802] which is supported by observations in Hamburg primary school education.[803] The religious orientation framework of the children in the kindergarten depends not only on the religious education of the children in the kindergarten but also on family contexts. It cannot be the point of religious education to hammer children with topics that do not interest them in their current phase of life, nor to deprive them of topics that concern them.

Considering the voice of kindergarten-age children in questions concerning children themselves can contribute to a culture of recognition.

> "Listening to young children offers children opportunities to participate in decision-making while at the same time learning a range of decision-making skills. They are not only expressing their perspectives of their experiences, but also learning how to listen respectfully to the views of others and to negotiate a way forward with those who hold competing or alternative views."[804]

Elisabeth Neurath emphasises the children's own perspectives which can advance the big picture of interreligious dialogue.[805]

Scheilke asks the question whether children first need an educational space in which they can develop their identity before they are confronted with an exciting pluralism?[806] On the one hand, there are views that children should first be at home in their own tradition and religion and their identity should be consolidated in it before they encounter other religions and traditions.[807] Rainer Möller points out that children can be overburdened by dealing with different religions. In order to avoid this, he proposes to first develop a reference to one's own religion by involving the children in the religious practice of their religious community before dealing with traditions and customs of other religions. Only in later childhood and adolescence should information about

---

802 Schweitzer, Friedrich (2009): Wie Kinder und Jugendliche religiöse Differenz wahrnehmen. In: Bucher, Anton A. et al. (Ed.): Jahrbuch der Kindertheologie: „In den Himmel kommen nur, die sich auch verstehen", 39–49, 45.

803 Cf. for example Jessen, Silke (2003): "Man redet viel über Gott und so ..." Schülermitbeteiligung im Religionsunterricht der Grundschule aus allgemein- und religionsdidaktischer Sicht. Münster et al.: Waxmann.

804 Lancaster, Penny Y. (⁵2010): Listening to young children: enabling children to be seen and heard. In: Pugh, Gillian/Duffy, Bernadette (Ed.): Contemporary Issues in the Early Years. Los Angeles/London/New Delhi/Singapore/Washington DC: Contemporary Issues in the Early Years [1992], 79–94, 80.

805 Cf. Neurath, Elisabeth (2009): „Wer früher stirbt, ist länger tot?" Was sich christliche und muslimische Kinder nach dem Tod erwarten. In: Bucher, Anton A. et al. (Ed.): Jahrbuch der Kindertheologie: „In den Himmel kommen nur, die sich auch verstehen", 60–70, 69.

806 Cf. Scheilke, Christoph Th./Schreiner, Peter (Ed.) (1994): Schule in multikultureller und interreligiöser Situation. Münster: Comenius-Institut, 4.

807 Cf. Evangelische Kirche in Deutschland (Ed.) (1994): Identität und Verständigung. Standort und Perspektiven des Religionsunterrichts in der Pluralität. Eine Denkschrift der Evangelischen Kirche in Deutschland. Gütersloh: Gütersloher Verlagshaus.

other religions be added.[808] The attempt to keep away children of other religions and to avoid thematising other religions in kindergarten are partly explained by processes of identification and the concern of confusing children in their identity formation.

On the other hand, importance is attached to getting to know and engaging in early dialogue with people of other religions and traditions.[809] It is emphasised that the determination of identity implies difference.[810] "I have argued that identities are forged through the marking of difference: [...] Identity, then, is not the opposite of, but *depends on*, difference."[811] The individuals are not fixed on a given identity of content, but *they* take part in a process of consciousness and will formation of an identity to be developed together,[812] which is never completed in life. The concern that having a confrontation with different religions too early could endanger the religious identity formation of the children or overburden the children can be refuted on the basis of the data obtained in this study. Children do not seem to be confused by the confrontation with different religions, but they can distinguish between "mine" and "yours". During the data collection, children were not irritated in any situation by the existence of other religions.[813] Either the existence of different religions is not thematised by the children and if they thematise these, preferably in the Islamic kindergarten, curiosity towards the other and the desire to know more about the other religion is the leading

---

808 Möller, Rainer (⁶2014): „Muss ich als Erzieherin auch religionspädagogisch qualifiziert sein?" Berufsrolle und religiöse Identität. In: Möller, Rainer/Tschirch, Reinmar (Ed.): Arbeitsbuch Religionspädagogik für ErzieherInnen. Stuttgart: Kohlhammer [2002], 13–60, 19.

809 The importance of dialogue is emphasised by various authors, although they also set different priorities. For a discussion of their positions see, for example, Asbrand, Barbara (2008): Zusammen leben und lernen im Religionsunterricht, 152–170; Bernhardt, Reinhold (2005): Pluralistische Theologie der Religionen. In: Schreiner, Peter/Sieg, Ursula/Elsenbast, Volker (Ed.): Handbuch Interreligiöses Lernen. Gütersloh: Gütersloher Verlagshaus, 168–178.

810 "On the one hand, this long-known insight that the determination of identity implies that of difference, has once again been remembered in the long term is, on the theoretical side, the philosophical and the like, which often operate as postmodern (e.g. by J.-F. Lyotard, J. Derrida and M. Foucault) and on the other hand to the different emancipation movements (e.g. the antiapartism movement, the feminist movement, the gay and lesbian movement)." (Mette, Norbert (2005): Einführung in die katholische Praktische Theologie, 73).

811 Woodward, Kathryn (1997): Concepts of Identity and Difference. In: Woodward, Kathryn (Ed.): Identity and difference. London/Thousand Oaks/New Delhi/Milton Keynes: Sage Publications in association with The Open University, 7–61, 29.

812 Cf. Mette, Norbert/Steinkamp, Hermann (1983): Sozialwissenschaften und Praktische Theologie, 44.

813 In a research project by Baumann, youths discussed religious ideas or festivals. They named the festival Divali a Hindoo Christmas, the Eid Al-Adha as the Muslim Easter. An imam or pandit were termed priests. Cf. Baumann, Gerd (1996): Contesting Culture. Discourses of Identity in Multi-Ethnic London. Cambridge: Cambridge University Press.

characteristic. A clear attribution of religious identity cannot take place,[814] since identity is never complete and no one is entitled to commit another person to one (religious) identity. Identity has to do with both subjective and social, psychological and intersubjective aspects.[815]

Structuring kindergarten as a *safe space*, by complementing the development of a culture of recognition with children's perspectives, can help to ensure that religious difference is experienced not exclusively as a challenge, but increasingly as an opportunity, both for the design of everyday kindergarten life and for (religious) identity development.

2.1.2 Support the development of the respective organisation

2.1.2.1 Support, advice and supervision of organisational development

Since organisational development is a long-lasting process, which is not completed by conceptual considerations,[816] support can be provided by a person not belonging to the organisation who, together with the members of the kindergarten, gets involved in the process and professionally accompanies it. In process consulting, the establishment of a helping relationship is important for Edgar Schein.[817] The personality of the participants, the group dynamics and cultural factors have an influence on process consulting, in which the decisive factor is the relationship between the person helping and the person seeking help.[818]

> "This means for me that we do not bring our customers a toolbox of advice and technology, but an attitude of questioning and investigation and a set of process intervention skills. It means that we identify the natural flow of these processes and go with it, that we maintain our flexibility and objectivity in order to intervene more effectively in the course of our own learning. We need to develop the observation and questioning skills of a good ethnographer and the intervention skills of a good analyst."[819]

The provision of advice for teachers and support for the process by outside persons who are involved in everyday life can be a helpful support for the development of

---

814 Asbrand, Barbara (2008): Zusammen leben und lernen im Religionsunterricht, 225.
815 Cf. Grümme, Bernhard (2012): Menschen bilden? Eine religionspädagogische Anthropologie. Freiburg i. Br.: Herder.
816 Cf. chapter "Conceptual reflections on religion and religious difference" (part V, 4.1.1). Although conceptual considerations and suggestions for change exist, these are not reflected in everyday kindergarten life.
817 Cf. Schein, Edgar H. (2003): Prozessberatung für die Organisation der Zukunft. Der Aufbau einer helfenden Beziehung. Bergisch Gladbach: Edition Humanistische Psychologie.
818 Cf. ibid., 297.
819 Schein, Edgar H. (2000): Organisationsentwicklung: Wissenschaft, Technologie oder Philosophie?. In: Trebesch, Karsten (Ed.): Organisationsentwicklung, 19–32, 28.

early childhood institutions by working out which areas could be further developed. Through support and external counselling services, the fears and concerns of the teachers and managers can be addressed, which can provide security in everyday kindergarten life in conflicts or challenging situations. This can reduce insecurity and fear[820] of talking to other people about religion and religious difference in kindergarten. Team meetings in which opportunities and challenges are discussed together, possibly with the involvement of a supervisor, make it clear that religious difference is not the concern of a single person in the kindergarten, but rather a common concern. Further training dedicated to the desires of a team can be context-sensitive to the specific kindergarten and its situation.

2.1.2.2 Support from the sponsorship and the management

Both the sponsorship and the management of the kindergarten have an influence on the dynamics of the respective institution.[821] An openness of the sponsorship for the discussion with religious difference can be an essential condition for an open and competent handling of religious difference in early childhood institutions . If, from the point of view of the sponsorship, religion generally has no place in everyday kindergarten life, or if only the religion or denomination of the sponsorship in kindergarten should be addressed and recognised, it is difficult to develop a difference-sensitive organisation in which those involved in kindergarten are open and give recognition to people of all religions. A sponsorship that promotes the importance of the discovery of religious difference and is prepared to recognise people of all religions, can form a good basis for a difference-sensitive approach in early childhood education. The sponsorship can sensitise for the meaning of the conscious perception, the argument and the topic of religious difference as well as encourage the teachers to participate in further training offers. The importance of support from the sponsors is also mentioned in the research project of Schweitzer, Edelbrock and Biesinger.[822]

2.1.2.3 Development of concepts for dealing with religious difference

Existing concepts focus on educational offers, and at times they also consider the personnel, but they ignore the level of the organisation that proves to be relevant with regard to how children address religious difference. The research results make it clear

---

820 Cf. section "Reasons for little thematisation of religious difference" (part V, 4.1.3).
821 Cf. chapter "Conceptual reflections on religion and religious difference" (part V, 4.1.1).
822 Cf. Blaicher, Hans-Peter/Haußmann, Annette/Wissner, Golde/Ilg, Wolfgang/Kaplan, Murat/Biesinger, Albert/Edelbrock, Anke/Schweitzer, Friedrich (2011): Interreligiöse Bildung in Kindertagesstätten in empirischer Perspektive. Vertiefte Auswertungen zur Tübinger Studie. In: Schweitzer, Friedrich/Edelbrock, Anke/Biesinger, Albert (Ed.): Interreligiöse und interkulturelle Bildung in der Kita, 147–222, 185.

that educational offers are only one part of a larger development affecting the entire kindergarten.[823] Interreligious concepts require a broader contextual framework in order to realise their intentions, which is why we need to look at the development of the entire kindergarten, which includes the sub-areas of the organisation, the staff and the educational offers.

Both Frieder Harz's[824] concept of interreligious learning, which favours the guest model for non-Christians or children without religious affiliation, and Matthias Hugoth's[825] concept sensitise for the perception of that children of different religious affiliations are in kindergarten and their religious background must be respected. They provide a variety of suggestions as to where interreligious learning is possible in kindergarten. On the basis of the present research results, in which the little thematisation of one's own religion by the children of minor religions becomes clear, greater consideration must be given to developing a culture of recognition in which children can thematise their religion and religious forms of expression, if they so wish. It requires the development of concepts that not only focus on the children and the teachers, but also on the organisation. Concepts that design the kindergarten as a *safe space* for the children and their themes can promote the recognition of children of all religions in kindergarten. The possibilities suggested by Frieder Harz[826] seem to be rather selectively anchored offers, with which children of the Christian religion can experience even the guest status.[827] Isolated offers are too few for experiencing religious difference;[828] rather, the self-evident thematisation of forms of expression of the minor religions would be desirable. Through the communicative involvement of all those involved in kindergarten activities, a concept for dealing with religious

---

823 Cf. chapter "Overview of the two core categories" (part V, 4.3).
824 Cf. Harz, Frieder (2001): Ist Allah auch der liebe Gott. Interreligiöse Erziehung in der Kindertagesstätte. Munich: Don Bosco; Harz, Frieder (2008): Religion in der interkulturellen Erziehung und Bildung. In: Hugoth, Matthias/Benedix, Monika (Ed.): Religion im Kindergarten. Begleitung und Unterstützung für Erzieherinnen. Munich: Kösel, 32–38; Harz, Frieder (2000): Kindergarten als Ort religiösen Lernens. *Zeitschrift für Pädagogik und Theologie 52*(4), 374–384; Harz, Frieder (2001): Feste der Religionen in der Kindertagesstätte. Professional roles in early childhood. *Theorie und Praxis der Sozialpädagogik 109*(4), 12–16.
825 Cf. Hugoth, Matthias/Benedix, Monika (Ed.) (2008): Religion im Kindergarten. Begleitung und Unterstützung für Erzieherinnen. Munich: Kösel; Hugoth, Matthias (2003): Fremde Religionen – fremde Kinder? Leitfaden für interreligiöse Erziehung. Freiburg i. Br.: Herder; Hugoth, Matthias (2012): Handbuch religiöse Bildung in Kita und Kindergarten. Freiburg i. Br.: Herder.
826 Harz, Frieder (2001): Ist Allah auch der liebe Gott, 128–137.
827 In her book, Doris Ziebritzki points out these possibilities of organising festivals where children of other religions are present as guests. Ziebritzki, Doris (2012): Wir wollen zusammen feiern. Feste der Weltreligionen im Kindergartenjahr. Freiburg/Basel/Vienna: Herder.
828 Cf. the celebration of the Festival of Eid Al-Adha or the clarification on the mosque in the Catholic kindergarten. Cf. chapter "Relevance of religious difference" (part V, 4.4.2).

difference can be developed. Once the concepts and the mission statement have been discussed, developed[829] and evaluated in a team, there is a good prerequisite for being supported by all those involved in the kindergarten.

2.1.3   Offer self-evaluation of the respective kindergarten

A self-evaluation of the respective kindergarten can help to identify areas in which further development of the kindergarten makes sense. John Keast and Heid Leganger-Krogstad prepared a checklist of key issues and questions for self-reflection that can help different educators identify their role in developing a suitable environment for teaching and learning.[830] The work "Religionspädagogische Kompetenzen" (Religious-educational competencies) by Biesinger and Schweitzer also contains a questionnaire that can help teachers reflect on their own practice in kindergarten and can be helpful in raising awareness of the importance of religious differences among teachers.[831] Since the checklist of Keast and Leganger-Krogstadt takes a closer look at the organisational level, it is used below as a basis for a checklist for the development of a culture of recognition in early childhood institutions. The questions are supplemented on the basis of the research results and adapted to the field of early childhood education from the perspective of religious difference.[832]

1. Ethos and values
- What is the value base of the kindergarten?
- Who defines and promotes these values?
- How do these values encourage and promote dialogue and respect?
- How do the values reflect the religious difference of the people in the kindergarten?
- Are these values publicised and agreed upon with parents, the society and the sponsorship of the kindergarten?
- How are the values that refer to religious difference part of the mission statement, the concept and the general vision of the kindergarten?

2. Educational policy
- How is religious difference taken into account and addressed in the admission of children to kindergarten?
- How far do policies promote values of religious difference and respect?
- To what extent does the kindergarten reflect the values of society?

---

829 Cf. Biesinger, Albert/Schweitzer, Friedrich (2013): Religionspädagogische Kompetenzen, 90–97.
830 Keast, John/Leganger-Krogstad, Heid (2007): Religious dimension of intercultural education: a whole school approach. In: Keast, John (Ed.): Religious diversity and intercultural education, 119–121.
831 Biesinger, Albert/Schweitzer, Friedrich (2013): Religionspädagogische Kompetenzen, 58f.
832 For use in early childhood institutions, it can be useful to select the questions that are most important for the respective organisation.

3. Kindergarten management
   - How does the kindergarten management take religious differences into account?
   - How does the sponsorship of the kindergarten influence the handling of religious difference?
   - To what extent does the kindergarten calendar reflect religious difference?
   - To what extent do holidays reflect the diversity of religious holy days?
   - To what extent is the religious difference in the range of meals offered in kindergarten considered?
   - How is the wearing of certain clothing or religious symbols dealt with?
   - How are conflicts and challenges arising from religious differences addressed?
   - To what extent is the difference between children in kindergarten taken into account in everyday kindergarten life?

4. Educational contents
   - How do educational opportunities deal with religious differences and how are they received by children?
   - How far is the kindergarten's tradition based on the dominant religion in the state?
   - When and in which areas is religious difference discussed?
   - To what extent are the regions represented in kindergarten addressed in educational programmes?
   - Which songs are sung in kindergarten?
   - What prayers are said in the kindergarten and what prayer posture is adopted?
   - What games are available in the kindergarten?
   - Which children participate in religious education of a particular religion and how do they participate in it?
   - Which children do not participate in religious education and how is this addressed?
   - How are the educational offers about religion and religious difference in kindergarten evaluated?

5. Religious education
   - How is religious education offered in kindergarten and how do children thematise the offer?
   - Which religions are addressed in everyday kindergarten life and why?
   - Which cooperations exist with religious communities?
   - To what extent is the religious background of the children taken into account?
   - To what extent are all religions seen to be on an equal footing in seeking truth?
   - To what extent is the religious development of the child seen as an objective of religious education?
   - To what extent is there a critical attitude towards religions?
   - How do children acquire knowledge about different religions?
   - How is the religious development of each child supported?

6. Education, training and further education
- How are teachers prepared to address religious difference?
- What opportunities are there for educators to educate themselves in relation to religious difference, and how are these opportunities taken advantage of?

7. Communication about religious difference[833]
- How is the cooperation with parents regarding religious differences?
- How and when do team meetings take place in kindergarten in which questions of religious difference are discussed?
- When do children address religious difference and how are children's themes addressed?
- How do arrangements take place with the sponsorship about religious difference?
- How do children and parents address their religious traditions and forms of expression in kindergarten?
- How do children and parents bring their desires for dealing with religious difference to the kindergarten?

2.2 Development of teaching

2.2.1 Recognising situations in everyday kindergarten life as a learning opportunity

The results of the study suggest that children are open and curious about religious difference insofar as they recognise it.[834] Thus, the children involved in the conversations in the Islamic kindergarten thematise objectively and as a matter of course that not all children go to Koran lessons. The results of Julia Ipgrave's[835] study also indicate that religious plurality is a matter of course for the children, although not always positive. As part of his research project, Gottfried Orth states that non-discriminatory difference experiences are a matter of course for children.[836] In the study „Gemeinsamkeiten stärken – Unterschieden gerecht werden" (Strengthen commonalities – do justice to differences), little prejudice against the other religion becomes visible in the conversations with the children.[837] In the interview with two girls of primary school age described

---

833 The sub item "communication about religious difference" does not appear in the original questionnaire. In view of the results of the study, communication is a key factor in a culture of recognition, which is why this area is added.
834 Cf. chapter "Relevance of religious difference" (part V, 4.2.1).
835 Ipgrave, Julia (2002): Inter faith encounter and religious understanding in an inner city primary school.
836 Cf. Orth, Gottfried (2000): Umgang mit religiöser Differenz. In: Fischer, Dietlind/Schöll, Albrecht (Ed.): Religiöse Vorstellungen bilden, 173–186, 182.
837 Schweitzer, Friedrich/Biesinger, Albert (with Boschki, Reinhold et al.) (2002): Gemeinsamkeiten stärken – Unterschieden gerecht werden.

by Hans Streib, they do not argue for the superiority of a religion, but enter into a playful interreligious exchange about ideas and images.[838] In Eva Hoffmann's study, unlike Julia Ipgrave's[839] research project, in which differences are not always viewed positively, the children show no explicit pride in their respective religious affiliation, although they are sometimes proud of individual ideas. These different results may be due to the different framework conditions and contexts of the studies: While Eva Hoffmann was doing research in Protestant-run kindergartens, Julia Ipgrave's study was conducted at a school with eight to eleven year-old children of the non-Muslim minority. Compared to Julia Ipgrave's[840] research project, this study shows no explicit pride in one's own religious affiliation. However, the Muslim children in the kindergarten are proud when they can recite sura well, and the children who speak Arabic appear to be proud of their language skills.

The naturalness and curiosity with which children encounter religious difference is a good foundation or learning processes about religious difference.[841] Curiosity is for Heinz Streib an important prerequisite for the beginning of an interreligious encounter.[842] The children's conversations or questions that suddenly arise during everyday kindergarten life can, provided that they are perceived and sensitively taken up by the educators, be opportunities for learning, in which an examination of religious difference can take place. Jonas Stier and others note in their study that the most fertile situations for intercultural learning arise unplanned and improvised.[843] Conflicts that arise in everyday kindergarten life in the context of religious difference can also be seen as opportunities for learning.

In kindergarten, there are religious forms of expression and action in which religious difference can be recognisable[844] for the children, but in which difference can also be hidden. Christa Dommel advocates applying the pedagogical concept of the situ-

---

838 Cf. Streib, Heinz (2001): Inter-Religious Negotiations. In: Heimbrock, Hans-Günter/Scheilke, Christoph/Schreiner, Peter (Ed.): Towards Religious Competence, 129–149, 138.

839 Ipgrave, Julia (2002): Inter faith encounter and religious understanding in an inner city primary school; Bock, Karin (2010): Kinderalltag – Kinderwelten.

840 Ipgrave, Julia (2002): Inter faith encounter and religious understanding in an inner city primary school.

841 Cf. chapter "Relevance of religious difference" (part V, 4.2.1).

842 Streib, Heinz (2001): Inter-Religious Negotiations. In: Heimbrock, Hans-Günter/Scheilke, Christoph/Schreiner, Peter (Ed.): Towards Religious Competence, 129–149, 140.

843 Cf. Stier, Jonas/Tryggvason, Marja-Terttu/Sandström, Margareta/Sandberg, Anette (2012): Diversity management in preschools using a critical incident approach. *Education* *23*(4), 285–296, 292.

844 Cf. chapter "Recognisable elements of religious difference" (part V, 4).

ational approach to the topic of religious diversity in institutions,[845] because she sees this as an instrument that avoids sorting children into drawers according to their religious affiliation and subordinating them to an abstract, unrelated concept of religion.[846] The children themselves are crucial for finding situations that are important for children.[847] Recognising situations in which children encounter religious differences and addressing them, if relevant to the children, can be conducive to dealing with religious differences. The present study shows, for example, that religious differences can be seen in the food, prayers, festivals and religious offerings.

In both kindergartens an attempt is made to find food that can be enjoyed by all children in the kindergarten. If it is organisationally possible, meals in kindergarten offer a chance to make religious differences visible in the different eating habits of the children. Martin Boltz, Hans Schrumpf and Martin Jäggle raised religious implications in everyday school life in primary schools and it became clear that the consideration of cultural (and religious) differences in school meals was an indicator for an appropriate handling of differences at the level of school management[848]. How religious eating habits are dealt with in meals can therefore be an important indication of how religious differences are dealt with in kindergarten.

Studies of prayers made it clear that the majority of children referred to these as positive activities.[849] The 5–7-year-olds do not yet have a fixed idea of what prayer means. They see, however, that prayer has to do with God. Furthermore, they particularly emphasize the outwardly perceptible forms and behaviours: Prayer means folding hands, using certain words, etc.[850] Surveys on the topic of prayer show,

> "that the outward appearance of prayer is particularly impressive and important for children before school. This suggests that praying with children at this age should be combined with externally perceptible forms or rituals – with certain language forms, postures or seating arrangements as well as with silence exercises. It seems that these are signs of identification that help the children accommodate themselves to prayer. In kindergarten especially, there are corresponding design possibilities."[851]

---

845 Cf. Dommel, Christa (2003): Kindergartenpädagogik und Religion in Deutschland. Von Fröbel zum Situationsansatz. In: Dommel, Christa/Heumann, Jürgen/Otto, Gert: WerteSchätzen. Religiöse Vielfalt und Öffentliche Bildung. Festschrift für Jürgen Lott zum 60. Geburtstag. Frankfurt/London: IKO, 206–222, 219.
846 Cf. ibid.
847 Cf. Ibid.
848 Cf. Jäggle, Martin (2000): Wie nimmt Schule kulturelle und religiöse Differenz wahr? In: Porzelt, Burkard/Güth, Ralph (Ed.): Empirische Religionspädagogik, 119–138, 127.
849 Cf. Moore, Kelsey/Talwar, Victoria/Bosacki, Sandra (2012): Canadian children's perceptions of spirituality: diverse voices. *International Journal of Children's Spirituality 17*(3), 217–234, 220; 225.
850 Cf. Schweitzer, Friedrich (2013): Das Recht des Kindes auf Religion, 168.
851 Ibid., 169.

Since the outward appearance of prayer is impressive and important for children, it makes sense to take this into account in kindergarten and to allow for religious difference. Offering prayers of different religious traditions is also an opportunity to make clear to children the recognition of their religion and their religious expressions. Silvia Habringer-Hagleitner recommends that the heterogeneity of religious traditions in the group should be taken into account when selecting songs and prayers.[852]

Festivals structure the year, are highlights and stopping points and children expect them with anticipation and excitement. The unique ccelebration of a festival of another religion without other consideration of religious difference in kindergarten seems to miss the desired intentions despite the positive intentions. When festivals are celebrated or thematised, the question arises how this is done so that the celebration is not perceived as an "exotic activity" but is based on the recognition of religious difference in kindergarten.

2.2.2 Offering factually correct explanations of religious difference

Children notice differences, but do not know the reason without explanation of the adults or invent their own reasons based on their experience.[853] Children need explanations from adults, which are often lacking, in order to understand religious difference. The study by Schweitzer and Biesinger[854] also finds that adults owe the children explanations. Children are not given an explanation on the religious background of why some children celebrate different festivals. The children still have experiences, even if they can't understand them.[855] Even if children cannot express their own religious affiliation or religious attitudes conceptually, some children may have experiences with it. "In all these cases, education means not only opening up the world in the sense of new experiences, but also a categorical exploitation of own experiences that already exist."[856]

> "It is undoubtedly an important pedagogical task to support children in processing experiences of difference. From the point of view of *religious* education, it is important that religious differences can also be understood religiously – in this case, the religious educational concern necessarily goes beyond merely intercultural learning."[857]

---

852 Cf. Habringer-Hagleitner, Silvia (2006): Zusammenleben im Kindergarten, 336.
853 Cf. section "Inquiries to children absent at celebrations" in chapter "Question of affiliation" (part V, 4.2.2).
854 Schweitzer, Friedrich/Biesinger, Albert (with Boschki, Reinhold et al.) (2002): Gemeinsamkeiten stärken – Unterschieden gerecht werden.
855 Cf. Schweitzer, Friedrich (2009): Wie Kinder und Jugendliche religiöse Differenz wahrnehmen. In: Bucher, Anton A. et al. (Ed.): Jahrbuch der Kindertheologie: „In den Himmel kommen nur, die sich auch verstehen", 39–49, 41.
856 Ibid., 42.
857 Schweitzer, Friedrich (2009): Wie Kinder und Jugendliche religiöse Differenz wahrnehmen. In: Bucher, Anton A. et al. (Ed.): Jahrbuch der Kindertheologie: „In den Himmel

If the children do not know the reason for the difference, they may unintentionally find an explanation that is hurtful or irritating for the children concerned. The present study shows to what extent children are dependent on explanations in some questions and how some of the statements of the children can be picked up and thematised by adults. Explanations and categorical assignments of adults are necessary for the education of children. In order to give children the opportunity to develop, the desideratum arises to offer them information that is new.[858]

> "Dealing with the theological constructions of children also makes us aware that the acquisition of knowledge, as well as world interpretation, takes place in the interplay of construction and reception. This means that everyone, whether child or adult, constructs the world within the framework of the structures already worked out by him – and at the same time repeatedly needs external stimulus in order to improve his own constructions."[859]

Sometimes it becomes apparent that children do not have the religious language skills to communicate on religious topics and have experiences for which they have no explanations. Also, the use of certain terms does not mean that the children know the meaning of the terms.

> "With children, the problem of *verbalism* has often been discussed: children use words whose meaning they do not understand. But is this only a problem with children? Is it not only true with many young and adult persons, especially when religious language is in question? On the other hand, the children often feel and think more than they are able to express. They do not have an adequate vocabulary at their disposal, and therefore their answers often give a poorer picture of their religiousness than is actually the case. In addition, words do not have the same meaning for children as they do have for older people, and they do not often have the fully same meaning even for people of same age."[860]

Religious education must therefore aim to practise acts of speech in which those who speak express themselves in their world of experience, in addition to establishing,

---

kommen nur, die sich auch verstehen", 39–49, 48.
858 Cf. Schambeck, Mirjam (2005): Wie Kinder glauben und theologisieren. In: Bahr, Matthias/Kropač, Ulrich/Schambeck, Mirjam (Ed.): Subjektwerdung und religiöses Lernen. Für eine Religionspädagogik, die den Menschen ernst nimmt. Munich: Kösel, 18–28, 23.
859 Ibid., 27.
860 Tamminen, Kalevi (1991): Religious Development in Childhood and Youth. An Empirical Study. Helsinki: Suomalainen Tiedeakatemia, 23. In addition to Tamminen, James W. Fowler and Fritz Oser and Paul Gmündner also dealt with the development of faith and religious development, cf. Fowler, James, W. (1995): Stages of Faith. The Psychology of Human Development and the Quest for Meaning. New York: HarperCollins Publisher [first published in San Francisco: HarperSanFrancisco 1981]; Oser, Fritz/Gmündner, Paul (²1996): Der Mensch, Stufen seiner religiösen Entwicklung. Gütersloh: Gütersloher Verlagshaus [1984].

teaching or specialist theological speaking.[861] Elisabeth Neurath notes that eschatological speech and picturelessness are not a way of religious education as the promotion of the ability to perceive, interpret, shape and discourse.[862]

> "In contrast, subject- and education-oriented religious education aims to respect children in their own activities, i.e. to examine their religious ideas and reflect on them in common theological conversation. By allowing children from different religious or denominational contexts to have their say, research in religious studies gains in relevance to reality."[863]

2.2.3 Guiding initiatives to promote the handling of difference

Initiatives and projects for dealing with religious differences in everyday kindergarten life can have a positive effect on the interaction of people in kindergarten. Aboud et al. produced a systematic overview of interventions aimed at reducing prejudice and promoting inclusion and respect for ethnic differences in early childhood.[864] There are various initiatives, which are mainly located in English-speaking countries.[865] For

---

861 Cf. Schambeck, Mirjam (2005): Wie Kinder glauben und theologisieren. In: Bahr, Matthias/Kropač, Ulrich/Schambeck, Mirjam (Ed.): Subjektwerdung und religiöses Lernen, 18–28, 25f.

862 Cf. Neurath, Elisabeth (2009): „Wer früher stirbt, ist länger tot?". In: Bucher, Anton A. et al. (Ed.): Jahrbuch der Kindertheologie: „In den Himmel kommen nur, die sich auch verstehen", 60–70, 68.

863 Ibid.

864 Aboud, Frances E./Tredoux, Colin/Tropp, Linda R./Brown, Christia Spears/Niens, Ulrike/Noor, Noraini M./the Una Global Evaluation Group (2012): Interventions to reduce prejudice and enhance inclusion and respect for ethnic differences in early childhood: A systematic review. *Developmental Review* 32, 307–336.

865 The brochure "Diversity and Social Inclusion Exploring Competences for Professional Practice in Early Childhood Education and Care" (DECET, www.decet.org/fileadmin/decetmedia/publications/Diversity-and-Social-Inclusion.pdf [01.07.2013]), funded by the Bernard van Leer Foundation, tries to define the competencies that are helpful for supporting diversity, social inclusion and professional work in Early Childhood Education and Care (ECEC). "The mission of the Bernard van Leer Foundation is 'to develop and support programmes that create significant positive change for children up to the age of 8 who are growing up in circumstances of social and economic disadvantage'. Many young children who live in such circumstances come from demographic groups which routinely experience exclusion and disrespect." (Bernard van Leer Foundation, http://www.bernardvanleer.org/ [21.07.2015]). Both the principles of the Diversity in Early Childhood Education and Training (DECET) network and the mission of the International Step by Step Association (ISSA) network are used. The DECET network aims to build communities where the knowledge, skills and characteristics of children and adults can be developed so that everyone can develop different aspects of identity, where learning from other cultures is possible, where everyone can participate as an active citizen, where

example, the evaluation of the Media Initiative for Children (MIFC)[866], founded by Early Years,[867] shows that initiatives can have a positive effect on mutual respect. Early Years is an organisation for young children in Northern Ireland in cooperation with the US-based Peace Initiatives Institute (Pii).[868] The "Media Initiative for Children: Respecting Difference Programme" is a pre-school programme for children aged three to four, which is based on the concern to promote awareness of diversity and difference among children, teachers, educators and parents and to contribute to more positive attitudes and behaviour.[869] The programme combines the use of five-minute animated films, a training programme for educators, parents and the management committee, an early childhood curriculum and a collection of culturally and contextually

---

prejudices are addressed and where people work together to challenge institutional forms of prejudice and discrimination. (Cf. DECET, www.decet.org [22.07.2015]). The International Step by Step Association (ISSA) is a global network. "ISSA promotes equal access to quality education and care for all children, especially in the early years of their lives, and supports family and early years practitioners' empowerment." (ISSA, http://www.issa.nl/global.html [10.07.2013]). The Joint Learning Initiative on Children and Ethnic Diversity (JLICED, Joint Learning Initiative on Children and Ethnic Diversity, http://www.qub.ac.uk/research-centres/JointLearningInitiativeonChildrenandEthnicDiversity/ [21.07.2015]) is a global network of early childhood researchers, practitioners, politicians who set the goal of reducing racial segregation, ethnic segregation and conflict and promoting socially inclusive and respectful communities through effective early childhood programmes. At the heart of the work are six study groups, which essentially deal with racial and ethnic differences with different emphases. The global initiative UNA (UNA, http://www.unaglobal.org/en [22.07.2015]) committed to the same goal. (Other organisations active as umbrella organisations or training institutes are ACEPP in Franc (ACEPP, www.acepp.asso.fr [22.07.2015]), Mutant in the Netherlands (Mutant, www.mutant.nl [22.07.2015] and VBJK in Belgium (VBJK, www.vbjk.be [22.07.2015]). The journal Early Childhood Matters has already dealt with the topic of plurality in several issues, cf. for example the journal: Promoting social inclusion and respect for diversity in the early years (2007). *Early Childhood Matters 108*, which contains various contributions by different authors on diversity. In political developments in Ireland the importance of focusing on diversity and interculturality has been highlighted: "Síolta, the National Quality Framework for Early Childhood Education (2006), Diversity and Equality Guidelines for Childcare Providers (2006), Aistear, The Early Childhood Curriculum Framework (2009) and the Intercultural Education Strategy (2010)" (Connolly, Paul/Miller, Sarah/Eakin, Angela (2010): A Cluster Randomised Trial Evaluation of the Media Initiative for Children: Respecting Difference Programme. Belfast: Centre for Effective Education, Queen's University Belfast, 53).

866 Cf. Connolly, Paul/Fitzpatrick, Siobhan/Gallagher, Tony/Harris, Paul (2006): Addressing diversity and inclusion in the early years in conflict affected societies: a case study of the Media Initiative for Children—Northern Ireland, *International Journal of Early Years Education 14*(3), 263–278.
867 Early years, http://www.early-years.org/ [22.07.2015].
868 Peace Initiative Institute, http://peaceii.org/ [22.07.2015].
869 Cf. Connolly, Paul/Miller, Sarah/Eakin, Angela (2010): A Cluster Randomised, 7.

appropriate resources for use in early childhood institutions and in the family environment.[870] Positive effects of the program on children's attitudes and consciousness in social-emotional development, cultural awareness and inclusive behaviour were observed. The effects were similar across the sample and no effect differences were found between boys and girls, between Catholic and Protestant children, between children of different socio-economic origins and children from Northern Ireland or the Republic of Ireland.[871]

> "Given the cumulative weight of evidence that now exists locally regarding how attitudes form at an early age, and in light of the strong evidence provided through this present trial of the role that early childhood initiatives can have in bringing about real and measurable positive change, it is imperative that issues of diversity and difference form a key component of any early childhood strategy and that such a strategy, in turn, represents a key element of any wider programme to promote community cohesion."[872]

When applying development programs, the specific contextual influences must be taken into account.

> "Rather, for such programmes to be effective, they need to be based upon a proper understanding of precisely how these divisions are affecting the lives of young children in particular contexts. Only by basing the development of early childhood programmes on evidence in this way can we be confident that they will engage meaningfully with the experiences and perspectives of the children themselves."[873]

2.3   Human resources development

The recognition of each person, including their religious attitudes in the organisation, cannot be taken for granted if some teachers take a positive view of religious difference, as the study has shown.[874] Although the directors and the teachers of religious difference express themselves positively, this is not reflected in everyday kindergarten life. This also becomes clear in Judith Weber's[875] research project, in which educators

---

870   Ibid.
871   For a detailed list of the results of the study see Connolly, Paul/Miller, Sarah/Eakin, Angela (2010): A Cluster Randomised, 29–44.
872   Connolly, Paul/Miller, Sarah/Eakin, Angela (2010): A Cluster Randomised, 53.
873   Connolly, Paul (2009): Developing programmes, 5f.
874   Cf. the positive view of religious difference of both kindergarten management (part IV, 2).
875   Weber, Judith (2014): Religionssensible Bildung in Kindertageseinrichtungen. Eine empirisch-qualitative Studie zur religiösen Bildung und Erziehung im Kontext der Elementarpädagogik. Interreligiöse und Interkulturelle Bildung im Kindesalter, vol. 4. Münster/New York: Waxmann, 169. The concrete religious education in child day care facilities is the subject of research. On the basis of guided interviews and participant observation, the question is explored which possibilities exist to integrate the concept of religious-educational action of religion-sensitive education as a component of the

emphasize the respectful handling and acceptance of this diversity as an important aspect of their pedagogical work, whereas some institutions take little account of the interreligious situation.[876] A research project in Greece shows that teachers theoretically know how to deal with religious diversity but do not always apply it in practice.[877]

A prerequisite for any development of early childhood education is the willingness of those working in kindergarten to work on themselves and on the organisation of kindergarten and to bring about change. Personnel development can help those working in kindergarten to develop themselves further.[878]

2.3.1 Recognise the importance and tasks of those working in the kindergarten

2.3.1.1 Significance and tasks of management

Management is particularly important in the respective kindergarten, as it is involved in the conceptual considerations and has a decisive influence on the organisational culture.[879]

> "In a learning organisation, leaders are designers, stewards, and teachers. They are responsible for building organizations where people continually expand their capabilities to understand complexity, clarify vision, and improve shared mental models – that is, they are responsible for learning."[880]

The management task begins with the principle of creative tension. Creative tension arises between the clear knowledge of the 'vision' and the clear statement of the given

---

pedagogical conception of day-care facilities for children, as well as to discuss the results in the current scientific elementary and religious-educational discourse. (Weber, Judith (2014): Religionssensible Bildung in Kindertageseinrichtungen, 169.) Child day care centres run by Catholics, Protestants and local authorities form the field of research. It is evaluated by means of content analytical procedures according to Mayring and Kuckartz.

876 Cf. Weber, Judith (2014): Religionssensible Bildung in Kindertageseinrichtungen, 298.
877 Lytsiousi, Stella/Tsioumis, Konstantinos/Kyridis, Argyris (2014): How teachers cope with the religious diversity in Greek kindergarten classes, from theory to reality. *International Journal of Education Learning and Development* 2(5), 18–32, 29f. In the study, 173 kindergarten teachers in different regions of Greece filled in questionnaires that were asking them for their opinions and ways of dealing with religious diversity.
878 With regard to personnel development in schools, see Buhren, Claus, G./Rolff, Hans-Günter (2002): Personalentwicklung in Schulen. Konzepte, Praxisbausteine, Methoden. Weinheim/Basel: Beltz, 7.
879 Cf. chapter "Conceptual reflections on religion and religious difference" (part V, 4.1.1).
880 Senge, Peter, M. (1990): The fifth discipline. The art and practice of the learning organization. New York/London/Toronto/Sydney/Auckland;Doubleday, 340.

reality. The gap between the two creates a natural tension.[881] Leadership is a quality feature of the system, a question of the interplay of management teams in horizontal and vertical terms, in common concern for the functioning of the respective units and for the survivability of the whole and not reduced to the ability of individuals.[882] The different phases of an organisation's life require different styles of leadership.[883] Edgar Schein sees the entrepreneurs as creators of culture insofar as the values of the founder become the basis of corporate management. In the second phase of the organisation's development, the communication structures, which in the founding phase were still based on face-to-face staff relations, must develop into a system of control and incentives. The third phase of management refers primarily to management. The main task is to take into account and combat employees' fears of change and loss of competence. The fourth phase of the leadership is about developing rules and standards in dealing with aspects such as safety and productivity.[884]

Depending on the phase of the organisation, it becomes clear in the list of the different tasks of the manager that there is not a single management style, but that managers adapt to the respective situations in the organisation.[885] As management, it is important to take into account and to take seriously the willingness of employees to change and their fears associated with change.[886] Changes should only be initiated when managers understand the norms, traditions and deviant practices of the group. To understand what's really going on, they have to ask.[887]

In an early childhood institution setting in which the recognition of religious difference was not given as a value when the kindergarten was founded, religious difference can subsequently be established as a value, whereby particular attention must be paid to the communication structures and reservations of the employees, and guiding ideas in dealing with religious difference must be developed.

---

881 Cf. Peter Senge (1993): Die fünfte Disziplin – die lernfähige Organisation. In: Fatzer, Gerhard (Ed.): Organisationsentwicklung für die Zukunft. Ein Handbuch. Cologne: Edition Humanistische Psychologie, 145–178, 149.
882 Wimmer, Rudolf (2000): Die Zukunft von Führung. In: Trebesch, Karsten (Ed.): Organisationsentwicklung, 161–178, 175f.
883 Cf. Schein, Edgar H. (2009): Die vier Gesichter der Führung. GDI Impuls. *Wissensmagazin für Wirtschaft, Gesellschaft, Handel 1*, 108–109.
884 Cf. Ibid, 108f.
885 Cf. ibid.
886 Cf. chapter "Verbal communication about religious difference" (part V, 4.1.3).
887 Cf. Schein, Edgar H. (2010): Prozess und Philosophie des Helfens. Bergisch Gladbach: Andreas Kohlhage, 127.

2.3.1.2 Importance and tasks of the pedagogues

The importance of teachers in dealing with religious difference[888] and in communicating about religion and religious difference became clear in the study.

> "The increasing knowledge-based nature of all social and economic processes increases the need for communication and interaction in organisations to control complex knowledge processes. The closer examination of the processes of knowledge generation, knowledge transfer and knowledge use as primarily socio-communicative and socially interactive processes make it urgently necessary that the perspective of competence and personnel development becomes central in organisations and thus offer options for further training to shape it adequately into its new role as an intermediary actor."[889]

Pedagogues from early childhood institutions who are familiar with the opportunities and challenges of the plural situation in kindergarten and who are aware of the different conditions and characteristics of children, especially the cultural and religious difference that has become even greater as a result of migration,[890] can express this diversity sensitively in their self-image. Responding to differences can contribute to successful cooperation.[891] Pedagogues can be a "bridge to society"[892] and the first point of contact for people who, for example, still have little social connection in the respective country due to recent migration. Some teachers are asked by parents how they should deal with situations in which children ask for religious difference. In a study by Jenny Berglund, in which 1,300 Swedish youth were asked about religion and leisure activities, 50 percent of those who called themselves Muslims trusted their teachers to help with personal problems, whereas only five percent of non-Muslims did so.

---

888 Cf. chapter "Recognisable elements of religious difference" (part V, 4.1.2) and chapter "Verbal communication about religious difference" (part V, 4.1.3).
889 Peters, Sibylle/Wahlstab, Sandra/Dengler, Sandra (2003): Perspektivenvielfalt betrieblicher Weiterbildung in der Wissensgesellschaft. In: Peters, Sibylle (Ed.): Lernen und Weiterbildung als permanente Personalentwicklung. Munich/Mering: Rainer Hamp, 7–28, 16.
890 The magazine *The Future of the children* deals with the well-being of immigrant children and what can be done to improve their educational performance, health status, social and cognitive development and long-term prospects for economic mobility, as it has been found that immigrant children often have problems with education, physical and mental health, poverty and integration into American society (The Future of the Children, http://www.princeton.edu/futureofchildren/publications/journals/journal_details/index.xml?journalid=74 [21.07.2015]).
891 Schweitzer, Friedrich (2008): Wozu brauchen Kinder Religion? Zur Grundlegung der religiösen Bildung in Kindertageseinrichtungen. In: Hugoth, Matthias/Benedix, Monika: Religion im Kindergarten. Begleitung und Unterstützung für Erzieherinnen. Munich: Kösel, 18-24, 23.
892 This phrase comes from the expert interview with the head of the Islamic kindergarten. Cf. chapter "Conceptual reflections on religion and religious difference" (part V, 4.1.1).

Muslim students ranked teachers in third place after parents and after God when asked who they went to when problems arise.[893] Berglund cites the fact that many of the young Muslims come from families that, due to national or cultural traditions, tend to show more respect in general and respect for teachers specifically, than is the case in Swedish society, where the current status of teachers is rather low.[894] Another explanation may be that younger Muslims find the help of teachers who have a better view of challenges and adaptations due to the demands of society more helpful than parents who have little contact with the social, cultural and practical realities of young people.[895] A third possibility is that the members of a "minority culture" feel more insecure and vulnerable than those of the "majority culture" and thus a teacher who belongs to the majority culture and is experienced as an interested, trustworthy adult person becomes a more important reference person and more important role model than for non-Muslim Swedes.[896]

> "Immigrant young people, including the second and third generations, sometimes feel like 'strangers in a strange land', a feeling that can be reinforced or weakened by the encounter with the majority society and its diverse social, cultural, political and economic institutions."[897]

People in educational institutions are often the first representatives of Western society to meet young immigrants. "Thus the teacher's ability to make immigrant pupils (and their parents) feel welcome, respected, confident, and included, may be of significant societal value at this particular time."[898] The results of Jenny Berglund's study show that it is the fairness, justice and professional interest of the teacher that bring about the recognition and trust of Muslim students and their parents. One boy tells that, unlike many other teachers, the theme of fasting was never a problem for one teacher, but rather that she discussed the matter with the student's mother and the student and thus they found a solution together.[899]

> "Significantly, Joseph noted that his mother also appreciated this teacher: 'She used to say that [the teacher] was one of the few who really trusted her as a parent and did not treat her differently because she wore the veil.' Regarding this teacher's approach to the matter of religious practice, Joseph recalled that 'fasting was never problematic for her, unlike for some of the other teachers I encountered. She simply discussed the matter with my mother and together they decided that I should fast on Fridays and

---

893 Berglund, Jenny (2014): Teachers only stand behind parents and God in the eyes of the Muslim pupils. In: Arweck, Elisabeth/Jackson, Robert: Religion, Education and Society. London/New York: Routledge Taylor & Francis Group, 109–118, 109f.; 111; 114.
894 Cf. ibid., 111.
895 Cf. ibid., 112.
896 Ibid., 114.
897 Ibid.
898 Ibid., 114f.
899 Cf. ibid., 113.

weekends.' Both of the above accounts show that it was the teacher's fairness, justness, and professional interest that inspired the appreciation, trust, and confidence of the Muslim pupils – and also, at least in Joseph's case, of the parents."[900]

In this example, it becomes clear how much a teacher can promote inclusion, which can affect not only the pupils but also the adult community: "Joseph's recollection that his mother also liked his teacher because she was inclusive and accepting of Muslim cultural differences is significant, indication that a teacher's potential to promote integration extends beyond the pupils to the adult immigrant community."[901]

Rudolf Englert distinguishes between two tasks for those responsible for education in a pluralistic society: empowering children and young people to meet others openly and empowering children and young people to take sides.[902] Religious education can be a contribution to peace.[903] The task of the teachers is to provide as much space and time for interreligious dialogue as is available for other forms of dialogue and thus to contribute to a *safe space* in which religion and religious difference can be addressed. "While the lecturer/facilitator may well have no personal religious convictions, their responsibility is not to impede the pedagogical possibilities of interfaith-dialogue when it occurs, but to give this space and air as much as is given to any other form of dialogue."[904]

2.3.2 Take causes of low thematisation of religious difference seriously

The reasons for the dominance of the major religion in kindergarten, the rare thematisation of religious difference and the lack of recognition of the minor religions were identified,[905] which can underlie the actions of the teachers and the director.

The claim not to exclude anyone and to treat all children equally can lead to the fear of treating children unfairly, and hence not addressing the issue of difference. Areas in which children differ are ignored and the environment is perceived and treated as being as homogeneous as possible, which cannot do justice to the difference that exists in kindergarten, although this concern is based on the claim of justice. "Insensitivity

---

900 Ibid.
901 Ibid., 115.
902 Cf. ibid., 172f.
903 In several contributions from different countries, the connection between education on religions and education for peace is put into relation with each other. Some of the authors see the current structural and political arrangements for religious education in their own countries as impairing education for justice and peace. Peace-building should include education for tolerance and look for ways to avoid misrepresentations and stereotypes, cf. Jackson, Robert/Fujiwara, Satoko (Ed.) (2008): Peace Education and Religious Plurality. International Perspectives. London/New York: Routledge.
904 Engebretson, Kath (2009): In your shoes, 166.
905 Cf. chapter "Communication about religious difference", section "Reasons for avoiding communication about religious difference" (part V, 4.1.3).

to difference, even that which arises from an egalitarian claim, contributes to unequal treatment of given differences."[906] If religious difference is not addressed because of the principle of equality that requires equal treatment, this can lead to the exclusion of areas that can be important for some children.

> "Out of concern that young people could be discriminated against, some teachers avoid addressing (religious) difference, while others see the integration of (religious) difference into the school space as a threat to peace at school. In both cases, an atmosphere of assimilation in the sense of religiously value-free thought, religious traditions but actually degrading secularism is reinforced."[907]

When difference is allowed and sensitively addressed in kindergarten, there is the possibility to talk to others, to inform oneself, to form one's own opinion in confrontation with others and to reflect one's own opinion. "In some kindergartens, one tries to educate in a value-free and neutral way, citing tolerance and liberal pedagogy. It is misunderstood that this demands the basic attitude of indifference; [...]."[908]

> "Educational practices that foster children's multiple identities need to avoid two pitfalls: colour-blindness and tokenism. Colour-blindness is the denial of differences, very often out of an honest concern to treat 'all children equal'. In practice this means that parents and children from minority communities are welcomed, but receive the (unintentional) message that they need to 'adapt' as soon as possible to what is considered 'normal' within the dominant culture. Tokenism on the contrary involves treating the 'culture' of a child's home life as fixed and static. Parents' and children's identities are thereby reduced to their origin by assuming there is something called 'the Magreb culture', 'the Asian way of doing things', or 'a typical lesbian family'. In practice this means that special, yet stereotypical, events or displays are set up for children and families (such as a festival celebrating Iraqi new year with traditional clothes and food). Such activities risk being both patronising and stigmatising, in that they overlook the complexities of children's personal histories and family cultures and ignore socioeconomic and other differences. An important way to avoid these pitfalls is to build real and symbolic bridges between the public culture of the early childhood centre and the private cultures of families, by negotiating all practices with the families involved."[909]

---

906 Mecheril, Paul/Plößer, Melanie (2009): Differenz. In: Andresen, Sabine et al. (Ed.): Handwörterbuch Erziehungswissenschaft, 194–208, 197.
907 Jäggle, Martin (2007): Religiöse Pluralität in Europa. In: Bock, Irmgard et al. (Ed.): Europa als Projekt, 51–67, 60.
908 Projektgruppe Religionsunterricht der österreichischen Kommission für Bildung und Erziehung (Project Group Religious Education of the Austrian Commission for Education) (1981): Österreichisches Katechetisches Direktorium für Kinder und Jugendarbeit. Vienna: Hausdruckerei der Erzdiözese Wien, 38.
909 Vandenbroeck, Michel (2008): Beyond colour-blindness and tokenism. In: Brooker, Liz/Woodhead, Martin (Ed.): Developing Positive Identities. Diversity and Young Children. Early Childhood in Focus, vol. 3. Milton Keynes: The Open University, 28.

The endeavour to offer religion to the satisfaction of all those involved, as well as the tradition-bound design of religion, make dealing with religious difference a challenge and not an opportunity. One's own approach is then determined by the desires of others, especially parents, and the satisfaction of all those involved or by unreflected traditions, and offers a false sense of security in dealing with religion. "Many people, adults as well as children and youngsters, experience the growing diversity and plurality as the burden of uncertainty, and make strong efforts to get rid of it."[910] One reason for the low thematisation of religious difference is the attempt to avoid conflicts and thus to ignore the area of religion, in which high vulnerability can exist. A religion that is not conspicuous causes no difficulties.

> "Thus, for example, the need for harmony that is often empirically established in primary school can become an addiction to harmony that is unable to tolerate differences or perhaps only at the price of indifference. What is distinctive does not have to be stylised as a dividing factor, but it should not fall victim to harmonisation either."[911]

If religion is marginalised at school, according to Martin Jäggle, its key function in terms of content and society "for shaping coexistence with migrants; for the intensity and quality of mutual understanding; for the acquisition of an attitude of critical respect towards others" cannot be expressed. "Causes and foundations of social and cultural conflicts" thus remain permanently hidden.[912] In evaluating Lischke-Eisinger's interviews, educators associate plurality predominantly with difficulties and conflicts. For example, some of the kindergarten teachers consider it positive that everyday kindergarten life is designed in such a way that interreligious questions can be omitted.[913]

If religion is ignored in organisations, the conflicts associated with or caused by religion remain subliminal. The social competence to avoid issues that may lead to conflicts can contribute to the fact that conflicts cannot be resolved and remain for a longer period of time. For example, in a long-running conflict like Northern Ireland, children develop specific social skills that allow them to determine whether or not the people with whom they are in contact belong to their own group. While this also helps to reduce conflicts that occur on a daily basis, it avoids communication between groups on the issues that separate them, thus helping to prolong the conflict.

---

910 Miedema, Siebren (2009): Religious Education between Certainty and Uncertainty. Towards a Pedagogy of Diversity. In: Meijer, Wilna A.J./Miedema, Siebren/Lanser-van der Velde, Alma: Religious Education in a World of Religious Diversity. Münster et al.: Waxmann, 195-205, 195.

911 Jäggle, Martin (2006): Schritte auf dem Weg. In: Bastel, Heribert u.a: Das Gemeinsame entdecken – Das Unterscheidende anerkennen, 31–42, 41.

912 Jäggle, Martin (2000): Wie nimmt Schule kulturelle und religiöse Differenz wahr?. In: Porzelt, Burkard/Güth, Ralph (Ed.): Empirische Religionspädagogik, 119–138, 137.

913 Cf. Lischke-Eisinger, Lisa (2012): Sinn, Werte und Religion in der Elementarpädagogik, 376.

"In certain circumstances, such as those outlined above, social competence may have short-term positive consequences but have negative consequences in the long-term. In particular in Northern Ireland becoming socially competent at 'telling' leads to a reduced level on conflict in day to day intergroup contact but also reduces intergroup communication about important divisive issues thus in the long-term prolonging the conflict."[914]

Conflicts that may arise due to differences are avoided in everyday life in the kindergarten if the children have adapted to a norm and the areas in which they are different are not addressed.

"(Religious) plurality does not mean idyll, but is perhaps only not a source of conflict where religion has been completely privatised, religions have become socially indifferent and ultimately meaningless. In dialogue, too, the harmony of 'understanding one another' will not be achieved, but rather the 'accompanying one another in strangeness' will be seen as a fruitful solution. Conflicts also hold opportunities. For this reason, too, it is not primarily a question of avoiding them, but of dealing with them appropriately".[915]

Communication about religious difference can bring challenges, which runs counter to the trend towards harmonisation. Dealing with conflicts, including dealing with religious conflicts, offers the opportunities and can be learned and tested in the kindergarten.[916]

If religious education in kindergarten is equated exclusively with the teaching of values, there is no need to address religious differences in kindergarten. The Global Ethic Project (1990) developed by Hans Küng corresponds to this approach, which tends towards a mediation of values that has been replaced by religions whereby difference is hardly discernible in this model[917] and the reality of the difference between religions and the resulting difference is not given special attention. In the programme of the Global Ethic project, "an attempt is made with great public resonance [...] to counter the often lamented ethical disorientation of our time by updating religious ethics, in which the common ethical conviction of the religions is brought up for discussion."[918] The Global Ethic project[919] "seeks the togetherness and common ground of the various religious communities in the ethically responsible practice of human

---

914 Cairns, Ed (2002): "What ever you say, say nothing": Social Competence and Communication in Northern Ireland. *Researching Early Childhood 4*, 75–81, 81.
915 Jäggle, Martin (2007): Religiöse Pluralität in Europa. In: Bock, Irmgard et al. (Ed.): Europa als Projekt, 51–67, 56.
916 Cf. chapter "Kindergarten as a *safe space*" (part VI, 4.1.1).
917 Initiative Weltethos Österreich (Global Ethic Initiative Austria), http://www.weltethos.org/ [25.11.2014].
918 Rehm, Johannes (2002): Erziehung zum Weltethos. Projekte interreligiösen Lernens in multikulturellen Kontexten. Göttingen: Vandenhoeck & Ruprecht, 11.
919 Cf. Initiative Weltethos Österreich, http://www.weltethos.org/ [21.07.2015].

action."[920] Materials are also available for the kindergarten, which are intended to make the children aware of the concerns of the Global Ethic project.[921] Religions differ considerably in some aspects and children recognise religious differences in their environment[922] in addition to emphasising the similarities, it is indispensable to address the differences and acknowledge them. It can be made clear to the children that religious difference allows a mutual element and a peaceful coexistence is possible. Barbara Asbrand, for example, points out that the similarities between the children which they find on the individual and relationship level make it possible to deal with plurality at the level of religions and religiosity.[923]

If religious education is regarded exclusively as a task of parents and religion is regarded as a "matter of privacy",[924] which does not play a role in public, the educators evade joint responsibility for religious education and thus an area of the educational mandate in the quantitative section of the Tübingen study „Auf die Eltern kommt es an" (It depends on the parents). 58 percent of the parents surveyed stated that religious education should take place at home in the family.[925] Early childhood institutions reflect trends in society. The fate of religion reveals a structural characteristic of modern society: the disintegration of the public and private spheres.[926] This view of privatising religion is criticised by several thinkers, so Habermas points out that religion is unfairly excluded from the public.[927]

In addition, educators do not feel sufficiently informed about different religions and cite a lack of knowledge about other religions as the reason for the lack of discussion of religious difference. They prefer not to talk about religion than to say something wrong. This is also shown in the study by Lischke-Eisinger, in which it becomes clear:

> "that many educators do not see themselves as competent contacts for dealing with religious diversity. For example, one educator argues that the authentic thematisation of a religion also requires belonging to it. Other educators assume that the discussion with the knowledge about other religions could possibly be initiated by them, but imply uncertainty here, both with regard to the contents and with regard to the ques-

---

920 Rehm, Johannes (2002): Erziehung zum Weltethos, 17.
921 Cf. http://www.weltethos.org/uploaded/documents/PM_Fruehe_Bildung_30.05_fin.pdf [25.11.2014].
922 Cf. chapter "Dealing with and thematising religious difference by children" (part V, 4.2).
923 Cf. Asbrand, Barbara (2008): Zusammen leben und lernen im Religionsunterricht, 229f.
924 Cf. Mette, Norbert/Steinkamp, Hermann (1983): Sozialwissenschaften und Praktische Theologie, 47.
925 Cf. Braun, Anne et al. (2011): Was Eltern erwarten und erfahren. In: Biesinger, Albert/Edelbrock, Anke/Schweitzer, Friedrich (Ed.): Auf die Eltern kommt es an!, 43–120, 120.
926 Mette, Norbert/Steinkamp, Hermann (1983): Sozialwissenschaften und Praktische Theologie, 48.
927 Cf. Habermas, Jürgen (2001): Glauben und Wissen. Friedenspreis des Deutschen Buchhandels 2001. Berlin: Suhrkamp.

tion of which kind of didactic preparation could be meaningful for the kindergarten children."[928]

All the reasons outlined why educators do not address religious difference in kindergarten should be taken up in religious education discourses and taken into consideration in reflections on personnel development.

2.3.3 Promote interreligious aspects of education and training

Due to the importance of teachers in early childhood institutions and the teacher's diverse tasks in dealing with religious differences, teachers require interreligious competence.[929] Dealing with difference should become a key qualification and a central area of pedagogical education and training[930] to support teachers in developing a sensitive perception of (religious) difference and a competent approach to it in kindergarten.[931] The challenges of professional pedagogical action associated with heterogene-

---

928 Lischke-Eisinger, Lisa (2012): Sinn, Werte und Religion in der Elementarpädagogik, 377.
929 Cf. Biesinger, Albert/Schweitzer, Friedrich (2013): Religionspädagogische Kompetenzen.
930 The examination of difference refers to a general educational problem of those working with children in the field of early childhood education, which is being countered by the current efforts to academies early childhood education.
931 In addition to the kindergartens, other forms of child care exist in Vienna, whereby the training of the persons responsible for this child care is alarmingly low, although this does not exclude the possibility that there are child group carers who are qualified for this work and provide it with a high level of personal commitment. A children's group is an extended family-like form of care which may comprise a maximum of 14 children cared for at the same time and is managed by a trained child group supervisor (Municipal Authorities of Vienna, http://www.wien.gv.at/bildung/kindergarten/private-angebote/ [22.07.2015]). The basic training as a child group supervisor, which enables them to practise their profession, for example comprises six seminars, one day of reflection or graduation and two evenings of supervision, at least 80 hours of practical training in a children's group and the preparation of an internship report (Children's groups in Vienna, http://www.wiener.kindergruppen. at/?page_id=33[22.07.2015]). Distinguished from these are the child-care workers. These are persons who "regularly and in return for payment look after and educate minors up to the age of 16 (day children) for part of the day individually in their own household" (Verordnung der Wiener Landesregierung über die Regelung der Tagesbetreuung nach dem Wiener Tagesbetreuungsgesetz, Ordinance of the Vienna State Government on the Regulation of Day Care according to the Vienna Day Care Act (WTBVO) 2001/94. Section 2, http://www.wien.gv.at/recht/landesrecht-wien/ rechtsvorschriften/html/s2700200.htm [21.07.2015]). The fourth article states "(1) Day-care mothers and fathers must provide proof of completion of training which must comprise at least 60 teaching units and must in any case cover basic knowledge [...]. (3) In addition to the training, child–care workers must provide evidence of regular, relevant advanced training of at least 16 teaching units per year (Ordinance of the Viennese Provincial

ity will not diminish in the future, but will grow.[932] Teachers are aware that an increase in competence in dealing with religious differences could make sense, but do not feel any need for further training. Although the training is considered negative in some areas, this leads to desire for further training in under 30 percent of cases.[933] Thus, in addition to the offer of further training that educators deem necessary, a further offer is needed, in that an examination of one's own prejudices, as is implemented in an Anti-Bias approach,[934] the training of awareness of religious difference and the expansion of knowledge about different religions can take place. In the following, two aspects of initial, continuing and further training are listed, the consideration of which appears to be particularly relevant on the basis of the research results.[935]

Government on the Regulation of Day Care under the Vienna Day Care Act (WTBVO) 2001/94. Section 4, http://www.wien.gv.at/recht/landesrecht-wien/rechtsvorschriften/html/s2700200.htm [21.07.2015]. Cf. also Municipal Authorities of Vienna, https://www.wien.gv.at/menschen/magelf/ahs-info/ausbildung.html [21.07.2015]). The extent of the required level of education does not seem to do justice to the complex activity and the diverse requirements in a group of children or as a child-care worker, mother or father. An examination of religious differences is not promoted in these courses. How can a child-care worker be sensitised to difference if diversity in education is not discussed in some way? Considerations regarding a change in the law would make sense. Parenthood does not qualify to work as a day care worker.

932 Cf. Gogolin, Ingrid/Krüger-Potratz, Marianne (2010): Einführung in die Interkulturelle Pädagogik. Opladen/Farmington Hills: Barbara Budrich, 26.

933 Cf. Blaicher, Hans-Peter et al. (2011): Interreligiöse Bildung in Kindertagesstätten in empirischer Perspektive. In: Schweitzer, Friedrich/Edelbrock, Anke/Biesinger, Albert (Ed.): Interreligiöse und interkulturelle Bildung in der Kita, 147–222, 206.

934 For a discussion of the Anti-Bias-approach cf. Derman-Sparks, Louise/A.B.C. Task Force (1989): Anti-Bias Curriculum: Tools for Empowering Young Children. Washington, DC: National Association for the Education of Young Children; Preissing, Christa/Wagner, Petra (Ed.) (2003): Kleine Kinder, keine Vorurteile? Interkulturelle und vorurteilsbewusste Arbeit in Kindertageseinrichtungen. Freiburg i. Br.: Herder; Gramelt, Katja (2010): Der Anti-Bias-Ansatz; Gramelt, Katja (2013): Diversity in early childhood education: a German perspective. Early Years. *An International Research Journal 33*(1), 45–58; Wagner, Petra (Ed.) (2010): Handbuch Kinderwelten; Vandenbroeck, Michel (2007): Beyond anti-bias education: Changing conceptions of diversity and equity in European early childhood education. European Early Childhood. *Education Research Journal 15*(1), 21–35; Wagner, Petra/Hahn, Stefanie/Enßlin, Ute (Ed.) (2006): Macker, Zicke, Trampeltier ... Vorurteilsbewusste Bildung und Erziehung in Kindertageseinrichtungen. Handbuch für die Fortbildung. Weimar: Verlag das Netz; Wagner, Petra (2003): Und was glaubst du? Religiöse Vielfalt und vorurteilsbewusste Arbeit in der Kita. In: Dommel, Christa/Heumann, Jürgen/Otto, Gert (Ed.): WerteSchätzen, 223–233. Dommel, Christa (2010): Religion – Diskriminierungsgrund oder kulturelle Ressource für Kinder?. In: Wagner, Petra (Ed.): Handbuch Kinderwelten, 148–159.

935 Cf. part V "Evaluation".

2.3.3.1 Acquiring knowledge about different religions

The enlightened man must, at least for the sake of his ability to understand, have dealt with religion himself, beyond a superficial knowledge of facts.[936] Knowledge that includes both awareness and understanding of different religions can encourage teachers to address different religions in kindergarten. In her research project on Muslim youth, Jenny Berglund emphasises the importance of knowledge about Islam, which also applies to knowledge about other religions.

> "As the formal education system constitutes one of the most encompassing of all social inclusions – a societal sphere that requires the participation of every young person and parent – it continues to be an area of great opportunity, in terms of being able to contribute to a successful outcome of these processes. However, in order to take advantage of this opportunity, the primary representatives of that institution – the teachers – must be prepared appropriately. In my view, one way of addressing this is to include courses in teacher training that provide specialised knowledge about Islam and the lifestyles, values, habits, and unique requirements of the diverse Muslim communities. Such programmes are of particular relevance at a time when the media portrayal of Muslims is often misleading and the phenomenon of 'Islamophobia' is becoming more widespread."[937]

To enable teachers to build trustful and meaningful relationships with Muslim students and their parents, knowledge and understanding of the respective religion can be helpful. If teachers lack knowledge about Islam or the differences that exist within the Islamic tradition, they may lack a basis to discuss with parents how the children can participate in special activities.[938] If teachers are informed about some aspects of Islam, this can lead to more trust and respect among Muslim parents, as they may be impressed that the teachers have taken the time to learn about their religion.[939] If the children are not given answers to their questions, misunderstandings and prejudices can arise or be intensified.[940]

---

936 Cf. Fischer, Dietlind/Schreiner, Peter/Doyé, Götz/Scheilke, Christoph Th. (1996): Auf dem Weg zur interkulturellen Schule. Fallstudien zur Situation interkulturellen und interreligiösen Lernens. Münster et al.: Waxmann, 22.
937 Berglund, Jenny (2014): Teachers only stand behind parents and God. In: Arweck, Elisabeth/Jackson, Robert: Religion, Education and Society, 109-118, 115.
938 Cf. Berglund, Jenny (2014): Teachers only stand behind parents and God. In: Arweck, Elisabeth/Jackson, Robert: Religion, Education and Society, 109-118, 116.
939 Cf. ibid.
940 Cf. Schweitzer, Friedrich et al. (2011): Interreligiöse und interkulturelle Bildung in Kindertagesstätten. In: Schweitzer, Friedrich/Edelbrock, Anke/Biesinger, Albert (Ed.): Interreligiöse und interkulturelle Bildung in der Kita, 29–54, 30.

One result of a study in Norway and Denmark[941] was that Danish early childhood teachers offered cultural activities which they themselves did well and not those they had mastered only to a certain extent. Only those teachers who played an instrument on a daily basis themselves invited a person from outside the kindergarten to play music with children. The results of 2001 and 2011 showed that more Christian activities were carried out in kindergartens than was expected.[942] In Denmark religion does not occur in the training of early childhood teachers, whereas in Norway it is taught as a subject. The results of the research project in 2011 show that the differences in the activities carried out are small and some are even more frequent in Denmark. In most kindergartens in Denmark and in most kindergartens in Norway, hymns are sung, the children are shown the church interior, they are taken to a church service and Easter is celebrated. Only in declaring the Easter Gospel did Norwegian early childhood teachers differ from Danish teachers: 61 percent of teachers in Norway and only 30 percent in Denmark explained the Easter Gospel. Perhaps a training would be needed for these explanations, since the background of Easter is not thematised among laymen.[943] The teachers therefore rely on religious offers in kindergarten even without training, design them according to their own ideas and often do so without explanations. This could mean that only action is taken within one's own cultural and religious frame of reference and one's own misconceptions are passed on if the teachers have not dealt with religion in a theoretical way.

> "One of the more daunting prospects for the teacher of studies of religion is the breadth of knowledge required to understand in any significant way the major world religions such as Christianity, Judaism, Buddhism, Islam, Hinduism and Sikhism. [...] Clearly a teacher cannot be expected to be an expert in all of these areas or to have a detailed competency in each. It is more important for the teacher to understand the range of methodologies available for studying religion and to appreciate the broad spectrum of world religions, together with a more detailed understanding of how a religious or non-religious world view informs a personal belief system and provides the infrastructure for a way of life. As with all subjects within the curriculum, it is important for the teacher to have a working knowledge of the studies of religion syllabus and be

---

941 In 2001, a research project on the extent of Christian values in the concept of kindergarten staff took place (cf. Boelskov, Jørgen/Boelskov, Birgit/Rosenberg, Finn (2002): Omfanget af kristne værdier i daginstitutionernes kulturformidling. København: Menighedernes Daginstitutioner) that was repeated in Norway and Denmark in 2011. (Boelskov, Jørgen/Tveiterås, Olav (2012): Omfanget af religiøse aktiviteter i danske og norske børnehavers kulturformidling: rapport. Kolding: University College Syddanmark). In 2001, teachers from 350 institutions were surveyed, with a response rate of 57 percent.
942 In 2011, teachers from 127 kindergartens in Denmark and 120 kindergartens in Norway were surveyed with a questionnaire; the response rate was 68 percent in Denmark and 52 percent in Norway.
943 The results of the study were presented by Jørgen Boelskov at the interdisciplinary-international symposium "Interreligious and intercultural competence in education for the elementary sector" on 19.09.2014 at the University of Tübingen.

prepared to work collaboratively with other teachers to ensure the subject is lively and challenging to students."[944]

Knowledge of other religions is a necessary but not a sufficient condition for a positive attitude towards religious difference.[945] "My point is also that no amount of knowledge and awareness will suffice if the teacher's task perception does not take into account the significant relational conditions that are involved in a given situation."[946] Only knowledge and information do not enable a positive approach, but, as shown in Julia Ipgrave's research project, can lead to the unintended action of being able to annoy and mock others better on the basis of existing knowledge and to deny the truthfulness of the other's religion.[947]

2.3.3.2 Dealing with religion and religious difference

Dealing with one's own religion and religiousness as well as the view of religious difference can help not to be determined by unreflected reasons when dealing with religious difference.[948] The reflected handling of one's own ideas of religion and religious difference can form the basis for not confusing one's own feelings with statements or actions of children, to be able to confront children's opinions as impartially as possible, to recognise the significance that religion could have for children and, in addition to the challenges that religious difference can bring, also to recognise the opportunities. In the study by Arniika Kuusisto and Silja Lamminmäku-Vartia[949] it becomes

---

944 Hobson, Peter R./Edwards, John S. (1999): Religious Education in a Pluralistic Society. The Key Philosophical Issues. London/Portland: Woburn Press, 169.
945 Cf. Schihalejev, Olga (2014): Contextuality of young people's attitudes. In: Arweck, Elisabeth/Jackson, Robert: Religion, Education and Society, 27–30, 29.
946 Frelin, Anneli (2013): Exploring Relational Professionalism at School. Rotterdam: Sense Publications, 122.
947 Cf. Ipgrave, Julia (2014): Relationships between local patterns. In: Arweck, Elisabeth/Jackson, Robert: Religion, Education and Society, 13–25.
948 Cf. chapter "Verbal communication about religious difference" (part V, 4.1.3).
949 Kuusisto, Arniika/Lamminmäki-Vartia, Silja (2012): Moral Foundation of the Kindergarten Teacher's Educational Approach: Self-Reflection Facilitated Educator Response to Pluralism in Educational Context. *Education Research International*. The study by Arniika Kuusisto and Silja Lamminmäku-Vartia examines the moral basis of kindergarten teachers' access to education from the perspective of sensitivity to religions and world views using ethnographic and action research. They investigate the research questions: "How do kindergarten teachers respond to pluralism in the educational context? What kinds of discourses and practical level approaches do they employ regarding the diversity of worldviews and worldview education in their work?" (Ibid., 4). In order to answer their research questions, Kuusisto and Lamminmäki survey the situation of Finnish "multi-faith kindergartens", which they surveyed using "mixed methods research" in five kindergartens in Helsinki. In a kindergarten, data were collected by means of an

clear that, in addition to knowledge, it is important for educators to examine their own values and attitudes in order to develop a sensitivity to different religions and world views. This is particularly necessary because the importance of certain world views for children is underestimated and the worldviews are experienced as restrictions in everyday kindergarten life.

> "[...] the personal meaning of worldviews to the children are often not realised, and the worldviews in general are still often seen through the perceived limitations to the everyday running of the kindergarten. This is why developing worldview sensitivity merely through the increase of knowledge on worldview traditions is not enough; rather the teachers need opportunities for pondering their own values and attitudes in relation to these [...]."[950]

The attitudes and assumptions of teachers towards cultures and world views that differ from their own become apparent in their daily encounters and actions in kindergarten,[951] which is why it is important that teachers develop a sensitivity towards other religions and world views.

> "However, as is true with many other theoretical lever goals, *employing an educational approach that consciously aims towards worldview sensitivity* should be in use as part of every teacher's moral competence for functioning in the present-day pluralistic education context. [...] Worldview sensitivity as an educational approach does not silence worldviews as taboos but preserves a position for them in the everyday life of the kindergarten or school. Although the most direct influences of this may often be visible in the religious or worldview education, sensitivity also reaches wider than this. It influences the teacher's approach towards openness and appreciation toward the diverse worldviews, both religious and nonreligious. In the kindergarten, worldview sensitive educational approach at its best includes aiming to detect and to support the needs of each individual child and family."[952]

Even if the educators seek to implement the principle of equality, equality is not possible if the educators are not aware of their own assumptions and prejudices.[953] In

---

ethnographic access. These were collected through participant observation, interviews with the employees and a questionnaire about the culturally and religiously diverse backgrounds of the children. In addition, data was collected in four kindergartens using an action research approach, using surveys and focus groups with employees, interviews with parents, participant observation and discussions with the children. In addition, the available national, municipal and kindergarten specific documents were used as part of the data. The data were evaluated by means of content analysis, including elements of discourse analysis.

950 Kuusisto, Arniika/Lamminmäki-Vartia, Silja (2012): Moral Foundation of the Kindergarten Teacher's Educational Approach. *Education Research International*, 10.
951 Ibid., 7.
952 Ibid., 11.
953 Cf. ibid.

addition to dealing with one's own attitude, it is important to have understanding and sensitivity for the views of people with other religions and religious attitudes, whereby it is important to meet the respective child and not a representative of a religion, "[...] the importance for the teacher to sensitively encounter each individual child, rather than seeing him as a representative of a particular tradition, and to positively recognize her culture and worldview from her particular starting points."[954]

According to Martin Jäggle, learning to see the world and oneself with each other's glasses, practising the change of perspective, can be very challenging and painful at the same time, but he asks the question whether self-knowledge and tolerance are possible otherwise.[955] The examination of one's own and other religious attitudes and the difference between them, as demanded by the situation of plurality, can contribute to learning something about one's own religion as well as about other religions and to developing further. This process is made possible when religious attitudes are recognisable and disclosed, and when there is a willingness to perceive these attitudes and to react appropriately to them.

> "However, accompanying the children in interreligious encounters will not only include an insight into the religious ideas of others – it will also have to pay attention to the questions that can arise for the child itself. If children want to know why some children believe in Allah, this also includes the question of the faith of their own family: 'And what are we? What do we believe?'"[956]

To be prepared to deal with one's own religious ideas and those of others is the prerequisite for meeting others honestly in dialogue, addressing conflicts and showing understanding. Learning processes are already designed to be interpretive in their basic structure. Differences in religious attitudes thus make an essential contribution to forming one's own religious ideas. Religious learning must not evade the plural or even fight it, but must make it the subject.[957]

3. Review – Outlook

3.1 View of children

The initial motivation for the work to increasingly include children's view of religious difference in research is still relevant at the end of the research. Children have their own voice, which should be listened to in research, if the children want to participate.

---

954 Ibid., 10.
955 Cf. Jäggle, Martin (2006): Schritte auf dem Weg. In: Bastel, Heribert et al. (Ed.): Das Gemeinsame entdecken – Das Unterscheidende anerkennen, 31–42, 42.
956 Schweitzer, Friedrich (2013): Das Recht des Kindes auf Religion, 71.
957 Cf. Ziebertz, Hans-Georg (1999): Religion, Christentum und Moderne. Veränderte Religionspräsenz als Herausforderung. Stuttgart:Kohlhammer, 82.

In order to perceive children's opinions and what actually concerns and interests children in a methodically controlled manner, the methodological possibilities of childhood research were examined. Due to the ethnographic approach and the attitude of openness implicit in this approach, it gradually became clear which methods were useful in order to gain insight into the children's perspective. This methodological diversity made it possible to gain an insight into how children address religious difference independently of the stimulus of an adult person. The children, who recognise religious difference, partly have no explanation for it and subordinate their behaviour as well as their thematisation of their religion to the desire for belonging, which becomes clear through the ethnographic approach of the study and the methodologically diverse view of the children. In particular, the ethnographic approach made it possible to perceive the children in their respective environment and to gain insights that would not have been possible with a selective data collection. The view of the organisation that emerged in the course of the research is also due to the ethnographic approach combined with the fundamentals of grounded theory and thematic coding.

3.2 View of the organisation

After some time in kindergarten and discussions with the children, it became apparent that the organisation cannot be ignored, which is why the research question has been adapted in line with grounded theory and further data collection is constantly being adapted in the course of research. Many data on other dimensions of difference such as gender, age, height, language, nationality, skin, hair and eye colour were also collected, especially during the participant observation spread over a school year, which are not addressed in this work with its focus on religious difference.[958]

In kindergarten, the religion of the majority tends to be dominant and this is the only one that is addressed in kindergarten, as the data in this study make clear. Children of the minor religions can adapt or are absent from certain offers, the potential of their own religion is not discernible in everyday kindergarten life. If difference is not addressed, the majority is automatically the "normal" and thus the "determining factor" in kindergarten.

The culture of the kindergarten, shaped by the dominant religion, must be developed into a culture of recognition in which there is no discrimination. Children need a *safe space* of recognition to address religious difference. In kindergarten it would be possible to recognise religious differences and to practice respect for different religions with children. Kindergarten has the chance to orientate itself on the metaphor *safe space* in which children can experience a space of recognition of their differences, including their religious differences.

---

[958] The evaluation of this data will be published in a separate article.

3.3 Research desiderata

The research results and the focus of the research question on the handling of religious difference in a Catholic kindergarten and an Islamic kindergarten refer to future research projects that provide deeper insights into dealing with religious difference on the part of the organisation and the children. The importance of the organisation as identified in the study must be taken into account in future projects, especially in the field of childhood research. Since the context and perspective of the children seem to be related, it is crucial not only to collect children's opinions, but also to consider and address the children's organisational context. It would be interesting to extend the research to other kindergartens. In this way, secular kindergartens could be included. In addition to kindergartens in a large city like Vienna, kindergartens in rural areas would also be relevant for further research.

Since the focus of this publication is on religious difference, it is important to focus more on worldviews in further works.

One area that could provide further insight into the context of the organisation, the opinions of children and their families, is the influence of parents or guardians on the organisation and perspective of children. It would be of interest to see how religion is addressed in the respective family and how religious education takes place and in what context this is related to the discussion of children in kindergarten.

The ethnographic approach proved to be particularly important in the present study, since the longer participation provided an insight into the field of research that would not have been possible by selective methodological survey. The method of ethnography, which places the human being at the centre of the study and is sensitive to the field of research and refers to it, must be increasingly integrated into religious education as a survey method. This method seems to be well suited to gain a comprehensive view of the organisation and the people involved in it, which is why further insights could be gained through the use of this method with regard to religious difference.

More intensive research on dealing with religious difference in early childhood institutions can raise awareness of the importance of the reflected and sensitive handling of religious difference in early childhood institutions, help children of the major religions to become more pluralistic and to escape the dominance trap and help children of minor religions gain their right to be recognised in kindergarten with what concerns them.

References

Abeldt, Sönke/Bauer, Walter/Heinrichs, Gesa/Knauth, Thorsten/Koch, Martina/Tiedemann, Holger/Weiße, Wolfram (Ed.) (2000): „... was es bedeutet, verletzbarer Mensch zu sein". Erziehungswissenschaft im Gespräch mit Theologie, Philosophie und Gesellschaftstheorie. Mainz: Matthias-Grünewald-Verlag.

Aboud, Frances E. (1988): Children and Prejudice. Oxford: Basil Blackwell.

Aboud, Frances E./Doyle, Anna Beth (1996): 'Does Talk of Race Foster Prejudice or Tolerance in Children?'. *Canadian Journal of Behavioural Science 28*(3), 161–170.

Aboud, Frances E./Tredoux, Colin/Tropp, Linda R./Brown, Christia Spears/Niens, Ulrike/Noor, Noraini M./the Una Global Evaluation Group (2012): Interventions to reduce prejudice and enhance inclusion and respect for ethnic differences in early childhood: A systematic review. *Developmental Review 32*, 307–336.

Abo-Zena, Mona M. (2012): Faith from the fringes: Religious minorities in school. *Kappanmagazin 93*(4), 15–19.

Albert, Mathias/Hurrelmann, Klaus/Quenzel, Gudrun/TNS Infratest Sozialforschung (2010): Jugend 2010–16. Hamburg: Deutsche Shell Holding GmbH.

Altmeyer, Stefan (2006): Von der Wahrnehmung zum Ausdruck. Zur ästhetischen Dimension von Glauben und Lernen. Stuttgart: Kohlhammer.

Altmeyer, Stefan (2007): Welche Wahrnehmung? Kontexte und Konturen eines praktisch-theologischen Grundbegriffs. In: Boschki, Reinhold/Gronover, Matthias (Ed.): Junge Wissenschaftstheorie der Religionspädagogik. Berlin: LIT, 214–237.

Altrichter, Herbert/Schley, Wilfried/Schratz, Michael (Ed.) (1998): Handbuch zur Schulentwicklung. Innsbruck/Vienna: Studienverlag.

Andresen, Sabine/Casale, Rita/Gabriel, Thomas/Horlacher, Rebekka/Larcher Klee, Sabina/Oelkers, Jürgen (Ed.) (2009): Handwörterbuch Erziehungswissenschaft. Weinheim/Basel: Beltz.

Ang, Lynn (2010): Critical perspectives on cultural diversity in early childhood: building an inclusive curriculum and provision. *Early Years: An International Research Journal 30*(1), 41–52.

Angel, Hans-Ferdinand (2006): Religiosität – Die Neuentdeckung eines Forschungsgegenstands. In: Angel, Hans-Ferdinand/Bröking-Bortfeldt, Martin/Hemel, Ulrich/Jakobs, Monika/Kunstmann, Joachim/Pirner, Manfred L./Rothgangel, Martin: Religiosität. Anthropologische, theologische und sozialwissenschaftliche Klärungen. Stuttgart: Kohlhammer, 7–15.

Angel, Hans-Ferdinand/Bröking-Bortfeldt, Martin/Hemel, Ulrich/Jakobs, Monika/Kunstmann, Joachim/Pirner, Manfred L./Rothgangel, Martin (2006): Religiosität. Anthropologische, theologische und sozialwissenschaftliche Klärungen. Stuttgart: Kohlhammer.

Argyris, Chris (^{2}1999): On Organizational Learning. Malden/Oxford/Carlton: Blackwell Publishing [1992].

Asbrand, Barbara (2008): Zusammen leben und lernen im Religionsunterricht. Eine empirische Studie zur grundschulpädagogischen Konzeption eines interreligiösen Religionsunterrichts in der Grundschule. Frankfurt am Main: Verlag für Interkulturelle Kommunikation.

Auernheimer, Georg (1989): Kulturelle Identität – ein gegenaufklärerischer Mythos?. *Das Argument 31*(3), 381–394.

Auernheimer, Georg (⁷2012): Einführung in die Interkulturelle Pädagogik. Darmstadt: Wissenschaftliche Buchgesellschaft [1990: Einführung in die Interkulturelle Erziehung].

Aukrust, Vibeke Grøver/Rydland, Veslemøy (2009): 'Does it matter?' Talking about ethnic diversity in preschool and first grade classrooms. *Journal of Pragmatics 41*(8), 1538–1556.

Arweck, Elisabeth/Jackson, Robert (2014): Religion, Education and Society. London/New York: Routledge Taylor & Francis Group.

Bahr, Matthias/Kropač, Ulrich/Schambeck, Mirjam (Ed.) (2005): Subjektwerdung und religiöses Lernen. Für eine Religionspädagogik, die den Menschen ernst nimmt. Munich: Kösel.

Balzer, Nicole/Ricken, Norbert (2010): Anerkennung als pädagogisches Problem. Markierungen im erziehungswissenschaftlichen Diskurs. In: Schäfer, Alfred/Thompson, Christiane (Ed.): Anerkennung. Paderborn/Munich/Vienna/Zurich: Ferdinand Schöningh, 35–87.

Bar-Tal, Daniel (1996): Development of social categories and stereotypes in early childhood: The case of "the Arab" concept formation, stereotype and attitudes by Jewish children in Israel. *International Journal of Intercultural Relations 20*(314), 341–370.

Bastel, Heribert/Göllner, Manfred/Jäggle, Martin/Miklas, Helene (Ed.) (2006): Das Gemeinsame entdecken – Das Unterscheidende anerkennen. Projekt eines konfessionell-kooperativen Religionsunterrichts. Einblicke – Hintergründe – Ansätze – Forschungsergebnisse. Münster: LIT.

Baumann, Gerd (1996): Contesting Culture. Discourses of Identity in Multi-Ethnic London. Cambridge: Cambridge University Press.

Beer, Peter (2003): Kinderfragen als Wegmarken religiöser Erziehung. Ein Entwurf für religionspädagogisches Arbeiten im Elementarbereich. Munich: Don Bosco.

Behnken, Imbke/Zinnecker, Jürgen (Ed.) (2001): Kinder. Kindheit. Lebensgeschichte. Seelze-Velber: Kallmeyersche Verlagsbuchhandlung.

Berger, Peter L./Weiße, Wolfram (2010): Im Gespräch: Religiöse Pluralität und gesellschaftlicher Zusammenhalt [Fußnote]. In: Weiße, Wolfram/Gutmann, Hans-Martin (Ed.): Religiöse Differenz als Chance? Positionen, Kontroversen, Perspektiven. Münster et al.: Waxmann, 17–26.

Berglund, Jenny (2014): Teachers only stand behind parents and God in the eyes of the Muslim pupils. In: Arweck, Elisabeth/Jackson, Robert: Religion, Education and Society. London/New York: Routledge Taylor & Francis Group, 109–118.

Bernhardt, Reinhold (2005): Pluralistische Theologie der Religionen. In: Schreiner, Peter/Sieg, Ursula/Elsenbast, Volker (Ed.): Handbuch Interreligiöses Lernen. Gütersloh: Gütersloher Verlagshaus, 168–178.

Bertram-Troost, Gerdien/Ipgrave, Julia/Josza, Dan-Paul/Knauth, Thorsten (2008): Encountering religious pluralism in school and society. A Qualitative Study of Teenage Perspectives in Europe. Background and Contextualisation. In: Knauth, Thorsten/Josza, Dan-Paul/Bertram-Troost, Gerdien/Ipgrave, Julia (Ed.): Encountering religious pluralism in school and society. A Qualitative Study of Teenage Perspectives in Europe. Münster et al.: Waxmann, 11–19.

Bertelsmann Stiftung (Ed.) (2008): Religion und Bildung. Orte, Medien und Experten religiöser Bildung. Gütersloh: Bertelsmann Stiftung.

Biehl, Peter (1998): Der phänomenologische Ansatz in der deutschen Religionspädagogik. In: Heimbrock, Hans-Günter (Ed.): Religionspädagogik und Phänomenologie. Weinheim: Deutscher Studien Verlag, 15–46.

Biehl, Peter (^{2}2005): Die Gottebenbildlichkeit des Menschen und das Problem der Bildung. In: Biehl, Peter/Nipkow, Karl Ernst: Bildung und Bildungspolitik in theologischer Perspektive. Münster: LIT, 9–102.

Biehl, Peter/Nipkow, Karl Ernst (2005): Bildung und Bildungspolitik in theologischer Perspektive. Münster: LIT.

Biesinger, Albert/Schweitzer, Friedrich (2013): Religionspädagogische Kompetenzen. Zehn Zugänge für pädagogische Fachkräfte in Kitas. Freiburg/Basel/Vienna: Herder.

Biesinger, Albert/Edelbrock, Anke/Schweitzer, Friedrich (2011): Auf die Eltern kommt es an! Interreligiöse und Interkulturelle Bildung in der Kita. Interreligiöse und Interkulturelle Bildung im Kindesalter, vol. 2. Münster et al.: Waxmann.

Biesinger, Albert/Schweitzer, Friedrich/Edelbrock, Anke (2010): Religiöse Differenzwahrnehmung im Kindesalter. Befunde aus der empirischen Untersuchung im Überblick. In: Edelbrock, Anke/Schweitzer, Friedrich/Biesinger, Albert (Ed.): Wie viele Götter sind im Himmel? Religiöse Differenzwahrnehmung im Kindesalter. Interreligiöse und interkulturelle Bildung im Kindesalter, vol. 1. Münster et al.: Waxmann, 23–38.

Bitter, Gottfried/Englert, Rudolf/Miller, Gabriele/Nipkow, Karl Ernst (Ed.) (^{2}2009): Neues Handbuch religionspädagogischer Grundbegriffe. Munich: Kösel [2002].

Bizer, Christoph (1993): Auf dem Weg zu einer praktischen Anthropologie des Kindes und des Jugendlichen. In: Riess, Richard/Fiedler, Kirsten (Ed.): Die verletzlichen Jahre. Handbuch zur Beratung und Seelsorge an Kindern und Jugendlichen. Gütersloh: Gütersloher Verlagshaus, 743–756.

Blaicher, Hans-Peter/Haußmann, Annette/Wissner, Golde/Ilg, Wolfgang/Kaplan, Murat/Biesinger, Albert/Edelbrock, Anke/Schweitzer, Friedrich (2011): Interreligiöse Bildung in Kindertagesstätten in empirischer Perspektive. Vertiefte Auswertungen zur Tübinger Studie. In: Schweitzer, Friedrich/Edelbrock, Anke/Biesinger, Albert (Ed.): Interreligiöse und interkulturelle Bildung in der Kita. Eine Repräsentativbefragung von Erzieherinnen in Deutschland – interdisziplinäre, interreligiöse und internationale Perspektiven. Interreligiöse und Interkulturelle Bildung im Kindesalter, vol. 3. Münster et al.: Waxmann, 147–222.

Blasberg-Kuhnke, Martina (2007): Kindertheologie – Zur pastoralen Bedeutung eines religionspädagogischen Programms. *Diakonia 38*, 305–308.

Bock, Karin (2010): Kinderalltag – Kinderwelten. Rekonstruktive Analysen von Gruppendiskussionen mit Kindern. Opladen/Farmington Hills: Barbara Budrich.

Boelskov, Jørgen/Tveiterås, Olav (2012): Omfanget af religiøse aktiviteter i danske og norske børnehavers kulturformidling: rapport. Kolding: University College Syddanmark.

Boelskov, Jørgen/Boelskov, Birgit/Rosenberg, Finn (2002): Omfanget af kristne værdier i daginstitutionernes kulturformidling. København: Menighedernes Daginstitutioner.

Bogner, Alexander/Menz, Wolfgang (^{2}2005): Das theoriegenerierende Experteninterview. Erkenntnisinteresse, Wissensform, Interview. In: Bogner, Alexander/Littig, Beate/Menz,

Wolfgang (Ed.): Das Experteninterview. Theorie, Methode, Anwendung. Wiesbaden: VS Verlag für Sozialwissenschaften [2002], 33–70.

Bogner, Alexander/Littig, Beate/Menz, Wolfgang (Ed.) (²2005): Das Experteninterview. Theorie, Methode, Anwendung. Wiesbaden: VS Verlag für Sozialwissenschaften [2002].

Böhm, Andreas (⁹2012): Theoretisches Codieren: Textanalyse in der Grounded Theory. In: Flick, Uwe/von Kardorff, Ernst/Steinke, Ines: Qualitative Forschung. Ein Handbuch. Reinbek bei Hamburg: Rowohlt Taschenbuch [2000], 475–485.

Bohnsack, Ralf (⁹2012): Gruppendiskussionen. In: Flick, Uwe/von Kardorff, Ernst/Steinke, Ines: Qualitative Forschung. Ein Handbuch. Reinbek bei Hamburg: Rowohlt Taschenbuch [2000], 369–384.

Bohnsack, Ralf/Nentwig-Gesemann, Iris/Nohl, Arnd-Michael (Ed.) (³2013): Die dokumentarische Methode und ihre Untersuchungspraxis. Grundlagen qualitativer Sozialforschung. Wiesbaden: VS Verlag für Sozialwissenschaften [2001].

Bohnsack, Ralf/Przyborski, Aglaja/Schäffer, Burkhard (²2010): Das Gruppendiskussionsverfahren in der Forschungspraxis. Opladen/Farmington Hills: Barbara Budrich [2006].

Boschki, Reinhold (2007): Der phänomenologische Blick: „Vierschritt" statt „Dreischritt" in der Religionspädagogik. In: Boschki, Reinhold/Gronover, Matthias (Ed.): Junge Wissenschaftstheorie der Religionspädagogik. Berlin: LIT, 25–47.

Boschki, Reinhold/Gronover, Matthias (2007): Junge Wissenschaftstheorie der Religionspädagogik. Berlin: LIT.

Bouma, Gary D. (2011): Being Faithful in Diversity. Religions and Social Policy in Multifaith Societies. The Lloyd Geering Lectures 2010. Hindmarsh: ATF Ltd.

Braun, Anne/Blaicher, Hans-Peter/Haußmann, Annette/Wissner, Golde/Ilg, Wolfgang/Biesinger, Albert/Edelbrock, Anke/Kaplan, Murat/Schweitzer, Friedrich/Stehle, Andreas (2011): Was Eltern erwarten und erfahren – Religiöse und interreligiöse Bildung in der Kita aus Elternsicht. In: Biesinger, Albert/Edelbrock, Anke/Schweitzer, Friedrich (Ed.): Auf die Eltern kommt es an! Interreligiöse und Interkulturelle Bildung in der Kita. Interreligiöse und Interkulturelle Bildung im Kindesalter, vol. 2. Münster et al.: Waxmann, 43–120.

Braunschweiger Zentrum für Gender Studies/Institut für Pädagogische Psychologie der Technischen Universität Braunschweig (Ed.) (2005): Geschlechtertrennung in der Kindheit: Empirische Forschung und pädagogische Praxis im Dialog. Abschlussbericht des Projekts „Identität und Geschlecht in der Kindheit". Braunschweig.

Brooker, Liz/Woodhead, Martin (Ed.) (2008): Developing Positive Identities. Diversity and Young Children. Early Childhood in Focus (3). Milton Keynes: The Open University.

Brüsemeister, Thomas (2008): Bildungssoziologie. Einführung in Perspektiven und Probleme. Wiesbaden: VS Verlag für Sozialwissenschaften.

Bucher, Anton A./Büttner, Gerhard/Freudenberger-Lötz, Petra/Schreiner, Martin (Ed.) (since 2002): Jahrbuch für Kindertheologie. Stuttgart: Calwer.

Bucher, Anton A./Büttner, Gerhard/Freudenberger-Lötz, Petra/Schreiner, Martin (Ed.) (2009): Jahrbuch der Kindertheologie: „In den Himmel kommen nur, die sich auch verstehen". Wie Kinder über religiöse Differenz denken und sprechen, vol. 8. Stuttgart: Calwer.

Buhren, Claus G./Rolff, Hans-Günter (2002): Personalentwicklung in Schulen. Konzepte, Praxisbausteine, Methoden. Weinheim/Basel: Beltz.

Cairns, Ed (2002): "Whatever you say, say nothing": Social Competence and Communication in Northern Ireland. *Researching Early Childhood 4*, 75–81.

Charter of Fundamental Rights of the European Union (2010/364/01). Official Journal of the European Union, article 10, http://www.awsg.at/Content.Node/files/sonstige/Charta_der_ Grundrechte_der_Europaeischen_Union.pdf [22.07.2015].

Coles, Robert (1990): The Spiritual Life of Children. Boston: Houghton Mifflin Company.

Collmar, Norbert (2004): Schulpädagogik und Religionspädagogik. Handlungstheoretische Analysen von Schule und Religionsunterricht. Göttingen: Vandenhoeck & Ruprecht.

Connolly, Paul (2008): Positive identities may lead to negative beliefs. In: Brooker, Liz/Woodhead, Martin (Ed.): Developing Positive Identities. Diversity and Young Children. Early Childhood in Focus, vol. 3. Milton Keynes: The Open University.

Connolly, Paul (2009): Developing programmes to promote ethnic diversity in early childhood: Lessons from Northern Ireland. Working Paper No. 52. The Hague: Bernard van Leer Foundation.

Connolly, Paul/Healy, July (2004): Children and the conflict in Northern Ireland: The Experiences and Perspectives of 3–11 Year Olds. Belfast: Office of the First Minister and Deputy First Minister.

Connolly, Paul/Miller, Sarah/Eakin, Angela (2010): A Cluster Randomised Trial Evaluation of the Media Initiative for Children: Respecting Difference Programme. Belfast: Centre for Effective Education, Queen's University Belfast.

Connolly, Paul/Smith, Alan/Kelly, Berni (2002): Too Young to Notice? The cultural and political awareness of 3–6 year olds in Northern Ireland. Belfast: Community Relations Council.

Connolly, Paul/Fitzpatrick, Siobhan/Gallagher, Tony/Harris, Paul (2006): Addressing diversity and inclusion in the early years in conflict affected societies: a case study of the Media Initiative for Children Northern Ireland. *International Journal of Early Years Education 14(3)*, 263–278.

Conrad, Jörg (2009): "As a Protestant, you somehow think a little less, somehow. Or "more or less the same" – how children perceive, understand and deal with denominational difference. In: Bucher, Anton A./Büttner, Gerhard/Freudenberger-Lötz, Petra/Schreiner, Martin (Ed.): Jahrbuch der Kindertheologie: „In den Himmel kommen nur, die sich auch verstehen". Wie Kinder über religiöse Differenz denken und sprechen, vol. 8. Stuttgart: Calwer, 60–70.

Convention on the Rights of the Child. Adopted and opened for signature, ratification and accession by General Assembly resolution 44/25 of 20 November 1989 entry into force 2 September 1990, http://www.ohchr.org/en/professionalinterest/pages/crc.aspx [22.07.2015].

Corbin, Juliet/Strauss, Anselm (^{3}2008): Basics of Qualitative Research. Los Angeles-London-New Delhi-Singapore: Sage Publications [1990 and 1998 eds. present Strauss as the first author and Corbin as second].

Cummings, Thomas G. (Ed.) (2008): Handbook of Organization Development. Thousand Oaks/London/New Delhi/Singapore: Sage Publications.

Dahlberg, Gunilla/Moss, Peter (2005): Ethics and Politics in Early Childhood Education. London/New York: RoutledgeFalmer.

Dalin, Per/Rolff, Hans-Günter/Bucher, Herbert (⁴1998): Institutioneller Schulentwicklungs-Prozeß. Ein Handbuch. Soest: Verlag für Schule und Weiterbildung [1990].

Deckert-Peaceman, Heike/Dietrich, Cornelia/Stenger, Ursula (2010): Einführung in die Kindheitsforschung. Darmstadt: Wissenschaftliche Buchgesellschaft.

de Graaff, Fuusje/van Keulen, Anke (2008): Making the road as we go. Parents and professionals as partners managing diversity in early childhood education. The Hague: Bernard van Leer Foundation.

Deinet, Ulrich/Sturzenhecker, Benedikt (Ed.) (⁴2013): Handbuch Offene Kinder- und Jugendarbeit. Wiesbaden: Springer Verlag für Sozialwissenschaften [1998].

Denzin, Norman K. (1989): The research act. A Theoretical Introduction to Sociological Methods. New Jersey: Prentice Hall.

Denzin, Norman K./Lincoln, Yvonna S. (Ed.) (⁴2011): The SAGE Handbook of Qualitative Research. Thousand Oaks/London/New Delhi/Singapore: SAGE, 1–19. [Denzin, Norman K./Lincoln, Yvonna S. (1994): Handbook of Qualitative Research. Thousand Oaks/London/New Delhi: SAGE].

Denzin, Norman K./Lincoln, Yvonna S. (⁴2011): Introduction. Disciplining the Practice of Qualitative Research. In: Denzin, Norman K./Lincoln, Yvonna S. (Ed.): The SAGE Handbook of Qualitative Research. Thousand Oaks/London/New Delhi/Singapore: SAGE, 1–19.

Derman-Sparks, Louise/A.B.C. Task Force (1989): Anti-Bias Curriculum: Tools for Empowering Young Children. Washington, DC: National Association for the Education of Young Children.

Deth, Jan W. van/Abendschön, Simone/Rathke, Julia/Vollmar, Meike (2007): Kinder und Politik. Politische Einstellungen von jungen Kindern im ersten Grundschuljahr. Wiesbaden: VS Verlag für Sozialwissenschaften.

Dethloff, Klaus/Langthaler, Rudolf/Nagl-Docekal, Herta/Wolfram, Friedrich (2005): Orte der Religion im philosophischen Diskurs der Gegenwart. Berlin: Parerga.

Dillen, Annemie (2009): Glaubensvorstellungen von Kindern und ihre Wahrnehmung von Multikulturalität. In: Bucher, Anton A./Büttner, Gerhard/Freudenberger-Lötz, Petra/Schreiner, Martin. (Ed.): Jahrbuch der Kindertheologie: „In den Himmel kommen nur, die sich auch verstehen". Wie Kinder über religiöse Differenz denken und sprechen, vol. 8. Stuttgart: Calwer, 50–59.

Dirks, Walter/Kogon, Eugen (Ed.) (1984): Nach 1984: Die Krise der Zivilisation und unserer Zukunft. *Frankfurter Hefte extra 6.*

Doherty, Martin (2009): Theory of Mind. How Children Understand Others' Thoughts and Feelings. East Sussex/New York: Psychology Press.

Dommel, Christa (2008): Religion und religiöse Unterschiede als „Weltwissen" im Kindergarten. In: Klöcker, Michael/Tworuschka, Udo: Handbuch der Religionen. Kirchen und andere Glaubensgemeinschaften in Deutschland/im deutschsprachigen Raum. Landsberg: Olzog, 1–14.

Dommel, Christa (2003): Kindergartenpädagogik und Religion in Deutschland. Von Fröbel zum Situationsansatz. In: Dommel, Christa/Heumann, Jürgen/Otto, Gert: WerteSchätzen. Religiöse Vielfalt und Öffentliche Bildung. Festschrift für Jürgen Lott zum 60. Geburtstag. Frankfurt/London: IKO, 206–222.

Dommel, Christa (²2010): Religion – Diskriminierungsgrund oder kulturelle Ressource für Kinder?. In: Wagner, Petra (Ed.): Handbuch Kinderwelten. Vielfalt als Chance – Grundlagen einer vorurteilsbewussten Bildung und Erziehung. Freiburg/Basel/Vienna: Herder [2008], 148–159.

Dommel, Christa/Heumann, Jürgen/Otto, Gert (Ed.) (2003): WerteSchätzen. Religiöse Vielfalt und Öffentliche Bildung. Festschrift für Jürgen Lott zum 60. Geburtstag. Frankfurt am Main/London: IKO – Verlag für interkulturelle Kommunikation.

Doppler, Klaus (2000): Kommunikation als Schlüsselfaktor der Organisationsentwicklung. In: Trebesch, Karsten (Ed.): Organisationsentwicklung. Konzepte, Strategien, Fallstudien. Stuttgart: Klett-Cotta, 281–307.

Dreher, Michael/Dreher, Eva (2013): Gruppendiskussionsverfahren. In: Flick, Uwe/von Kardorff, Ernst/Keupp, Heiner/von Rosenstiel, Lutz/Wolff, Stephan (Ed.): Handbuch qualitative Sozialforschung: Grundlagen, Konzepte, Methoden und Anwendungen. Munich: Psychologie Verlags Union, 186–188.

Drury, Rose/Miller, Linda/Campbell, Robin (2000): Looking at Early Years Education and Care. Professional roles in early childhood. London: David Fulton Publishers.

Dubiski, Katja/Essich, Ibtissame/Schweitzer, Friedrich/Edelbrock, Anke/Biesinger, Albert (2010): Religiöse Differenzwahrnehmung im Kindesalter. Befunde aus der empirischen Untersuchung im Überblick. In: Edelbrock, Anke/Schweitzer, Friedrich/Biesinger, Albert (Ed.): Wie viele Götter sind im Himmel? Religiöse Differenzwahrnehmung im Kindesalter. Interreligiöse und Interkulturelle Bildung im Kindesalter, vol. 1. Münster et al.: Waxmann, 23–38.

Dubiski, Katja/Essich, Ibtisamme/Schweitzer, Friedrich/Edelbrock, Anke/Biesinger, Albert (2010): Religiöse Differenzwahrnehmung im Kindesalter. Eine qualitativ-empirische Untersuchung mit Kindern im Alter zwischen 4 und 6 Jahren. In: Edelbrock, Anke/Schweitzer, Friedrich/Biesinger, Albert (Ed.): Wie viele Götter sind im Himmel? Religiöse Differenzwahrnehmung im Kindesalter. Interreligiöse und Interkulturelle Bildung im Kindesalter, vol. 1. Münster et al.: Waxmann, 122–194.

Dunn, Judy (1988): The Beginnings of Social Understanding. Oxford: Basil Blackwell.

Edelbrock, Anke/Schweitzer, Friedrich/Biesinger, Albert (Ed.) (2010): Wie viele Götter sind im Himmel? Religiöse Differenzwahrnehmung im Kindesalter. Interreligiöse und interkulturelle Bildung im Kindesalter, vol. 1. Münster et al.: Waxmann.

Edelbrock, Anke/Schweitzer, Friedrich/Biesinger, Albert (Ed.) (2011): Interreligiöse und interkulturelle Bildung in der Kita. Eine Repräsentativbefragung von Erzieherinnen in Deutschland – interdisziplinäre, interreligiöse und internationale Perspektive. Interreligiöse und interkulturelle Bildung im Kindesalter, vol. 3. Münster et al.: Waxmann.

Edelbrock, Anke/Biesinger, Albert/Schweitzer, Friedrich (Ed.) (2012): Religiöse Vielfalt in der Kita. So gelingt interreligiöse und interkulturelle Bildung in der Praxis. Berlin: Cornelson Verlag Scriptor.

Elkind, David (1964): Age changes in the meaning of religious identity. *Review of Religious Research* 6(1), 36–40.

Engebretson, Kath (2009): In your shoes: inter-faith education for Australian religious educators. Ballan: Connor Court Publishing.

Engebretson, Kath/de Souza, Marian/Durka, Gloria/Gearon, Liam (Ed.) (2010): International Handbook of Inter-religious Education. Part One. Dordrecht/Heidelberg/London/New York: Springer.

Engebretson, Kath/de Souza, Marian/Durka, Gloria/Gearon, Liam (Ed.) (2010): International Handbook of Inter-religious Education. Part Two. Dordrecht/Heidelberg/London/New York: Springer.

Englert, Rudolf (1995): Religiöse Erziehung als Erziehung zu Toleranz. In: Hilpert, Konrad/Werbick, Jürgen (Ed.): Mit den Anderen leben. Wege zur Toleranz. Düsseldorf: Patmos, 161–177.

Englert, Rudolf (2002): Dimensionen religiöser Pluralität. In: Schweitzer, Friedrich/Englert, Rudolf/Schwab, Ulrich/Ziebertz, Hans-Georg: Entwurf einer pluralitätsfähigen Religionspädagogik. Gütersloh/Freiburg i. Br.: Gütersloher Verlagshaus/Herder, 17–50.

Englert, Rudolf (2012): Religion gibt zu denken. Eine Religionsdidaktik in 19 Lehrstücken. Munich: Kösel.

Erickson, Frederick (^{4}2011): A history of qualitative inquiry in social and educational research. In: Denzin, Norman K./Lincoln, Yvonna S. (Ed.): The SAGE Handbook of Qualitative Research. Thousand Oaks/London/New Delhi/Singapore: SAGE, 43–59, 43.

Evangelische Kirche in Deutschland (Ed.) (1994): Identität und Verständigung. Standort und Perspektiven des Religionsunterrichts in der Pluralität. Eine Denkschrift der Evangelischen Kirche in Deutschland. Gütersloh: Gütersloher Verlagshaus.

Exeler, Adolf (1983): Religiöse Erziehung als Hilfe zur Menschwerdung. Munich: Kösel.

Exeler, Adolf (^{2}1977): Fehlformen religiöser Erziehung. In: Feifel, Erich/Leuenberger, Robert/Stachel, Günter/Wegenast, Klaus (Ed.): Handbuch Religionspädagogik, vol. 1 (Religiöse Bildung und Erziehung: Theorie und Faktoren). Gütersloh/Zurich/Einsiedeln/Cologne: Gütersloher Verlagshaus, 135-144.

Facer, Keri (2011): Learning Futures. Education, technology and social change. London: Routledge.

Fatzer, Gerhard (Ed.) (1993): Organisationsentwicklung für die Zukunft. Ein Handbuch. Cologne: Edition Humanistische Psychologie.

Fatzer, Gerhard (1993): Organisationsentwicklung als Beitrag für die lernfähige Organisation. In: Fatzer, Gerhard (Ed.): Organisationsentwicklung für die Zukunft. Ein Handbuch. Cologne: Edition Humanistische Psychologie, 125–127.

Fatzer, Gerhard (1993): Einleitung. Organisationsentwicklung und ihre Herausforderungen. In: Fatzer, Gerhard (Ed.): Organisationsentwicklung für die Zukunft, 13–34.

Federal Constitutional Act on the Rights of Children. In: Federal Law Gazette I No. 4/2011, http://www.ris.bka.gv.at/Dokument.wxe?Abfrage=BgblAuth&Dokumentnummer=BG-BLA_2011_I_4 [22.07.2015].Feifel, Erich/Leuenberger, Robert/Stachel, Günter/Wegenast, Klaus (Ed.) (^{2}1977): Handbuch Religionspädagogik, vol. 1 (Religiöse Bildung und Erziehung: Theorie und Faktoren). Gütersloh/Zurich/Einsiedeln/Cologne: Gütersloher Verlagshaus [1973].

Fischer, Dietlind/Schöll, Albrecht (Ed.) (2000): Religiöse Vorstellungen bilden. Erkundungen zur Religion von Kindern über Bilder. Münster: Comenius-Institut.

Fischer, Dietlind/Schreiner, Peter/Doyé, Götz/Scheilke, Christoph Th. (1996): Auf dem Weg zur interkulturellen Schule. Fallstudien zur Situation interkulturellen und interreligiösen Lernens. Münster et al.: Waxmann.

Flavell, John H./Everett, Barbara A./Croft, Karen/Flavell, Eleanor R. (1981): Young children's knowledge about visual perception: further evidence for the level 1–level 2 distinction. *Developmental Psychology 17*(1), 99–103.

Fleck, Carola (2011): Religiöse Bildung in der Frühpädagogik. Berlin: LIT.

Flick, Uwe (⁴2009): An Introduction to Qualitative Research. London u.a.: Sage [originally published as Qualitative Forschung 1995].

Flick, Uwe (³2011): Triangulation. Eine Einführung. Wiesbaden: VS Verlag für Sozialwissenschaften.

Flick, Uwe (⁵2012): Qualitative Sozialforschung. Eine Einführung. Reinbek bei Hamburg: Rowohlt [1995; revised and amended edition 2007].

Flick, Uwe (⁹2012): Triangulation in der qualitativen Forschung. In: Flick, Uwe/von Kardorff, Ernst/Steinke, Ines: Qualitative Forschung. Ein Handbuch. Reinbek bei Hamburg: Rowohlt Taschenbuch [2000], 309–318.

Flick, Uwe/von Kardorff, Ernst/Steinke, Ines (Ed.) (⁹2012): Qualitative Sozialforschung. Ein Handbuch. Reinbek bei Hamburg: Rowohlt [2000].

Flick, Uwe/von Kardorff, Ernst/Keupp, Heiner/von Rosenstiel, Lutz/Wolff, Stephan (Ed.) (2013): Handbuch qualitative Sozialforschung: Grundlagen, Konzepte, Methoden und Anwendungen. Munich: Psychologie Verlags Union.

Foley, Pam/Roche, Jeremy/Tucker, Stanley (Ed.) (2001): Children in Society. Contemporary Theory, Policy and Practice. London: Palgrave in association with The Open University.

Follari, Lissanna (2015): Valuing Diversity in Early Childhood Education. Boston et al.: Pearson Education.

Forgas, Joseph P. (1995): Mood and judgement: The affect infusion model (AIM). *Psychological Bulletin 117*(1), 39–66.

Fowler, James W. (1995): Stages of Faith. The Psychology of Human Development and the Quest for Meaning. New York: HarperCollins Publisher [first published in San Francisco: HarperSanFrancisco 1981].

Frelin, Anneli (2013): Exploring Relational Professionalism at School. Rotterdam: Sense Publications.

Friebertshäuser, Barbara/Langer, Antje/Prengel, Annedore (Ed.) (⁴2013): Handbuch. Qualitative Forschungsmethoden in der Erziehungswissenschaft. Weinheim/Basel: Beltz Juventa [1997].

Friebertshäuser, Barbara/von Felden, Heide/Schäffer, Burkhard (Ed.) (2007): Bild und Text. Methoden und Methodologien visueller Sozialforschung in der Erziehungswissenschaft. Opladen/Farmington Hills: Barbara Budrich.

Friese, Susanne (QUARC Consulting) (2014): Atlas.ti 7. User Guide and Reference. Berlin: ATLAS.ti Scientific Software Development GmbH.

Friese, Susanne (²2014): Qualitative Data Analysis with Atlas ti. London: Sage Publications Ltd [2012].

Fuhs, Burkhard (2012): Kinder im qualitativen Interview – Zur Erforschung subjektiver kindlicher Lebenswelten. In: Heinzel, Friederike (Ed.): Methoden der Kindheitsforschung. Ein

Überblick über Forschungszugänge zur kindlichen Perspektive. Weinheim/Basel: Beltz Juventa, 80–103.

García Coll, Cynthia/Lamberty, Gontran/Jenkins, Renee/McAdoo, Harriet Pipes/Crnic, Keith/Wasik, Barbara Hanna/Vázquez García, Heidie (1996): An Integrative Model for the Study of Developmental Competencies in Minority Children. *Child Development 67*(5), 1891–1914.

Geertz, Clifford (1973): The interpretation of cultures. Selected essays. New York: Basic Books.

Geiling, Ute/Hinz, Andreas (Ed.) (2005): Integrationspädagogik im Diskurs. Auf dem Weg zu einer inklusiven Pädagogik. Bad Heilbrunn: Julius Klinkhardt.

Geneva Declaration of the Rights of the Child of 1924, adopted Sept. 26, 1924, League of Nations O.J. Spec. Supp. 21, at 43 (1924), http://www.kinderrechte.gv.at/wp-content/uploads/2013/01/genfer_erklaerung_1924_englisch1.pdf [22.07.2015].

Gierden-Jülich, Marion (2008): „Von Kindesbeinen an: Von der Notwendigkeit, den Umgang mit Pluralität zu erlernen". Politische Optionen für interkulturelle und interreligiöse Bildung. In: Schweitzer, Friedrich/Biesinger, Albert/Edelbrock, Anke (Ed.): Mein Gott – Dein Gott. Interkulturelle und interreligiöse Bildung in Kindertagesstätten. Weinheim/Basel: Beltz, 142–145.

Girtler, Roland (^{3}1992): Methoden der qualitativen Sozialforschung. Vienna/Cologne/Weimar: Böhlau [1984].

Glaser, Barney G./Strauss, Anselm (1967): The Discovery of Grounded Theory. Strategies for Qualitative Research. New York: Aldine Publishing.

Gogolin, Ingrid/Krüger-Potratz, Marianne (2010): Einführung in die Interkulturelle Pädagogik. Opladen/Farmington Hills: Barbara Budrich.

Gramelt, Katja (2010): Der Anti-Bias-Ansatz. Zu Konzept und Praxis einer Pädagogik für den Umgang mit (kultureller) Vielfalt. Wiesbaden: VS Verlag für Sozialwissenschaften.

Gramelt, Katja (2013): Diversity in early childhood education: a German perspective. *Early Years. An International Research Journal 33*(1), 45–58.

Griese, Hartmut M. (^{4}2013): Kinder und Jugendliche mit Migrationshintergrund. In: Deinet, Ulrich/Sturzenhecker, Benedikt (Ed.): Handbuch Offene Kinder- und Jugendarbeit. Wiesbaden: Springer Verlag für Sozialwissenschaften [1998], 143–148.

Grom, Bernhard (^{5}2000): Religionspädagogische Psychologie des Kleinkind-, Schul- und Jugendalters. Düsseldorf: Patmos [1981].

Grümme, Bernhard (2012): Menschen bilden? Eine religionspädagogische Anthropologie. Freiburg i. Br.: Herder.

Gutmann, Hans-Martin/Weiße, Wolfram (2010): Einleitung. In: Weiße, Wolfram/Gutmann, Hans-Martin (Ed.): Religiöse Differenz als Chance? Positionen, Kontroversen, Perspektiven. Münster et al.: Waxmann, 7–14.

Guzzoni, Ute (1981): Identität oder nicht: zur kritischen Theologie der Ontologie. Freiburg i. Br.: Alber.

Habermas, Jürgen (2001): Glauben und Wissen. Friedenspreis des Deutschen Buchhandels 2001. Berlin: Suhrkamp.

Habringer-Hagleitner, Silvia (2006): Zusammenleben im Kindergarten. Modelle religionspädagogischer Praxis. Stuttgart: Kohlhammer.

Habringer-Hagleitner, Silvia (2009): Geschlechtergerechte Religionspädagogik im Kindergarten. Möglichkeiten, Grenzen und Chancen. In: Pithan, Annebelle/Arzt, Silvia/Jakobs, Monika/Knauth, Thorsten (Ed.): Gender – Religion – Bildung. Beiträge zu einer Religionspädagogik der Vielfalt. Eine Veröffentlichung des Comenius Instituts. Gütersloh: Gütersloher Verlagshaus, 306–316.

Hadwin, Julie/Perner, Josef (1991): Pleased and surprised: Children's cognitive theory of emotion. *British Journal of Developmental Psychology 9*(2), 215–234.

Hafeneger, Benno/Henkenborg, Peter/Scherr, Albert (Ed.) (2007): Pädagogik der Anerkennung. Grundlagen, Konzepte, Praxisfelder. Schwalbach/Ts.: Wochenschauverlag.

Hammersley, Martyn/Atkinson, Paul (^{3}2007): Ethnography. Principles in practice. London/ New York: Routledge [1983].

Harz, Frieder (2000): Kindergarten als Ort religiösen Lernens. *Zeitschrift für Pädagogik und Theologie 52*(4), 374–384.

Harz, Frieder (2001): Feste der Religionen in der Kindertagesstätte. Professional roles in early childhood. *Theorie und Praxis der Sozialpädagogik 109*(4), 12–16.

Harz, Frieder (2001): Ist Allah auch der liebe Gott? Interreligiöse Erziehung in der Kindertagesstätte. Munich: Don Bosco.

Harz, Frieder (2008): Religion in der interkulturellen Erziehung und Bildung. In: Hugoth, Matthias/Benedix, Monika (Ed.): Religion im Kindergarten. Begleitung und Unterstützung für Erzieherinnen. Munich: Kösel, 32–38.

Haug, Lena (2011): Junge StaatsbürgerInnen. Politik in Zukunftsvorstellungen von Kindern. Wiesbaden: VS Verlag für Sozialwissenschaften.

Heimbrock, Hans-Guenter/Scheilke, Christoph/Schreiner, Peter (Ed.) (2001): Towards Religious Competence. Diversity as a Challenge for Education in Europe. Münster: LIT.

Heinzel, Friederike (1997): Qualitative Interviews mit Kindern. In: Friebertshäuser, Barbara/ Prengel, Annedore (Ed.): Handbuch Qualitative Forschungsmethoden in der Erziehungswissenschaft. Weinheim/Munich: Juventa, 396–413.

Heinzel, Friederike (Ed.) (^{2}2012): Methoden der Kindheitsforschung. Ein Überblick über Forschungszugänge zur kindlichen Perspektive. Weinheim/Basel: Beltz Juventa [2000].

Heinzel, Friederike (^{2}2012): Qualitative Methoden der Kindheitsforschung. Ein Überblick. In: Heinzel, Friederike (Ed.): Methoden der Kindheitsforschung. Ein Überblick über Forschungszugänge zur kindlichen Perspektive. Weinheim/Basel: Beltz Juventa [2000], 22–35.

Hemel, Ulrich (2001): Religiosität. In: Mette, Norbert/Rickers, Folkert (Ed.): Lexikon der Religionspädagogik, vol. 2. Neukirchen-Vluyn: Neukirchener Verlag, 1839–1844.

Hemel, Ulrich (2006): Religionsphilosophie und Philosophie der Religiosität. In: Angel, Hans-Ferdinand/Bröking-Bortfeldt, Martin/Hemel, Ulrich/Jakobs, Monika/Kunstmann, Joachim/Pirner, Manfred L./Rothgangel, Martin: Religiosität: Anthropologische, theologische und sozialwissenschaftliche Klärungen. Stuttgart: Kohlhammer, 92–115.

Henckens, Reinhilde/Pollefeyt Didier/Hutsebaut, Dirk/Dillen, Annemie/Maex, Joke/De Boeck, Ellen (2011): Geloof in kinderen? Levensbeschouwelijke perspectieven van kinderen in kaart gebracht. Opzet, methode en resultaten van empirisch onderzoek bij leerkrachten rooms-katholieke godsdienst en hun leerlingen in de derde graad lager onderwijs en de eerste graad secundair onderwijs. Instrumenta Theologica 33. Leuven: Uitgeverij Peeters.

Hess-Maier, Dorothee (2011): Mein Gott – Dein Gott, kein Gott? Religion in Kita und Elternhaus. In: Biesinger, Albert/Edelbrock, Anke/Schweitzer, Friedrich (Ed.): Auf die Eltern kommt es an! Interreligiöse und interkulturelle Bildung in der Kita. Münster et al.: Waxmann, 13–14.

Hilpert, Konrad/Werbick, Jürgen (Ed.) (1995): Mit den Anderen leben. Wege zur Toleranz. Düsseldorf: Patmos.

Hirschfeld, Lawrence (1994): The child's representation of human groups. In: Medin, Douglas L. (Ed.): The psychology of learning and motivation, vol. 31. San Diego: Academic Press, 133–183.

Hobson, Peter R./Edwards, John S. (1999): Religious Education in a Pluralistic Society. The Key Philosophical Issues. London/Portland: Woburn Press.

Hoffmann, Eva (2009): Interreligiöses Lernen im Kindergarten? Eine empirische Studie zum Umgang mit religiöser Vielfalt in Diskussionen mit Kindern zum Thema Tod. Berlin: LIT.

Hofmeier, Johann (1987): Religiöse Erziehung im Elementarbereich. Munich: Kösel.

Honig, Michael-Sebastian/Leu, Hans Rudolf/Nissen, Ursula (Ed.) (1999): Kinder und Kindheit. Soziokulturelle Muster – sozialisationstheoretische Perspektiven. Weinheim/Munich: Juventa.

Honig, Michael-Sebastian/Leu, Hans Rudolf/Nissen, Ursula (1999): Kindheit als Sozialisationsphase und als kulturelles Muster. Zur Strukturierung eines Forschungsfeldes. In: Honig, Michael-Sebastian/Leu, Hans Rudolf/Nissen, Ursula (Ed.): Kinder und Kindheit. Soziokulturelle Muster – sozialisationstheoretische Perspektiven. Weinheim/Munich: Juventa, 9–29.

Honneth, Axel (^{6}2010): Kampf um Anerkennung. Zur moralischen Grammatik sozialer Konflikte. Frankfurt am Main: Suhrkamp [1992].

Houskamp, Fisher, Stuber (2004): Spirituality in children and adolescents: research findings and implications for clinicians and researches. *Child & Adolescent Psychiatric Clinics of North America 13*(1), 221–230.

Hugoth, Matthias (2003): Fremde Religionen – fremde Kinder? Leitfaden für interreligiöse Erziehung. Freiburg i. Br.: Herder.

Hugoth, Matthias (2012): Handbuch religiöse Bildung in Kita und Kindergarten. Freiburg i. Br.: Herder.

Hugoth, Matthias/Benedix, Monika (2008): Religion im Kindergarten. Begleitung und Unterstützung für Erzieherinnen. Munich: Kösel.

Hull, John (1997): Wie Kinder über Gott reden: ein Ratgeber für Eltern und Erziehende. Aus dem Engl. übersetzt von Sieglinde Denzel und Susanne Naumann. Gütersloh: Gütersloher Verlagshaus [English first edition: Hull. John: God talk with young children. Philadelphia: Trinity Press International 1991].

Hülst, Dirk (2012): Das wissenschaftliche Verstehen von Kindern. In: Heinzel, Friederike (Ed.): Methoden der Kindheitsforschung. Ein Überblick über Forschungszugänge zur kindlichen Perspektive. Weinheim/Basel: Beltz Juventa, 52–77.

Hurrelmann, Klaus/Bründel, Heidrun (^{2}2003): Einführung in die Kindheitsforschung. Weinheim/Basel/Berlin: Beltz [1996].

Ipgrave, Julia (2002): Inter faith encounter and religious understanding in an inner city primary school. PhD thesis. University of Warwick.

Ipgrave, Julia (2013): The Language of Interfaith Encounter Among Inner City Primary School. *Children, Religion & Education 40*(1), 35–49.

Ipgrave, Julia (2014): Relationships between local patterns of religious practice and young people's attitudes to the religiosity of their peers. In: Arweck, Elisabeth/Jackson, Robert: Religion, Education and Society. London/New York: Routledge, 5–11.

Jackson, Robert/Fujiwara, Satoko (Ed.) (2008): Peace Education and Religious Plurality. International Perspectives. London/New York: Routledge.

Jäggle, Martin (2000): Wie nimmt Schule kulturelle und religiöse Differenz wahr? Grundsätzliche Vorbemerkungen und Einblick in ein Forschungsprojekt in Wien. In: Porzelt, Burkard/Güth, Ralph (Ed.): Empirische Religionspädagogik. Grundlagen – Zugänge – Aktuelle Projekte. Münster: LIT, 119–138.

Jäggle, Martin (2006): Schritte auf dem Weg zu einer Kultur gegenseitiger Anerkennung. In: Bastel, Heribert/Göllner, Manfred/Jäggle, Martin/Miklas, Helene (Ed.): Das Gemeinsame entdecken – Das Unterscheidende anerkennen. Projekt eines konfessionell-kooperativen Religionsunterrichts. Einblicke – Hintergründe – Ansätze – Forschungsergebnisse. Münster: LIT, 31–42.

Jäggle, Martin (2007): Religiöse Pluralität in Europa – Religionen – Religionslosigkeit. In: Bock, Irmgard/Dichtl, Johanna/Herion, Horst/Prügger, Walter (Ed.): Europa als Projekt. Berlin: LIT, 51–67.

Jäggle, Martin (2015): Religionsbedingte Heterogenität als Thema der Forschung in der LehrerInnenbildung. In: Lindner, Doris/Krobath, Thomas (Ed.): Vielfalt(en) erforschen. Tag der Forschung 2014. Series: Schriften der Kirchlichen Pädagogischen Hochschule Wien/Krems, Band 10. Vienna/Berlin: LIT, 28–37.

Jäggle, Martin/Krobath, Thomas/Stockinger, Helena/Schelander, Robert (2013): Kultur der Anerkennung. Würde – Gerechtigkeit – Partizipation für Schulkultur, Schulentwicklung und Religion. Baltmannsweiler: Schneider Hohengehren.

Jessen, Silke (2003): „Man redet viel über Gott und so …" Schülermitbeteiligung im Religionsunterricht der Grundschule aus allgemein- und religionsdidaktischer Sicht. Münster et al.: Waxmann.

Johnson, R. Burke/Onwuegbuzie, Anthony J. (2004): Mixed Methods Research: A Research Paradigm Whose Time Has Come. *Educational Researcher 33*(7), 14–26.

Kalloch, Christina (2009): Kindertheologie als religionsdidaktisches Prinzip. In: Kalloch, Christina/Leimgruber, Stephan/Schwab, Ulrich (Ed.): Lehrbuch der Religionsdidaktik. Für Studium und Praxis in ökumenischer Perspektive. Freiburg: Herder, 314–327.

Kalloch, Christina/Leimgruber, Stephan/Schwab, Ulrich (Ed.) (2009): Lehrbuch der Religionsdidaktik. Für Studium und Praxis in ökumenischer Perspektive. Freiburg: Herder.

Karstadt, Lyn/Medd, Jo (2000): Children in the family and society. In: Drury, Rose/Miller, Linda/Campbell, Robin: Looking at Early Years Education and Care. Professional roles in early childhood. London: David Fulton Publishers, 35–40.

Kauffeld, Simone/Ebner, Katharina (^{5}2014): Organisationsentwicklung. In: Schuler, Heinz/Moser, Klaus (Ed.): Lehrbuch Organisationspsychologie. Bern: Hans Huber, 457–507.

Keast, John (Ed.) (2007): Religious diversity and intercultural education: a reference book for schools. Strasbourg: Council of Europe Publishing CDED.

Keast, John/Leganger-Krogstad, Heid (2007): Religious dimension of intercultural education: a whole school approach. In: Keast, John (Ed.): Religious diversity and intercultural education: a reference book for schools. Strasbourg Cedex: Council of Europe, 119–121.

Keller, Heidi (Ed.) (⁴2011): Handbuch der Kleinkindforschung. Bern: Huber [1997].

Kernan, Margaret/Singer, Elly (Ed.) (2011): Peer Relationships in Early Childhood Education and Care. London/New York: Routledge.

Kirchenamt der Evangelischen Kirche in Deutschland (Hg.) (2007): Religion, Werte und religiöse Bildung im Elementarbereich. 10 Thesen des Rates der Evangelischen Kirche in Deutschland. Hannover: Kirchenamt der EKD.

King Jr., James E./Bell, Myrtle P./Lawrence, Ericka (2009): Religion as an aspect of workplace diversity: an examination of the US context and a call for international research. *Journal of Management, Spirituality & Religion 6*(1), 43–57.

King, Katherine/Hemming, Peter J. (2012): Exploring Multiple Religious Identities through Mixed Qualitative Methods. *Fieldwork in Religion 7*(1), 29–47.

Kjørholt, Anne Trine (2011): Rethinking young children's rights for participation in diverse cultural contexts. In: Kernan, Margaret/Singer, Elly (Ed.): Peer Relationships in Early Childhood Education and Care. London/New York: Routledge, 38–48.

Klein, Stephanie (2005): Erkenntnis und Methode in der Praktischen Theologie. Stuttgart: Kohlhammer.

Klöcker, Michael/Tworuschka, Udo (Ed.) (2008): Handbuch der Religionen. Kirchen und andere Glaubensgemeinschaften in Deutschland/im deutschsprachigen Raum. Landsberg: Olzog.

Kloeters, Ulrike/Lüddecke, Julian/Quehl, Thomas (Ed.) (2003): Schulwege in die Vielfalt. Handreichung zur Interkulturellen und Antirassistischen Pädagogik in der Schule IKO. Frankfurt am Main: Verlag für interkulturelle Kommunikation.

Knauth, Thorsten/Josza, Dan-Paul/Bertram-Troost, Gerdien/Ipgrave, Julia (Ed.) (2008): Encountering religious pluralism in school and society. A Qualitative Study of Teenage Perspectives in Europe. Münster et al.: Waxmann.

Kolb, Jonas/Mattausch-Yıldız, Birgit: Muslimische Alltagspraxis in Österreich. Ein Kompass zu religiöser Diversität. Zwischenbericht für das Projektjahr 2013. University of Vienna, Department for Islamic-Theological Studies (https://iis.univie.ac.at/fileadmin/user_upload/p_iis/muslimische_alltagspraxis_in_oesterreich.projektbericht.pdf [21.08.2015]).

Korczak, Janusz (1999): Sämtliche Werke, vol. 4. Gütersloh: Gütersloher Verlagshaus.

Kowalski, Kurt (1998): The Impact of Vicarious Exposure to Diversity on Preschoolers' Emerging Ethnic/Racial Attitudes. *Early Child Development and Care 146*(1), 41–51.

Krappmann, Lothar/Oswald, Hans (1995): Alltag der Schulkinder. Weinheim/Munich: Juventa.

Krause, Anke (²2010): "Woher kommst du?" – Wie junge Kinder Herkunftsfragen begreifen. In: Wagner, Petra: Handbuch Kinderwelten. Vielfalt als Chance – Grundlagen einer vorurteilsbewussten Bildung und Erziehung. Freiburg/Basel/Vienna: Herder [2008], 92–101.

Krüger, Heinz-Hermann/Grunert, Cathleen (Ed.) (2002): Handbuch Kindheits- und Jugendforschung. Opladen: Leske + Budrich.

Kühl, Stefan/Strodtholz, Petra/Taffertshofer, Andreas (Ed.) (2009): Handbuch Methoden der Organisationsforschung. Quantitative und Qualitative Methoden. Wiesbaden: VS Verlag für Sozialwissenschaften.

Kunstmann, Joachim (2002): Religion und Bildung. Zur ästhetischen Signatur religiöser Bildungsprozesse. Gütersloh/Freiburg: Gütersloher Verlagshaus/Herder.

Kuusisto, Arniika/Lamminmäki-Vartia, Silja (2012): Moral Foundation of the Kindergarten Teacher's Educational Approach: Self-Reflection Facilitated Educator Response to Pluralism in Educational Context. *Education Research International.*

Lamnek, Siegfried (^{3}1995): Qualitative Sozialforschung; vol. 1. Methodologie. Weinheim: Beltz BVU [1988].

Lamnek, Siegfried (^{2}2005): Gruppendiskussion. Theorie und Praxis. Weinheim: Beltz.

Lamnek, Siegfried (^{5}2010): Qualitative Sozialforschung. Weinheim/Basel: Beltz [1988].

Lancaster, Penny Y. (^{5}2010): Listening to young children: enabling children to be seen and heard. In: Pugh, Gillian/Duffy, Bernadette (Ed.): Contemporary Issues in the Early Years. Los Angeles/London/New Delhi/Singapore/Washington DC: Contemporary Issues in the Early Years [1992], 79–94.

Lange, Jochen/Wiesemann, Jutta (2012): Ethnografie. In: Heinzel, Friederike (Ed.): Methoden der Kindheitsforschung. Ein Überblick über Forschungszugänge zur kindlichen Perspektive. Weinheim/Basel: Beltz Juventa, 262–277.

LBS-Gruppe: LBS-Kinderbarometer Deutschland 2016: So sehen wir das! Stimmungen, Trends und Meinungen von Kindern aus Deutschland.

Leira, Arnlaug/Saraceno, Chiara (Ed.) (2008): Childhood: Changing Contexts. Bingley: Emerald Group Publishing Limited.

Lempp-Würschum, Christiane/Stehle, Andreas (2011): Interreligiöse und interkulturelle Bildungsarbeit – Ohne die Eltern kann es nicht gelingen. In: Biesinger, Albert/Edelbrock, Anke/Schweitzer, Friedrich (Ed.): Auf die Eltern kommt es an! Interreligiöse und Interkulturelle Bildung in der Kita. Interreligiöse und Interkulturelle Bildung im Kindesalter, vol. 2. Münster et al.: Waxmann, 132–139.

Lewis, Ann/Lindsay, Geoff (Ed.) (2000): Researching children's perspectives. Buckingham-Philadelphia: Open University.

Lewis, Ann/Lindsay, Geoff (2000): Emerging Issues. In: Lewis, Ann/Lindsay, Geoff (Ed.): Researching children's perspectives. Buckingham/Philadelphia: Open University, 189–197.

Liebig, Brigitte/Nentwig-Gesemann, Iris (2009): Gruppendiskussion. In: Kühl, Stefan/Strodtholz, Petra/Taffertshofer, Andreas (Ed.): Handbuch Methoden der Organisationsforschung. Quantitative und Qualitative Methoden. Wiesbaden: VS Verlag für Sozialwissenschaften, 102–123.

Liegle, Ludwig (2006): Bildung und Erziehung in früher Kindheit. Stuttgart: Kohlhammer.

Lischke-Eisinger, Lisa (2012): Sinn, Werte und Religion in der Elementarpädagogik. Religion, Interreligiosität und Religionsfreiheit im Kontext der Bildungs- und Orientierungspläne. Wiesbaden: Springer VS.

Loos, Peter/Schäffer, Burkhard (2001): Das Gruppendiskussionsverfahren. Theoretische Grundlagen und empirische Anwendung. Opladen: Leske + Budrich.

Lüders, Christian (^{9}2012): Beobachten im Feld und Ethnographie. In: Flick, Uwe/von Kardorff, Ernst/Steinke, Ines (Ed.): Qualitative Forschung. Ein Handbuch. Reinbek bei Hamburg: Rowohlt Taschenbuch [2000], 384–401.

Lytsiousi, Stella/Tsioumis, Konstantinos/Kyridis, Argyris (2014): How teachers cope with the religious diversity in Greek kindergarten classes, from theory to reality. *International Journal of Education Learning and Development* 2(5), 18–32.

Mangold, Werner (1960): Gegenstand und Methode des Gruppendiskussionsverfahrens: aus der Arbeit des Instituts für Sozialforschung, vol. 9. Frankfurt am Main: Europäische Verlagsanstalt.

Markefka, Manfred/Nauck, Bernhard (1993): Handbuch der Kindheitsforschung. Neuwied/Kriftel/Berlin: Luchterhand.

Mata, Jennifer (2015): Spiritual Experiences in Early Childhood Education. Four Kindergarteners, One Classroom. New York/Oxon: Routledge.

Matthes, Joachim (2005): Das Eigene und das Fremde. Gesammelte Aufsätze zu Gesellschaft, Kultur und Religion. Published by Rüdiger Schloz. Würzburg: Ergon.

McKenna, Ursula/Ipgrave, Julia/Jackson, Robert (2008): Interfaith Dialogue by Email in Primary Schools: An Evaluation of the Building E-Bridges Project. Religious diversity and education in Europe, vol. 6. Münster et al.: Waxmann.

MacNaughton, Glenda/Davis, Karina (Ed.) (2009): "Race" and Early Childhood Education. An International Approach to Identity, Politics, and Pedagogy. New York: Palgrave Macmillan.

Mc Wirther, Liz/Gamble, Roberta (1982): Development of ethnic awareness in the absence of physical cues. *Irish Journal of Psychology* 5(2), 109–127.

Mecheril, Paul/Plößer, Melanie (2009): Differenz. In: Andresen, Sabine/Casale, Rita/Gabriel, Thomas/Horlacher, Rebekka/Larcher Klee, Sabina/Oelkers, Jürgen (Ed.): Handwörterbuch Erziehungswissenschaft. Weinheim/Basel: Beltz, 194–208.

Medin, Douglas L. (Ed.) (1994): The psychology of learning and motivation Vol. 31. San Diego: Academic Press.

Meijer, Wilna A.J./Miedema, Siebren/Lanser-van der Velde, Alma (2009): Religious Education in a World of Religious Diversity. Münster et al.: Waxmann.

Merkens, Hans (1992): Teilnehmende Beobachtung: Analyse von Protokollen teilnehmender Beobachter. In: Hoffmeyer-Zlotnik, Jürgen H.P. (Ed.): Analyse verbaler Daten. Über den Umgang mit qualitativen Daten. Opladen: Westdeutscher Verlag, 216–247.

Merz, Vreni (Ed.) (1994): Alter Gott für neue Kinder? Das traditionelle Gottesbild und die nachwachsende Generation. Fribourg/Switzerland: Paulusverlag.

Mette, Norbert (1983): Voraussetzungen christlicher Elementarerziehung. Vorbereitende Studien zu einer Religionspädagogik des Kleinkindalters. Düsseldorf: Patmos.

Mette, Norbert (2000): Praktische Theologie – Ästhetische Theorie oder Handlungstheorie?. In: Abeldt, Sönke/Bauer, Walter/Heinrichs, Gesa/Knauth, Thorsten/Koch, Martina/Tiedemann, Holger/Weiße, Wolfram (Ed.): „… was es bedeutet, verletzbarer Mensch zu sein". Erziehungswissenschaft im Gespräch mit Theologie, Philosophie und Gesellschaftstheorie. Helmut Peukert zum 65. Geburtstag. Mainz: Matthias-Grünewald-Verlag, 37–46.

Mette, Norbert (2005): Einführung in die katholische Praktische Theologie. Darmstadt: Wissenschaftliche Buchgesellschaft.

Mette, Norbert (^{3}2006): Religionspädagogik. Düsseldorf: Patmos [1994].

Mette, Norbert/Steinkamp, Hermann (1983): Sozialwissenschaften und Praktische Theologie. Düsseldorf: Patmos.

Metz, Johann Baptist (1976): Theologie als Biographie. Eine These und ein Paradigma. *Concilium 12*, 311–315.

Metz, Johann Baptist (^{5}1992): Glaube in Geschichte und Gesellschaft. Studien zu einer praktischen Fundamentaltheologie. Mainz: Matthias-Grünewald-Verlag [1977].

Meuser, Michael/Nagel, Ulrike (^{2}2005): ExpertInneninterviews – vielfach erprobt, wenig bedacht. Ein Beitrag zur qualitativen Methodendiskussion. In: Bogner, Alexander/Littig, Beate/Menz, Wolfgang (Ed.): Das Experteninterview. Theorie, Methode, Anwendung. Wiesbaden: VS Verlag für Sozialwissenschaften [2002], 71–93.

Mey, Günter/Mruck, Katja (Ed.) (^{2}2011): Grounded Theory Reader. Wiesbaden: VS Verlag für Sozialwissenschaften-Springer Fachmedien [2007].

Miedema, Siebren (2009): Religious Education between Certainty and Uncertainty. Towards a Pedagogy of Diversity. In: Meijer, Wilna A.J./Miedema, Siebren/Lanser-van der Velde, Alma (Ed.): Religious Education in a World of Religious Diversity. Münster et al.: Waxmann, 195–205.

Moleiro, Carla/Marques, Susana/Pacheco, Pedro (2011): Cultural diversity competencies in child and youth care services in Portugal: Development of two measures and a brief training program. *Children and Youth Services Reviews 33*, 767–773.

Möller, Rainer/Tschirch, Reinmar (^{6}2014): Arbeitsbuch Religionspädagogik für ErzieherInnen. Stuttgart: Kohlhammer.

Möller, Rainer (^{6}2014): „Muss ich als Erzieherin auch religionspädagogisch qualifiziert sein?" Berufsrolle und religiöse Identität. In: Möller, Rainer/Tschirch, Reinmar (Ed.): Arbeitsbuch Religionspädagogik für ErzieherInnen. Stuttgart: Kohlhammer [2002], 13–60.

Moore, Kelsey/Talwar, Victoria/Bosacki, Sandra (2012): Canadian children's perceptions of spirituality: diverse voices. *International Journal of Children's Spirituality 17*(3), 217–234.

Muckel, Petra (^{2}2011): Die Entwicklung von Kategorien mit der Methode der Grounded Theory. In: Mey, Günter/Mruck, Katja (Ed.): Grounded Theory Reader. Wiesbaden: VS Verlag für Sozialwissenschaften-Springer Fachmedien [2007], 333–352.

Murray, Jaclyn (2012): Learning to live together: an exploration and analysis of managing cultural diversity in centre-based early childhood development programmes. *Intercultural Education 23*(2), 89–103.

Nentwig-Gesemann, Iris (2002): Gruppendiskussionen mit Kindern. Die dokumentarische Interpretation von Spielpraxis und Diskursorganisation. *Zeitschrift für qualitative Bildungs-, Beratungs- und Sozialforschung 3*(1), 41–63.

Nentwig-Gesemann, Iris (2007): Sprach- und Körperdiskurse von Kindern – Verstehen und Verständigung zwischen Textförmigkeit und Ikonizität. In: Friebertshäuser, Barbara/von Felden, Heide/Schäffer, Burkhard (Ed.): Bild und Text. Methoden und Methodologien visueller Sozialforschung in der Erziehungswissenschaft. Opladen/Farmington Hills: Barbara Budrich, 105–120.

Neurath, Elisabeth (2009): „Wer früher stirbt, ist länger tot?" Was sich christliche und muslimische Kinder nach dem Tod erwarten. In: Bucher, Anton A./Büttner, Gerhard/Freudenberger-Lötz, Petra/Schreiner, Martin (Ed.): Jahrbuch der Kindertheologie: „In den Himmel kommen nur, die sich auch verstehen". Wie Kinder über religiöse Differenz denken und sprechen, vol. 8. Stuttgart: Calwer, 60–70.

Neuss, Norbert (Ed.) (2007): Bildung und Lerngeschichten im Kindergarten. Konzepte – Methoden – Beispiele. Berlin: Cornelsen Skriptor.

Nigel, Thomas (2001): Listening to Children. In: Foley, Pam/Roche, Jeremy/Tucker, Stanley (Ed.): Children in Society. Contemporary Theory, Policy and Practice. London: Palgrave in association with The Open University, 104–111.

Nipkow, Karl Ernst (1998): Bildung in einer pluralen Welt, vol. 1. Moralpädagogik im Pluralismus. Gütersloh: Chr. Kaiser/Gütersloher Verlagshaus.

Nipkow, Karl Ernst (1998): Bildung in einer pluralen Welt, vol. 2. Religionspädagogik im Pluralismus. Gütersloh: Chr. Kaiser/Gütersloher Verlagshaus.

Nipkow, Karl Ernst (^{2}2009): Pädagogische Grundbegriffe – religionspädagogische Grundmuster. In: Bitter, Gottfried/Englert, Rudolf/Miller, Gabriele/Nipkow, Karl Ernst (Ed.): Neues Handbuch religionspädagogischer Grundbegriffe. Munich: Kösel [2002], 25–30.

Oelkers, Jürgen (1994): Die Frage nach Gott. Über die natürliche Religion von Kindern. In: Merz, Vreni (Ed.): Alter Gott für neue Kinder? Das traditionelle Gottesbild und die nachwachsende Generation. Fribourg/Switzerland: Paulusverlag, 13–22.

Oerter, Rolf/Montada, Leo (Ed.) (^{6}2008): Entwicklungspsychologie. Weinheim: Beltz [1983].

Orth, Gottfried (2000): Umgang mit religiöser Differenz in Gesprächen über Bilder von Gott. In: Fischer, Dietlind/Schöll, Albrecht (Ed.): Religiöse Vorstellungen bilden. Erkundungen zur Religion von Kindern über Bilder. Münster: Comenius-Institut, 173–186.

Oser, Fritz/Gmündner, Paul (^{2}1996): Der Mensch, Stufen seiner religiösen Entwicklung. Gütersloh: Gütersloher Verlagshaus [1984].

Ossowski, Ekkehard/Rösler, Winfried (2002): Kindheit. Interdisziplinäre Perspektiven zu einem Forschungsgegenstand. Baltmannsweiler: Schneider Hohengehren.

Pastoral Constitution on the church in the modern world: Gaudium et Spes, promulgated by Pope Paul VI, 7th December 1965.

Perlman, Michal/Kankesan, Tharsni/Zhang, Jing (2010): Promoting diversity in early child care education. *Early Child Development and Care 180*(6), 753–766.

Peters, Sibylle (Ed.) (2003): Lernen und Weiterbildung als permanente Personalentwicklung. Munich/Mering: Rainer Hamp.

Peters, Sibylle/Wahlstab, Sandra/Dengler, Sandra (2003): Perspektivenvielfalt betrieblicher Weiterbildung in der Wissensgesellschaft. In: Peters, Sibylle: Lernen und Weiterbildung als permanente Personalentwicklung. Munich/Mering: Rainer Hamp, 7–28.

Peukert, Helmut (1984): Über die Zukunft der Bildung. In: Dirks, Walter/Kogon, Eugen (Ed.): Nach 1984: Die Krise der Zivilisation und unserer Zukunft. *Frankfurter Hefte extra 6*, 129–137.

Peukert, Helmut (1987): Die Frage nach der Allgemeinbildung als Frage nach dem Verhältnis von Bildung und Vernunft. In: Pleines, Jürgen-Eckardt (Ed.): Das Problem des Allgemeinen in der Bildungstheorie. Würzburg: Königshausen & Neumann, 69–88.

Peukert, Helmut (2004): Bildung und Religion. Reflexionen zu einem bildungstheoretischen Religionsbegriff. In: Dethloff, Klaus/Langthaler, Rudolf/Nagl-Docekal, Herta/Wolfram, Friedrich: Orte der Religion im philosophischen Diskurs der Gegenwart. Berlin: Parerga, 363–386.

Piaget, Jean (1999): The stages of the intellectual development of the child. In: Slater, Alan/Muir, Darwin (Ed.): The Blackwell Reader in Developmental Psychology. Malden-Oxford: Blackwell Publishing, 35–42, 38–40. (From *Bulletin of the Menninger Clinic 26* (1962), 120–128).

Pirner, Manfred L. (2006): Religiosität als Gegenstand empirischer Forschung. In: Angel, Hans-Ferdinand/Bröking-Bortfeldt, Martin/Hemel, Ulrich/Jakobs, Monika/Kunstmann, Joachim/Pirner, Manfred L./Rothgangel, Martin: Religiosität. Anthropologische, theologische und sozialwissenschaftliche Klärungen. Stuttgart: Kohlhammer, 30–52.

Pithan, Annebelle (2007): Kinder als Jungen und Mädchen. In: Spenn, Matthias/Beneke, Doris/Harz, Frieder/Schweitzer, Friedrich (Ed.): Handbuch Arbeit mit Kindern – Evangelische Perspektiven. Gütersloh: Gütersloher Verlagshaus, 63–70.

Pithan, Annebelle/Schweiker, Wolfhard (Ed.) (2011): Evangelische Bildungsverantwortung: Inklusion. Ein Lesebuch. Münster: Comenius-Institut.

Pithan, Annebelle/Arzt, Silvia/Jakobs, Monika/Knauth, Thorsten (Ed.) (2009): Gender – Religion – Bildung. Beiträge zu einer Religionspädagogik der Vielfalt. Eine Veröffentlichung des Comenius Instituts. Gütersloh: Gütersloher Verlagshaus.

Pleines, Jürgen-Eckardt (Ed.) (1987): Das Problem des Allgemeinen in der Bildungstheorie. Würzburg: Königshausen & Neumann.

Pohlkamp, Ines (2012): Differenzsensible/intersektionale Bildung – Ein Theorie-Praxis-Dilemma? Vortrag im Rahmen der Ringvorlesung „Behinderung ohne Behinderte?! Perspektiven der Disability Studies", University of Hamburg, 29.10.2012, http://www.zedis-ev-hochschule-hh.de/files/pohlkamp_29102012.pdf [29.06.2015].

Pollack, Detlef/Friedrich, Nils (2013): Religiöse Vielfalt – Bedrohung oder Chance. *Forschung. Spezial Demografie 38*(1), 34–37.

Pollock, Friedrich (Ed.) (1995): Gruppenexperiment: Ein Studienbericht. Bearbeitet von Friedrich Pollock. Mit einem Geleitwort von Franz Böhm. Frankfurter Beiträge zur Soziologie, im Auftrag des Instituts für Sozialforschung. Published by Theodor W. Adorno and Walter Dirks, vol. 2. Frankfurt am Main: Europäische Verlagsanstalt.

Porzelt, Burkard (2000): Qualitativ-empirische Methoden in der Religionspädagogik. In: Porzelt, Burkard/Güth, Ralph (Ed.): Empirische Religionspädagogik. Grundlagen – Zugänge – Aktuelle Projekte. Münster: LIT, 63–81.

Porzelt, Burkard/Güth, Ralph (Ed.) (2000): Empirische Religionspädagogik. Grundlagen – Zugänge – Aktuelle Projekte. Münster: LIT.

Preissing, Christa/Wagner, Petra (Ed.) (2003): Kleine Kinder, keine Vorurteile? Interkulturelle und vorurteilsbewusste Arbeit in Kindertageseinrichtungen. Freiburg i. Br.: Herder.

Prengel, Annedore (1993): Pädagogik der Vielfalt. Verschiedenheit und Gleichberechtigung in Interkultureller, Feministischer und Integrativer Pädagogik. Wiesbaden: VS Verlag für Sozialwissenschaften.

Prengel, Annedore (2005): Anerkennung von Anfang an – Egalität, Heterogenität und Hierarchie im Anfangsunterricht und darüber hinaus. In: Geiling, Ute/Hinz, Andreas (Ed.): Integrationspädagogik im Diskurs. Auf dem Weg zu einer inklusiven Pädagogik. Bad Heilbrunn: Julius Klinkhardt, 15–34.

Prengel, Annedore (^{3}2006): Pädagogik der Vielfalt. Verschiedenheit und Gleichberechtigung in Interkultureller, Feministischer und Integrativer Pädagogik. Wiesbaden: VS Verlag für Sozialwissenschaften [1993].

Prengel, Annedore (2007): „Ohne Angst verschieden sein?" – Mehrperspektivische Anerkennung von Schulleistungen in einer Pädagogik der Vielfalt. In: Hafeneger, Benno/Henkenborg, Peter/Scherr, Albert (Ed.): Pädagogik der Anerkennung. Grundlagen, Konzepte, Praxisfelder. Schwalbach/Ts.: Wochenschauverlag, 203–221.

Prengel, Annedore (2010): Inklusion in der Frühpädagogik. Bildungstheoretische, empirische und pädagogische Grundlagen. Munich: Deutsches Jugendinstitut e. V. (DJI).

Project Group Religious Education of the Austrian Commission for Education and Upbringing (1981): Österreichisches Katechetisches Direktorium für Kinder und Jugendarbeit. Vienna: Hausdruckerei der Erzdiözese Wien.

Promoting social inclusion and respect for diversity in the early years (2007). *Early Childhood Matters 108.*

Promoting social inclusion and respect for diversity in young children's environments (2007). *Early Childhood Matters 108*, 5–6.

Przyborsky, Aglaja/Wohlrab-Sahr, Monika (^{4}2014): Qualitative Sozialforschung. Ein Arbeitsbuch. Munich: Oldenbourg [2008].

Pugh, Gillian/Duffy, Bernadette (Ed.) (^{5}2010): Contemporary Issues in the Early Years. Los Angeles/London/New Delhi/Singapore/Washington DC: Contemporary Issues in the Early Years [1992].

Puttalaz, Martha/Gottman, John M. (1981): An interactional model of children's entry into peergroups. *Child development 52*, 986–994.

Pyke, Alice (2013): Assessing and understanding young people's attitudes toward religious diversity in the United Kingdom. PhD thesis, University of Warwick.

Qvortrup, Jens (Ed.) (1993): Childhood as a social phenomenon: lessons from an international project: international conference Billund, Denmark, 24–16 September 1992. Vienna: European Centre of Social Welfare Policy and Research.

Qvortrup, Jens/Corsaro, William A./Honig, Michael-Sebastian (Ed.) (2011): The Palgrave Handbook of Childhood Studies. Basingstoke/New York: Palgrave Macmillan.

Ramsey, Patricia (1991): The Salience of Race in Young Children Growing Up in All-White Community. *Journal of Educational Psychology 83*(1), 28–34.

Council of the Evangelical Church in Germany (Ed.) (2014): Religiöse Orientierung gewinnen. Evangelischer Religionsunterricht als Beitrag zu einer pluralitätsfähigen Schule. (2014). Eine Denkschrift des Rates der Evangelischen Kirche in Deutschland. Gütersloh: Gütersloher Verlagshaus.

Rehm, Johannes (2002): Erziehung zum Weltethos. Projekte interreligiösen Lernens in multikulturellen Kontexten. Göttingen: Vandenhoeck & Ruprecht.

Riegel, Christine/Geisen, Thomas (Ed.) (2007): Jugend, Zugehörigkeit und Migration. Subjektpositionierung im Kontext von Jugendkultur, Ethnizitäts- und Geschlechterkonstruktionen. Wiesbaden: VS Verlag für Sozialwissenschaften.

Riegel, Christine/Geisen, Thomas (2007): Zugehörigkeit(en) im Kontext von Jugend und Migration – eine Einführung. In: Riegel, Christine/Geisen, Thomas (Ed.): Jugend, Zugehörigkeit und Migration. Subjektpositionierung im Kontext von Jugendkultur, Ethnizitäts- und Geschlechterkonstruktionen. Wiesbaden: VS Verlag für Sozialwissenschaften, 7–23.

Riess, Richard/Fiedler, Kirsten (Ed.) (1993): Die verletzlichen Jahre. Handbuch zur Beratung und Seelsorge an Kindern und Jugendlichen. Gütersloh: Chr. Kaiser/Gütersloher Verlagshaus.

Riitaoja, Anna-Leena/Dervin, Fred (2014): Interreligious dialogue in schools: beyond asymmetry and categorisation?. *Language and Intercultural Communication 14*(1), 76–90.

Rolff, Hans-Günter/Buhren, Claus G./Lindau-Bank, Detlev/Müller, Sabine (^{4}2011): Manual Schulentwicklung. Handlungskonzept zur pädagogischen Schulentwicklungsberatung (SchuB). Weinheim/Basel: Beltz [1998].

Rothgangel, Martin (2006): Religiosität als menschliches Gesicht der Offenbarung Gottes. In: Angel, Hans-Ferdinand/Bröking-Bortfeldt, Martin/Hemel, Ulrich/Jakobs, Monika/Kunstmann, Joachim/Pirner, Manfred L./Rothgangel, Martin: Religiosität: Anthropologische, theologische und sozialwissenschaftliche Klärungen. Stuttgart: Kohlhammer, 175–198.

Rothgangel, Martin/Angel, Hans-Ferdinand/Hemel, Ulrich (2006): Die Bedeutung von Religiosität im Horizont religionspädagogischer Theorie und Praxis. In: Angel, Hans-Ferdinand/Bröking-Bortfeldt, Martin/Hemel, Ulrich/Jakobs, Monika/Kunstmann, Joachim/ Pirner, Manfred L./Rothgangel, Martin: Religiosität. Anthropologische, theologische und sozialwissenschaftliche Klärungen. Stuttgart: Kohlhammer, 199–212.

Rothgangel, Martin/Aslan, Ednan/Jäggle, Martin (Ed.) (2013): Religion und Gemeinschaft. Die Frage der Integration aus christlicher und muslimischer Perspektive (RaT-Reihe vol. 3). Göttingen: Vienna University Press bei V&R unipress.

Schäfer, Alfred/Thompson, Christiane (Ed.) (2010): Anerkennung. Paderborn/Munich/Vienna/Zurich: Ferdinand Schöningh.

Schambeck, Mirjam (2005): Wie Kinder glauben und theologisieren. In: Bahr, Matthias/Kropač, Ulrich/Schambeck, Mirjam (Ed.): Subjektwerdung und religiöses Lernen. Für eine Religionspädagogik, die den Menschen ernst nimmt. Munich: Kösel.

Schein, Edgar H. (^{3}1980): Organizational Psychology. Englewood Cliffs, New Jersey: Prentice Hall [1965].

Schein, Edgar. H. (^{2}1992): Organizational Culture and Leadership. San Francisco: Jossey-Bass.

Schein, Edgar H. (2000): Organisationsentwicklung: Wissenschaft, Technologie oder Philosophie?. In: Trebesch, Karsten (Ed.): Organisationsentwicklung. Konzepte, Strategien, Fallstudien. Stuttgart: Klett-Cotta, 19–32.

Schein, Edgar H. (2003): Prozessberatung für die Organisation der Zukunft. Der Aufbau einer helfenden Beziehung. Bergisch Gladbach: Edition Humanistische Psychologie.

Schein, Edgar H. (2009): Die vier Gesichter der Führung. GDI Impuls. *Wissensmagazin für Wirtschaft, Gesellschaft, Handel 1*, 108–109.

Schein, Edgar H. (2009): Führung und Veränderungsmanagement. Bergisch Gladbach: Andreas Kohlhage.

Schein, Edgar H. (2010): Prozess und Philosophie des Helfens. Bergisch Gladbach: Andreas Kohlhage.

Schieder, Rolf (2001): Wieviel Religion verträgt Deutschland?. Frankfurt am Main: Suhrkamp.

Schihalejev, Olga (2010): From Indifference to Dialogue? Estonian Young People, the School and Religious Diversity. Münster et al.: Waxmann.

Schihalejev, Olga (2014): Contextuality of young people's attitudes and its implications for research on religion: a response to Julia Ipgrave. In: Arweck, Elisabeth/Jackson, Robert: Religion, Education and Society. London/New York: Routledge, 13–25.

Schley, Wilfried (1998): Schule als lernende Organisation. In: Altrichter, Herbert/Schley, Wilfried/Schratz, Michael (Ed.): Handbuch zur Schulentwicklung. Innsbruck/Vienna: Studienverlag, 13–53.

Schluß, Henning (2005): Ein Vorschlag. Gegenstand und Grenze der Kindertheologie anhand eines systematischen Leitgedankens zu entwickeln. *Zeitschrift für Pädagogik und Theologie 37*, 23–35.

Schneider, Wolfgang/Lindenberger, Ulman (Ed.) (^{6}2008): Entwicklungspsychologie. Weinheim: Beltz ^{7}2012 (formerly Oerter, Rolf/Montada, Leo (Ed.): Entwicklungspsychologie, Weinheim: Beltz [1983]).

Scholz, Gerold (2012): Teilnehmende Beobachtung. In: Heinzel, Friederike (Ed.): Methoden der Kindheitsforschung. Ein Überblick über Forschungszugänge zur kindlichen Perspektive. Weinheim/Basel: Beltz Juventa, 116–134.

Schori, Kurt (1998): Religiöses Lernen und kindliches Erleben. Eine empirische Untersuchung religiöser Lernprozesse bei Kindern im Alter von vier bis acht Jahren. Stuttgart/Berlin/Cologne: Kohlhammer.

Schreyögg, Georg (^{3}1999): Organisation. Grundlagen moderner Organisationsgestaltung. Mit Fallstudien. Wiesbaden: Gabler [1996].

Schreiner, Peter (2007): A "safe space" to foster self-expression. In: Keast, John (Ed.): Religious diversity and intercultural education: a reference book for schools. Strasbourg: Council of Europe Publishing CDED, 57–66.

Schreiner, Peter (2012): Religion im Kontext einer Europäisierung von Bildung. Eine Rekonstruktion europäischer Diskurse und Entwicklungen aus protestantischer Perspektive. Münster et al.: Waxmann.

Schreiner, Peter/Sieg, Ursula/Elsenbast, Volker (Ed.) (2005): Handbuch Interreligiöses Lernen. Gütersloh: Gütersloher Verlagshaus.

Schuler, Heinz/Moser, Klaus (Ed.) (2014): Lehrbuch Organisationspsychologie. Bern: Hans Huber.

Schweitzer, Friedrich/Biesinger, Albert (with Boschki, Reinhold/Schlenker, Claudia/Edelbrock, Anke/Kliss, Oliver/Scheidler, Monika) (2002): Gemeinsamkeiten stärken – Unterschieden gerecht werden. Erfahrungen und Perspektiven zum konfessionell-kooperativen Religionsunterricht. Freiburg i. Br./Basel/Vienna: Herder – Gütersloh: Gütersloher Verlagshaus.

Schweitzer, Friedrich (2002): Ausblick: Internationale Perspektiven. In: Schweitzer, Friedrich/Englert, Rudolf/Schwab, Ulrich/Ziebertz, Hans-Georg: Entwurf einer pluralitätsfähigen Religionspädagogik. Gütersloh/Freiburg i. Br.: Gütersloher Verlagshaus/Herder, 229–237.

Schweitzer, Friedrich (2006): Religionspädagogik. Gütersloh: Gütersloher Verlagshaus.

Schweitzer, Friedrich (2008): Den Anfang schon verpasst? Religiöse Bildung in der Kindheit. In: Bertelsmann Stiftung (Ed.): Religion und Bildung. Orte, Medien und Experten religiöser Bildung. Gütersloh: Bertelsmann Stiftung, 23–28.

Schweitzer, Friedrich (2008): Wozu brauchen Kinder Religion. Zur Grundlegung der religiösen Bildung in Kindertageseinrichtungen. In: Hugoth, Matthias/Benedix, Monika (Ed.): Religion im Kindergarten. Begleitung und Unterstützung für Erzieherinnen. Munich: Kösel, 18–24.

Schweitzer, Friedrich (2009): Wie Kinder und Jugendliche religiöse Differenz wahrnehmen – Möglichkeiten und Grenzen der Orientierung in der religiösen Pluralität. In: Bucher, Anton A./Büttner, Gerhard/Freudenberger-Lötz, Petra/Schreiner, Martin (Ed.): Jahrbuch der Kindertheologie: „In den Himmel kommen nur, die sich auch verstehen". Wie Kinder über religiöse Differenz denken und sprechen, vol. 8. Stuttgart: Calwer, 39–49.

Schweitzer, Friedrich (2010): Children's Right to Religion and Religious Education. In: Engebretson, Kath/de Souza, Marian/Durka, Gloria/Gearon, Liam: International Handbook of Inter-religious Education. Part Two. Dordrecht/Heidelberg/London/New York: Springer, 1071–1086.

Schweitzer, Friedrich (2013): Das Recht des Kindes auf Religion. Gütersloh: Gütersloher Verlagshaus [new edition of Schweitzer, Friedrich (2000): Das Recht des Kindes auf Religion. Ermutigungen für Eltern und Erzieher. Gütersloh: Gütersloher Verlagshaus].

Schweitzer, Friedrich (2013): Religiöse Bildung als Integrationsfaktor? Aufgaben und Möglichkeiten Interreligiösen Lernens im Kindes- und Jugendalter. In: Rothgangel, Martin/Aslan, Ednan/Jäggle, Martin (Ed.): Religion und Gemeinschaft. Die Frage der Integration aus christlicher und muslimischer Perspektive. RaT-Reihe, vol. 3. Göttingen: Vienna University Press bei V&R unipress, 149–165.

Schweitzer, Friedrich/Biesinger, Albert (Ed.) (2015): Kulturell und religiös sensibel? Interreligiöse und Interkulturelle Kompetenz in der Ausbildung für den Elementarbereich. Interreligiöse und interkulturelle Bildung im Kindesalter, vol. 5. Münster/New York: Waxmann.

Schweitzer, Friedrich/Biesinger, Albert (with Boschki, Reinhold/Schlenker, Claudia/Edelbrock, Anke/Kliss, Oliver/Scheidler, Monika) (2002): Gemeinsamkeiten stärken – Unterschieden gerecht werden. Erfahrungen und Perspektiven zum konfessionell-kooperativen Religionsunterricht. Freiburg i.Br./Basel/Vienna: Herder – Gütersloh: Gütersloher Verlagshaus.

Schweitzer, Friedrich/Biesinger, Albert/Edelbrock, Anke (Ed.) (2008): Mein Gott – Dein Gott. Interkulturelle und interreligiöse Bildung in Kindertagesstätten. Weinheim/Basel: Beltz.

Schweitzer, Friedrich/Edelbrock, Anke/Biesinger, Albert (Ed.) (2011): Interreligiöse und Interkulturelle Bildung in der Kita. Eine Repräsentativbefragung von Erzieherinnen in Deutschland – interdisziplinäre, interreligiöse und internationale Perspektiven. Interreligiöse und Interkulturelle Bildung im Kindesalter, vol. 3. Münster et al.: Waxmann.

Schweitzer, Friedrich/Biesinger, Albert/Conrad, Jörg/Gronover, Matthias (2006): Dialogischer Religionsunterricht. Analyse und Praxis konfessionell-kooperativen Religionsunterricht im Jugendalter. Freiburg i. Br.: Herder.

Schweitzer, Friedrich/Englert, Rudolf/Schwab, Ulrich/Ziebertz, Hans-Georg (2002): Entwurf einer pluralitätsfähigen Religionspädagogik. Gütersloh/Freiburg i.Br.: Gütersloher Verlagshaus/Herder.

Schweitzer, Friedrich/Biesinger, Albert/Blaicher, Hans-Peter/Edelbrock, Anke/Haußmann, Annette/Ilg Wolfgang/Kaplan, Murat/Wissner, Golde (2011): Interreligiöse und interkulturelle Bildung in Kindertagesstätten – Befunde aus der Erzieherinnenbefragung. In: Schweitzer, Friedrich/Edelbrock, Anke/Biesinger, Albert (Ed.): Interreligiöse und interkulturelle Bildung in der Kita. Eine Repräsentativbefragung von Erzieherinnen in Deutschland – interdisziplinäre, interreligiöse und internationale Perspektiven. Interreligiöse und Interkulturelle Bildung im Kindesalter, vol. 3. Münster et al.: Waxmann, 29–54.

Senge, Peter M. (1990): The fifth discipline. The art and practice of the learning organization. New York/London/Toronto/Sydney/Auckland: Doubleday.

Senge, Peter M. (1993): Die fünfte Disziplin – die lernfähige Organisation. In: Fatzer, Gerhard (Ed.): Organisationsentwicklung für die Zukunft. Ein Handbuch. Cologne: Edition Humanistische Psychologie, 145–178.

Senge, Peter/Cambron McCabe, Nelda/Lucas. Timothy/Smith, Bryan/Dutton, Janis/Kleiner, Art (2012): Schools that learn. A Fifth Discipline Fieldbook for Educators, Parents, and Everyone who Cares About Education. New York: Crown Business.

Shaffer, David R./Kipp, Katherine (^{9}2014): Developmental Psychology. Childhood and Adolescence. International Edition. Belmont: Wadsworth.

Siegler, Robert/DeLoache, Judy/Eisenberg, Nancy (^{3}2011): Entwicklungspsychologie im Kindes- und Jugendalter. Heidelberg: Spektrum Akademischer Verlag [2005].

Sievers, Burkard (2000): Organisationsentwicklung als Lernprozeß personaler und sozialer Systeme – oder: Wie läßt sich OE denken?. In: Trebesch, Karsten (Ed.): Organisationsentwicklung. Konzepte, Strategien, Fallstudien. Stuttgart: Klett-Cotta, 33–49.

Singer, Elly/de Haan, Dorian (2011): Fostering a sense of belonging in multicultural childcare settings. In: Kernan, Margaret/Singer, Elly (Ed.): Peer Relationships in Early Childhood Education and Care. London/New York: Routledge, 88–101.

Slater, Alan/Muir, Darwin (Ed.) (1999): The Blackwell Reader in Developmental Psychology. Malden/Oxford: Blackwell Publishing.

Spenn, Matthias/Beneke, Doris/Harz, Frieder/Schweitzer, Friedrich (Ed.) (2007): Handbuch Arbeit mit Kindern – Evangelische Perspektiven. Gütersloh: Gütersloher Verlagshaus.

Stengel, Barbara S. (2010): The Complex case of Fear and Safe Space, in: Studies in Philosophy and Education 29(6), 523–540.

St. Nikolaus-Kindertagesheimstiftung, Wien/Caritas für Kinder und Jugendliche, Linz (2010): Religionspädagogischer BildungsRahmenPlan für elementare Bildungseinrichtungen in Österreich. Linz: Unsere Kinder.

Stockinger, Helena (2013): Die wechselseitige Verwiesenheit einer Kultur der Anerkennung und einer Kindheitsforschung. In: Jäggle, Martin/Krobath, Thomas/Stockinger, Helena/Schelander, Robert (Ed.): Kultur der Anerkennung. Würde – Gerechtigkeit – Partizipation. Schulkultur, Schulentwicklung und Religion. Baltmannsweiler: Schneider Hohengehren, 191–201.

Stockinger, Helena (2014): Religiöse Differenz in elementarpädagogischen Einrichtungen. Was der Religionspädagogik zu denken geben kann. *ÖRF 22*, 85–91.

Strauss, Anselm/Corbin, Juliette (1990): Basics of Qualitative Research. Grounded Theory Procedures and Techniques. London u.a.:Sage.

Strauss, Anselm/Corbin, Juliet (1996): Grounded Theory. Grundlagen Qualitativer Sozialforschung. Weinheim: Psychologie Verlags Union.

Streib, Heinz (2000):Gottesbilder fallen nicht vom Himmel. Kindliche Malprozesse als Gestaltung von Religion. In: Fischer, Dietlind/Schöll, Albrecht (Ed.): Religiöse Vorstellungen bilden. Erkundungen zur Religion von Kindern über Bilder. Münster: Comenius-Institut, 129–141.

Streib, Heinz (2001): Inter-Religious Negotiations: Case Studies on Students' Perception of and Dealing with Religious Diversity. In: Heimbrock, Hans-Guenter/Scheilke, Christoph/Schreiner, Peter (Ed.): Towards Religious Competence. Diversity as a Challenge for Education in Europe. Münster: LIT, 129–149.

Strübing, Jörg (^{2}2011): Zwei Varianten von Grounded Theory? Zu den methodologischen und methodischen Differenzen zwischen Barney Glaser und Anselm Strauss. In: Mey, Günter/Mruck, Katja (Ed.): Grounded Theory Reader, 262–277.

Stier, Jonas/Tryggvason, Marja-Terttu/Sandström, Margareta/Sandberg, Anette (2012): Diversity management in preschools using a critical incident approach. *Intercultural Education* 23(4), 285–296.

Stringer, Martin D. (2013): Discourses on Religious Diversity. Explorations in an Urban Ecology. Farnham/Burlington: Ashgate.

Tamminen, Kalevi (1991): Religious Development in Childhood and Youth. An Empirical Study. Helsinki: Suomalainen Tiedeakatemia.

Tashakkori, Abbas/Teddlie, Charles (Ed.) (^{2}2010): SAGE Handbook of Mixed Methods in Social & Behavioral Research Overview of contemporary issues in mixed methods research. Thousand Oaks/London/New Delhi/Singapore: SAGE Publications [2003].

ter Avest, Ina (2010): Der Andere – fast so wie ich? Der Unterschied zwischen dem Ich und dem Anderen aus der Sicht von Kindergartenkindern. In: Edelbrock, Anke/Schweitzer, Friedrich/Biesinger, Albert (Ed.): Wie viele Götter sind im Himmel? Religiöse Differenzwahrnehmung im Kindesalter. Interreligiöse und Interkulturelle Bildung im Kindesalter, vol. .1 Münster et al.: Waxmann, 89–103.

ter Avest, K.H. Ina/Miedema, Siebren (2010): Learn Young, Learn Fair. Interreligious Encounter and Learning in Dutch Kindergarten. In: Engebretson, Kath/de Souza, Marian/Durka, Gloria/Gearon, Liam (Ed.): International Handbook of Inter-religious Education. Part One. Dordrecht/Heidelberg/London/New York: Springer, 513–527.

Tillich, Paul (1962): Religionsphilosophie. Stuttgart: Kohlhammer [first published in: Dessoir Max (Ed.): Lehrbuch der Philosophie, vol. 2. Berlin: Ullstein 1925].

Tillich, Paul (1964): Die Frage nach dem Unbedingten. Schriften zur Religionsphilosophie. Gesammelte Werke, vol. V. Stuttgart: Evangelisches Verlagswerk.

Tillich, Paul (1967): Die religiöse Substanz der Kultur. Schriften zur Theologie der Kultur. Gesammelte Werke, vol. IX. Stuttgart: Evangelisches Verlagswerk.

Tisdall, E. Kay M./Davis, John/Gallagher, Michael (2009): Researching with Children and Young People. Research Design, Methods and Analysis. Los Angeles/London/New Delhi/Singapore/Washington DC: SAGE.

Tisdall, E. Kay M./Davis, John/Gallagher, Michael (2009): Introduction. In: Tisdall, E. Kay M./Davis, John/Gallagher, Michael (Ed.): Researching with Children and Young People. Research Design, Methods and Analysis. Los Angeles/London/New Delhi/Singapore/Washington DC: SAGE, 1–10.

Trebesch, Karsten (Ed.) (2000): Organisationsentwicklung. Konzepte, Strategien, Fallstudien. Stuttgart: Klett-Cotta.

Trebesch, Karsten (2000): 50 Definitionen der Organisationsentwicklung. In: Trebesch, Karsten (Ed.): Organisationsentwicklung. Konzepte, Strategien, Fallstudien. Stuttgart: Klett-Cotta, 50–62.

Ullrich, Carsten G. (2009): Deutungsmusteranalyse und diskursives Interview. *Zeitschrift für Soziologie 28*(6), 429–447.

United Nations General Assembly: Universal Declaration of Human Rights 1948, www.un.org/en/universal-declaration-human-rights/[22.07.2015].

Uslucan, Haci-Halil (2008): Religiöse Werteerziehung in islamischen Familien. Commissioned by: Federal Ministry for Family Affairs, Senior Citizens, Women and Youth. Berlin.

Van Ausdale, Debra/Feagin, Joe R. (1996): Using Racial and Ethnic Concepts: The Critical Case of Very Young Children. *American Sociological Review 61*(5), 779–793.

Van Ausdale, Debra/Feagin, Joe R. (2001): The First R: How Children Learn Race and Racism. Maryland: Rowman and Littlefield.

Vandenbroeck, Michel (2007): Beyond anti-bias education: Changing conceptions of diversity and equity in European early childhood education. European Early Childhood. *Education Research Journal 15*(1), 21–35.

Vandenbroeck, Michel (2008): Beyond colour-blindness and tokenism. In: Developing positive identities. Early childhood in focus 3. Diversity and young children. The Hague: The Open University, 28.

van Deth, Jan W./Abendschön, Simone/Rathke, Julia/Vollmar, Meike (2007): Kinder und Politik. Politische Einstellungen von jungen Kindern im ersten Grundschuljahr. Wiesbaden: VS Verlag für Sozialwissenschaften.

Ven, Johannes A. van der (^{2}1994): Entwurf einer empirischen Theologie. Kampen: Kok [1990].

Verordnung der Wiener Landesregierung über die Regelung der Tagesbetreuung nach dem Wiener Tagesbetreuungsgesetz (WTBVO) 2001/94. Section 4; http://www.wien.gv.at/recht/landesrecht-wien/rechtsvorschriften/html/s2700200.htm [21.07.2015].

Wagner, Petra (2003): Und was glaubst du? Religiöse Vielfalt und vorurteilsbewusste Arbeit in der Kita. In: Dommel, Christa/Heumann, Jürgen/Otto, Gert (Ed.): WerteSchätzen. Religiöse Vielfalt und öffentliche Bildung. Festschrift für Jürgen Lott zum 60. Geburtstag. Frankfurt/London: IKO Verlag für Interkulturelle Kommunikation, 223–233.

Wagner, Petra (Ed.) (^{2}2010): Handbuch Kinderwelten. Vielfalt als Chance – Grundlagen einer vorurteilsbewussten Bildung und Erziehung. Freiburg/Basel/Vienna: Herder [2008].

Wagner, Petra (^{2}2010): Vielfalt und Diskriminierung im Erleben von Kindern. In: Petra Wagner (Ed.): Handbuch Kinderwelten. Vielfalt als Chance – Grundlagen einer vorurteilsbewussten Bildung und Erziehung. Freiburg/Basel/Vienna: Herder [2008], 56–58.

Wagner, Petra/Hahn, Stefanie/Enßlin, Ute (Ed.) (2006): Macker, Zicke, Trampeltier … Vorurteilsbewusste Bildung und Erziehung in Kindertageseinrichtungen. Handbuch für die Fortbildung. Weimar: Verlag das Netz.

Weber, Judith (2014): Religionssensible Bildung in Kindertageseinrichtungen. Eine empirisch-qualitative Studie zur religiösen Bildung und Erziehung im Kontext der Elementarpädagogik. Interreligiöse und interkulturelle Bildung im Kindesalter, vol. 4. Münster/New York: Waxmann.

Wehr, Hans (^{4}1968): Arabisches Wörterbuch für die Schriftsprache der Gegenwart. Wiesbaden: Otto Harrassowitz [1952].

Weiße, Wolfram/Gutmann, Hans-Martin (Ed.) (2010): Religiöse Differenz als Chance? Positionen, Kontroversen, Perspektiven. Münster et al.: Waxmann.

West, Andy/O'Kaine Claire/Hyder, Tina (2008): Diverse childhoods: Implications for childcare, protection, participation and research practice. In: Leira, Arnlaug/Saraceno, Chiara (Ed.): Childhood: Changing Contexts. Bingley: Emerald Group Publishing Limited, 268–292.

Wilk, Liselotte/Wintersberger, Helmut (1996): Paradigmenwechsel in Kindheitsforschung und -politik. Das Beispiel Österreich. In: Zeiher, Helga/Büchner, Peter/Zinnecker, Jürgen (Ed.): Kinder als Außenseiter? Umbrüche in der gesellschaftlichen Wahrnehmung von Kindern und Kindheit. Weinheim/Munich: Juventa, 29–55.

Wimmer, Rudolf (2000): Die Zukunft von Führung: Brauchen wir noch Vorgesetzte im herkömmlichen Sinn?. In: Trebesch, Karsten (Ed.): Organisationsentwicklung. Konzepte, Strategien, Fallstudien. Stuttgart: Klett-Cotta, 161–178.

Witte, Markus (Ed.) (2001): Religionskultur – zur Beziehung von Religion und Kultur in der Gesellschaft. Beiträge des Fachbereichs Evangelische Theologie an der Universität Frankfurt am Main. Würzburg: Religion und Kultur.

Witte, Markus (2001): Zu diesem Buch. In: Witte, Markus (Ed.): Religionskultur – zur Beziehung von Religion und Kultur in der Gesellschaft. Beiträge des Fachbereichs Evangelische Theologie an der Universität Frankfurt am Main. Würzburg: Religion und Kultur 2001, 11–17.

Wolff, Stephan (^{9}2012): Wege ins Feld und ihre Varianten. In: Flick, Uwe/von Kardorff, Ernst/Steinke, Ines (Ed.): Qualitative Forschung. Ein Handbuch. Reinbek bei Hamburg: Rowohlt Taschenbuch [2000], 334–349.

Woodhead, Martin (2008): Identity at birth – and identity in development. In: Brooker, Liz/Woodhead, Martin (Ed.): Developing positive identities. Diversity and young children. Early childhood in focus, vol. 3. The Hagues: The Open University, 4–5.

Woodward, Kathryn (Ed.) (1997): Identity and difference. London/Thousand Oaks/New Delhi/Milton Keynes: Sage Publications in association with The Open University.

Woodward, Kathryn (1997): Concepts of Identity and Difference. In: Woodward, Kathryn (Ed.): Identity and difference. London/Thousand Oaks/New Delhi/Milton Keynes: Sage Publications in association with The Open University, 7–61.

Wustmann, Cornelia/Bamler, Vera (2010): Lehrbuch Kindheitsforschung. Weinheim/Munich: Juventa.

Zeiher, Helga/Büchner, Peter/Zinnecker, Jürgen (Ed.) (1996): Kinder als Außenseiter? Umbrüche in der gesellschaftlichen Wahrnehmung von Kindern und Kindheit. Weinheim/Munich: Juventa.

Zeiher, Helga (1996): Von Natur aus Außenseiter oder gesellschaftlich marginalisiert? Zur Einführung. In: Zeiher, Helga/Büchner, Peter/Zinnecker, Jürgen (Ed.): Kinder als Außenseiter? Umbrüche in der gesellschaftlichen Wahrnehmung von Kindern und Kindheit. Weinheim/Munich: Juventa, 7–27.

Ziebertz, Hans-Georg (1999): Religion, Christentum und Moderne. Veränderte Religionspräsenz als Herausforderung. Stuttgart: Kohlhammer.

Ziebertz, Hans-Georg (2002): Grenzen des Säkularisierungstheorems. In: Schweitzer, Friedrich/Englert, Rudolf/Schwab, Ulrich/Ziebertz, Hans-Georg: Entwurf einer pluralitätsfähigen Religionspädagogik. Gütersloh/Freiburg i. Br.: Gütersloher Verlagshaus/Herder, 51–85.

Ziebertz, Hans-Georg (2002): Gesellschaft und Öffentlichkeit. In: Schweitzer, Friedrich/ Englert, Rudolf/Schwab, Ulrich/Ziebertz, Hans-Georg: Entwurf einer pluralitätsfähigen Religionspädagogik. Gütersloh/Freiburg i. Br.: Gütersloher Verlagshaus/Herder, 204-226.

Ziebertz, Hans-Georg (Ed.) (2011): Praktische Theologie – empirisch. Methoden, Ergebnisse und Nutzen. Berlin: LIT.

Ziebertz, Hans-Georg (2011): Preface. In: Ziebertz, Hans-Georg (Ed.): Praktische Theologie – empirisch. Methoden, Ergebnisse und Nutzen. Berlin: LIT, 3–4.

Ziebritzki, Doris (2012): Wir wollen zusammen feiern. Feste der Weltreligionen im Kindergartenjahr. Freiburg/Basel/Vienna: Herder.

Zimmermann, Mirjam (Ed.) (2013): Fragen im Religionsunterricht. Unterrichtsideen zu einer schülerorientierten Didaktik. Göttingen: Vandenhoeck & Ruprecht.

Zirker, Hans (2001): Religion, Religionskritik. In: Mette, Norbert/Rickens, Folkert (Ed.): Lexikon der Religionspädagogik, vol. 2. Neukirchen-Vluyn: Neukirchener, 1672–1677.

Zonne, Erna (2006): Interreligiöses und interkulturelles Lernen an Grundschulen in Rotterdam-Rijnmond. Münster et al.: Waxmann.

Online sources

ACEPP, www.acepp.asso.fr [22.07.2015].
Bernard van Leer Foundation, http://www.bernardvanleer.org/ [21.07.2015].
DECET, www.decet.org [22.07.2015].
Early years, http://www.early-years.org/ [22.07.2015].
Protestant Church in Austria, http://www.evang.at/kirche/zahlen-fakten [21.07.2015].
Initiative Weltethos Österreich, http://www.weltethos.org/ [21.07.2015].
Islamic community in Austria, http://www.derislam.at/?c=content&cssid= Kinderg%E4rten/ Hort%20&navid=460&par=40 [21.07.2015].
ISSA, http://www.issa.nl/ [10.07.2013].
ISSA, [http://www.issa.nl/global.html [10.07.2013].
Joint Learning Initiative on Children and Ethnic Diversity, http://www.qub.ac.uk/ research-centres/JointLearningInitiativeonChildrenandEthnicDiversity/ [21.07.2015].
Catholic church in Austria, http://www.katholisch.at/site/kirche/article/102078.html [21.07.2015].
City Administration of Vienna, http://www.wien.gv.at/bildung/kindergarten/private-angebote/ index.html [21.07.2015].
City Administration of Vienna, http://www.wien.gv.at/bildung/kindergarten/staedtisches-angebot/index.html [21.07.2015].
City Administration of Vienna, http://www.wien.gv.at/statistik/pdf/wieninzahlen.pdf [21.07.2015].
City Administration of Vienna, http://www.wien.gv.at/bildung/kindergarten/private-angebote/ [22.07.2015].
City Administration of Vienna, https://www.wien.gv.at/menschen/magelf/ahs-info/ausbildung.html [21.07.2015].

City Administration of Vienna, https://www.wien.gv.at/menschen/magelf/ahs-info/pdf/kindergruppe-ausbildung.pdf [21.07.2015].

Mutant, www.mutant.nl [22.07.2015].

Paul Connolly, http://www.paulconnolly.net/publications/ [21.07.2015].

Peace Initiative Institute, http://peaceii.org/ [22.07.2015].

Persona Doll Training, http://www.persona-doll-training.org/ [21.07.2015].

Portal Intersektionalität, http://portal-intersektionalitaet.de/startseite/ [22.07.2015].

Religion and Society, http://www.religionandsociety.org.uk/uploads/docs/2012_12/1355390760_Jackson_Phase_2_Large_Grant.pdf [07.02.2014].

Statistics Austria, http://www.statistik.at/web_de/statistiken/bildung_und_kultur/index.html [16.08.2013].

Statistics Austria, http://www.statistik.at/web_de/statistiken/bevoelkerung/volkszaehlungen_registerzaehlungen_abgestimmte_erwerbsstatistik/bevoelkerungsstand/index.html [30.04.2015].

The Future of the Children, http://www.futureofchildren.org/futureofchildren/publications/journals/journal_details/index.xml?journalid=74 [21.07.2015].

UNA, http://www.unaglobal.org/en [21.07.2015].

United Nations. Treaty Collection, http://treaties.un.org/Pages/ViewDetails.aspx?src=TREATY&mtdsg_no=IV-11&chapter=4&lang=en [21.07.2015].

VBJK, www.vbjk.be [22.07.2015].

Wiener Kindergruppen, http://www.wiener.kindergruppen.at/?page_id=33 [22.07.2015].

World Vision Annual Review 2013, http://www.worldvision-institut.de/kinderstudien-kinderstudie-2013.php [16.07.2015].

Zeitschrift für qualitative Forschung, http://www.budrich-journals.de/index.php/zqf [21.07.2015].

List of tables and figures

Table 1: Population of Austria and population of Vienna by religious affiliation by the last conventional census 2001 103

Table 2: Population of Austria and population of Vienna by religious affiliation by own census or projection 104

Table 3: Religious affiliation of children in the Catholic kindergarten 115

Table 4: Countries of origin of the children in the Catholic kindergarten .. 116

Table 5: Religious affiliation of children in the Islamic kindergarten 119

Table 6: Countries of origin of the children in the Islamic kindergarten ... 119

Fig. 1: Presentation of the procedure by linking the research approaches of grounded theory and thematic coding 88

Appendix

Re: Declaration of consent

A research project on diversity in kindergartens is being conducted at the University of Vienna.

With my signature, I agree that the data collected in the kindergarten may be used anonymously for research and teaching purposes.

Date: _____ Signature: _____

Re: Participation in the study "Living together"   16.12.2013

Dear parents and guardians,

the University of Vienna will conduct a study on the topic of "Living together" and gives children the opportunity to express themselves. The aim of the study is to better understand children in order to provide them with the best possible conditions in kindergarten. In this context, group discussions are conducted with children, which are documented by means of audio and video recordings.

I completed my training as a kindergarten teacher in 2004, studied psychology, philosophy, theology and religious education, am currently a research assistant at the University of Vienna, teach Catholic religion at BAKIP Kenyongasse and I am responsible for early childhood education at the KPH Vienna/Krems Centre for teacher training in religion for the field of early childhood education . The study is part of my dissertation project at the University of Vienna.

I ask for your consent by handing in the signed lower section at kindergarten. Please do not hesitate to contact me if you have any questions: helena.stockinger@univie.ac.at

I look forward to good cooperation!

Yours sincerely,
Helena Stockinger

With my signature, I agree that my child participates in the study "Living together", which is carried out at the university. In the course of this research project, group discussions are conducted with children, whereby the activities are documented by means of audio and video recordings. By signing this form, I agree that the data collected may be used anonymously for research and teaching purposes. For questions etc. please contact helena.stockinger@univie.ac.at

Date: _____   Signature: _____

Abstract

Religious plurality is a fact of society, whereby the core of this plurality is difference (Nipkow 1998). Being able to act sensitive to differences and thus contribute to peaceful coexistence seems to be an essential challenge of the present. Based on the research results to date on religious difference (Hoffmann 2009, Edelbrock/Schweitzer/Biesinger 2010; Connolly 2009 and others) and developmental psychological findings (Elkind 1964; Schneider 2012) it becomes clear that children can recognise religious difference and deal with it. In order to further develop a difference-sensitive approach within the organisation kindergarten, empirical basic research is needed that takes the entire organisation into account from the perspective of religious difference. The research project makes this claim by guiding the research question of how kindergartens deal with religious differences and how children address them.

Taking into account the findings of childhood research (Heinzel 2012), an ethnographic approach was chosen in conjunction with grounded theory (Strauss/Corbin 1996) and thematic coding (Flick 2012). Data collection and data evaluation were thus an interdependent process, which was regarded as complete with thematic saturation in the two kindergartens.

The research design, which developed in the course of the research process, consisted of participant observation, which took place for one year, expert interviews with the heads of the two kindergartens, group discussions with the teachers and group discussions with the children. The field research took place in a Catholic kindergarten and an Islamic kindergarten in the same district in Vienna, with children of different religious backgrounds attending the two kindergartens.

The results point to a connection between the willingness of children to address their own religion and religious forms of expression and the organisation's handling of religious difference. In the two kindergartens, the religion of sponsorship, which is also the major religion in the respective kindergarten, is dominant, while other religions are hardly recognisable and thematised in kindergarten. Accordingly, the children feel that they belong to the major religion in kindergarten, while the children of the minor religions remain silent about their religion and their religious expressions and do not stand out in their religious difference, in which the desire for belonging becomes clear.

The work concludes with an outlook on how this disadvantage in early childhood institutions can be countered in a sensitive manner and contributed to a culture of recognition. The necessary development of early childhood institutions is taken into consideration by using school development processes (Rolff et al. 2011) from the perspectives of organisational, personnel and educational offer development.